The Culture of Ancient Egypt

By

JOHN A. WILSON

(First published as *The Burden of Egypt*)

Phoenix Books

THE UNIVERSITY OF CHICAGO PRESS

AN ORIENTAL INSTITUTE ESSAY

First published as

THE BURDEN OF EGYPT

This book is also available under that title in a clothbound edition from

THE UNIVERSITY OF CHICAGO PRESS

THE UNIVERSITY OF CHICAGO PRESS, CHICAGO 37
Cambridge University Press, London, N.W. 1, England
The University of Toronto Press, Toronto 5, Canada

To Mary

The burden of Egypt. Behold, the Lord rideth upon a swift cloud, and shall come into Egypt.

ISAIAH, 19:1

How say ye unto Pharaoh: "I am the son of the wise, the son of ancient kings"? Where then are thy wise men?

ISAIAH, 19:11–12

Contents

INTRODUCTION

THIS is not a history of ancient Egypt, but rather a book about ancient Egyptian history. The interest of the writer has not been in searching out and attempting to establish facts, in selecting chains of the most pertinent facts, and then in weaving those chains into a consecutive and meaningful story. Certainly, the writer is aware of the importance of working on historical fact, but his chief interest is not in validating facts. He takes certain data as given and then attempts to seek the significance of such assumed truth. Is there any justification for such a procedure and such an attitude?

A history book proper would attempt to maintain a maximum of scientific procedure and of objectivity. It could serve as a reference book for observations which had been recorded and checked for various periods of historical time. Such observed data would be presented in such a way that they could be verified, analyzed, and tested by other persons. Interpretation of the data, that is, the historian's attempt to give them consequence and value, would be clearly defined, so that it might be discounted by other persons who desired to form their own independent opinions on the basis of the facts presented. The ideal would present a library of books on ancient Egypt, with source books and volumes of special studies leading up to a cultural history. Thus there would be the following: volumes of translations of all categories of ancient Egyptian texts, brought up to date and provided with adequate commentary to give the reader a control of the validity of the translations; volumes of systematic arrangement and analysis of the physical remains of ancient Egypt, including works of art, with adequate illustration and chronological specification to give the reader control of the data; volumes of special studies on religion, government, economics, social organization, industry, science, art, literature, etc., as well as various phases of those subjects; and the summing-up of the preceding materials in a sober cultural history, in which the source materials would, in so far as possible, "speak for themselves." Only after such a presentation in objective terms should the subjectivity of the historian appear in speculative studies which pretend to give the significance and "value" of the story. Here we put the cart before the horse. In large measure the present study is such a speculative and subjective cart, which should have been preceded by the horses of detailed source materials and sober history.

Now most of our horses are lacking or sadly aged. Up-to-date translations of original Egyptian records are lacking. Analyses of physical remains appear somewhat haphazardly and incompletely. Systematic treatises on phases of ancient Egyptian culture are scanty or scattered. And there is no recent and first-rate history of ancient Egypt in English. The forthcoming new edition of the *Cambridge Ancient History* will meet a great need. Meanwhile, Breasted's *A History of Egypt* remains a standard, after forty years, because it is a single and consecutive telling of a story. Collaborative projects by different scholars, as in the *Cambridge Ancient History*, gain in authority at specific points by sacrificing unity and continuity. However, the raw materials upon which history is based have become so voluminous that it is increasingly difficult for one scholar to write adequately and comprehensively on all of ancient Egypt. For better and worse, we have become a generation of specialists.

Another problem which the ancient historian recognizes with increasing clarity is the peculiar nature of the sources upon which he must base his writing. What is a "fact" or what is a "historical record" from ancient Egypt? We have come to understand a little better—perhaps only a little better—the psychology within which the ancient wrote his records. Our definition of a fact or of the truth would not be his. His motivations in his world were quite different from those in our world. In part, the present volume will try to show how the ancient's psychology differed from ours; in part, the difference may be indicated here. The essential point for the present argument is that the ancient had an entirely different attitude toward any kind of observed process. We have come to think in terms of movement and consecution, of antecedents and consequents, of cause and effect. In order to understand an observed phenomenon, we want to know what preceded it and what brought it into being. We have come to think kinematically: that this particular frame of our experience has its proper setting within a strip of film. To the ancient, observed phenomena were not parts of a consecutive chain, so that their antecedents were not related and significant. To the ancient, phenomena were momentary flashes of a timeless and boundless universe, the realm of the gods and therefore always subject to divine control or intervention. He thought in terms of a mirror image: that this experience was an illustration of the plans of the gods as revealed from the beginning. If one accepts the principle of complete revelation, that the gods created a universe which has been essentially static from the beginnings, and if one is able to account for any phenomenon as effected by divine agency and therefore not open to human questioning, then there will be little occasion to seek out impersonal causes for our effects, and there will be no interest in the movement of time.

The ancient oriental mentality has been called a "mythmaking" mentality. The ancient related his personal experiences to myths which he told about the activities and interests of the gods. He found a real security in considering the particular only an aspect of the vast and undifferentiated. The reference of some observation or experience to a myth of divine agency relieved man of the responsibility of seeking impersonal causation in the past or of taking any exceptional measures for the future.

Since he lacked a sense of time, relativity, or impersonal causation, he was no historian. He was not interested in going back to a beginning to explain a phenomenon, but he was satisfied to find divine beginnings. He did not seek mundane origins and then try to trace events, chronologically and systematically, down to the present. Nor, apart from mythmaking, did he attempt to work out some philosophy of history, explaining the consecution of events through an interpretation of basic causes.

This means that our two basic sources—written records and records in art—will be innocent of any concern with the progress of time and of any concern with the concatenation of cause and effect. It means, further, that the ancient's understanding of historical truth was different from ours. Where truth lies in divine revelation and activity, the element of the miraculous is fundamental. Where, as in ancient Egypt, the king was a god, the king was the state, and the supreme energies of the state were directed toward supporting such a dogma, the written records will have a perfectly good conscience in presenting the divine, miraculous, and unchanging. This may be called "propaganda" to uphold the dogma of the divine kingship; one may point out clear cases where it leads to distortions of the truth or to absolute untruths; but one must recognize that in the ancient setting it was sincere and consistent.

Unfortunately, it places question marks against the historical data which we have to use. If fact has been presented in a way which varies all the way from the tendentious to the unblushingly deceptive, how can we establish what is fact? We cannot hale the ancient record-writers into court and then try to find two or more contemporary, competent, and disinterested witnesses, who are not self-deceived themselves. Such objective evidence does not exist. It certainly does not exist in the art of ancient Egypt, which was as timeless and propagandistic as the literature. It does exist in the physical remains resulting from excavation, but this is an extremely limited witness, which only occasionally can deny or corroborate the written record.

What we have to do, then, is to learn our material as thoroughly as its vast bulk will permit; test it constantly against itself, against evidence known from other peoples and cultures, and against good common sense; then form certain tentative generalizations about ancient Egyptian culture; and, finally, apply those generalizations to the material as a broad interpretation of the specific. This may appear to be shocking, for the suggested methodology is as much deductive as it is inductive; it is as much subjective as it is objective. We do not place the cart before the horse; instead, we harness ourselves to the cart and start blithely out on a self-directed journey.

Perhaps such arrogance is not unseemly when one considers the difference between ancient Egyptian history and, for example, modern European history. When the ancient data are partial, biased, and saturated with the mythmaking psychology, can we permit those data to speak for themselves? It might easily be argued that for the pre-Greek world there is no history in the strict sense, there are only historians, moderns who try to organize, understand, and interpret that which refuses to speak for itself but insists upon talking about the gods. If that be the case, then we might honestly recognize it and work in a frankly subjective and deductive atmosphere. This book is full of personal speculation about the significance of ancient Egypt, and it will be clear very early that many more questions can be raised than can be answered with success.

Another question should be raised in advance: If this book is so highly speculative and tentative, dealing with a culture so remote from us in time and space, is the effort worth while? We live in a crowded and breathless age, with an uneasy sense of crisis sounding distant thunder over our left shoulder. We live in basic ways quite differently from the ancient Egyptians, for the typical unit of power has changed from man or animal to the fuel-fed machine and the typical mode of life has changed from agricultural subsistence to urban trading. We seem to stand on the threshold of a radically new life in a world tightly contracted by communications and experimenting with new sources of power. Perhaps the past is a dead hand, which should not be permitted to hinder our advance into the future. Perhaps the preclassical past is so different that it has no relevance to the present or future. Perhaps the study of ancient Egypt is merely an unrelated diversion about something quaint, exotic, and amusingly at variance with our life. Can we justify another book about ancient Egypt, especially a book of random questionings?

The volume itself must present the answer to that question, because we are here attempting to discover the values inherent in Egyptian culture and inevitably we shall consider value in a modern sense. However, it may be pertinent to say something at this point about the study of ancient history in general.

The broad argument is that we are men striving to work out for ourselves better adjustments of life, so that any culture which men have previously established has interest and significance to us, particularly if that culture proved satisfactory enough to last many long centuries. We should have a gain if we could establish the principles which provided that long satisfaction and which ultimately failed to maintain the culture. Even if we should determine that these principles were no longer applicable, we should have made a negative gain in our understanding.

We live in days which demand good judgment, and good judgment rests against the steadfast knowledge of that which has long-range value. Judgment may falter if fears, prejudices, or ambitions are too immediate and urgent; it may be made more stable by solid and far-reaching background. That background is the essential. If it proves to be a continuation of the foreground, there is firm stability. If it proves to be different, the immediate foreground stands out in bold relief.

Thus we are talking about perspective rather than specific information. Therefore, it is not strictly relevant whether ancient Egyptian medicine was the grandfather of modern medicine, whether the concept of social justice comes down to us in an unbroken line from the Middle Kingdom, or whether monotheism was first introduced to the world by the Eighteenth Dynasty. Those are interesting and important problems for special studies, and they will be approached as questions

in this book, but they are debatable questions and therefore are of reserved value for the present day. What we today need is a sense of our
relative position in the process of human existence and a sense of general values which will help us in moving through that position. For
such a need the generalized and long-range impression of human history is basic.

This does not mean that the statement about ancient Egypt or about
any other culture should itself be vague, loose, and generalized. Good
judgment has to rest on confidence, and we must have confidence that
historians have done their honest and painstaking best in collecting the
data reverently, sorting them conscientiously, and weaving them together into a firm fabric upon which the design of generalizations may
be set. Unless we feel that the historians are learned and sound in
method and attitude, we cannot use their findings for that sense of position in time, that sense of relative values, and that resultant good
judgment. However, it is not necessary that everybody try to know
all the details. We need the assurance only that the historian has tried
to encompass all the details possible. On that assurance we may rest our
generalized sense of the aims and directions of human process.

In that understanding, the cultural history of ancient Egypt for three
thousand years becomes a kind of external parable, a story of other men
who made great achievements, who experienced success, failure, optimism, and disillusion. That story is detached from us, so that we can
study it and understand it without prejudice, and it thereby becomes a
teaching which has relevance and application to our life. A long process
of man's striving in other times, other places, and other circumstances
is a parable of what happens to mankind, specifically to us. We can
approve or deplore what the Egyptians did over these thousands of
years, and when we do so, we inevitably cast a shadow of value criticism upon our own doings. Whether the ancient Egyptians had different sources of power from ourselves, whether their social and economic
organization was at variance with ours, or whether their psychological
attitude to their universe was distinct from ours, they were humans
seeking a life of richness and adjustment, so that there is an unbroken
line of endeavor from their times to ours. The burden of Egypt which
Isaiah proclaimed is also our burden.

The background for this kind of interpretative essay may appear in
certain writings coming from the Oriental Institute of the University
of Chicago: J. A. Wilson, "Archeology as a Tool in Humanistic and

Social Studies," *JNES*, I (1942), 3 ff.; Th. Jacobsen and J. A. Wilson, "The Oriental Institute: Thirty Years and the Present," *JNES*, VIII (1949), 236 ff.; and H. and H. A. Frankfort, J. A. Wilson, Th. Jacobsen, and W. A. Irwin, *The Intellectual Adventure of Ancient Man: An Essay on Speculative Thought in the Ancient Near East* (Chicago, 1946), which was abridged as *Before Philosophy* (Penguin Books, 1949). If I fail to give my individual colleagues credit for the very real contributions which they have made to my knowledge and to my thinking, it is not through lack of gratitude. In a highly personalized interpretation, I may spare them any share of my responsibility for what may be tentative, unstable, or tendentious.

I

THE BLACK LAND

Geographic Factors of Egypt

Most visitors to Egypt are distinctly aware of the exceptional nature of climate and topography along the Nile. They have come from lands of normal rainfall, where meadows run from valley to hill without break and where the clouds may conceal the sun, moon, and stars for days on end. They have come from lands where the roads may run in any direction. Their expectations in terms of terrain or weather have allowed for a wide variety of chance: they have looked to all four directions of the compass; they may have experienced rain in March or August; they are uncertain about the weather for their week-end outing; they may have planted their crops in a riverside meadow or in a highland meadow. Now they find Egypt a land essentially rainless, confined closely to the banks of the Nile River, and thus restricted to a single north-and-south axis. They find the sharpest possible contrast between riverside meadow and highland desert (Fig. 1). That contrast between the fertile black land and the red desert sands is marked by a definite margin, which is the extreme limit to which the waters of the Nile may reach. It is possible to stand with one foot on the fruitful alluvial soil and one foot on the lifeless desert sands. As one looks inward toward the river valley, one is conscious of bustling and teeming life. As one looks outward toward the sandstone hills, one is aware of vast desolate stretches where no life is possible. Inevitably, the polarity of attention is the great muddy river which brings the life-giving water and soil. If the Nile were by some chance cut off, that soil would dry to dust and blow away. The land of

Egypt would become a vast dry wadi of the great North African desert.

Because of this dramatic contrast between the desert and the sown, we all repeat Herodotus' observation that Egypt is the gift of the Nile.[1] One is scarcely aware of the few little oases spotting the Libyan Desert. The Nile has come with pulsing prodigality out of equatorial Africa and the highlands of Abyssinia and has flung fabled riches across one of the world's poorest areas. Only that surging summer inundation of the River makes a land possible here, and the annual gifts of refreshing water and refertilizing soil in a semitropical climate give an agricultural richness which has been proverbial in all times. With the proper use of the soil, two or three crops a year are a happy expectation.

However, as one lives in Egypt, one is conscious that the Nile's gift lays heavy obligations upon the Egyptian peasant. The inundation rushes through the valley on its way to the sea. Unless its waters are captured and retained, the fertility of the soil will last for a few months only. In the spring one hears the ceaseless musical groaning of the water wheel bringing moisture up from deep wells; one sees the back of a peasant, bending and lifting all day long at the well sweep (Fig. 3b); one sees the heavy work of mending little water channels, which carry moisture off to the outlying fields. Incessant toil is the responsibility laid on the Egyptian peasant by the Nile's great gift. Without that labor to make the most lasting and economical use of the waters, Egypt would be a much narrower country, snatching at a single crop immediately after the inundation.

That observation leads us back into distant prehistoric times, in an attempt to imagine the valley of the Nile before man had developed any system of irrigation. Life then must have been concentrated even more closely at the margins of the River. Each summer the inundation must have rushed through without restraint, spreading thinly beyond the riverside marshes and draining off quickly. The red desert must have come down much closer toward the River, close to a thick, jungle-like tangle of marsh at the edge of the stream. The two banks must have been a thicket of reeds and brush, and the profusion of waterfowl and jungle fowl must have provided a happy hunting ground for the smaller animals. That this riverine jungle did exist before man drained the marshes and carried the water up toward the foot of the hills is evidenced by pictures of historic times (Fig. 2a). There, in scenes of hunting in the swamps, we see the vestiges of earlier conditions, with

1. Herodotus ii. 5.

the tangle of reeds and brush and the swarming of game and fowl. The flora and fauna of Egypt down into historic times were much like the life now present in the southern Sudan. For example, the ibis and the papyrus, so symbolic of ancient Egypt, are now found in the jungle-like Nile reaches fifteen hundred miles to the south.[2]

Thus earliest man in Egypt was trapped between the encroaching desert sands and the riotous riverine jungle. To gain any permanent foothold, he had to drain and root out the jungle, and he had annually to thrust and hold the water out against the greedy desert sands. This was hard work, and it probably was a slow, dogged effort covering thousands of years of prehistory. Indeed, we have no clear evidence of any really important irrigation, involving community effort on canals and catch basins, before historic times. Before then, one infers a clearing-out of swamps by an inching process. It is an inference that late prehistoric times saw major developments in irrigation—but only an inference. The supporting argument would run as follows: large-scale irrigation extended the arable land and produced the necessary food for a larger population and for that element of surplus which goes with civilized living; but large-scale irrigation requires a common effort, binding together different communities, and is a factor promoting the growth of a state; the visible elements of historic times argue that, for several centuries back, there must have been a widespread economy in the utilization of water, to make those historic factors possible. We shall return to this theme in the next chapter.

The Nile lays another obligation upon the Egyptian. The River is not precise in the timing of its inundation or in the volume of its waters. Man must be on the alert against its antic behavior. In particular, its volume is a matter of serious concern. Only a few inches of maximum height separate the normal Nile from famine or riotous destruction. In modern times, before the Assuan Dam was built, a high Nile at the First Cataract, rising 25 or 26 feet above a zero datum, meant a good, normal inundation, easily controlled and covering enough ground for bountiful crops. A high Nile which fell 30 inches below this normal meant insufficient crops and a pinched year. A drop of 60 inches—80 per cent of normal—meant a fatal famine, with starvation stalking the Egyptians for a year. Too high an inundation was also a peril. The levels of canals and protective dikes were fixed on the expectation of a good, normal flood; only a foot above normal would mean damage to

2. P. E. Newberry, *Egypt as a Field for Anthropological Research* (Smithsonian Report for 1924 [Washington, 1925]), pp. 435 ff.

the earth embankments; a 30-foot Nile—20 per cent above normal—would sweep away dikes and canal banks and bring the mud-brick villages tumbling down. The legend of the seven years of plenty and the seven lean years was no fantasy for Egypt; it was always a threatening possibility. The margin between abundant life and hollow death was a very narrow one. Constant vigilance against the antic behavior of the life-giving River was necessary, and only an orderly government could provide that vigilance for the entire land. Again the gift of the River imposed its hard obligations.

This was the setting in which the ancient Egyptian civilization flourished, and these were the incentives which led the Egyptians to struggle upward toward a fuller life based on the fertile potentiality of their soil. It was no warm and drowsy land of lotus-eaters. In Toynbee's terms of an environmental challenge and a human response, there were problems to be met progressively. The full potentiality of climate, water, and soil was a challenge which demanded long centuries of back-bending toil to drain the jungle marshes and reclaim the land nearest the River, then centuries of weary labor to carry the River water against the greedy desert by canals and catch basins. Thereby the ancient won great richness of crops, and these, in turn, set new challenges. How was the resultant large population to be organized, and how was the surplus of wealth to be applied? For the present our concern is to describe the geographic factors of the land and to suggest how they were conditioning factors. In the next chapter we shall take up the social and governmental responses which the ancients made to the challenges of greater population and wealth.

Another environmental factor which needs attention is the physical isolation of the land of Egypt. The Nile Valley was a tube, loosely sealed against important outside contact. To the west and east of the valley lay forbidding deserts, passable for small caravans of traders but insuperable barriers for any people coming in force. Along the northern frontiers the Sinai desert thinned out and weakened contact with Asia, while the Libyan coast provided a slightly greater potential of traffic for pastoral and nonaggressive peoples. Land communication east or west meant five to eight days of desert caravaning—across Sinai to Palestine, through the Wadi Hammamat to the Red Sea, or out to the nearest of the western oases.

There were also barriers to contact by water. Prehistoric man, with his flexible little boats and his lack of experience in navigation, would not venture across the Mediterranean in force. The Egyptians themselves built boats for the Nile River and adapted them inadequately for the sea. The earliest boats may well have hugged the coast for protection and direction. If that be true, the overseas communication between the Egyptian Delta and the Phoenician coast, instead of being four days' direct sailing, may have been twice as long. Contact with Crete presents a distinct problem, since a crossing between that island and Africa would require open seas. Possibly the Cretans themselves, living in the midst of the sea, were the first to open that contact. It still required four or more days' sailing.

To the south of Egypt proper there were also barriers. The First Cataract was not a serious obstacle, as it could easily be navigated or by-passed. However, the land south of the First Cataract is relatively inhospitable, with the desert cliffs cutting in close to the Nile and limiting the arable land to meager strips. No large and powerful culture was possible between the First and Third Cataracts. South of the Third Cataract the land opens out and provides wider fields and greater pasture land, but the Third Cataract itself, the Second Cataract, and the Nubian deserts were all serious obstacles to movement north and south. There was always the possibility of infiltration from the south, just as there was the possibility of infiltration from Libya or through Sinai. However, the elements which strained out these threats were strong, and a normal Egyptian government was able to handle the threats as a police problem. In earliest times Egypt was well sealed against invasion.

The many generalizations made in this book are subject to modification, exception, or different interpretation. The generalization that Egypt was secure against attack from outside is relative to time and place. There were periods in ancient history when the movements of peoples exerted such pressure that forces broke through the barriers of desert or sea. However, such great folk wanderings as the Hyksos movement or the Sea Peoples' attack come much later in Egyptian history; in earlier times the complacent sense of security was a dominant psychology. Further, there were parts of Egypt where infiltration might be a constant problem: at the First Cataract, at the northwestern frontier against the Libyans, or on the Suez frontier against the Asiatics. In those areas frontier police were necessary, and constant vigilance was an element of the psychology of the region.

Security from foreign threat is also relative in the comparison of different cultures. In contrast to their contemporary neighbors—the Mesopotamians, the Syro-Palestinians, or the Anatolians—the Egyp-

tians were in a happy position of geographic isolation. It was not necessary for them to maintain major and constant force against attack. Any
potential threat could be seen at a considerable distance, and it was unlikely that that threat would penetrate Egypt with damaging force.
This relative sense of security bred in the ancient Egyptian an essential
optimism about his career in this world and the next, and it permitted
a marked element of individual freedom for the ordinary Egyptian.
In contrast to his neighbors—the Babylonians and the Hebrews—the
ancient Egyptian was not constrained to slavish obedience to authority,
in the interests of the complete conformance of the community. His
rules were general and well understood, but within those rules he enjoyed a relatively high degree of liberty to exercise his own personality. This freedom arose out of his basic confidence in himself and in
his world, and this optimism, in turn, was possible because of his relatively high degree of geographic security. As we shall see in a subsequent chapter, when that sense of security was finally shaken, the entire attitude of the Egyptian was reversed, and the mailed hand of national demand closed down upon his optimism and his freedom. But
that is a story of the end rather than of the beginning.

One must make a distinction between the sense of insecurity which
arises out of the threat of invasion from abroad and the sense of insecurity which arises out of the possibility of a low Nile and famine conditions. The Egyptian did not have the first threat; the second threat
was always a lurking possibility. However, that second threat was constantly countered by the hope and expectation that a year of low Nile
might be followed by a year of good Nile. It was possible to face the
low Nile by a cautious husbanding of Egyptian resources, in order
to tide over the famine months of the year until another Nile came.
Another Nile always came in its season. That element of periodicity
of the life-bringing inundation strongly promoted the Egyptian sense
of confidence. Every spring the River would shrink down into its bed
and leave the fields to the fury of the hot desert winds—the invader
from without—but every summer the Nile would surge again with
floodwaters, lift high above its bed, and revive the fields with moisture
and new soil. The Nile never refused its great task of revivification.
In its periodicity it promoted the Egyptian's sense of confidence; in its
rebirth it gave him a faith that he, too, would be victorious over death
and go on into eternal life. True, the Nile might fall short of its full
bounty for years of famine, but it never ceased altogether, and ultimately it always came back with full prodigality.

The reassuring periodicity of the River was supported by the periodicity of the sun. In a sky carrying few or no clouds, the sun sank into darkness every evening but surged back in power every morning. The Egyptian might be respectful of the sun's heat; he might be grateful for the cooling north wind or for cooling water; but he was happy in the warmth of the sun after the cool darkness of night. He stretched himself thankfully in the morning rays and observed that his animals did likewise. The grateful sense that daylight was the time of life and that night was a time of arrested life was marked in a land where the distinction between night and day came suddenly and clearly. The sun was the great governing factor of his day-by-day life. Its conquest of death every night and its brilliant rebirth every morning were factors of importance; they renewed the Egyptian's confidence that he, too, would conquer death, as did the sun and the Nile.

Let us look at the land of Egypt from a different viewpoint. Only one-thirtieth of the modern state of Egypt is black land, where man may live and plant crops; more than 95 per cent is barren desert. It is as if our entire Atlantic coast were a country, of which only the state of Maryland was habitable territory. At the present day, 99 per cent of Egypt's population lives on this one-thirtieth of the whole land. The density of habitation is more than twelve hundred to the square mile. This is nearly seven times the density of Maryland's population. Egypt is still agricultural, but it has an extraordinary concentration of population, so that the little agricultural towns lie close together and are packed with people. Except in the back districts, there is a kind of semi-urbanism, through the intensity of contacts.

The population of modern Egypt has grown extraordinarily in the past century, and it is certain that ancient Egypt had nothing like the same density of habitation. The point, however, is that its density was relative to its ancient scene. There was still a sharp and dramatic contrast between the teeming life of the sown and the uninhabited stretches of the desert. Modern Egypt has a population of sixteen million. If ancient Egypt had had only one-tenth that population, its density of habitation on the habitable land would have been about twice the density of modern Virginia or nearly three times the density of Mississippi. Such a concentration, sharply separated from the barren desert, promoted internal contacts and led to a kind of urbanity of thought through the constant iteration of such contacts.

One of the ancient Egyptian terms for their country was "the Two Lands," and this expresses a real geographic truth. Egypt was a single land in its uniform dependence upon the Nile and in its isolation from other cultures. Internally, however, it divided into two contrasting regions, the long, narrow trough of Upper Egypt to the south and the broad, spreading delta of Lower Egypt to the north. Throughout history these two areas have been distinct and have been conscious of their distinction.[3] Upper Egypt may be only four to twenty miles wide; it is always within immediate reach of the Nile and always within immediate contact with the desert cliffs which inclose it; it has only a north-and-south axis. Lower Egypt loses this axis in its broad stretches running out flat in every direction as far as the eye can reach. Still moldering stretches of marshland in the Delta today remind us of a prehistoric situation in which Lower Egypt must have been an almost uninterrupted flat jungle. In the north the great River breaks down into a number of smaller branches or canals, and there is no one artery of movement. Lower Egypt faces out toward the Mediterranean Sea, toward Asia and Europe; its agricultural richness has an overlay of brisk commercial interest. Its contacts are more cosmopolitan. Upper Egypt, held viselike between two deserts, is restrained to Africa; its commerce moves toward the south or toward Lower Egypt; its agricultural richness retains vestiges of a past in which there was a greater interest in cattle-herding. Anciently and modernly, the two regions spoke markedly different dialects and had different outlooks on life. In a true sense, they were "the Two Lands" which were made into one land.

The proximity of the desert to the habitations of the Upper Egyptians, contrasting with the broad expanses of fertile soil in the Delta, accounts for two factors in the survival of evidence on ancient Egypt. In Upper Egypt the desert was always near at hand for the burial of the dead and for the building of great temples; people might live and carry on their business on the black soil, but they were buried in the preserving sand of the hillside, and their temples lay at the foot of the hillside. The result is that our evidence on the ancient Egyptians is disproportionately strong in material on their mortuary beliefs and formal temple worship but weak on such lay matters as business, government, economics, and social organization. The view that the ancient Egyptians

3. In the Middle Kingdom an exile expressed his sense of bewilderment at finding himself in a foreign country: "I do not know what separated me from my place. It was like a dream, as if a man of the Delta were to see himself in Elephantine, or a man of the (northern) marshes in Nubia." In the Empire period, the difference in speech between northern and southern Egypt was expressed in the words: "Your speeches . . . are confused when heard, and there is no interpreter who can explain them. They are like the words of a man of the Delta marshes with a man of Elephantine" (Erman, *LAE*, pp. 25, 233 f.).

were excessively concerned with death and the next world is conditioned by the accident that materials dealing with death and the next world lay out in the desert sands and survived down to our day, whereas materials dealing with life in this world lay chiefly on the fertile alluvial soil; were subject to moisture, chemical destruction, and human wear and tear; and so did not survive.

The second disproportion of evidence arises out of the contrast between Upper and Lower Egypt. By far the vast bulk of our evidence comes from the preserving sands of Upper Egypt, the more provincial part of the land. Similar evidence in the north lay in the moist soil and perished, so that the part of Egypt which was in closest contact with Asia and the Mediterranean tells us the least. We have to reconstruct our story out of the materials which have come down to our time, and these materials are limited in more ways than one. The history of the Delta as such must be inferred very largely out of the materials coming from the south.

The tragedy of the moldering destructiveness of the Delta mud becomes apparent when one remembers that the Delta was the pivotal point for contacts between Egypt and other important cultures. The biblical account places the sojourn of the Children of Israel in the Delta; the settlements of Greeks were in the Delta; and, under the Egyptian Empire, the main capital of Egypt was in the Delta, with the city of Thebes a seasonal or provincial capital. One of the theories advanced in this book is that there was little transmission of essential and important cultural elements by Egypt to younger neighboring peoples. Perhaps that theory would be stated differently if a proper proportion of our evidence did come from Lower Egypt, where the contacts with Hebrews, Phoenicians, Aegeans, Ionians, and other peoples were fresher and closer. We believe that the theory would still stand as a working hypothesis in the terms in which it is stated in our final chapter, but we might have to qualify the argument if we had a clearer knowledge of the cultural interplay in the Egyptian Delta.

The Egyptian culture as it came into its characteristic form was an amalgam of the Asiatic-Mediterranean influences which had play in Lower Egypt and the African influences which affected Upper Egypt. The ancient Egyptians were related to the Semites but were not true Semites; they were related to the Hamites but were not true Hamites. Scholars disagree on the precise elements in the Egyptian culture which are attributable to Asia or Africa, but they recognize this dual nature in the culture. Even the Egyptian Delta was exposed on its eastern frontier to the Asiatic influences of Sinai and on its western frontier to the African influences of Libya. Factors of common cultural expression may be pointed out between Egypt and the Hamites to the south, between Egypt and the Libyans to the west, between Egypt and the Minoans to the north, and between Egypt and the Semites to the east. For us the important observation is that Egypt, despite her relative isolation, was subject to relational influences from different directions and, in turn, exerted her influence in different directions.

In another place[4] we have tried to explain the ancient Egyptian's love of geometric parallelism in art or literature as the product of his geographic setting, where the east bank of the Nile confronted the west bank, where the eastern desert cliff confronted the western. The Egyptian love of counterposition or of dualism is clearly visible, but we have come to doubt our explanation as being the sole factor producing the aesthetic enjoyment of balance or dualism in art, literature, or mythology. In the long trough of Upper Egypt, where the axis of the River exerts such strong polarity, the balance of eastern and western sides is a visible phenomenon. However, the same would not be true of the Delta, where the fields stretch as far as the eye can reach and where there are no sharply defined desert cliffs. Perhaps the duality of "the Two Lands" was a stronger factor in producing the dualism of Egyptian psychology. Perhaps there were other elements just as strong.

This chapter has discussed the geography of Egypt, not so much in terms of physiography, as in terms of the influence of the environment upon the inhabitants. We should not like to leave the impression that physical environment was here considered the sole determinant of cultural expression, or even the major determinant. Geographic factors are easy to see and describe and certainly are influential forces playing upon peoples. There are also psychological and spiritual forces which are strong shaping factors. They are less easy to describe, and there is less agreement among scholars in selecting them. This book will try to suggest some of them in passing.

4. H. Frankfort *et al.*, *The Intellectual Adventure of Ancient Man* (Chicago, 1946), pp. 41 f.

II

OUT OF THE MUD

The Long Prehistoric Struggle

THE fruitful green valley of the Nile was not there in distant geological ages. Before there were any Egyptians, nature had to carve out a land in which they might live. This she accomplished over slow eons of time by two prodigious heavings of a land mass. One visualizes northeastern Africa long ago as a great limestone plateau, watered with abundant rain and with the waters draining off in many different directions. As the ages passed, that plateau slowly rose, and the waters had to dig their way to the sea. So an enormous gorge was gouged out, cutting north across the limestone plateau and carrying a tremendous river as the force which eroded out the Nile Valley. Further ages passed, and the land majestically sank, until the sea backed up into the great limestone gorge. The valley became a fjord for six hundred of the seven hundred miles which are now Egypt—all the way to Esneh. The sea laid down its characteristic deposits, and it is possible to find marine fossils as far up as Assiut in Middle Egypt. As time passed, nature reversed herself again, and the land mass rose once more. There was still an abundance of rain, although the volume of water was not so mighty as it had been in Oligocene and Miocene times. This new Nile cut its channel north through the marine deposits which had been laid down in Pliocene times.[1]

This majestically slow scouring-out of a valley had, of course, been innocent of any traces of man. Such plant and animal life as had appeared in northeastern Africa could exist in the forests which cloaked

1. K. S. Sandford in *AJSL*, XLVIII (1932), 170 ff.: *Palaeolithic Man and the Nile Valley in Upper and Middle Egypt* (*OIP*, Vol. XVIII [1934]), p. 126.

the plateau. However, a new slow process had already set in, for the rains were not holding up in volume and the mighty Nile could not maintain its mass. A long process of desiccation set in over a wide belt of the earth's surface, and a shrinking Nile is indicated by river banks successively lower and successively closer together. Eight of these shrinking banks cut into the old marine deposits in a series of terraces or steps leading down from the limestone cliffs to the present bed of the River. This narrowing focus of life-giving water must have exerted its strong magnetic polarity on plant and animal life. Yet we look in vain for any indication of man in the uppermost four of the eight terraces. He may have paused there, at the edge of one of those vast prehistoric Niles, paused in his restless food-gathering through the shrinking forest, but he was too poor in physical equipment to leave us any trace of his passage. Then, in geological formation in the fifth of the terraces from the top, there appear man-made artifacts, and our geology turns to prehistory. Here are imbedded flint hand axes of types recognizable as being practically the same as those found in Europe and there called "Abbevillian." A creature far enough developed to carry a weapon of respectable technique and efficiency had come out of the woods, pursuing game or snatching at reeds. He left us not a bone of himself, so that we can only guess at his appearance from "Stone Age man" in other parts of the world. Probably he tarried only briefly at the unfamiliar jungle thicket that screened his upland hunting ground from a strange and terrible body of moving water. The next terrace lower shows a later type of flint implement, similar to the European Acheulean, while the two lowest terraces show still later techniques, like the European Levalloisian and Mousterian. That is all the evidence until we come down and stand on the present black alluvial silt. A few scattered paleoliths are very incomplete testimony for man, but they are all we have, and their limited evidence is that his life must have been the same in northeastern Africa as in other parts of the world: hunting timidly or with a certain frantic courage over wide ranges of forest, stuffing his mouth with edible wild plants, or grubbing for roots. It would be romantic nonsense to think of that first hunter, "like some watcher of the skies when a new planet swims into his ken," staring down at the future home of his distant descendants "with a wild surmise." No; the wild surmise is in us, as we try to bridge the gap between his tiny existence and the towering ambitions of those who were to build the pyramids. He saw no boundless and glorious future along the Nile. Nature had to drive him down relentlessly to its banks.

That was effected by the continuing desiccation of Africa, with forest giving way to savanna, savanna to prairie, and prairie to desert, with the slow drying-up of water holes out in the desert.[2] This drying-up occurred first to the south, in the Sudan and Nubia and in Upper Egypt, whereas the rains persisted longer in the northern area near the Mediterranean. This meant that a more sluggish Nile came out of Africa, so that the fertile silt which it carried was not swept out to sea but was deposited in an increasing bed, in the stream itself, and along the banks of the stream through the inundation. This alluvial soil has tantalizingly covered and hidden some of the most interesting evidence of all: the data on man's final settlement along the banks of the Nile as a relatively sedentary creature, the first evidence of his transition from a life based on pursuing food or gathering it in transit to a life based on nurturing food in the place where he lived. In the gap of evidence, we are limited to speculation. Desiccation of the desert must have cut off plant foods except at the margin of the River. The animals of the upland, including man, were thus herded down to the river bank, pursuing plant food and pursuing each other. A much closer juxtaposition meant greater acquaintance: man found that it was advantageous to keep certain animals close at hand for his future food supply; he found that certain plants could be teased into greater productivity for his feeding and the feeding of those animals which he was holding beside him. Slowly—probably without invention but with unconscious transition—food-gathering gave way to food-production, the essential element of historical life. But the evidence on this transition is lost to us beneath the alluvium.

When finally the curtain does rise again for a few scattered views of man, he has his feet firmly planted in the black alluvial mud along the Nile, he has domestic animals, and he is cultivating plants. In his dietary essentials and in the physical bases of life, he is modern man—or, at least, man as he was up to the industrial revolution. He still had a long way to go in achieving the full physical values of the life he had, and he still had to work out his new social organization, and he still had vast unexplored stretches in his intellectual and spiritual life. But the gap in our evidence hides a major revolution—the transition from the food-

2. On the desiccation of Egypt and the climate of the region in prehistoric times see S. A. Huzzayin, *The Place of Egypt in Prehistory* ("Mémoires présentés à l'Institut d'Égypte," Vol. XLIII [1941]). According to his analysis of the evidence, there was somewhat more moisture than modernly all the way into historic times, and the contemporary conditions of aridity did not set in until after 2500 B.C.

gathering economy of hunters, fishers, trappers, and grubbers for roots and pluckers of berries to the food-producing economy of farming and herding cattle. In the food-gathering economy the social unit had necessarily been limited to the family or tribe, ranging over a considerable area of land and necessarily limited to light, portable equipment. Now man was settled, and he could begin to accumulate goods in greater quantity. He was more definitely in control of his food, since he himself produced it, so that there could be more food. More people could live within any given area, so that the family or tribe need not be the essential element. Unrelated families could live side by side, without difficult competition, perhaps even to mutual advantage. Such a transition must have taken long thousands of years. It was still incomplete when our evidence begins once more.

Diligent search along the margins of the cultivated land, in the Faiyum, on the edges of the Delta, and in pockets of land in Middle Egypt, has given us some incomplete evidence on prehistoric man's dim gropings for a fuller life. Roving food-gatherers came out of the north African prairie and paused at the margins of the Faiyum lake. Before they departed again, they left a kitchen midden of elephant or hippopotamus bones, with scanty traces of their simple artifacts: microlithic flints, with little or no pottery. At a later stage—probably many centuries later—the inhospitable desert cast them forth, and they settled down at the edge of the jungle swamps which lined the Nile Valley. The artifacts were somewhat more numerous, but still primitive and crude. We have tools and weapons, beads, baskets, pottery, granaries, and the bones of domestic animals. The last two are very important because they show that man no longer roamed in pursuit of his food but stayed in one place to produce his food. At Merimdeh Beni-Salameh at the southwestern margin of the Delta, there was even a village of crude oval huts made of big lumps of mud. It was no garden city. The entire village covered about six acres, and the ungainly huts were of a single, smoke-filled room about fourteen by nine feet. There was a jar sunk into the flooring to drain off the rain water coming through the roof. It was not a cheery place.

The village had a communal granary, consisting of woven baskets sunk into the ground. The individual huts had no granaries beside them. Apparently the first attempts at village life retained some of the elements of tribal custom: the individual sense of property had not yet replaced the community sense of property. The cereals included the same kind of barley as is grown today, emmer wheat, and a common vetch. Flax was also grown, spun into thread, and woven into linen on some kind of crude loom. So we have already had the revolution in life produced by the discovery that certain kinds of wild plants could be protected, nurtured, and teased into greater productivity for man's food and clothing. The other discovery had also taken place: that certain kinds of animals could be held close beside man and cultivated for their meat, hides, or wool. However, the Merimdeh village and the Faiyum middens show an incomplete transition to food-producing. The small amount of grain indicated by the granaries and the profusion of bones of wild animals suggest that the cereals of his fields and the meat of his cattle and pigs did not yet provide a sufficient diet for man. The jungle and the desert were still close at hand, and man was still animated by a primitive restlessness; he went hunting and fishing for additional food.

Probably his fields were tiny pockets of soil, adventitiously watered by the Nile, and he had not yet set himself to the formidable tasks of draining the jungle marshes and then channeling water to the cleared fields. That was to be a long, slow process, still incomplete at the time when history began. For the moment he took what was easiest to his hand.

If we jump all the way down into historic times and look at the wall carvings of the Old Kingdom, we can see that the process of domestication was still uncompleted after some two thousand years. These Old Kingdom scenes show the nobles of historic times hunting in lush swamps teeming with wild life: hippopotamus, crocodile, and wild fowl. To be sure, the ancient artist may have allowed himself the luxury of exaggeration; but he must have had models upon which to draw, the models of a land not yet completely drained and tamed. Further, such scenes show a continuing experimentation in the domestication of wild animals. There are stables containing gazelles and hyenas, fattened by forcible feeding. Man did not give up the attempt to add new animals to his domestic menage until history had run a full millennium and the strong hand of tradition halted further experimentation.[3]

We return to the primitive and prehistoric. It is not the purpose of this book to detail the successive cultures of predynastic Egypt, with the elements of change in each. We wish only to make a few points. The first is that the struggle was a native struggle within Egypt and—until the end of the predynastic period—not affected to any appreciable degree by stimuli from outside. Long, slow change of culture may be a

3. J. H. Breasted in *Scientific Monthly*, November, 1919, pp. 416 ff.

matter of unconscious inner drive, without invasion of "superior" or of goading peoples from abroad. We do not know very much about race in predynastic Egypt. What we do know is chiefly negative, that changes of race in the early Nile Valley were negligible in quantity or quality. For the most part, there was an "Egyptian," short, slight, long-headed, and dark, a mongrel of Africa, Asia, and the Mediterranean. Whatever motivation there was toward civilization burned deep within him, a slow fire of which he was quite unconscious. Gradually, without deliberate invention on his part and without any early stimulation from abroad, he was to grope his way upward toward a life of greater maturity, of greater physical comfort, and of greater interdependent complexity. Until the very end of the predynastic period, the process was unconscious and terribly slow. Man's feet were mired in the mud of the river banks, and he had to move deliberately.

And so the archeologist lists a series of successive predynastic cultures with formidable names: Tasian, Badarian, Amratian, Gerzean, and Semainean; and he lists the physical phenomena which appear in each culture: flints, pottery, the earliest metal, amulets, graves, houses, and works of art. There was constant change, and—with qualifications—there was constant enrichment. Certain forms, such as houses and metal implements, became more numerous, larger, and more varied. Other forms, however, suffered through competition with new elements; flint weapons and decorated pottery reached climaxes of achievement at an early stage and then faded away in quality as man's energies were diverted into other lines. This was particularly true of pottery, where man's creative artistry produced ware of the greatest skill, beauty, and utility; but then his craftsman's impulse was drawn into other channels, and the pottery became dull and merely utilitarian.

Before we discuss art further, perhaps we should gain a clearer picture of the artist. What do we know about the predynastic Egyptian, since he has left us no writing and we have to learn about him through the objects he left buried in Egyptian soil? The picture is, of course, quite incomplete, but it does have contours. Let us pick a point toward the end of the predynastic stretch, but before the final transition into history, and set down what we know about the man who lived along the Nile.

To begin with, he was no physical giant. The men stood less than five feet six inches in height, the women were closer to five feet tall. They were slight, but strong-boned, with relatively long heads and oval, rather birdlike faces. The men had no great amount of hair on face or body and probably had slight or patchy beards. Their clothing was relatively scanty but was of linen. For dress occasions they wore strings of simple beads and adorned their faces with an eye cosmetic, preferably green. Physically, as in other respects, they showed relations to the Hamites, the Semites, and the Mediterraneans.

Those crude oval huts of rough lumps of mud had now become rectangular houses of shaped mud bricks. One model house which has come down to us has a door lined with wood and small windows framed in wood. Its original must have been large enough for inner partitioning into rooms, with a central timber supporting a flat roof. Most of the essentials of the historical house were present.[4]

This man was a farmer, but he probably had little to sell or trade, so that each domestic unit must have been self-sufficient in the necessities of life. Armed with a homemade hoe of wood and a sickle set with flint teeth, he cultivated barley, emmer wheat, vetch, a few vegetables, and flax. The cereals gave him bread and beer; the flax gave him the linen which was spun and woven into cloth.

Perhaps every family had a domestic animal or two, which might be pooled into a village herd. It must have been a rarely wealthy man who had a herd of his own. The animals were the African long-horned cattle, the sheep, the goose, the goat, the donkey, and—chiefly in the north—the pig. Perhaps we may credit the prehistoric Egyptian with the selective breeding of two animals, a naturally hornless kind of cattle and the Egyptian greyhound.[5] Despite the presence of domestic animals, it is a fair assumption that meat was not a normal element of diet but was reserved for feasts and sacrifices. Fishing, fowling in the marshes, and hunting in the desert supplemented the meat provision.

Although this man was self-sufficient for his domestic and field tools, there was one category of goods which he probably could secure only by trading, and that embraced the implements of metal. Metallurgy must have been a skilled craft confined to a few technicians. The smelting of copper required great heat in a closed space, and it has been assumed that some of the techniques were the same as in the fusing of sands and ores for glazing.[6] The copper was cast in a mold, and the closed mold was shortly to replace the open mold. Having conquered

---

4. D. Randall-MacIver and A. C. Mace, *El Amrah and Abydos* (*EES*, Vol. XXIII [1902]), p. 42, Pl. X; H. Schäfer and W. Andrae, *Die Kunst des alten Orients* (3d ed., Berlin, 1942), p. 173.

5. E. O. Orenander in *Sphinx*, XXII (1931), 8 ff.; M. Hilzheimer in *Antiquity*, VI (1932), 411 ff.

6. A. Lucas in *JEA*, XXXI (1945), 96 f.

metal, man was now able to bend it to his needs and make knives, daggers, axes, chisels, etc., with the metal assuming a shape for its necessary function and not following the old shapes set by stone implements. Stone tools and weapons were on the way out, no longer able to compete with copper; but, before the stone disappeared, it had a final triumph of technical skill, particularly because religious custom eschewed the new medium and clung to stone for such practices as sacrifice or circumcision. The final flint blades are superb pieces, thin, beautifully ground, and rippled to perfection. Such delicately beautiful flints may have been purely show-pieces. The ordinary farmer had to content himself with wooden tools or with implements of wood set with flint points or edges. Metal and the finest flints belonged to the community or to the overlord.

This little Egyptian had his times of aggressiveness and adventure. Archeology produces a great amount of arrowheads and mace-heads, and the skeletons of the predynastic Egyptians show an extraordinary number of broken bones. Apparently, communities had come into competitive contact with other communities, so that there was already that warfare which built little states into larger states and was ultimately to produce a nation. We do not know anything about the authority under whom the Egyptian fought. Theoretically, there were already local rulers of small states, distinct from the tribal chieftains of an earlier stage.

If we define a "machine" as an instrument which unites two distinct elements for a single merged force, this man commanded several simple machines. Of course, he had inherited the bow and arrow from long-distant ancestors. He had also the harpoon with attached cord, the hoe, the spindle, the loom, and—most complicated of all—the drill for hollowing out stone vases or for piercing small beads. These are all of a fairly elementary mechanical nature, but they have advanced beyond a club or a hand ax or a digging stick.

In one respect this late predynastic Egyptian had fallen short of the achievements of his ancestors, and that was in the craftsmanship of containers, vessels of pottery and stone. His loving artisanry had been diverted to other channels. The pottery had declined in the fineness of the ware, in the boldness of the form, and in the pains taken with decoration. The stone vessels were not so commonly in the very refractory materials, nor were they so successful in form; it was now sufficient to make a container of routine shape out of soft stone. Artistic talents had gone into the shaping of figurines or into the decoration of ceremonial slate palettes, an artistry which required the new technique of relief sculpture. To a degree, art was separating itself from function and was becoming a skilled craft for the purposes of the state or the overlord.

This man was earth-bound to his little fields, except at such times as he was led forth to war. However, he was not cut off from contact with distant regions. The boats which plied the Nile now carried sails, and some of them may have adventured out into the "Great Green" Sea, hugging the coast as long as possible. There was commerce the whole length of Egypt, and somehow goods trickled in from other areas: gold and copper from the eastern mountains, ivory and myrrh from the distant south, olive oil from Libya and from Palestine, cedar woods from the Phoenician coast, lapis lazuli and obsidian from lands far to the east. Such goods may have passed only from community to community, but the means were already present, in shipping, for more direct contact and thus for greater influence of one culture on another. It is already possible to see a remarkable similarity of form between Egypt and Palestine in the shapes of pots, stone vessels, and stone palettes.[7]

We know very little about the religion of this man. Most of what we list we guess from his burials. Certainly, a belief in some kind of future life was important to him. His graves became increasingly elaborate, and increasingly he took goods with him into his grave. Food and drink were most important; but clothing, ornamentation, cosmetics, weapons, and tools accompanied him to the next world. Sometimes such objects were broken or pierced and thus "killed," so that they might share their owner's fate. At times dogs were buried with their masters. Whether servants were killed and buried at the same time as their masters we do not know. This was a practice which disappeared early in historical times, and one assumes that it was a prehistoric practice, in order to maintain a lord's household in the future life. The predynastic evidence for the custom is, however, lacking. We shall revert presently to the other evidence on religion as shown by art.

Was life a grim business for this predynastic Egyptian, with his back bent to the hoe or the loom? Yes, it must have been drudgery, but the monotony was relieved by the celebration of feasts, which surely marked the fortunes of the Nile and the agricultural year. There were fishing and hunting and warring. There were even games. Excavation has produced a crude kind of checkerboard. It is a table of unbaked

7. H. J. Kantor in *JNES*, I (1942), 174 ff.

clay with four stumpy legs, its surface divided into eighteen squares, and accompanied by about a dozen game pieces of clay coated with wax.[8] Such an apparatus for amusement is significant. There must already have been the slight surplus of wealth which relieved the pressure of endless toil; there must already have been the leisure time for entertainment. Such a transitional point and such a state of mind are also indicated by the development of an art for its own sake. Let us go back and look at the art of earlier predynastic times.

The urge toward beauty appeared first in the manufacture of useful things, such as a graceful pot with an applied decoration or a stone jug which made skilful use of the natural graining of the stone. A rounded pot offered an irresistible surface for the early artist. He could build up the form with applied clay, he could incise the pot when it was still damp, he could fire the vessel in such a way as to give two tones, he could apply a shiny slip or burnish his ware, or he could paint the surface. Thus we have a great variety of wares, decorated with a great variety of motifs. A bowl may show a primitively blocked-out painting of a hunter with his hounds on leash, while a jug may depict an adorned boat plying the waters of the Nile. This repertoire of paintings on pottery offers a great deal of our information on the culture of predynastic Egypt (Fig. 3a). It certainly affords plenty of speculation for the prehistorian. Are the connections of this "Cross Lined" ware with Africa to the south and the Sahara to the west? Does this "Decorated" ware derive from the northern part of Egypt? Just how are these "Wavy Handled" pots related to Palestine? Such questions illustrate again the variety of contacts possible in a relatively primitive culture. It is easy to say that Egypt's early development was essentially internal, without important outside influence, but it is also clear that there were outside contacts which must have been mutually refreshing to both parties.

The pots which show pictures of boats are especially important as indicating a river commerce from one end of Egypt to the other. The boats carry simple ensigns which probably give the place of origin, that is, the home port. In so far as we can identify these ensigns, they show that there was river commerce along the entire course of the Nile from the Mediterranean to the First Cataract, at a time long before Egypt was a unified nation.[9] Under relatively primitive conditions, with local

8. Of middle predynastic times (E. R. Ayrton and W. L. S. Loat, *Pre-dynastic Cemetery at El Mahasna* [EES, Vol. XXXI (1911)], p. 30, Pl. XVII).

9. P. E. Newberry in *Annals of Archaeology and Anthropology*, V (Liverpool, 1912–13), 132 ff.; in *Ancient Egypt* (1914), pp. 5 ff.

rule only, the river merchants of Egypt were able to move about freely with their wares. Nor was trading contact restricted to the Nile Valley alone. The presence in predynastic Egyptian graves of foreign materials, such as lapis lazuli, obsidian, ivory, and olive oil, shows that there was a range of commerce extending ultimately to lands as distant as Persia. This does not imply caravans of Egyptians ranging hundreds of miles away from Egypt or merchants from Iran bringing their wares to the Nile Valley, nor does it mean commercial ships plying the Mediterranean several centuries before history. It is more likely that distant wares were passed from one area to another by immediate, rather than long-range, contact. Nevertheless, the closed tube of the Nile Valley was not hermetically sealed against all contact, and outside influences would have some slow cumulative pressure as time went on.

It is difficult to talk about the religion of predynastic Egypt because the evidence is so slight and because the modern concept of religion fits the ancient scene so imperfectly. With ancient man, religion permeated every part of life and yet was hardly formalized into a theological system. Predynastic Egypt has left us no writings, so that we must make our guesses from the few material remains and on the supposition that the later theological system had had its prehistoric beginnings. This is insecure ground for speculation. The Egyptian graves have provided art objects which are undoubtedly connected with a belief in unseen and powerful forces. This is particularly true of figurines of humans, animals, and standardized symbols. Arguing from the analogy of primitive peoples known to the anthropologist today, one assumes that religion held three strong forces: protection from known and unknown perils, success in the enterprise of food-gathering or food-producing, and the enlargement and continuance of one's own people. The Egyptians were agricultural and must have invoked the forces promoting growth of their crops and enlargement of their herds. They must have given consideration to the force of reproduction of their own kind. And they must have offered fearful propitiation to the vast perils of a great world. These attitudes toward mysteries which were partly within their control but were largely controlled by the unknowable whims of nature would make up the beginnings of their religion. We can see a few of their attitudes in the figurines of females or of animals having to do with reproduction. But other figurines or amulets are less meaningful and may have been forces which would protect them from the many perils of existence. Their religion was as simple in essential elements and as complicated in daily and hourly forms as are the observances of most primitive peoples.

We cannot know what political struggles went on in predynastic Egypt. Beyond doubt, there was a reaching-out for power on the part of small units, and the process of conquest and assimilation built up constantly larger units. In theory there would be an evolutionary process, with the village-state growing into a district-state and the district-state growing into a large province; ultimately, at the beginning of history, a full nation would have come into being. We do not know that this expansive process moved according to such a theory. Certainly, there was a governmental change when men settled down to agriculture, won some surplus, and engaged in a struggle for larger territory. The tribal unit of most primitive times, a unit related by blood or immediate intimacy, certainly gave way to a wider governmental unit, in which people were not necessarily related by blood, did not necessarily know one another, but had sufficient economic and social interests in common that they were willing to act under one ruler. However, it is possible that the unit of rule was still relatively small only a few centuries before dynastic times and that the large provincial state came into being rather suddenly and only in the latest predynastic period.

This question about the size of the governmental and social and economic unit is linked with another problem which is equally a matter of speculation: When did large-scale irrigation works come into Egypt? It has been suggested that the first settlers in the Nile Valley lived on the edge of a thick jungle swamp and cultivated such pockets of land as were readily available. Such a location and such a life would provide small and unrelated communities, confined in size by limited food. The initial draining of the swamps would be the prerequisite to the gaining of greater agricultural territory, and this process of cutting away and draining the jungle may well have been a constant one. There is, however, a second step which was the essential for the winning of the fullest possible agricultural territory, and that was the bringing of major irrigation works to the land—large catch basins or canals which cut across miles of land and brought the Nile waters to the edge of the desert hills. The draining of the swamps won fertile soil for agriculture, but that soil could be kept fertile and extended in area only by large-scale irrigation. Large-scale irrigation demands planning and agency by a strong governmental organization, and, when once undertaken, it maintains and fosters that strong governmental unit.

The question is then: At what stage in the long centuries of predynastic process did the Egyptian attain such a degree of widespread co-operation, such an ability to plan ahead and carry out his plans, and such an ambition for more power, land, and food that he was able to undertake large irrigation projects? The answer to that question must be personal and subjective because we have no data to permit more than speculation. We can see man's abilities through his artifacts—pots and stone vessels, stone and copper implements, amulets and ornaments, houses and clothing—and we still do not have the answer. How intelligent was he, in our critical terms? The former assumption that the ancient Egyptian invented a 365-day calendar several centuries before dynastic times has been shown to be untenable. That calendar was initiated after the dynasties had begun. To be sure, such a calendar had to be based on a long period of observation, on recording by some kind of notation, and on the ability to work out the records into a consistent system. But if this 365-day calendar was initiated sometime in the first three dynasties, the preceding period of observations and records need not have extended very far into the late predynastic period. The invention of the calendar cannot be used for the argument that the Egyptian of the middle predynastic period had extraordinary intellectual powers.[10]

What can we say about his abilities, beyond the observed facts of skill in local arts and crafts and the acceptance of a widespread commerce? He had a number of simple skills, which involved logical process and experimentation along new lines. As a biologist, he was able to bring into being new species of plants and animals. As a chemist, he could make bread, brew beer, and mix paints or clays. As a geologist, he sought out the stones for knives and jars, mineral compounds for cosmetics, gold, and copper. As a physicist, he could work exquisite flint knives, drill small beads, glaze stone or pottery surfaces, and smelt and cast copper. As a mathematician, he could lay out fields and construct huts. At some time in his prehistoric career he had advanced to the stage of using machines, that is, instruments which combined more than one principle of force. A drill for hollowing out stone vessels is a machine in this sense, for it combines the cutting point, the downward pressure, and a rocking or rotary motion, all for a single purpose. This drill must have come in quite early in the predynastic period, if we may judge from the magnificent stone vessels. On the other hand, the potter's wheel apparently did not enter Egypt until historic times. We do not

10. O. Neugebauer in *Acta orientalia*, XVII (Copenhagen, 1938), 169 ff.; A. Scharff in *Historische Zeitschrift*, CLXI (Munich and Berlin, 1940), 3 ff.

know when such machines as the plow and the standing loom appeared in Egypt. It is possible that the plow was a late predynastic development, depending upon that other unsettled problem of the time when large-scale irrigation and agriculture began.

At any rate, it is correct to say that our Egyptian primitive had latent abilities and a willingness to experiment along modest lines. If he must be called a "barbarian" because he was not yet literate and civilized, he was not a doltish savage; he was an earth-bound peasant of limited range and imagination, but his gaze was sometimes raised above the mud, and vaguely he pressed toward the enrichment of his life. Even so, we do not have enough data to decide at what point he took the two major steps of extensive irrigation works and government of a far-reaching and impersonal nature. The dynasties begin with a union of the parts of Egypt into a single nation. At about the same time we have pictorial evidence that the king of Egypt was interested in irrigation and would take ceremonial part in the opening of a new canal.[11] It is a personal judgment that large governmental units and large irrigation projects were relatively new at the time and that the slow processes of building ever larger communities and of clearing the jungle had gone on very deliberately for a long time and then had a final spurt of energy, a spurt which flung man into history itself.

As we have pointed out above, the wall reliefs of historical times show a clear vestige of jungle conditions, suggesting that the complete clearing of the swamps had not yet been effected. Further, it is possible to argue that irrigation works on a grand scale were a concomitant of an important social revolution: some pressure of population demanded more land; more land was won by irrigation; increased crops permitted a much greater population; and greater population produced profound political, economic, and social changes in life. This is the kind of revolution which starts very slowly, finally picks up momentum, and then accelerates rapidly. It cannot be proved or disproved at present, but it is possible that the important changes in agriculture through irrigation were an immediate forerunner of historic times and, in fact, produced the historic times. This does not mean that the digging of large canals produced history; the process was far more complex than that. It does mean that man reached a certain stage of maturity or of internal pressure when he was moved to undertake such a co-operative activity

11. J. E. Quibell, *Hierakonpolis*, I ("Egyptian Research Account," Vol. IV [London, 1900]), Pl. XXVI, *c*; Schäfer and Andrae, *op. cit.*, p. 188.

and that his maturity, interacting with the products of irrigation, won for him a new kind of life.

What was that new kind of life? In attempting to answer that question, one must consider certain concepts suggested by certain scholars. Toynbee has laid down the principle of "Challenge and Response" for the evocation of ancient Egyptian society.[12] For him, the first challenge was a physical one: the clearing of the river jungle along the Nile, the taming of the fertile black soil, and the extension and control of the river floodwaters. Through such a response of activity, a uniform culture was constructed, and the energies of the responders continued unabated into historic times, with the great achievements of the Pyramid Age.

Beyond doubt, there is an important principle here. Nevertheless, it would still seem to leave a number of unanswered questions. Why did the prehistoric people of Egypt respond to the challenge, whereas their southern neighbors in the Sudan did not respond? Did the prehistoric Egyptians ignore the challenge of a fertile soil blanketed by jungle marshes for a long period of time; and, when they finally responded positively to the challenge, what new factors made them respond? Obviously, we are dealing with a spiritual agent which can be seen and described after the fact but which cannot be predicted before the fact. It would seem that an environment might offer oportunities which could be ignored until some catalytic force precipitated the energies of a people in a useful way. What could such a catalyst be—the product of gradual economic change, the product of gradually increasing population, a stimulus from abroad, or a gradual spiritual maturing? Perhaps there was no one catalyst but rather a combination of some of these suggested forces. If so, the slow change of past ages would become a rapid change of late predynastic into dynastic times.

12. Arnold J. Toynbee, *A Study of History*, I (Oxford University Press, 1935), 302–15; or one-volume abridgment (Oxford Press, 1947), pp. 68–73. In subsequent chapters it may be noted that we have not found some of Toynbee's concepts or principles sufficiently applicable to ancient Egypt to warrant detailed discussion. For example, we have difficulty in accepting the sequence of "time of troubles" (First Intermediate Period), "universal state" (Middle Kingdom), "interregnum" (Hyksos invasion), and "universal state" reasserted (Empire); for us, the effectively disturbing troubles which wrecked Egyptian culture grew out of the Empire and the attempt to maintain it. Even less valid seems the concept of the worship of Osiris as a kind of "universal church created by an internal proletariat"; the Osirian religion was mortuary and could not be the genesis of a "new society," and it was originally created by and for Toynbee's "dominant minority." These criticisms do scant justice to Toynbee's enormously refreshing influence in assailing formerly fixed ideas. The thinking of this book owes much to him, even though his societal pattern for Egypt is rejected.

Another concept which should be considered at this point is Childe's "urban revolution."[13] This view would see the beginning of history as marked by a basic social change, in which the undifferentiated agricultural society came to cluster around villages which were agricultural, political, and economic centers. In a very general sense every man in the preceding society had been his own self-sufficient master, producing his own food and clothing; making his own tools, weapons, and containers; building his own hut; and trading his own goods directly. With Childe's urban revolution, there came specialization of function. Instead of the farmer's undertaking a whole series of domestic avocations, certain men embraced the professions of weapon-maker, potter, weaver, builder, sailor, merchant, etc. This theory would see agricultural improvement as producing both a surplus of wealth and a surplus of population. The surplus of wealth created a ruling class with leisure time and an interest in the arts, and the surplus of population provided the specialists who would serve each need of the crafts and arts as a main vocation. Further, the larger communities were based on interdependent, but impersonal, interests instead of a single common interest of a personally related group. Thus there was a need for new sanctions to control such impersonally organized communities, so that there was a growth of governmental organization, of impersonal law, and of the constraints of a national religion. Thus Childe's urban revolution called into being an elaborated state, with a civil and ecclesiastical bureaucracy and a police force to elicit conformance to the ritual of religion and law. Ultimately, the professionalization of the government and of commerce would produce a final by-product of the urban revolution, since the necessity for keeping administrative and business records demanded writing.

The urban revolution contained two apparently conflicting currents. On the one hand, the individual had become a specialist in some vocation, and higher talents were called forth from him as a specialist. On the other hand, as society moved away from the smaller community, which had been intimate and related, and became a large state, with the awful impersonality of formalized law and religious dogma, there was a depersonalization of the individual, who became, as it were, a mere statistic of the state. That conflict between individual and group was present at the beginning of history, just as it is today.

What can one say about this theory of the urban revolution? Obvi-

13. V. Gordon Childe, *Man Makes Himself* (London, 1936), pp. 157–201, and *What Happened in History* (Penguin Books, 1946), pp. 106–17.

ously, as a theory it has much that is acute and just. Yet it is too absolute. It has two essentials: markedly increased population, tending toward an urban economy, and specialization of function. The term "urban," however, implies too much; it seems to say that agriculture ceased to be basic and that commerce replaced agriculture in importance. Actually, agriculture did not lose its essential importance, and one may doubt whether any community in earliest Egypt deserved the term "city." They were all agricultural villages of greater or less degree. Probably one would have to come far down into history—possibly down to the Eighteenth Egyptian Dynasty—before one could be sure of a city in the modern sense. Further, specialization of profession had surely been present in the earlier economy, even though in a lesser degree. The small tribal community must have had its farmer who was more skilful than any other in making weapons, its farmer whose hand turned more readily to painting, and its farmer who was a priest and medicine man. The differences between the earlier agricultural period and the historical period are not differences of kind but differences of degree. Thus one may accept a truth in Childe's "urban revolution," provided that it is understood that it was not "urban" and was not a "revolution." There was a change in the direction of greater concentration of population in centers, there was a change toward greater professionalism, there was an increase in wealth, and there was an elaboration of administrative machinery to control the new elements.

Let us consider one more concept, Redfield's "folk society."[14] This is an abstraction, constructed for the purpose of understanding modern urban society in contrast to a simpler and more primitive society. This ideal folk society is homogeneous, small, and has a strong sense of community. It is nonliterate, and its economy is one of self-sufficiency rather than of buying and selling. In general, the ties of family provide the community. The society is deeply rooted in religious belief and custom, and relations are personal, so that the secular and impersonal have not yet come into being. The behavior of such a society is strongly traditional, so that there is no encouragement to speculation or to experimentation, since sanctified tradition has provided all the answers. Such a folk society could exist as a pure culture only if the conditions of its maintenance and security from disturbance were assured.

Over against the abstraction of the folk society is placed the concept of its opposite—modern urban society, large, amorphous, heterogene-

14. Robert Redfield, "The Folk Society," *American Journal of Sociology*, LII (1947), 293–308.

ous, and lacking a sense of community. Urban society is secular, highly impersonal in relationships, and very complicated in its interdependence of commercial transactions. Family and tradition are of little importance. The society is, of course, literate and, at its ideal best, speculative, experimental, and fluid.

How did ancient Egypt at its crucial point between prehistory and history fit into the concept of the folk society or of the urban society? Clearly, it was in a transitional stage between the two. In its entire historical course ancient Egypt never reached the full urban stage. It was always strongly agricultural. Although increasingly secularized, it always had a strongly controlling element of the sacred. In few other cultures was the force of tradition so binding, and after its first historical spurt of energies it dropped any dangerous tendencies toward speculation or experimentation. Despite its practices of a semisecular government, of an intricate interdependence of economics, of literacy, and of the union of two disparate sections of Egypt under a single rule, ancient Egypt was always at heart a sacred society, clinging passionately to hallowed tradition.

Even in the predynastic period, however, it seems clear that Egypt was not a pure folk society. It was relatively fluid and was willing to try out new methods of plant or animal breeding, of architecture, or of art. In fact, there may have been less hostility to change in the prehistoric than there was in historic times, when a codified and enforced dogma began to set its disapproval upon deviations from the traditional. Further, predynastic Egypt saw an increasing amount of commerce and thus an increasing interweaving of persons and communities which were not related by blood. Basically, the economy of any one unit was that of self-sufficiency, but the role of the market was already strong, and the essential element of the folk culture—a strong sense of group solidarity as over against outsiders—had already weakened. Whether in the predynastic or the dynastic period, ancient Egypt was transitional between the folk society and urban society, and no sharp break appeared at the beginning of history.

Thus the three concepts of challenge and response, the urban revolution, and the folk society are useful and instructive about that important transition between prehistoric "barbarism" and historic "civilization," but none of them provides a full and satisfying explanation of the phenomenon of such a transition within a comparatively brief time. No one can give that satisfying explanation, first, because our information is too slight on the times and, second, because there were certain spiritual imponderables at which we can only guess. It would provide a certain satisfaction if we could lay down a series of observations on economic, social, and political changes, add them up, and achieve a result which was clearly determinant: here were the forces which brought man into civilization, which gave him a maturity of mind and outlook, which produced national governments, which called forth writing, which gave the rudiments of science, and which produced a sophisticated world outlook, art, and literature. Perhaps we simply do not know enough to list such visible determinants of historical change, but we suspect that we shall never know enough because the essential motivating forces will always be invisible, the outreaching of man's mind and spirit. Those spiritual and intellectual impulses would never be recorded because they lie too deep in the human heart and mind; early man was quite unconscious of them.

The phenomenal determinants of economics, environment, diet, and governmental and social organization seem to produce different results in different places. The civilization which emerged in Egypt was different from that which emerged in Mesopotamia, or the Indus Valley, or China, or Yucatan. The physical cultures of these different areas were distinct, and their spiritual settings were markedly varied. Further, there were some barbarisms—as in the Sudan—which were given a whole series of favorable determinants and still did not emerge into civilized life. It is possible to argue that each case is extraordinarily complex and that the series of phenomenal determinants is different in each case, so that—if we could know enough—we could explain the differences in each civilization or each barbarism on the basis of a highly complicated mathematical equation. But we suspect that every equation would contain an unknown value, the x of the mind and spirit of man. The totality of our visible observations would still leave us short of a historical or sociological answer to the phenomenon of the emergence of a culture into civilization.

The process of predynastic Egypt seems like a chemical action of slow change and final sudden reaction. It is as if there were drops of a chemical falling into a solution over a long period without producing any compositional change. Then, with relative abruptness, the solution changed, and we had a structurally different substance. What we do not know is whether this was a quantitative or a qualitative change. Was it simply a matter of saturation, and the accumulating drops abruptly became sufficient to produce a reaction? Or was it a matter of a new substance introduced at just the proper point, acting as a catalyst to make a different chemical composition?

We cannot answer this question, except subjectively. It seems likely that the whole process was quantitative and that ancient Egypt reached a point of accumulated small changes where the culture looked markedly different. A sufficient volume of quantitative change effects a difference which seems to be qualitative. However, we cannot reject the possibility that the very end of Egypt's predynastic period witnessed a new element which was the catalyst producing civilized life in the Nile Valley. That new element was a visible stimulus of the predynastic Egyptian culture by factors deriving from Mesopotamia.

No one knows how long the succession of predynastic periods lasted in Egypt, from the crude little village of Merimdeh to the beginnings of the dynasties. Let us assume that this stretch of time occupied two thousand years. For the great majority of that time—for perhaps the first eighteen hundred years—the development of Egyptian culture was internal. To be sure, there are evidences of commercial contacts reaching to far-distant lands, but the succession of visible elements is logically native and may be charted in terms of progress or retrogression of physical forms. Even the introduction of a new kind of pottery at a certain stage of prehistory appears to be rooted in the area of northeastern Africa. One can see analogies between pot forms or forms of stone vessels between Egypt and Palestine; but the analogies cannot be pressed to conclusive derivations, and, if there were derivations, it would be difficult to establish the direction of influence. No; Egypt's development was native and internal for most of her prehistory.

Then, at the very end of her prehistory, she accepted certain visible elements of definite Mesopotamian character.

The elements which Egypt borrowed from her eastern neighbor are quite clear.[15] There was the cylinder seal, an idea and an instrument which had already had a career in Mesopotamia. There was monumental architecture, using bricks in a decorative paneling, a technique which can be traced to its origins in Mesopotamia but which appeared fully developed in Egypt at this final predynastic period (Fig. 4a). And there were certain artistic motifs which were native to Mesopotamia but foreign to Egypt: balanced, antithetic groups; a hero dominating two balanced beasts; composite and fabulous animals or animals with intertwined necks; and boats of distinctively Mesopotamian type.

15. See the article by H. Frankfort in *AJSL*, LVIII (1941), 329–58, esp. 355.

All these elements had their history in the Babylonian scene and appeared full-fledged in Egypt as borrowings.

There are other elements which may belong to the same period of borrowing but where our argument rests on minor uncertainties. Mesopotamia already had the potter's wheel, which was not to appear in Egypt until dynastic times. Metallurgy in Asia was distinctly in advance of that craft in Egypt, and the latter country may have been influenced by better methods abroad. However, the most important critical factor which Egypt may have taken from Mesopotamia was the idea of writing. The most that one can say is that there was visible priority in writing in Mesopotamia, where there had been some centuries of notation on clay tablets, gradually developing into fuller record. In Egypt, writing appeared rather abruptly at the transitional point between prehistory and history; and when it appeared, it seemed already to have certain elements which—in theory, at least—belong to an advanced stage of writing. That is to say, the theory of writing assumes that the first stage must be pictographic, with each element standing for itself: the picture of a house meaning "house," the picture of a star meaning "star," etc.; and that a second stage uses the rebus-principle to construct words which cannot easily be depicted. To use the classical example applying to the English language, we can picture a *bee* and a *leaf*, but we cannot picture a *belief*. We can, however, put together the pictures of a bee and a leaf to make the sounds *bee-leaf*. At the very beginning of history, Egyptian hieroglyphic writing appeared on stone and clay with this rebus-principle already accepted. And yet the pictures which went into hieroglyphic writing were all good Egyptian pictures: the Egyptian forms of hoe and plow and stone drill. How could this writing appear thus in its adolescence, without any traces of infancy? Some have assumed that its infancy must have existed but been lost to us because the first writing was on perishable material like wood or hide. There is perhaps an element of truth in this assumption, but another theory would greatly shorten that period of infancy, the theory that the principles of picture writing, including the rebus-principle, had been borrowed from Mesopotamia at the time of the other borrowings in the late predynastic. None of the Mesopotamian pictures was taken over, only the two ideas that a standardized picture may be used as a symbol to convey a specific word and that words which cannot easily be pictured may be conveyed phonetically by the rebus-principle. If Egypt did thus borrow the idea of writing from Babylonia, it brought her abruptly into literacy and was a powerful factor in the construction of history.

We have, then, certain clear and definite borrowings from Mesopotamia and other borrowings which look entirely possible. On the other hand, archeology has thus far found no indications of Babylonian borrowing from Egypt. The cultural history of Mesopotamia showed a straightforward, normal progress through her predynastic and early dynastic periods, with no sharp break or twist at any point. The cultural history of Egypt showed a straightforward, normal progress, using native materials and methods, for the greater part of her predynastic, but at the very end of her predynastic there was—to our subjective feeling—a certain repetitiveness and uncertainty in the use of her native forms and native art. Perhaps she was groping for change. At this point there was an artistic, intellectual, and technical fructification from Babylonia, and Egypt made a great spurt toward history. Within a few generations there came the union of Egypt under the dynasties. Thus it seems that Babylonia had reached a certain cultural level which contained elements and ideas which Egypt was ready and eager to borrow, but we see no reciprocal tendency on Babylonia's part to borrow from Egypt. The cultural leadership was all on the Mesopotamian side at a time when Egypt needed such leadership. Further, we may note that the elements which Egypt borrowed just before her dynastic period continued in greater or less degree to express her culture under the first two dynasties, but then were discarded in the Third and Fourth Dynasties, when the classical Egyptian style was instituted. By that time Egypt had attained her own self-confident maturity and knew what forms she wished to use in order to express that maturity. Thanks to a stimulus from Babylonia, she was able to stand upon her own feet and work out her own forms of expression. When she did work out her own forms under the Third and Fourth Dynasties, she set for herself a style which became the cherished and rigorously maintained Egyptian expression for most of her historical career, a style which was quite independent of any Mesopotamian models. Her art of the Old Kingdom was more composed and consistent than were the artistic products of contemporary Mesopotamia.

If it be true that the last Egyptian predynastic period was affected by intellectual, technical, and artistic stimuli from Mesopotamia and that almost immediately Egypt went into her historic period, what is the meaning of this observation? Did Mesopotamian cultural leadership raise Egypt from barbarism into civilization? Our own answer to that question is qualified. On the affirmative side, Egypt's debt to Babylonia is obvious, is roughly coincident with the transition from prehistory into history, and thus may be credited with formative influence. The qualifications may be indicated by phrasing a different question: Would Egypt have passed from barbarism to civilization without Mesopotamian stimulation? Of course, the answer to that question must be speculative, since there was Mesopotamian stimulation. However, it is our belief that internal impulses are far more compelling than external pressures; that the urge toward change must be strong within a culture; and that, in the absence of that inner urge, no amount of foreign example could effect any essential spiritual change. A savage may be taught forms and techniques, but he will remain a savage because he is so in mind and heart. But one who is hungering and thirsting for change will eagerly accept forms and techniques from another in order to gain greater self-expression. If true and satisfactory self-expression is thus attained, that self-expression will work out its own forms and techniques with new self-confidence.

It is thus our belief that Egypt had been building up the maturity of outlook and the complexity of social and economic life to the point where the next step was what we call "civilization." She was at the critical point of her adolescence. At this critical point, seeking further maturity, she gladly accepted certain forms of expression from Mesopotamia and used these forms to carry over into the historical period. For some centuries they were her most important forms of expression, until she had stabilized her new life and gained the necessary sense of security and continuity. Then she worked out and standardized her own way of life, quite independently of any outside models. Her debt to the influence of Mesopotamia was very great, but the inner spiritual urge to a new way of life was the essential factor—really the only motivating factor—in the great change.

There is a related problem to this question of the nature and force of the influence of one culture upon another, and that is the problem of the means by which the influence was effected. Was there Mesopotamian conquest or colonization of Egypt, or commercial exploitation, or simply an outreaching cultural priority? It is a very simple solution to a problem if we can ascribe cultural change under outside influence to an actual penetration by immigrants, either an invading and conquering army or a colonizing incursion. Then the numerical weight and authority of the foreigners easily explains the change.

Egypt was not easy to invade. Any conquering army would have to cross difficult desert barriers or seas, where they would be cut off from bases or from adequate supplies. Looking back into predynastic days and attempting to guess what an armed force might have been, one cannot believe that a sufficient body of invaders could have penetrated the Nile Valley to overpower the Egyptians and set up a dominating rule.

The problem of colonization, either through the infiltration of wandering peoples or through the setting-up of commercial posts, is less easy to dispose of. It is true that a new racial element appeared in Egypt about this time, a people having a broader head than the Egyptians themselves. However, this broadheaded stock is assumed to have entered Egypt from the north, whereas the evidences of Mesopotamian influence which can be localized are in Upper Egypt. Further, the broadheaded stock could not have been Babylonian but could have been a northern or mountain people.

It is a slender thread to go on, but the pictured presence of boats of Mesopotamian type on monuments in the Nile Valley seems to indicate an acquaintance with such boats in or near to Egypt. The best theory which one can devise to meet the problem is that the Babylonians or some people in close touch with the Babylonians came as sailing merchants to Egypt. They would coast down the Persian Gulf and up the Red Sea. They would make their contact with the Egyptians either at a Red Sea port, such as Suez or Kosseir at the eastern end of the Wadi Hammamat, or in the Nile Valley itself if they could caravan across the eastern desert. Such merchants had knowledge of some of the recent changes in Mesopotamia. The Egyptians were at a restless, transitional point and seized eagerly on the elements of Mesopotamian culture which they could use for themselves. Thus there might have been a kind of cultural conquest without physical conquest. But, as so often, one must admit that we do not know enough to go beyond a vague speculation.

Thus we have seen several forces which were instrumental in lifting the Egyptian out of the clinging mud of his prehistory and onto the paving stones of history. The ultimate large-scale irrigation produced profound economic and social changes, bringing a much larger population, a surplus of wealth, a ruling class, and skilled professions. The stimulation from Mesopotamia was the final catalyst which precipitated the solution. But the final mystery still remains: What inner forces lifted the Egyptian toward a new life? Is the entire explanation visible before our eyes in the "urban revolution" and the Mesopotamian catalyst? Or is there still an unknown factor, which is the presence or absence of a spiritual urge toward a new way of life? It is clear that the answer must be subjective. Such an answer would be that some cultures have accepted opportunity and stimulation, whereas other cultures have simply bogged down stubbornly in the mud of the past. The only explanation that can be offered for such a difference is a dangerous one because it may seem to give a repeatable pattern to the processes of cultural development. It is possible that there is a kind of maturing of cultural experience, in which there is youth, willing to try change and experimentation, and there is a more cautious old age, which rejects the new. That might be a general rule, but one would prudently have to note that cultures may be as different essentially as persons are, with some conservative youth and some adventurous old age. On the whole, it is safer to record the How of historical occurrences and to disavow any professional concern with the Why. Let us settle down to the firm ground that Egypt ended her long predynastic period and emerged into world history with the beginning of the dynasties.

III

THE SEARCH FOR SECURITY AND ORDER

Dynasties 1–3 (about 3100–2700 B.C.)

WHAT happened at the beginning of the First Dynasty? At a
certain date we change from predynastic to dynastic, from
prehistory to history, from the unrecorded prologue to a
stage with the curtain up but the lights dimmed down to a minimum.
Why did Egyptian historical tradition claim that a certain Menes
united the Two Lands into a single nation and began the first of a series
of dynasties? We can give certain answers based on our limited range
of observations, but the essentials of the process must evade us. We can
see much of what happened, but we cannot establish the driving forces
which produced the nation.

To be sure, a single date for the beginning of a nation is always an
arbitrary figure, selected from a number of different dates: that is, at
this point we consider that the nation really became effective. There
must have been a long process of preparation before that time, and
there was probably a long process of consolidation and justification
after that time. If we could establish our early Egyptian chronology
with certainty and state that Menes held a ceremonial of "the Uniting
of the Two Lands" on certain days in some specific year in the range of
3100 B.C., we should still have to face the problems of what went before
and what came after that date.

What we do know is fragmentary and has little true significance.
A ruling family of Upper Egypt came north, by conquest united the
two parts of the land, set up a capital at Memphis near the junction of
the Two Lands, and thus started the long series of dynasties, a series

43

which lasted for about three thousand years. However, we do not know the antecedents of these conquerors from the south; we do not know whether Menes was an actual historical figure or only a later composition of legend; we do not know precisely what the word "conquest" means; we do not know whether the conquest was effected in a generation or two or lasted some centuries; and we do not know whether the role of Memphis was suddenly and immediately effective or whether it had long antecedents and later development. Above all, we lack the psychology of the process: was this a painful imposition of rule by force against long-drawn-out opposition or was Egypt ready and ripe for nationhood, with the only question one of internal competition for the rule?

We can only bring certain observations to play upon these questions. It seems that the first two dynasties were times of consolidation; for perhaps four hundred years after the founding of the First Dynasty, the culture of final predynastic times continued; then, in the Third and Fourth Dynasties, the new state was stable and secure enough to express itself in a distinctively new and "Egyptian" way. This change to new cultural expression appears to have come about with relative abruptness. The inference is that the new state could not at first address itself to matters of culture, such as architecture, art, and literature, while it was preoccupied with matters of government, such as the setting-up of force and bureaus and the securing of the acceptance of rule. This is a negative argument, but it can be bolstered with the positive observation that there are scattered records of fighting and an apparent rebellion within the First and Second Dynasties.[1] It would seem that the new state had to have plenty of time to discover and extend its powers.

Another problem, very difficult to state, is the role of the newly established king within this newly established state. In later times he was stated by the official dogma to be of other nature, a god reigning over humans. Was he so accepted from the beginnings? Probably not, for the conquest should have been more rapid if the conqueror had been widely accepted as a god. Did dogma from the beginning claim that he was a god, but did this claim gain slow acceptance because of competing claims? Or was the dogma of the divinity of the pharaoh a concept which the new state worked out over the early dynasties, in order to establish securely the new rule? In other words, did this new ruler find it necessary to promote himself from the role of the paramount mortal, whose authority might be challenged by other strong mortals, to the role of the god who could not be challenged?

1. Breasted, *ARE*, I, §§ 104, 112, 125.

This question is important because it deals with the central doctrine of the Egyptian state in all its aspects, the doctrine of the god-king. To understand that concept, we should like to know how, when, and why it came into being. It is false to assume that the divinity of the ruler belongs to a certain developmental stage of any culture. When we look at the comparable and contemporary cultures of Mesopotamia and Israel, we see that they looked upon their kings quite differently from the way the Egyptians did.[2] In those other cultures the king ruled *for* the gods but not *as* a god. In Egypt the pharaoh ruled as the god who was upon earth and among mortals. Can we understand why the Egyptians fixed upon this dogma? Can we discover when the dogma came into being?

We can give no firm and final answers to these questions. We can only pose certain hypotheses, which may or may not fit the case. The chief of these hypotheses goes back to the geographic nature of Egypt, at once isolated and divided. Egypt was the land which was cut off from major contacts and thus enjoyed a happy sense of security and special election. Her destiny was exceptional because divine providence had set her apart—distinctly apart—from her neighbors. The gods of the larger cosmos did not need to hover over her, cautiously deputizing a mortal to rule on their behalf but retaining to themselves the functional elements of power and control. No; they could go confidently about their cosmic business because one of their number, the pharaoh who was himself a god, carried the functions of power and control and resided in Egypt. The geographic security of the land, so different from Israel or Mesopotamia, gave the gods a sense of confidence about the land, so that rule could safely come down to earth *de jure* and need not be extended through a deputy on earth.

However, the geographic nature of Egypt provides a paradox, which may seem to vitiate both ends of our argument. Viewed in her external isolation, Egypt was a unity, a land apart. Viewed in her internal dualism, Egypt was a disunity, a land split apart. To the Egyptian, Egypt was at the same time "the land" and "the Two Lands." Upper Egypt and Lower Egypt were always distinctly conscious that they were different, one from the other. In any time of weakened rule they broke apart. What held them together was their common dependence upon the Nile and the accepted dogma that Egypt was ruled not by an Upper Egyptian nor by a Lower Egyptian but by a god, in whom could reside the essential forces of each part of the Two Lands. If Lower Egypt accepted this dogma, it could not object to being ruled by a being whose

2. H. Frankfort, *Kingship and the Gods* (Chicago, 1948).

family seemed to have been resident in Upper Egypt but who was, by definition, not of a geographic region in this world but of the realm of the gods.

If this be true, it is probable that it took some time to secure nation-wide acceptance of the dogma that this apparent human was not a mortal but was of other being. He proclaimed himself to be a Horus, a god of the distant spaces, of the sky, like a falcon. He proclaimed him-self to be "the Two Ladies"; that is, his being incorporated the beings of the two goddesses who stood, respectively, for Upper and Lower Egypt. These two claims took him away from any part of the soil of Egypt and yet rooted him in both parts of Egypt. Ultimately, by the Fifth Dynasty, he would claim to be the divine son of the sun-god Re, the supreme god. How did such dogma secure acceptance?

To answer that question, we must make a distinction between the acceptance of the dogma as a theory of rule and the acceptance of the dogma as applying specifically to one conquering dynasty. We have argued above that the geography of Egypt supplied a propensity to-ward acceptance of divine kingship. An added argument would flow out of the psychology of the ancient Egyptian mind. Those people were neither mystics nor modern scientific rationalists. They were basically practical, eager to accept what worked in practice and to try several different approaches to attain an end. What was useful, effec-tive, or advantageous was good. This does not mean that they were hardheaded, efficient, and categorical in a modern sense. Their reason-ing never sought to penetrate to the essence of phenomena, and their easy-going pragmatism did not attempt to find the one single way; rather, different and disparate ways were acceptable if they gave some indication of practical effectiveness.[3] Unlike their Asiatic neighbors, Babylonians and Hebrews, the Egyptians made little attempt to system-atize a coherent scheme, with separate categories for distinct phenom-ena. Under a warmer sun the Egyptians blandly blended phenomena which might have been kept resolutely apart. They were lazily tolerant and catholic-minded. Ancient psychology gave animation to every-thing in the universe—sun, wind, water, tree, rock—and made no sharp boundaries among states of being—human and animal, living and dead, human and divine. Therefore, the Egyptian's all-embracing catholicity saw no essential difference in substance in the several components of the universe. To him the various visible and tangible phenomena of his existence were only superficially or temporarily different, but essen-

3. See note at end of chapter, pp. 67–68.

tially of one substance, blended into a great spectrum of overlapping colors without sharp margins.[4] Since he felt no necessity for making clear-cut categories, it was easy for him to move comfortably from the human to the divine and to accept the dogma that this pharaoh, who lived among men as if of mortal flesh and blood, was actually a god, graciously residing upon earth in order to rule the land of Egypt. One may believe that the dogma of divine kingship was easy and natural for the Egyptian and thus may have had its roots deep in his prehistoric past.

However, it is a different question when we come to the application of the dogma to a new and conquering dynasty. When the First Dynasty came out of Upper Egypt and set up its claim to divine rule over all of Egypt, did that easygoing tolerance of the conquered territories promote immediate acceptance? Did they say to themselves: "This works; we're a practical people; we accept these rulers as our divine kings"? We do not know the answer to this question. Was there any precedent for uniting the two parts of Egypt into a single nation? It has been claimed that there had been a predynastic union of the land, probably several centuries before the First Dynasty and followed by some centuries of disunion. Unfortunately, it is impossible to say whether that predynastic union was historical fact or later historical fiction. If it was fact, then there was a precedent for the union of Egypt by the rule of a god on earth, but the precedent had been broken by a long period of disunion. If the predynastic union was not fact, then the fiction of such a union must have been built up under the earliest dynasties to justify the dynastic union by a mythical prototype.

It has already been noted in this chapter that the first two dynasties appear to have been concerned with conquest and consolidation. We should therefore propose the working theory that the idea of divine kingship was native to Egypt and had long been present as a loosely formulated concept, that the first dynasties seized upon that concept to give sanction to their new rule, and that the dogma of the divine pharaoh as we know it was therefore worked out in detailed application and achieved formal acceptance under the earliest dynasties. It must be admitted that this cannot be proved, but it can stand as a theory until additional evidence may be adduced to prove or disprove it.

Before picking up the loose thread of historical narrative, we must wrestle with another concept which, like the divine kingship, gave

4. Wilson in H. Frankfort *et al., The Intellectual Adventure of Ancient Man* (Chicago, 1946), pp. 62 ff.

stability and authority to the new state. That concept lies in the Egyptian word *ma‹at*, variously translated as "truth," "justice," "righteousness," "order," and so on. Each of those translations may be apt in a certain context, but no one English word is always applicable. *Ma‹at* was a quality which belonged to good rule or administration, but it cannot be translated as "rule," "government," "administration," or "law." *Ma‹at* was the proper quality of such applied functions. Basically, *ma‹at* had some of the same flexibility as our English terms "right," "just," "true," and "in order." It was the cosmic force of harmony, order, stability, and security, coming down from the first creation as the organizing quality of created phenomena and reaffirmed at the accession of each god-king of Egypt. In the temple scenes the pharaoh exhibited *ma‹at* to the other gods every day, as the visible evidence that he was carrying out his divine function of rule on their behalf. Thus there was something of the unchanging, eternal, and cosmic about *ma‹at*. If we render it "order," it was the order of created things, physical and spiritual, established at the beginning and valid for all time. If we render it "justice," it was not simply justice in terms of legal administration; it was the just and proper relationship of cosmic phenomena, including the relationship of the rulers and the ruled. If we render it "truth," we must remember that, to the ancient, things were true not because they were susceptible of testing and verification but because they were recognized as being in their true and proper places in the order created and maintained by the gods. *Ma‹at*, then, was a created and inherited rightness, which tradition built up into a concept of orderly stability, in order to confirm and consolidate the *status quo*, particularly the continuing rule of the pharaoh. The opposites of *ma‹at* were words which we translate as "lying," "falsehood," and "deceit." That which was not consonant with the established and accepted order could be denied as being false. *Ma‹at* comes closest to the moral connotation of our word "good."

To the human mind the future has fearful uncertainty, and passing time brings change, even decay. If man could arrest the flight of time, he would discharge some of his feeling of uncertainty and insecurity. It is possible to cut down on the ravages of time and the peril of the future by asserting the eternal and unchanging. If temporary and transitory phenomena can be related to the timeless and stable, doubts and fears can be reduced. The ancient did this by the process of myth-making, whereby the phenomena and activities of his little world were asserted to be momentary flashes of the everlasting, rocklike order of the gods. So this little pharaoh who sat upon the throne of Egypt was no transitory human but was the same "good god" that he had been from the Beginning and would be for all time. So the relationship of beings was not something which had to be worked out painfully in an evolution toward even better conditions but was magnificently free from change, experiment, or evolution, since it had been fully good from the Beginning and needed only to be reaffirmed in its unchanging rightness. Aspects of the divine kingship and of *maʿat* might be subject to temporary misfortune or challenge, but the generalities of these two concepts came to be fundamental in acceptance because they gave timid man freedom from doubt through the operation of the immutable.

It is our theory that these two concepts had already been present in Egyptian consciousness before the dynasties, because they seem natural to Egypt and not artificial constructions, but that the early dynasties had the problem of articulating the concepts to that new nation which they were constructing. Until that specific application had been worked out in its many relationships and interpretations, the new nation was tentative and formative. When, finally, the application had become accepted as the eternal tradition of Egypt, the state was truly in being, and ancient Egypt ended her adolescence and entered upon her characteristic career of essential sameness for fifteen hundred years. We believe that the adolescence took up much of the energies of the new state for the first two dynasties, perhaps four centuries, and that it was not until the Third Dynasty that Egypt really became Egypt.

Thus we assume the process of the first two or three dynasties to have been highly centripetal, with the setting-up of a state with the pharaoh as its essential nucleus. He, as a god, *was* the state. To be sure, it was necessary for him to have officials of a government which had spread and which would become increasingly elaborated, but our evidence indicates that they were his officers, appointed by him, responsible to him alone, and holding office subject to his divine pleasure. To be sure, it was necessary for a new state to have rules and regulations for administrative procedure and precedent, but our negative evidence suggests that there was no codification of law, impersonally conceived and referable by magistrates without consideration of the crown. Rather, the customary law of the land was conceived to be the word of the pharaoh, articulated by him in conformance with the concept of *maʿat* and ever subject to his divine pleasure, within his interpretation of *maʿat* and of his function as a god. These suggestions derive from observations of later times and from our theory that the construction of the state was achieved in these earliest dynasties, to be valid for all later times. In later times there was visible no impersonal and continuing body of law, like one of the Mesopotamian codes, until we come down into Persian and Greek days; the centralization of the state in the person of the king apparently forbade such impersonal law. The authority of codified law would have competed with the personal authority of the pharaoh. We theorize that magistrates operated under customs and practices as locally known to them, all conceived to be the expression of royal will and immediately changeable by royal whim. The only qualification to such rigidly personalized and centralized government was the concept of *ma‹at*, that which was right and true and in conformance with divine order; but, since the king was himself a god, he was the earthly interpreter of *ma‹at* and—in theory, at least—was subject to the control of *ma‹at* only within the limits of his conscience, if a god needs to have a conscience.

These forms and this philosophy of rule are invisible to us in the earliest dynasties. It is the analogy of visible forms which leads us to suggest that the invisible forms were being worked out at this time. Physically, the culture of the first three dynasties is shown in architecture, sculpture, minor arts, and a small amount of writing. Such forms show the first two dynasties to have been a continuation of the physical culture of the final predynastic period, particularly as affected by the stimulation from Mesopotamia. Those borrowings of monumental architecture with recessed brick paneling, of cylinder seals, and of certain motifs in relief sculpture continued through the first two dynasties and only began to receive alteration or substitution in the Third and Fourth Dynasties. Our argument is, thus, that the first three dynasties were too busy setting up the state and the tradition of the state to undertake any modification of the forms of culture. When that state was finally and firmly set upon its base of the divine kingship, then Egypt was ready to express her own characteristic forms, worked out independently upon native soil.

The royal and noble tombs of the final predynastic and earliest dynastic times are the largest visible sign of the physical culture. These were low, flat-topped structures of thick brick walls and sloping sides, called *mastabas* in Egyptian archeology. The sides were relieved by decorative paneling, with bricks set into recessed niches. All this was Mesopotamian in origin. Mesopotamia had only brick. Egypt, of course, had brick, but stone was abundant and easy to work. It is significant that stone came in only slowly, first as a mere adjunct of a brick structure. Under the First Dynasty one pharaoh tried the experiment of flooring his burial pit with slabs of cut and fitted granite. Thus the central chamber in his eternal home had a pavement of more enduring material than the rest of the brick tomb. Under the Second Dynasty a pharaoh had a complete chamber of his brick tomb constructed of hewn and fitted limestone, and for the same period there is literary evidence of a temple or shrine built in stone. Such construction was unusual enough to warrant significant mention in the royal annals.[5] It was in the Third Dynasty that stone really came into its own, in the great complex around the Step Pyramid of King Djoser at Sakkarah (Fig. 9b). Perhaps it is wrong to say that stone "came into its own," because the stone of this structure was cut into small bricks, laid as if the stone blocks were mud bricks, and paneled in the same way as the previous brick tombs were. However, the great complex was built entirely in stone, even though experience and tradition dictated that stone should be treated as though it were brick. As yet, the architects and masons had not dared to realize the qualities of stone for massiveness, strength, and durability. There were also decorative elements in the brick construction which told of the weight of conservatism in an architecture which had dared to be revolutionary in the medium used. The columns supporting the roof blocks were pieced together out of limestone bricks and carved with flutings, to represent a bundle column of reeds smeared with mud, an earlier architectural form from a much simpler structure. The stone roof blocks were carved and painted on their undersides to represent palm logs, the earlier roofing material. This great complex of buildings was a magnificent achievement, and the architect who conceived it and laid it out was an inventive and bold genius. However, even an adventurer may explore new territory in ways that are familiar to him, with due regard for precedent, particularly if the sacred sanctions are involved.[6]

As a generalization, the ancient Egyptian was neither adventurous nor experimental; he preferred to continue the pattern which had been handed down through long ages. However, that pattern must have been developed through experimentation at some time, and the earliest dynasties were a period of trial and discovery. Then the Egyptian worked out the forms of expression which were so thoroughly to his

5. Breasted, *ARE*, I, §134.

6. E. Baldwin Smith, *Egyptian Architecture as Cultural Expression* (New York, 1938), pp. 60 ff.

liking that he attempted to hold them unchanging for the rest of his cultural existence. It is a great pity that we know so little about this earliest historical period and that most of our knowledge is derived by inference or reference from later periods. Over the many centuries of ancient Egyptian history the charge that this people was not adventurous or creative[7] is true. They preferred to cling firmly to the status which they had inherited—from the gods, in their dogma. The great majority of those new elements which came into the physical culture of later pharaonic Egypt consisted of borrowings and adaptations from abroad, not local inventions. But, of course, the status to which they clung so fervidly had been worked out at some time. For the most part, that time was the first five dynasties. If that is true, we do face the question of whether this status which made up the characteristic Egyptian culture was also a borrowing from abroad. We have seen the effect of the fructification from Mesopotamia at the end of the predynastic period. Was the "Egyptian cultural expression" which was devised in the earliest dynasties also a borrowing or adaptation from abroad?

The answer to that question is in part an argument from silence. It is difficult to see anything in that Egyptian cultural expression which can be referred to any foreign neighbor, and it is possible to ascribe every new development to domestic activity only. Thus far we have mentioned only monumental architecture in stone, taking the place of construction in brick. It was pointed out that Mesopotamia had been forced to build in brick, because of the absence of stone, whereas Egypt had an abundance of building stone in great variety. It might further be pointed out that the architectural types worked out in stone were Egyptian in spirit. The columns imitating reed bundles, the roof slabs imitating palm trunks, the cornice roll, and the torus molding— all went back to Nilotic models and not to any known antecedents elsewhere. Further, the characteristic batter of the walls of tombs and temples has its direct analogy in the sloping cliff walls which border the Nile, so that these structures were artistically fitted to their setting against or upon those cliffs. Ultimately, that battered wall found its logical expression in the sloping sides of the pyramid, a structure which is characteristically Egyptian and has no sensible analogies elsewhere.

Sculpture in the round may be viewed with the same eye as architecture, and relief sculpture was subject to some of the same principles

7. For example, H. E. Winlock, *The Rise and Fall of the Middle Kingdom at Thebes* (Macmillan, 1947), pp. 150 ff., and, by inference, H. Frankfort, *Ancient Egyptian Religion* (New York, 1948), pp. vii f.

which governed statuary. Before the Fourth Dynasty the typical Egyptian figure in sculpture or painting had not yet been devised. Statues gave the impression of a compact cylinder, of well-rounded surfaces. Figures in the flat were soft, moist gingerbread men in feeling—plastic, pliable, lithe. By the Fourth Dynasty new forms had been set, and a canon of dignified art, with a feeling of strong permanency, had been laid down. We use the word "canon" because the acceptance of the new forms was as absolute as though there had been a royal decree, prescribing and proscribing forms of artistic technique and expression. Actually, the process was probably less formal and consisted of royal acceptance of certain forms over a generation or two, which acceptance was as binding as law. At any rate, the cylindrical in statuary gave way to the cubic, with the impression of flat planes and corners. Statues were to be viewed in direct full-face or in direct profile. It is probable that statues were never set out in the open, where they might be viewed from any angle, but were always designed as essential parts of some structure, to which they belonged as an artistic composition and in which they should be seen only in setting. Thus a statue might be inserted into a niche, where it could be seen only from the front, or might be set up against a wall, where it should be seen only from the front. In this way the flat plane became essential, and that distinctive angularity which marks Egyptian art came into being. There is no indication of any outside influence; the forms which were achieved derived from the use of blocks of stone of any size, so plentiful in Egypt, and from the setting of statues as dictated by Egyptian religion.[8]

Sculpture in the round is inseparable from relief sculpture, which, in turn, is inseparable from painting. The essential cubism of Egyptian statuary produced that squared, static, and solid flat figure which covers the walls of Egyptian tombs and temples. The flat planes of statuary appeared here skilfully twisted, with eye and shoulders in full frontal view, the rest of the body in profile. For its purpose, this figure was wonderfully successful. Like the statue, it was designed for eternity. Each figure claimed eternal life by solidity and stolidity; by avoiding the appearance of flexibility, momentary action, or passing emotion; and by standing massive and motionless, sublimely freed from a single location in space or a single moment in time. As the Egyptian myths made momentary activities timeless and everlasting, so Egyptian art

8. Cf. H. Frankfort, *Sculpture of the Third Millennium B.C. from Tell Asmar and Khafājah* (*OIP*, Vol. XLIV [Chicago, 1939]), pp. 34 ff.

made the depicted individual a stereotype, and thus immortal. This does not mean that there was no characterization of individuals in Egyptian art; such individuality of portraiture as did not violate the essential of eternal repose was permitted. However, if we speak of portraiture, we must not use the modern sense, which brings in the photographic, temporary, and emotional, but we must remember that the ancient Egyptian desired the representation which best served the purposes of eternal life and that this necessarily had a great deal of the static and idealized. Playing children, servants, and persons of little dignity might be depicted in activity or excitation, but the lord whom the art served was shown in timeless and untiring majesty. For that purpose, the squared-off, striding profile, with its wide, unblinking eye, was beautifully adapted.

This new art came into being with extraordinary rapidity and achieved grace and sophistication of line and feeling within a relatively brief time. Few artistic compositions are so successful for the purposes of sublime majesty as is the seated figure of the Pharaoh Khaf-Re of the Fourth Dynasty in the Cairo Museum or for massive and eternal repose as is the Hem-Iunu in Hildesheim. Yet we should like to emphasize that there was a good deal of experimentation within the set canons and standards of this art. The Sheikh el-Beled in Cairo and the Ankh-haf in Boston (Fig. 8b) are no slavish stereotypes. One has the feeling that these early artists did not feel chained by the absolute dictates of this art but took delight in creating a subsurface feeling under the prescribed formula. Experimentation and creativity were still possible in a period when the art was new, before the dead hand of the past became too heavy a burden.[9]

Probably there were other elements in the culture in which this period of trial and new life produced works of real value. Returning to architecture, it could be noted that the pyramids and pyramid temples of the earlier period were more truly and conscientiously constructed than were those of the later Old Kingdom. In particular, the Great Pyramid, near the beginning of the Fourth Dynasty, is a tremendous mass of stone finished with the most delicate precision. Here were six and a quarter million tons of stone, with casing blocks averaging as much as two and a half tons each; yet those casing blocks were dressed and fitted with a joint of one-fiftieth of an inch—a scrupulous nicety worthy of the jeweler's craft. Here the margin of error in the square-

9. See W. S. Smith, *A History of Egyptian Sculpture and Painting in the Old Kingdom* (Oxford University Press, 1946), and the review in *JNES*, VI (1947), 247 ff.

ness of the north and south sides was 0.09 per cent and of the east and west sides, 0.03 per cent. This mighty mass of stone was set upon a dressed-rock pavement which, from opposite corners, had a deviation from a true plane of only 0.004 per cent. The craftsman's conscience could not humanly have done better.[10] Such cold statistics reveal to us an almost superhuman fidelity and devotion to the physical task at hand. Certainly, such exactness and conscientiousness were not characteristics of Egyptian builders in later times, who were frequently guilty of hasty, showy, but insecure construction.[11] The earliest dynasties constituted ancient Egypt's trial of strength and were the one period in which her physical achievements were marked by the greatest honesty and care. The several pyramids of the Third and Fourth Dynasties far surpass later pyramids in technical craftsmanship. Viewed as the supreme efforts of the state, they show that earliest historical Egypt was once capable of scrupulous intellectual honesty. For a short time she was activated by what we call the "scientific spirit," experimental and conscientious. After she had thus discovered her powers and the forms which suited her, the spirit was limited to conservative repetition, subject to change only within known and tested forms. We of the age which glorifies progress to ever better forms and conditions may deplore such a slackening of spirit. But we must understand the ancient mythmaking mind, which sought security in arresting time by clinging to the divinely set origins and thus ignoring the future and which did not inquire too closely into the unknown because that belonged to gods rather than men. In that setting we should give all credit to Egypt's earliest achievements and to her success in working out forms which lasted for long centuries. After all, stability was what she desired, and she effected a culture which gave her satisfaction for some fifteen hundred years.

Now one line of argument does not make a case, particularly an argument resting on a few selected data. We have claimed that earliest historical Egypt was of high intellect, conscience, and daring; that claim has been based solely upon a few observations in architecture and art. Are there any other data visible from the first dynasties which would corroborate these observations? We believe that there are, although we must confess that they are not easy to establish or even to date with certainty. Such data may be found in a scientific treatise, the

10. I. E. S. Edwards, *The Pyramids of Egypt* (Penguin Books, 1947), esp. p. 87.

11. S. Clarke and R. Engelbach, *Ancient Egyptian Masonry: The Building Craft* (Oxford University Press, 1930), esp. pp. 132 ff.

Edwin Smith Surgical Papyrus, and in a philosophical discourse, the Memphite Theology. If only these two could be dated with finality to the first four dynasties, they would establish that earliest culture as equaling—perhaps even surpassing—anything in the ancient world down to the Greeks in intellectual-spiritual expression. Unfortunately, both texts come down to us in documents which were written in later times, so that it is first necessary to argue that they derive from very early originals.

The Edwin Smith Surgical Papyrus is known in a manuscript probably of the seventeenth century B.C. From the language, grammar, and syntax it may easily be argued that there was an original document of the early Old Kingdom. It is certain that the text is much older than the extant manuscript. The tendency of such medical documents to claim a legendary origin in the First to Fourth Dynasties may have a basis of fact in the beginnings of formal Egyptian medicine in that early period. At any rate, nothing in the basic text of this papyrus points to a document composed as late as the seventeenth century, the time when the extant manuscript was written down; several elements in that text point to a very early origin, to a period before the Egyptian language received its classical cast. We believe that the basic text precedes the Fifth Dynasty and may go back to the first two dynasties.

Egyptian medical documents contain a hodge-podge of home remedies based on a lore of herbs and of sympathetic magic, outright witch-doctoring in the forms of charms and incantations, and shrewd observation on the functions of the body. In both the Edwin Smith Surgical Papyrus and the Ebers Medical Papyrus there is a treatise on the functions of the heart, pointing out how the heart "speaks" in various parts of the body and thus the physician may "measure for the heart" in those parts of the body. This does not quite reach the concept of the circulation of the blood, since there was no recognition of a circuit to and from the heart and since it was believed that the heart supplied other fluids as well as blood. However, the recognition of the organic relation of the heart and parts of the body and the recognition of the importance of the heart as a source of life-material surpass any physiological observation until one comes down to the Greeks. Further, when the ancient physician examined the patient by "measuring for the heart," he probably did not count the pulse in our modern sense—so many beats to some unit of time—but rather gained an impression of the patient's general condition, observing that the heart beat was markedly too fast or too slow. These qualifications should not blind our eyes to an appraisal of this treatise on the heart as a remarkable pre-Greek scientific document.[12]

The Edwin Smith Surgical Papyrus concerns itself chiefly with broken bones. The surgeon describes each break, states whether he believes that he can deal with it successfully, and gives the indicated treatment. The text is full of glosses, explaining the technical or strange terms which were no longer in the language of the day. There is remarkably little magic in the treatise. With one glaring exception, the surgeon confined himself to manual treatment, rest, diet, and medicaments. Further, in certain cases where the surgeon confessed himself unable to deal successfully with a serious fracture, he went on to observe the progressive stages of the ailment. This is very significant: he did not ascribe a hopeless case to the malignant activity of some divine or demoniac force; he did not resort to a magico-religious hocus-pocus; with dispassionate scientific curiosity, he noted the succession of purely physical symptoms. Within the mythmaking mind of the times, this matter-of-fact attitude was rare and very creditable.

One case in the papyrus highlights the practical spirit of the early surgeon.[13] The patient had incurred a compound fracture of the skull, resulting in a partial paralysis on one side of the body. A mysterious aspect of the ailment was that there was no external evidence of the serious fracture; the skin was not broken or bleeding. It might further have been mysterious in that an unseen break in the skull produced paralysis in the neck, shoulder, hand, and foot—on one side only. The surgeon confessed that he could not cure this fracture. He could only recommend relaxation and continued observation. Yet he makes this curious remark: "Thou shouldst distinguish him from one whom something entering from outside has smitten, (but simply) as one the head of whose shoulder-fork is not released, as well as one whose nail has fallen into the middle of his hand, while he discharges blood from his nostrils and his ears, and he suffers a stiffness in his neck." Here it is denied that the mysterious and alarming ailment is the result of a "smiting" by "something entering from outside." What does that mean? Fortunately, we are provided with an explanatory gloss: "As for 'something entering from outside,' it means the breath of an outside god or death, and not the introduction of something which his (own) flesh has pro-

12. J. H. Breasted, *The Edwin Smith Surgical Papyrus* (*OIP*, Vol. III [Chicago, 1930]), I, 1–29.

13. Case 8, *ibid.*, pp. 201–16. Our translation differs from that of Breasted in the critical words, "thou shouldst distinguish him from. . . ."

duced." In other words, the surgeon was not separated from his dispassionate scientific state of mind by the strange aspects of the case. He said that these phenomena were purely physical and not a product of divine or demoniacal force. The unseen fracture and the partial paralysis were products of flesh and blood suffering from a physical blow and not the unaccountable and intruding "breath of an outside god or death." Again we must note that this was a remarkable approach to the scientific attitude in an age which rarely sought physical or physiological causes but which was normally content to seek explanations in the activity of unseen forces. Egyptian medicine never surpassed the detached and scholarly state of mind shown in the Edwin Smith Papyrus. Indeed, no later Egyptian medical document came up to the general scholarly attitude of that treatise. If we can accept the argument that the treatise derived from the earliest dynasties, this is an added reason for prizing the spirit and achievements of that period so highly.

The text known as the "Memphite Theology" also comes down to us in a late copy, but here we are even more confident that the original must be dated to the early Old Kingdom. Not only are the language and textual construction very early, but the internal evidence of the text places it at the beginning of Egyptian history. In large part the inscription deals with the importance of Memphis, the Memphite god Ptah (Fig. 7b), and the ceremonies which took place at that city. Now Memphis was the new capital of Egypt at the beginning of the dynasties. This, then, was the text giving the theological justification for the location of the national capital. The very early date is clearly validated.

The particular section of the text in which we are interested is that part which deals with the creation. Now it was not unusual that an important shrine, like that at the new capital of Memphis, should claim participation in the creation myth. Mythmaking is a process of relating the localized and temporal to the cosmic and eternal. Every important shrine in Egypt seems to have had its creation mound, recognized as the Place of the Creation,[14] and various gods were blended in various ways with the creator-god, so that their claims to priority might have some show of validity. Thus it would not be surprising to find that Ptah, the "Opener," was somehow concerned with that creation usually attributed to Atum, the cosmic "All."

What is remarkable in the Memphite Theology is the statement of the mechanism and purpose of creation. The customary myth of creation is of a nature which probably goes back to simple and earthy pre-

14. H. Frankfort *et al.*, *The Intellectual Adventure of Ancient Man*, pp. 21-23.

dynastic beginnings. It tells that before the creation there was a watery void, accompanied by darkness, formlessness, and invisibility. Then, just as the floodwaters of the Nile subside and permit little hillocks of mud to appear as the first promise of annual life in Egypt, so the primeval watery void subsided, and the first primordial hillock of earth appeared amid the surrounding nothingness. On that island hillock was the creator-god Atum, whose name means that he was All within himself. There was no other being but Atum. On that mud hillock he brought into existence all the other beings and phenomena of the universe. The various versions differ on how he did this. A rather earthy concept takes the viewpoint that Atum was male and that there was no female with whom he might mate for procreation, so that he produced his seed by self-pollution; the resulting male and female deities then took up the task of generation and produced the further phenomena. Another version carries the idea somewhat away from the physical by observing that Atum was All within himself, so that he brought the other gods into being by naming the parts of his body. The utterance of a name which has never before been spoken is in itself an act of creation; it gives form and identity to that which previously had been unknown. However, even this version is basically physical, since Atum effectively dismembered himself to make other and separate beings.

Now we turn to the new Memphite Theology, which must have been fully aware of the normally accepted Atumic creation myth and which had to adapt or incorporate that myth into its elevation of Ptah and Memphis to priority. It faced the questions: Where did Atum himself come from? Why was there creation? In other words, it sought for a First Principle. It stated that Ptah, the god of Memphis, was the heart and tongue of the gods. Egyptian thought could deal with abstracts but tended to give them concrete location. "Heart and tongue" was the Egyptian's pictorial way of saying mind and speech. There was an articulate intelligence behind the creation. Through the thought of the heart and the expression of the tongue, Atum himself and all the other gods came into being. This idea of a rational principle behind creation constitutes the Egyptians' closest approach to the Logos doctrine— "in the beginning was the Word, and the Word was with God, and the Word was God." The heart, which was to the Egyptian the seat of mind, will, and emotion, conceived the idea of a universe, separated into its various phenomena, peopled by its various beings, and regulated by divine order. The tongue gave birth to that idea by the process of uttering a command.

It is (the heart) which causes every completed (concept) to come forth, and it is the tongue which announces what the heart thinks. Thus all the gods were formed. . . . Indeed, all the divine order came into being through what the heart thought and the tongue commanded. . . . (Thus justice was given to) him who does what is desired, (and punishment to) him who does what is not desired. Thus life was given to him who has peace, and death was given to him who has sin. Thus were made all work and all crafts, the action of the arms, the movement of the legs, and the activity of every member of the body, in conformance with the command which the heart thought, which came forth through the tongue, and which gives the value of everything. (And so) it comes to pass that it is said of Ptah: "He who made everything and brought the gods into being." . . . So Ptah was satisfied, after he had made everything, as well as the divine order.[15]

What we have in the Memphite Theology is of the greatest importance. It is a search for the First Principle, the intelligence underlying the universe. As such, it was inquisitive and exploratory beyond the normal Egyptian placidity with the universe as created. Within its definite circumscription, it was philosophical beyond anything which came later in ancient Egypt. It was an approach to abstract thinking—only an approach, because the pragmatic Egyptian still used his limited range of physical concepts like "heart" and "tongue" in his search for mind and purpose behind the creation of the cosmos and human existence. But we must remember that the Memphite Theology lies two thousand years before the Greeks or Hebrews. Its insistence that there was a creative and controlling intelligence, which fashioned the phenomena of nature and which provided, from the beginning, rule and rationale, was a high peak of pre-Greek thinking, a peak which was not surpassed in later Egyptian history. From that achievement it may be argued that ancient Egypt exhibited its best at the beginning of its history, in the first three or four dynasties, when its culture was still tentative and exploratory, in search of national expression. Later, when it had discovered the satisfactory forms of expression, speculation about purposes and goals fell under a kind of tacit interdict, and the world and heavenly order had to be accepted as given, as belonging to the realm of divine myth and therefore not to be examined or questioned by mere man.

We credit these initial dynasties with another achievement of great cultural importance, and that is the invention of the 365-day calendar. It is easy to exaggerate the importance of this calendar to the Egyptian; the new calendar was simply for official precision in keeping records and had little application to daily life. Agricultural activity was regu-

15. K. Sethe, *Dramatische Texte zur altägyptischen Mysterienspielen* (*Untersuch.*, X [1928]), pp. 59 ff.

lated by the rise and fall of the Nile, and lunar months were basic for briefer periodicity in the lives of the masses and even in most of the festivals. However, the Nile year was erratic, sometimes falling short of a true solar year and sometimes exceeding it, and a year constructed of lunar months would not coincide with an average Nile year; the state needed to keep its records more precisely. Gradually, over the centuries, the Egyptians must have kept records of the number of days between each high Nile, worked out an average, which came close to 365 days, and established an arbitrary year, which they pegged at first to an annual phenomenon, the visibility of the Dog Star on the eastern horizon at dawn. The lack of a leap year would not be felt for a few generations, and, since the official 365-day year had no agricultural or seasonal importance but was simply used for governmental and business records, there was no necessity to try for greater precision. Nevertheless, we must give the Egyptians credit for the observations and calculations by which, nearly five thousand years ago, they invented and set in motion the direct ancestor of our own calendar year.

If it be true that the earliest dynasties were a period in which the characteristic structure of the Egyptian culture was worked out in its historical form, what do we know about the beginnings of institutions in that period? What do we know about the setting-up of a national government, of the articulation of the former local states into the nation, of the building-up of an officialdom, of the legal sanctions whereby the state controlled the people? What do we know about the social and economic status of the people? Did a new government bring into being new ruling classes, and therefore new social classes? Did a single government, controlling the land from the First Cataract to the Mediterranean, so improve the economic standing of the nation that there was a newly rich class and a notable increase in population? These are highly important questions, but we cannot answer any of them. Documentary evidence in the form of records is virtually lacking for the first three dynasties and is very scarce in the fourth. Evidence from art or from physical remains is too scanty to bear much weight. It is again necessary to ignore such questions in the lack of evidence or to resort to pure speculation; and it must be stressed that speculation is highly subjective.

In the first chapter we noted that the wall reliefs of the Old Kingdom, in the Fifth and Sixth Dynasties, showed scenes of hunting in jungle marshes, suggesting that the task of draining such jungles and then irrigating the resultant land was still incomplete. It seems possible that the arable land of Egypt was relatively slight before there was a unified state. With national order established for the length of Egypt, there would be domestic peace and an opportunity to concentrate on agricultural advance, and there would be one single government regulating the use of water and land, forbidding malpractice, and encouraging wider irrigation and planting, in the interests of higher taxes. There would be a freer flow of commerce, more urban centers for the distribution of goods, and thus a greater market for increasing products. We have already discussed the concept of an "urban revolution" and have seen that it was probably a slow process of evolution rather than of revolution. When we consider the factor of one strong, central, and regulating government, it seems likely that a great stimulation to the process of the urban revolution lay in the union of Egypt under the dynasties. If that be true, a major part of the draining of the swamps, the irrigating of new land, the increase in crops and in population, the stimulation of commerce, the specialization of working function, and the appearance of a wealthy and leisured class may have been a result of national government rather than a process leading to national government. In any case, the beginnings of this urban revolution lay in prehistory, even though we may assume that the setting-up of a state was an essential to the progress of the revolution.

In the process of winning new agricultural land, the pharaoh was a leader. Credit went to him, as the embodiment of the state, for the presence and control of the life-giving waters.[16] An early relief shows him active in the ceremonial of opening a new canal (Fig. 5a). His government had a definite interest in the annual height of the Nile and the consequent prosperity of the land. The early royal annals give a measurement for each year, which can only be the height of the River above or below some fixed datum. Prosperity belonged to the pharaoh and had to be credited to his divine activity on behalf of his land; adversity was probably ascribed to the hostile activity of other gods, whom the pharaoh would have to propitiate in order to rescue his land.

Mention has been made of royal annals, and we do possess a fragmentary and cryptic series of notations for the reigns of a few kings from the First to the Fifth Dynasty, in the Palermo Stone and related fragments. Each year was memorialized because of some significant happening and was marked with a record of the height of the Nile. At any rate, the happening was significant at the time when the record

16. G. A. Wainwright, *The Sky Religion in Egypt* (Cambridge University Press, 1938).

was made, although many of the notations have little meaning to us. Most of them seem to belong to religious ceremonials related to the kingship. Perhaps it is significant that there is very little of political history, in the sense of wars and conquests. For the recording of the years, the peaceful activity of royal ritual, journeys, and buildings was of major importance.[17]

For the first three dynasties we know little about the kings, less about the nobility, and practically nothing about the people. We must stifle our curiosity about social conditions in a changing age. One small series of observations must bear an inordinate amount of weight, because it is all that we have to go on. That deals with the relation of pharaoh to his people at the point of death.

The Egyptian belief in a life after death, an immortality which repeated the best features of the life in this world, was one of the extraordinary factors in the culture. In its developed form it promised every good man a happy eternity. There may be some question as to the definition of that term "good man," particularly as it related to the common masses, but the evidence which comes down to us from the articulate populace indicates that any man might win for himself immortality. When and how did that belief originate? Are its origins lost in the predynastic past, or can we see some development of the idea in historic times?

Like so many of the questions in this book, these can receive only tentative answers. The first observation is that there was a belief in some kind of survival in the earliest predynastic period, as evidenced by the equipment which accompanied the dead in burial and the fact that the burial position was commonly in relation to the rising sun. Whether that survival was thought to be limited in time or in scope we do not know. At any rate, in the predynastic period burial was localized in the several provinces in an apparent independence of rulers. The final predynastic and the first dynasties show a contrast, in that the burial of important personages was commonly in close juxtaposition to the royal tomb. It would seem that the development of the idea of the state and of the divinity of the pharaoh was reflected in a burial custom in which the noble clearly expressed his dependence upon his god-king. What does this mean?

We may accompany this observation with the recent discovery of

17. Breasted, *ARE*, I, §§ 76 ff.; H. Schäfer, *Ein Bruchstück altägyptischer Annalen* (*Berlin Abh.*, 1902); H. Gauthier, *Quatre nouveaux fragments de la Pierre de Palerme* ("Musée Égyptien," III [Cairo, 1915]), pp. 29 ff., Pls. XXIV-XXXI.

the burial of a First Dynasty princess together with her personal and domestic servants, each having the tools and materials of his or her trade and apparently all put to death at the time of the princess' interment.[18] In other words, the princess, as the daughter or wife or mother of the god-king, was assured of a continuing existence after death in essentially the same terms as in this life. For that afterlife she needed her own physical equipment, which was placed in her tomb, and she needed her own servants, who were slaughtered to accompany her. We cannot know their state of mind at this mass execution on behalf of their lady. Presumably, there was a doctrine that their afterlife was nonexistent or very limited unless they were needed by someone who was certain of immortality. Therefore, their chance of immortality rested solely on their physical and temporal juxtaposition to her in death. This discovery is the clearest indication of a primitive custom which had been suspected from other evidence.[19] However, the practice of mass sacrifice seems not to have survived into later times in Egypt. The accompaniment of the lord by the servant thereafter became ritual, magical, and symbolic.

Thus the close juxtaposition of the tomb of the noble to the tomb of the pharaoh, particularly in early times down into the Fifth Dynasty, has its meaning. There was no mass sacrifice at the time of the king's death or burial; the accompaniment was spatial rather than temporal. The pharaoh, as a god, was assured of eternal and blessed existence. At the beginning of Egyptian history the noble was not so assured; his best chance of happy immortality lay in his close relation to and service of his god-king. If he could be buried close to the royal *mastaba* or pyramid, if his titles as carved on his tomb clearly stated his service to the pharaoh, and if the inscriptions of his tomb expressed his dependence upon royal pleasure, he might then be needed as an agent in that continued rule which the deceased pharaoh would enjoy in other realm. In the next chapter we shall note the Pyramid Texts, which served to beatify the pharaoh after death, and the absence of similar texts in the tombs of nobles; and we shall there note the beginnings of a process of decentralization and independence of the king. Here we claim that, in the earliest dynasties, only those were sure of eternal life after death

18. *Illustrated London News*, June 25, 1947, p. 91; *American Journal of Archaeology*, LI (1947), 192.

19. For example, under the Middle Kingdom an Egyptian official was buried in the Sudan, together with more than a hundred slaughtered servants (G. A. Reisner, *Excavations at Kerma, I–III* ["Harvard African Studies," Vol. V (Cambridge, 1923)], pp. 141 ff.). See also pp. 139–40 below.

who carried within them the germ of divinity—king and queen, prince and princess—and that the noble class apparently depended upon royal need of their services in order to gain such eternal life. This was the doctrine of divine kingship carried out in grim earnest.

As to the lower grades of society—merchants, artisans, peasants, serfs, and slaves—we have no real evidence on their hopes of immortality at this early period. Probably, they, like the nobles, depended upon their immediate overlords. If a Queen Meres-enekh was graciously pleased to record the name, title, and figure of her mortuary priest Khemetnu in her tomb, she had some need of him and he had some chance of survival in her service.[20] Carrying out the same principle, when a noble had the figures of domestic servants placed in his tomb or carved on the walls of the tomb, his servants in this world might have hope of continued existence in accompanying and waiting upon him, just as he himself lived on because he accompanied and waited upon the pharaoh. This, however, is an argument based on rather slim evidence. It assumes that the next world was essentially the same as this world in its happiest and most successful aspects. Since the central factor in this world was the divine nature of the king, who owned and controlled everything within Egypt, the next world would be based on the same absolute authority. Life after death, independent of the pharaoh, would thus be out of the question for this early period.

Many of our arguments in this chapter have been derived from fragmentary and slim evidence. We might similarly speculate on the political tensions and struggles of the first three or four dynasties, as indicated in the apparent popularity of certain gods, some of whom had geographic or functional location. For example, the pharaoh was the god Horus, embodiment of far-reaching rule. What does it mean that briefly in the Second Dynasty the pharaoh was also the god Seth, a factor opposite to Horus? Was this a rebellion by a part of Egypt devoted to Seth or a rebellion within the doctrine of divine kingship? Here we simply note the fact as indicating the struggle of the state to work out national acceptance.[21]

A different problem, which may be of far greater importance, lay in the struggle between two religious systems, the solar and the Osirian. That some such struggle went on, down into historic times, seems

20. G. A. Reisner in *Bulletin of the Museum of Fine Arts, Boston*, XXV (October, 1927), 76.

21. P. E. Newberry, "The Set Rebellion of the IInd Dynasty," *Ancient Egypt* (1922), pp. 40 ff.

highly probable. To be sure, the struggle is visible chiefly as a conflict between two different mortuary religions, the relation of the dead to the sun, which sinks to rest but rises again in glory every day, and the relation of the dead to Osiris, a mortuary god of obscure origins. Whether Osiris was originally an earthly king, who died and thus became the king of the dead; was a god of the earth, in which the dead were buried; or was the god of the Nile, which also died and came to life again is uncertain. By the beginning of the dynasties he had come to be the god who was dead but still lived and therefore to be the dead ruler and ruler of the dead. Thus the deceased pharaoh came to be Osiris, and his son who followed him on the throne came to be the dutiful son Horus, who took action to keep his deceased father alive in another world. Increasingly this concept of death overshadowed the concept in which the deceased went into the company of the sun. It is clear that the two doctrines were, to our modern minds, competing and therefore irreconcilable. However, it is not necessary that the tolerant and catholic Egyptian found them irreconcilable. To him it may simply have been an enlargement of the idea of life in death that there were alternatives, that the deceased had wide scope and different phases of being. Perhaps this conflict between two different mortuary systems was no bitter struggle at all.

Certainly, the conflict between the solar god Re and the mortuary god Osiris was no social and economic class struggle between the haves and the have-nots, between the king and the state religion, on the one side, and the people and the religion of the masses, on the other. That is clear from the fact that the earliest mortuary religion that we can read in the texts limits both the solar and the Osirian phases of future life to the pharaoh alone. He was the only one who, as a god, went to join the sun-god in his journeys; he was the only one who, as a dead king, became Osiris, the king of the dead. At the beginning and for most of the course of the Old Kingdom, these were royal religions, denied to the masses. That "democratization" which was to come at the end of the Old Kingdom and in the First Intermediate Period was quite a different process. It may have seized upon the Osirian faith for its extension of future happiness to wider numbers of the populace, but the Osirian faith was not in itself "democratic." On the contrary, it began in the highest degree as a limitation to the god-king alone.

It is a great tragedy that we know so little about these first dynasties, because there are clear indications that this formative period of ancient

Egyptian history was of critical importance and that, for once, the Egyptian spirit was one of eager adventure and advance. Now that the prologue has been read, the stage lights become brighter, and we see a culture which had already been formed in its essentials, which was satisfied with those essentials, and which embarked upon a long career of attempting to maintain those essentials unchanged against the wear of time and changing circumstance. Of course, that attempt could not be absolutely successful, for the centuries did bring constant change and reinterpretation of the essentials of the culture; but Egypt was basically the same in her outlook on life from about 2700 to about 1200 B.C., and that is an extraordinarily long time to maintain a status. The social-political essential was the assertion that Egypt was owned and ruled by a god, who assured the land of divine blessings and whose knowledge, power, and oversight were complete and absolute. The spiritual essential was that Egypt was the most blessed of lands, so that setbacks could be only temporary and one might be free to relish life in its simple and homely terms. That basic optimism about life in this world was soon to be extended to an optimism about the life to come as eternally blessed for all good Egyptians.

A NOTE ON UTILITY AND GLORY

It was stated above that the Egyptian looked upon the useful as the good. The idea of a rule-of-thumb pragmatism, with no trace of a reasoned and reasoning experimentalism, and the idea that a single word might mean both "celestial glory" and mundane "utility" are so foreign to modern thought that they should be argued more extensively. The precise translations of words which possessed a range of meaning are always difficult. The concept *ma'at* might be "order" in one context and "righteousness" in another. One authority translates the adjective *akh* as "beneficial, advantageous, glorious," and the adjective *menekh* as "efficient, beneficent, excellent."[22] One could reason that to the mythmaking mind a state of glory, splendor, or blessedness was *ipso facto* effective for any function, so that "glory" was the basic idea in *akh*; or one could reason that some kind of effective power brought about the state of glory, so that "effectiveness" was the basic idea. In either case the range of meaning from unearthly luster to earthly utility is present. A good case can be worked out that the root meaning of each word was "useful efficiency." In the Instruction of Ptah-hotep, eloquence is prescribed "as of advantage (*akh*) to him who will hearken

22. A. H. Gardiner, *Egyptian Grammar* (Oxford, 1927), pp. 532, 543.

and of disadvantage to him who may neglect it," the contented wife is described as "a profitable (akh) field for her lord," and the fool is blamed because "he regards knowledge as ignorance and profit (akhet) as loss."[23] If a noble does what the king wishes, his majesty "will carry out many important petitions of thine, to benefit (akh) the son of thy son forever."[24] A man asks for mortuary prayers, "inasmuch as it is more advantageous (akh) for him who does (it) than for him for whom (it) is done; the breath of the mouth is beneficial (akh) for the dead."[25] As a noun this word was applied to the blessed dead, and it is sometimes translated "soul" or "spirit." A more precise translation would be "effective personality." A noble is able to threaten with vengeance from the next world anyone who violates his tomb because "I am an able effective-personality (akh), I know all magic useful (akh) to me in the necropolis, and I have done everything of advantage (akh) for myself."[26] In like manner, King "Pepi is an effective-personality with his prepared mouth."[27] It was said to a dead person: "I have given thee magic as thy protection and the abilities (akhu) of Isis as thy strength."[28] Those mortuary texts which were recited for the benefit of a dead man were called sakhu, spells for "conferring effective personality" in the next world.

The word menekh had similar applicability. The dead king was a being of capability: King "Unis is completely competent (menekh menekhet); his arms are not broken."[29] In scenes in the Old Kingdom tombs, those who slaughtered cattle were urged to "seize hold effectively (menekh)."[30] A noble boasted that he was "trustworthy and serviceable (menekh) to the king."[31]

In addition to these meanings of applied usefulness, there are many instances in which a translation is indicated along the lines of "admirable, noble, pleasing, splendid, glorious." Again we have a spectrum reaching from earth to heaven, with functional value at one end and supernal brightness at the other.

23. Erman, LAE, pp. 56, 61, 64.

24. K. Sethe, Urkunden des alten Reichs (Urk. I [Leipzig, 1903]), I, 122.

25. K. Sethe, Aegyptische Lesestücke (Leipzig, 1924), p. 88.

26. Sethe, Urkunden des alten Reichs, p. 263; cf. also pp. 122, 142–43.

27. Sethe, Die altägyptischen Pyramidentexte (Leipzig, 1908–10), II, §930.

28. A. de Buck, The Egyptian Coffin Texts (OIC, XXXIV [Chicago, 1935]), I, 194; cf. A. H. Gardiner in JEA, XXIV (1938), 157, n. 5.

29. Sethe, Die altägyptischen Pyramidentexte, I, §357.

30. A. Erman, Reden, Rufe und Lieder auf Gräberbildern des alten Reiches (Berlin Abh., 1919), p. 11.

31. Sethe, Urkunden der 18. Dynastie (Urk. IV [Leipzig, 1909]), p. 962.

IV

THE KING AND GOD

Dynasties 4–6 (about 2700–2200 B.C.)

THIS chapter deals with the Old Kingdom, the period of Egypt's rich and abundant youth, the period of the most centralized absolutism in the person of the king, and, at the same time, the period of a progressive decentralization away from the king. In the preceding chapter we anticipated much of the statement on this period, in dealing with the construction of a national system which was to be valid for all future time. Here we shall give further details on that system, in which the concept of the divine king was nuclear.

On the rock plateau of Gizeh, to the north of the capital city at Memphis, rise the three great pyramids of the Fourth Dynasty. Artificial mountains designed to resist decay to the maximum, they are symbolic in two respects. Their enduring shape and construction asserted very successfully an eternal life for the mortal being who was buried within; and the investment in labor and materials in each pyramid was a ringing insistence that the service of the king was the most important task of the state. No other activity visibly and enduringly claimed the energies of the Egyptian people. It was the eternal home of their god-king, which was worthy of their supreme efforts in time, in materials, in manpower, and in craftsmanship. In sublime arrogance the royal pyramids dominated the Old Kingdom and sent their shadows down the ages.

If one charts the Old Kingdom pyramids in size and technique, one makes a further observation. The royal tombs and the great pyramids of Gizeh progress on up to the climax of the Pyramid of Khufu, with the immediately preceding monuments of Snefru and the immediately succeeding tomb of Khaf-Re of the same sublime character. The rise was astonishingly fast. The first serious stone masonry may have been about 100 or 125 years before Khufu; the first significant structure of stone—Djoser's Step Pyramid—was about 75 years before Khufu. In that brief span the Egyptians had learned how to handle tremendous masses of stone, without any of that tackle which we moderns would consider essential. They abandoned the handling of stone as if it were brick and treated the new material for its own qualities of mass and durability. And they learned how to finish off myriads of blocks with a perfection that presented a single unified mass. This sudden development seems to have been entirely native within Egypt. It was called forth by two devotions: the acceptance of the dogma that the king was a god and thus deserving of a supreme offering of energies, and the excitement of a new adventure in art and technique. The sudden and brilliant rise of achievement was a glorious chapter of Egyptian history.

Carrying on the chart of pyramids after Khufu and Khaf-Re, we see a corresponding decline of size and technique. The tombs of the later Fourth Dynasty and of the Fifth and Sixth Dynasties were much smaller and decidedly inferior in technical perfection. In this respect of a supreme national effort on behalf of the king, we see clearly the sudden beginnings of decentralization. The texts which asserted the dogma of his divinity would insist that he suffered no loss in his godliness or in the reverence of his people for him, but we shall observe other indications of the centrifugal tendencies which began early in this period.

In the previous chapter we cited some of the statistics with regard to the Great Pyramid, as an index to the search for technical perfection. Something more might be said about the application of power to a single project. A significant factor in the building of the pyramids was the lack of any such machines as we should consider essential for the movement of huge masses of stone. The missing element was the wheel, in a vehicle for the delivery of stone, in a pulley, or in a crane. Without wheeled carriages, pulleys, or cranes, how could they deliver heavy blocks into precise place at high elevations? They used sloping ramps of brick and earth, ramps which could later be destroyed. For the maneuvering of blocks, they had ropes, sledges, levers, and cradles, and they used a mortar of sand and gypsum as a lubricating medium, a slippery surface for the sliding of blocks into precise place. They enjoyed all the manpower which could be employed within any one space for any one operation. Above all, they took the needed time to do each little job with their "primitive" means: the calculation of a particular operation, the cutting and rebuilding of the ramp to deliver a five- or ten-ton block exactly, and the delicate measuring and cutting of stone for the most refined fitting. We moderns could duplicate their result with their methods, if we thought it worth while to use such limited resources and if we had the patience to undertake the task in terms of a lifetime.

The ancient engineer faced other unprecedented problems of stress. The pyramid form was ideal in overcoming some of the difficulties of great weight, built up to 480 feet and thus crushing downward with brutal mass. Burial chambers within a pyramid were successfully protected against the downward thrust of the mountain of stone. There was also consolidation inside the pyramid by "accretion faces," that is, solid retaining walls constructed in the form of a stepped pyramid and holding different segments of the structure in place.

Calculations were made in units of measurement originally of the simplest nature but formalized by this time into officially accepted standards, the royal cubit or forearm of 20.6 inches, subdividing into 7 palms or 28 fingers. In the Great Pyramid this unit provides us with good round numbers for major elements: 280 cubits for the height, 440 for a side of the base, 90 for the longest inner passage, and a burial chamber of 20 × 10 × 11. What has been said about construction methods applies also to the mathematics with which the engineers made their calculations. There were two awkward factors. They added and subtracted as we do, but their multiplication and division used a process of doubling and doubling again as long as necessary, and then adding those pairs of numbers which came closest to the required factors.[1] It may be easier to illustrate this process than to explain it further. In the following example of multiplication they doubled as often as indicated, then sought in the left-hand column those numbers—here marked with asterisks—which added up to the required 9, and then added the corresponding figures in the right-hand column to gain the desired result.

To multiply 50 by 9:

$$
\begin{array}{r}
1- \ \ 50 \\
2-100 \\
4-200 \\
8-400 \\
\hline
9-450
\end{array}
$$

For division, they again used doubling, but now ticked off the right-hand column to equal or approximate the dividend. The corresponding

1. T. E. Peet in *Bulletin of the John Rylands Library, Manchester,* XV (1931), 409 ff.; O. Neugebauer in *Quellen und Studien zur Geschichte der Mathematik, Astronomie und Physik,* B,1 (1930), 301 ff.

numbers in the left-hand column then added up to the required result.

To divide 550 by 9:

```
*  1—   9*
   2—  18
*  4—  36*
*  8—  72*
* 16— 144*
* 32— 288*
  64— 576
  ‾‾‾‾‾‾‾
  61— 549, that is, 61, with remainder 1.
```

The other difficulty was the lack of complex fractions. Except for 2/3 and 3/4, the ancients had only simple fractions of the type 1/5 or 1/27 or 1/65. The complex fraction was broken down into a series of simple fractions. Thus 3/8 was written 1/4 plus 1/8, and 11/16 was written 1/2 plus 1/8 plus 1/16. Although this seems unbelievably cumbersome, it does not take long for one to work himself into the system and to acquire some speed. With an arithmetic of this kind, the Egyptians were able to calculate exactly the volume of a truncated pyramid and, within an extraordinarily close approximation, the volume of a cylinder.

The point we are driving at is that mathematically and mechanically the Egyptian method fell far short of modern requirements but that the ancient made the best possible use of his means. The value of his product in terms of working conscience is very considerably enhanced when we think of the methods and equipment which he was able to employ.

The preceding chapter discussed the setting-up of a system of life, embracing government, literature, art, and religion, and the backing of that system by divine sanctions sufficient to justify the expression, "the canonization of a national system." The essential support of the system was, of course, the doctrine that the state belonged to a ruler who was a god. The Egyptians, for all their surface trappings of myth and ceremonial mystery, were basically a pragmatic people, interested in what worked. The system of life and nationhood which they worked out seemed to them highly effective; they gave it divine sanction through the person of the god who was owner and ruler of the land. There was no written and detailed statecraft for Egypt; there needed to be none where the state was summed up in the person of a god, ever present to voice the purposes and practices of the state by his divine utterance. His alone was the authority by dogma, which is another way of saying that his alone was the responsibility for the maintenance and nurture of his property. He was the sole intermediary between the people and the gods, the only being shown by texts and scenes in the service of the other gods. Good government rested upon his success in bringing fertility to the soil, a profitable commerce, and the peace for normal internal development.

Of course, actual practice made it impossible for the pharaoh to perform every official and magisterial function in the entire land, just as it was impossible for him to perform the daily service for every god in every temple. Responsibilities had to be delegated to ordinary mortals, who might be charged to act for the king and in his name. Practically, the symbol of the pyramid, with its single capstone, will serve as the description of state and society. In the organization of government, the pharaoh stood above his national ministers, who were above the governors of the several provinces, who were above the mayors of the villages. Socially, the pharaoh was over the nobles, who were above the serfs, although here we have some questions about the existence of a separate class of artisans, small merchants, and factors. In terms of the religious organization of the state, the pharaoh was the only point of contact with the gods, surmounting the priests, who were above the people. These several pyramidal descriptions are, of course, really one, because higher officials, nobles, large landlords, and priests were the same; they constituted that group directly under the pharaoh, to whom he delegated the carrying-out of those functions which belonged to him by definition.

There are unknowns and uncertainties in this loose description. We know very little about the great masses of the people, who were illiterate and inarticulate. Except for the depiction of servants and peasants in the tomb scenes, what little we know about the common people comes from later times. In fact, our process of attempting to guess the life of the common people is a rather strained analogy; we observe the Egyptian peasant of the past century, before he was exposed to modern forces; we carry that impression back through documents on Egypt in Coptic, Hellenistic, and Late-Egyptian times, until our written sources begin to diminish as we go back to about 1300 B.C.; and then we seek isolated analogies in earlier Egypt. Although it is partly an argument from silence, it is a fairly good one that the peasant of the twenty-seventh century B.C. lived much the same as did the peasant of the nineteenth century after Christ, despite the enormous changes in superficial expression. With this line of tradition in mind, we look at the tomb reliefs of the Old Kingdom, and we see the Egyptian peasant as undemanding, improvident, quick-tempered but not holding his wrath, lighthearted and loving gayety, capable of very hard work but incapable of long sustained effort. His feet were ever sunk into the mud of the river bank, planting or reaping his master's crops, building in mudbrick for his master, or driving his master's cattle. He lived ever close to nature, with the peasant's mystic and superstitious sense of community with plant and animal. He was slender and not fully nourished, much of his work was heavy on his back, and his reward in payment in kind was slight. At the low point of the year, before the first autumn crops came in, he was probably close to starvation. Periodic famine and pestilence made him the fearful victim of unknown and sudden peril from vast forces which he took to be gods.[2] Every act of his daily life was circumscribed by the fear of jealous little forces—on the threshold of his hut, in the whirling dust storm, in fire, in running water, in the cattle he herded, and in his first fruits. Yet through it all he was able to laugh and sing. Driving his cattle through the swamp, he sang a little song addressed to the crocodile and fish. Carrying his master in the palanquin, he joined in a song of flattery, with an impudent grin and an eye on the reward. Bending his back to tugging ropes, he joined in a workers' litany, with a musical cadence that made for unified effort. At the periodic festivals he danced and played with animal energy and stuffed himself overfull with the banquet provided by his master. Perhaps his life was closely akin to the lives of the animals who were beside him day and night. He was a chattel, a beast of burden, a draught animal, intimately dependent upon the amount of green fodder on the valley floor. The peasant certainly had far less opportunity than the skilled artisan, the household servant, or the noble's personal slave. And yet, as the basic Egyptian element, his fortunes were those of his lord, in common dependence upon the Nile and the sun, upon the forces of growth and reproduction. In the preceding chapter we suggested that the Egyptians looked on the phenomena of the universe as one continuous blending spectrum, without sharp dividing lines. In that spectrum the peasant will have stood between the animals and the gentry, sharing intimately with each and never set off in opposition to either.

This brings up another problem and another hypothesis. We have argued that the earliest dynasties laid down a system of life valid for all future generations, a system which had broad application to every

2. For an Old Kingdom relief depicting the emaciated peasants in a famine see *Illustrated London News*, February 26, 1944, p. 249; see our Fig. 2b.

phase of life, and that that system worked successfully for about fifteen hundred years. One might ask how a rigid and static order could possibly stand the wear and tear of change over so many centuries. Surely, a comprehensive way of life based dogmatically on divine revelation and therefore held to be eternally satisfactory would be so rigid and inflexible that it would break under the pressure of changing times. The answer here given is that the system could not have survived if it had been unbending in actual practice. A tolerant and easygoing people could not be categorically absolute. The system was both general, admitting exception, and flexible, admitting modification. In art, for example, the broad general rules and practices were followed with fidelity from the Fourth Dynasty down into Hellenistic times, and yet there was always variety and individuality; there was sufficient change, so that modern critics may date an Egyptian sculpture on the basis of style. As we can see that it was so in the visible expression of art, thus we believe that it was so in less visible expressions of life. The sun-given tolerance of the ancient Egyptian and his easygoing refusal to make sharp and binding categories gave him a system of life which was adaptable to the changes enforced by time. Oh, to be sure, the dogma might be stated in terms which were flat, eternal, and absolute, but the dogma was of general nature, and the actual practice was flexible, tolerant, catholic, and pragmatic.

One great element of this flexibility and fluidity, if we are right, lay in the common substance of all known phenomena, that spectrum of being which reached from the highest gods down through humans, animals, and plants to inorganic objects. The application of this hypothesis to society would be that ancient Egypt had no rigid caste system, in which nobles, artisans, peasants, and slaves were restrained to a single class for generation upon generation. Society would normally be organized on the basis of continuing and inherited relations, so that the son of a peasant would continue to be a peasant and would himself produce peasants-to-be. The same continuum would be normal for the noble class. But a pragmatic and tolerant people would not constrain any person to remain eternally in his inherited class, if circumstances gave opportunity or necessity of change. Periods in which the Egyptian state grew and advanced demanded the services of men of ability and reliability. Artisans would be recruited from the peasants, household servants would become trusted factors, superior artisans and efficient factors would be rewarded with property, position, and privilege and would thus move into the aristocracy. We shall shortly deal further with the successful rise in career of originally obscure men. The one exception to such flexibility from class to class should lie in the kingship, where the dogma asserted that this was no man but a god. Even there the presence of royal children and relatives blurred the dividing line by presenting doubts about the royal succession, and we shall see the process by which the nobility gradually absorbed privileges which had originally been reserved for the pharaoh alone. In every respect, a cultural expression which was timeless, changeless, and dogmatically static was actually subject to constant change, as it bent to the winds of passing time. Thus ancient Egypt survived "unchanged" for long centuries by changing constantly and ignoring such change.

Writing and literature would be further examples of the static, yet fluid, character of Egyptian culture. The Old Kingdom saw the formation of a classical language which was still in relatively successful official use nearly twenty-five hundred years later. When writing became fairly common in the Fifth and Sixth Dynasties, a primitive language was already dying, a highly inflected language which survived sporadically only in certain archaic forms like religious and medical texts. The classical language, called "Middle Egyptian," which received acceptance in the Old Kingdom, continued with minor change down to the cosmopolitan excitation under the Egyptian Empire and thereafter was maintained for religious and official purposes as long as men carved hieroglyphs on temple walls. And yet it is possible to date inscriptions to their periods of original composition or existing expression by criteria of paleography, vocabulary, "spelling," syntax, or style; it is possible to point out contemporary colloquialisms in a classical text or archaisms in a relatively colloquial text. To be sure, we have about three thousand years of texts to deal with, and constant change within so long a time would seem inevitable to a modern, but the extraordinary phenomenon is the broad consistency and continuity over so long a time. A text of 700 B.C. very successfully reproduced the language of 2700 B.C., with remarkably few intrusive vulgarisms of the day. A deliberate revolution of vulgarization, such as we shall see in chapter ix, violated the generalities of the Egyptian system and became heresy, but slow change within an outwardly static order was always taken with complacency.[3]

What has been said about language applies also to literature. Change

3. On the historical development of the Egyptian language there is a thesis (in Dutch) by B. H. Stricker, in *Oudheidkundige Mededeelingen uit het Rijksmuseum van Oudheden te Leiden*, Nieuwe Reeks, Vol. XXV (1944).

Fig. 1.—*The Nile Valley at Thebes, Held Viselike between the Two Deserts*

Fig. 2a.—The Abundant Life of the Marshes

Fig. 2b.—The Deadly Effects of a Famine

Fig. 3a.—A Group of Prehistoric Pots

Fig. 3b.—The Never Ending Toil of Bringing Water to the Fields

Fig. 4a.—The Façade of a Tomb Decorated with Paneling in Mud Brick

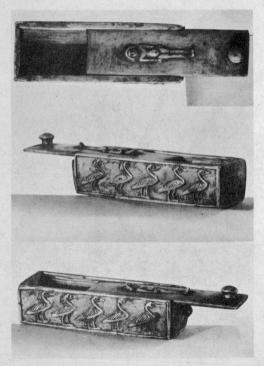

Fig. 4b.—An Ivory Box of Predynastic Times

Fig. 4c.—The Writing Equipment of an
Egyptian Scribe

Fig. 5a.—Predynastic or Early Dynastic Mace, Showing the
King as a God Opening a Canal

Fig. 5b.—Ivory Figurine of
a First Dynasty King

Fig. 5c.—An Egyptian Scribe Ready To
Take Dictation

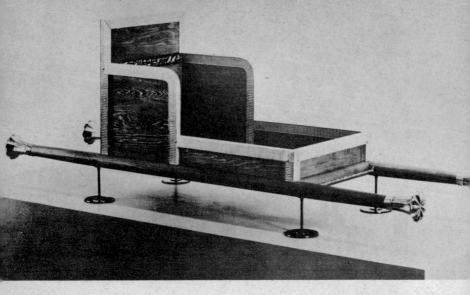

Fig. 6a.—The Carrying-Chair of Queen Hetep-hires, Mother of King Khufu,
Reconstructed from the Materials Found in Her Tomb

Fig. 6b.—A Bed of the Earliest Historical Period

Fig. 7a.—The Potter at His Wheel

Fig. 7b.—The God Ptah of Memphis

Fig. 7c.—The Fifth Dynasty Noble
En-khefet-kai and His Wife

Fig. 7d.—The Sixth Dynasty Noble
Seneb, a Dwarf, with His Family

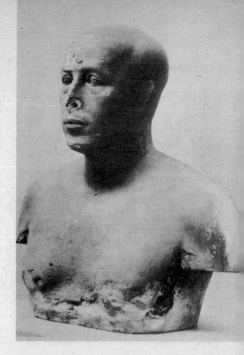

Fig. 8a.—The Lady Seshseshet, Wife of Mereruka

Fig. 8b.—Bust of the Fourth Dynasty Noble Ankh-haf

Fig. 8c.—Statuette of the Fifth Dynasty Architect Nekhebu

Fig. 8d.—Model in Plaster from the Mummy of an Old Kingdom Noble

Fig. 9a.—The Pyramids at Gizeh, Seen from the Air

Fig. 9b.—Reconstruction of the Step Pyramid at Sakkarah, with Its
Complex of Temple Buildings

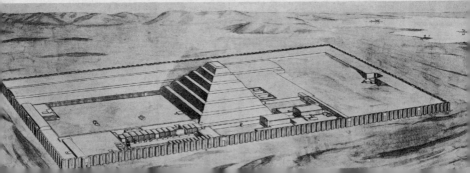

Fig. 10a.—Boys Playing Games, from the Tomb of Mereruka

Fig. 10b.—Trussing Up and Herding Cattle, from the Tomb of Mereruka

Fig. 11a.—Stela of the Noble Uha, Expressing the Independent
Spirit of the First Intermediate Period

Fig. 11b.—A Group of Wooden Figures, Showing a Bakery of
the Middle Kingdom

Fig. 12a.—Head of a Limestone Statuette
of a Twelfth Dynasty King

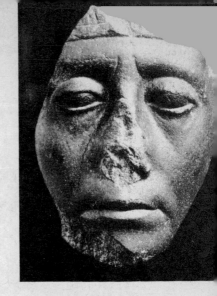

Fig. 12b.—Quartzite Head of Sen-Usert
of the Twelfth Dynasty

Fig. 12c.—Granite Statue of the Lady
Sennui, Wife of Djefa-Hapi,
Found at Kerma

Fig. 12d.—Pottery Head of an Old
Kingdom Dancing Girl

Fig. 13.—An Eleventh Dynasty Group of Model Figures, as They Appeared in Excavations by the Metropolitan Museum of Art at Deir el-Bahri

Fig. 14a.—Head of a Statue of a Middle Kingdom Noble

Fig. 14b.—Head of a Statuette of a Middle Kingdom Lady, Found at Megiddo in Palestine

Fig. 15a.—*An Emaciated Desert Herdsman Leading Cattle;
from the Middle Kingdom Tombs at Meir*

Fig. 15b.—*Old Man Gossiping with Boat-Builders; from the
Middle Kingdom Tombs at Meir*

Fig. 16a.—An Ostracon of Empire Times. Showing a Mouse as a Magistrate,
a Small Boy as a Culprit, and a Cat as a Policeman

Fig. 16b.—An Empire Wall Painting, Showing the Trapper Ptah-mose
with Pelicans

and the unchanging were both present. There were certain literary modes and genres which were characteristic of single periods and disappeared when their popularity had faded. Such were the didactic stories of skepticism and social challenge in the First Intermediate Period and in the early Middle Kingdom and the dashing and eupeptic autobiographies in the tombs of the early Empire. On the other hand, the Old Kingdom Pyramid Texts were still in active use in Saite and Persian times, and schoolboys had to copy the Instruction of Amen-em-het I seven centuries after that pharaoh had died.

A generalization which might be made at this point and which applies not only to literature but also to art is that earlier Egypt provided no strictly secular products, no literature of idle entertainment, and no art for art's sake. Art and literature had an applied purpose, and that purpose was indissolubly related to religion. All phases of life carried a strong coloration of the sacred, from the beginnings down to the first important secularization under the Empire. Every work of art, in line or word, fitted somewhere into the pervading religiosity of the age. Even stories which we might read for enjoyment, like the Tale of the Shipwrecked Sailor,[4] have a strong mythological pattern and were didactic in stressing the centrality of Egypt within the universe. Modern categories lead us to think in terms of the sacred and the secular; no such opposing purposes were possible in a society which long continued to be essentially sacred.

Art is one of the easier categories for generalizations, because it is abundant and decisively visible. The one generalization which we wish to lay down now is the rapidity with which art, like architecture, achieved a full maturity. In the first three dynasties the aspect of the composition was often conditioned by the medium used: figures in ivory might be soft, free, fluid, and naturalistic, whereas statues in stone would be lumplike and massive. This difference disappeared in the Fourth Dynasty in a thoroughly sophisticated expression in any medium. The royal statues of Khaf-Re and Men-kau-Re were carved in the most obdurate stones and in softer stones; yet all achieved a product unconditioned by the material, a product which expressed the religious purposes of the sculptor with complete satisfaction. Statues and reliefs of the Fourth and Fifth Dynasties uttered the desired expression of dignity, authority, and eternal life as successfully as at any period of Egyptian history. It may be claimed that the Old Kingdom products were the most Egyptian, most successful, and most sophisti-

4. Erman, *LAE*, pp. 29 ff.

cated of all ancient Egyptian history; but such a claim will involve aesthetic judgments and the ability of the modern to project himself into the ancient criteria.[5] The point which we are here pressing is the sudden flowering of maturity as shown in technique and in ability to convey spirit. Different scholars will assign different reasons for a sudden coming-of-age of a culture. Here we shall content ourselves with the suggestion that the first two or three dynasties had solved Egypt's problems about her national spiritual identity and had given her a security against disturbance, two achievements which permitted sudden maturing. Concomitants of the process of coming-of-age were optimism and self-confidence bordering upon bumptiousness and an assurance that the Egyptian way was so good that it was valid for all time.

That optimism deserves further stress. The apparent Egyptian preoccupation with death and their elaboration of funerary equipment and service might leave the impression that the ancient Egyptians were a morbid people, obsessed with the idea of death, gloomily and solemnly bending their times of life in preparation for the end of life. Nothing could be further from the truth. They did spend an extraordinary amount of time and energy in denying and circumventing death, but the spirit was not one of gloomy foreboding. On the contrary, it was a spirit of hopeful triumph, a vigorous relish of life, and an expectant assertion of continued future life as over against the finality or doom of death. Self-assurance, optimism, and a lust for life produced an energetic assertion of eternally continuing life rather than elaborate defenses against death.[6] For the moment we shall advance this claim without qualification of any difference between the god-king, the nobles, and the masses; later in this chapter we shall consider the question of different hereafters in separate categories. The unqualified claim rests upon the spirit displayed in Old Kingdom tombs, both in scenes and in texts. The total impression is confident, lively, and gay. Through the formal expression of language and art emerges a delight in the bustle and activity of this life and a flat determination to continue this life after death. The tomb scenes do not stress burial and mortuary services; they stress the pleasure in an abounding harvest, delight in nature, enjoyment of

5. W. S. Smith, *A History of Egyptian Sculpture and Painting in the Old Kingdom* (Oxford University Press, 1946), p. xv: "Nowhere in the ancient world until the time of the new spirit of Greek civilization is there anything comparable to the technical accomplishment, the naturalism, and the productivity of Egyptian art as exemplified in the first of its great periods of achievement, the Old Kingdom."

6. A. H. Gardiner, *The Attitude of the Ancient Egyptians to Death and the Dead* (Cambridge University Press, 1935).

the hunt, and the excitement of feasts and games (Fig. 10*b*). Here is life and the ardent pursuit of more abundant life. This was no hypochondriac people, in mortal terror. This was a people who embraced existence joyfully and confidently, assured that they were under the favored care of the gods, particularly of the one god who was their king. That buoyant optimism was so strong and so ingrained that it survived that first national illness which we shall outline in the next chapter. It survived as long as Egypt was secure within her borders and was able to enjoy a sense of special election, and it disappeared only when a feeling of insecurity became chronic and when the insistent pressure of an outside world cast doubt upon the sense of special election. As long as that gay and assured relish of daily life continued in the land, the Egyptians lived intensely in the present, made grateful but brief gestures to the past, and denied the future by projecting the present into the future. In the final disillusion, when the present became burdensome, they turned back and clung nostalgically to the past, and they looked somberly to the future as a release and justification. But for most of the period covered by this book the life given to them by their gods was their joy and their desire.

Any discussion of the state under the Old Kingdom starts by reiterating the doctrine that the king was the state. There were no words for "government," "state," or "nation," impersonally conceived. There were geographic terms—"the land," "the Black Land," etc.; and there were terms applying to the pharaoh—"kingship" and "rule." Since the theory of government was that the king was everywhere and did everything, a large proportion of the officials who acted for him carried titles expressing their direct responsibility to him: "Overseer of the Domain of the Palace," "Overseer of All (Construction) Works of the King," or "Sealbearer of the King of Lower Egypt." That last title signified the delegated authority of certain royal officials to conduct business away from the king and the capital, certifying their transactions with the king's seal. At first, only the king's son may have held this office; later it became widespread. Of course, in practice, responsible decisions had to be made by responsible officials. As time went on, there was a great proliferation of royal officials carrying out the extensive business of a great and bustling government. The fiction of a direct delegation of duty and of a direct report to the king was impossible to maintain in practice; but in the theory of government it was no fiction, it was a working reality. Commissioners sent south in the Sudan had to act with

independent judgment in transacting their business with foreign chieftains, but they sincerely expressed the conviction that they were under
the orders of pharaoh and subject to his divine pleasure.[7] Of course,
such majestic and awful backing was of advantage to them in treating
with others at a distance, but, until the breakdown of authority at the
end of the Old Kingdom, they acted in the full conviction that they
were pharaoh's servants.

As the royal pyramid symbolized the soaring supremacy of the king,
so the tombs of nobles and officials symbolized the centralization of the
state and their dependence upon the king by clustering close around the
pyramid. In the Fourth and early Fifth Dynasties it was the rule that
the great officials sought close community with their ruler in death as in
life. They sued for his royal grace to permit them to erect their eternal
homes inside his pyramid domain. He was a god in life, and he would
continue to be a ruling god in death. As they had been his servants in
life, so they hoped to be his servants in death, and so they sought the
equivalent of servants' quarters with him. The royal bureaucracy seems
to have been relatively small in the earlier part of the Old Kingdom.
A greater degree of intimacy with the king was possible. Perhaps "intimacy" is the wrong term, as there is evidence that the divine person
was normally untouchable and unapproachable.[8] But there was the
possibility of closer approach at a time when the official family was of
more modest proportions. Into the Fifth Dynasty, only the king's highest official, the Vizier, was the "Sealbearer of the King of Lower
Egypt," authorized to supervise the movement of official parties or
goods through Egypt. In the late Fifth and Sixth Dynasties, we find
dozens of such Sealbearers. Into the Sixth Dynasty, there was only one
"Governor of Upper Egypt," a viceroy in the more distant part of the
realm. At the end of the Sixth Dynasty, we find a score of local rulers
enjoying the title of "Governor of Upper Egypt," asserting a wider
rule than their own little province. This late process rests partly upon
the change of functional titles into honorary titles; in part it is a feature
of decentralization and the self-arrogation of authority by local rulers;
but in part it came about through the elaboration of government and
the consequent multiplication of offices. Obviously, it had reciprocal
relations of cause and effect with the decentralization of the state.

However, we are still concerned with the earlier period, when cen-

---

7. Breasted, *ARE*, I, §§ 333 ff., 358 ff.

8. Wilson in H. Frankfort *et al.*, *The Intellectual Adventure of Ancient Man* (Chicago, 1946), pp. 75 ff.

tralization remained strong. The economic theory of the state probably expressed the doctrine of divine rule. Surely, goods moved locally and within a circumscribed range of village and neighboring village without specific royal authorization. It is likely that the major movement of goods—thereby resorting to the Nile traffic—was controlled by the royal Sealbearer and thereby by the king. If so, we do not know whether the state's advantage was one of control only or of an exacted price for such traffic. Foreign commerce was probably a royal monopoly, although our evidence is slight and comes from texts which express attachment to the king. The movement of caravans into Nubia and the Sudan and the passage of sailing ships from Egypt to the cedar-bearing areas in Phoenicia were royal enterprises, and we have no indication of any private enterprise outside the frontier. The exploitation of the turquoise and copper mines in Sinai was definitely an activity of the king from the First Dynasty onward, manned by royal officials and policed by the army. On analogy, the exploitation of the gold mines in the eastern deserts must have been a royal monopoly. The production of these two metals would give the palace inestimable economic advantage. At a much later date foreign rulers remarked on the abundance of gold owned by Egypt, and copper was even more important. Down to the Middle Kingdom, copper was the basic metal medium of the ancient world, with bronze continuing to be basic down to the fourteenth or thirteenth century B.C. It is not a mere coincidence that Egypt, which possessed copper in the desert to her east, dominated the eastern Mediterranean down to the fourteenth or thirteenth century B.C. and that the period of her weakening vis-à-vis other countries was synchronous with the coming of the iron age, for Egypt possessed no iron. Thus a monopoly by the palace in the exploitation of the copper mines was an effective factor in pharaoh's domination.

The amount of copper ore won from the Sinai mines has been illustrated by the recent discovery of a stunning hoard of tools and weapons in the tomb of a First Dynasty king at Sakkarah. There were scores of knives and swords with wooden handles, ranging in length from nine inches to two feet; quantities of saws; dozens of copper daggers with wooden handles; scores of vases, bowls, and ewers; dozens of hoes; up to hundreds of adzes, chisels, borers, needles, and so on. In addition, there were seventy-five rectangular slabs of copper for the pharaoh to take into the next world, so that his otherworldly coppersmith might make such additional tools and weapons as might be required over there. The discovery of such an amassing of metal is extraordinary, and yet there is nothing to show that this hoard was exceptional at that time. It simply happened to survive to our day.[9]

The Old Kingdom sent commercial and military expeditions into Libya, the Sudan, and Asia. It was not, however, imperialistic in a political or military sense. It did not attempt to conquer and hold foreign territory by resident governors and garrisons. Indeed, its contact with neighboring countries was very attentuated. Except for the commercial colony at Byblos in Phoenicia, there is little Old Kingdom Egyptian material to be discovered on foreign soil. Pharaoh did send royal gifts to the prince of Byblos, and an Egyptian temple at that port tells us that Egyptians were perhaps resident there. We believe them to have been merchants sent by pharaoh to promote a flow of goods from Phoenicia and other parts of Asia, resident in a city-state which was sovereign and independent of Egypt. Elsewhere in Asia there is extremely little Egyptian material of the period. Only one piece of recognizable Old Kingdom material has been found on Palestinian soil, as against twenty of the Middle Kingdom and more than five hundred of the Empire.[10] To the south of Egypt, Nubia was a stagnant backwater culturally, unmoved by the extraordinary advances made by pharaoh's land. The only imperialism of the time was commercial, and the few military operations known to us were raids undertaken to protect the channels upon which goods moved. As yet, there was no effective challenge to Egypt's security within her borders. As yet, her cultural superiority over her nearest neighbors was sufficient, so that she needed policing rather than conquest, so that trade flowed to her as if by right. As yet, she reclined serenely along the bed of the Nile, assured that the gods had made her superior to other peoples, mistress of all that she could survey.

Commercially and fiscally it was an age of barter, whether in the market place or through the payment of taxes in kind. Biennially and then later annually, there was a fiscal census, a governmental counting of arable land, cattle, and gold. On the basis of this inventory there would be an assessment of taxes, payable in kind—grain, hides, gold, and so on—or in labor. If later evidence is valid, such taxes were rendered by the provinces to the state, so that it is legitimate to suppose that there was a progressive farming-out of taxes.

Although transactions were conducted by barter, there was already

9. W. B. Emery in *ASAE*, XXXIX (1939), 427 ff.

10. A. Rowe, *A Catalogue of Egyptian Scarabs . . . in the Palestine Archaeological Museum* (Cairo, 1936), graph following Pl. XXXVIII, pp. xiii ff.

a referable medium of exchange in the Old Kingdom, a "piece" of metal of fixed material and weight—not a coin, because it was not stamped. A man sold a house near the Great Pyramid and received ten "pieces" for it. What he actually received was a bed valued at four pieces and two different lots of linen valued at three pieces each. Thus there was a fixed and accepted unit of value for price quotations, even though a transaction might be carried through entirely with goods in kind and without the "piece" being handled by either party.[11] This was an economic advance, and the unit of value was a precursor of money proper, which would not appear for another two thousand years.

We have spoken about taxes being paid in labor; and it is important that we consider another problem, the mobilization of manpower for the enterprises of the state. Greek tradition made the building of the pyramids a grievous burden upon the Egyptian masses, who were forced to bend their backs to an uneconomic task. On the other hand, it has recently been suggested that the tremendous amount of labor which went into the largest pyramids was conditioned by a kind of autocratic benevolence on the part of the pharaoh.[12] This argument would suggest that the dynastic union and the organization of the Egyptian state produced a security and prosperity which increased the population suddenly and drastically, that there was a period of maladjustment when the population was too great for the food production, so that Egypt was in great distress. In this crisis, the argument would run, the pharaoh greatly extended his public works, that is, his pyramid-building, in order to provide employment for added thousands of peasants, who would be housed and fed at government expense. This is the kind of work relief with which we are familiar in modern times.

The truth probably lies between these two concepts, but closer to the Greek tradition than to the modern theorist. It is true that pharaoh had to house and feed the workers whom he drafted for his construction work, but it is surely a very modern concept to believe that this was work relief. Rather, the answer lies in the dogma of the divine kingship and the highly centripetal force of the Pyramid Age. If the state had finally succeeded in gaining complete and enthusiastic support for the idea that this pharaoh was the state, owned the nation and all that was therein, and that the major hope of eternal reward lay in serving the

11. K. Sethe, *Aegyptische Inschrift auf den Kauf eines Hauses* (*Königliche Sächsische Gesellschaft der Wissenschaften, Sitzungsberichte. Phil.-hist. Klasse* [Leipzig, 1911], pp. 133 ff.); T. E. Peet in *Mélanges Maspero*, I (*MIFAO*, LXVI), 185 ff.

12. R. Engelbach in *ASAE*, XLII (1943), 193 ff.

pharaoh and advancing his immortality, then the supreme energies of the nation would go into the building of pharaoh's eternal home. As he was incomparably great, wise, and eternal, so his lasting home must be incomparably great, skilfully constructed, and enduring. So flat and mandatory became this doctrine that any idea of a work relief project is seen to be an absurdity. To be sure, its derivative product was akin to work relief, because a major endeavor of pyramid construction was at the period of high Nile, when the great blocks of stone could be floated from the quarries to a point near the pyramid plateau. The period of high Nile was the low point of the year from the standpoint of crop production, that time when the River was bringing its promise of renewed crops but when the granaries of last year were at their lowest. When the state drafted labor at such a time and had to feed its workers, the workers enjoyed a small dietary relief. But the purpose of the work was solely the service of the god-king, and the labor was undoubtedly conscripted and worked to the last pound of energy. The analogy of the First Dynasty princess for whose burial personal and household servants were slaughtered suggests that any Egyptian should have been happy to give his utmost effort for his divine ruler. Of course, we are privileged to doubt whether such a doctrine would appeal to a worker under the foreman's lash, but it was the officially accepted doctrine of Egypt.

The accent on the king is shown further in the difference between the mortuary texts of the pharaoh and those of his nobles. From the Fourth Dynasty onward, we have inscribed tombs for the nobles, containing the statement of their hope of continued life. From the end of the Fifth Dynasty onward, we have the Pyramid Texts, carved within the royal tombs; their form of expression and their content clearly show them to be much older than this, but originally not carved on pyramid walls. In the Old Kingdom the mortuary texts of the pharaohs were quite distinct from those of the nobles. The latter were more mundane, designed to extend the activities of this life into the next, including the devoted service of the king. Such texts carried a considerable element of autobiography and a statement of official positions held, which served to give the noble successful momentum into the future life and to propose a continuation of his services to the king in another existence. The scenes and texts of daily life affirmed prosperity and worldly success and proposed a continuation of earthly riches into the future life. Death made no change in the essential lives of Egyptian nobles, unless there might be a hope and expectation that the future life

would hold only the happier and more successful phases of this existence. Riches and success in the service of the king were the greatest
goods of this life and of the next.

In one respect death made no change in the existence of the king: he
was a god on earth in this life, and he would join the circle of the gods
in the next life; he ruled in this world, and he would be a ruler in the
next. However, the Pyramid Texts have an elaborate provision for in-
suring his happiness and success in that next life. They resorted to
every ritual, religious, or magical utterance which might seem to promote eternal life. There are ritualistic texts to accompany the feeding,
provisioning, and service of the deceased king. There are exorcisms
against snakes, scorpions, and other dangerous forces which might in-
fest the ground in which the king was buried. There are very old
hymns, fragments of myths, and rituals of predynastic kings, intended
both to relate the deceased king to the glorious past and to project his
kingship into the next existence. And there are many promotional texts,
intended to advance the pharaoh's acceptability or authority in the next
world and to make him an *akh*, that is, both a "being of glory" and a
continuingly "effective personality." Such beatifications placed him in
the company of the gods as a god. In the Egyptians' all-inclusive range
of endeavor, such texts ran from the most humble to the most arrogant.
They promised that the deceased king would bale out the boat of the
sun-god, would sit as the sun-god's scribe, would be the ugly and
amusing little pygmy who dances for the gods' entertainment—anything to associate him with the divine company. At the other extreme,
they made him the most powerful of all gods, taking over the throne of
the sun-god or cannibalistically devouring the gods and thus incorpo-
rating all their powers into himself. From two different theological
systems they placed him within the company of the sun-god Re or they
made him the ruler of the dead, Osiris. To us much of this is incompatible or competitive, but, as we have said in the preceding chapter, the
Egyptian looked upon such alternatives as complementary rather than
conflicting. Whatever would promote the effective and eternal life of
the dead pharaoh was valid.

When we examine the scenes and inscriptions in the tombs of Old
Kingdom nobles, we find that their future life did not possess the same
boundless scope as that of the pharaoh. They did not become an Osiris
at death, did not become gods of any kind. They did become *akh*'s,
"effective" or "glorious" beings. But this simply states that their personalities carried on effectively and successfully after death and did

not promote them to more transcendent existence. Unlike the dead kings, the dead nobles did not have a *ba* in the Old Kingdom.[13] For lack of a better term, we translate the Egyptian word *ba* as "soul," but it was an expression of continued function after death or an expression of some aspect of a god's being. Since it had power, scope, and range and was originally divine, it could belong to the god-king but not to ordinary circumscribed mortals. Both kings and nobles did have *ka*'s, guiding and protecting forces in life and death, but the *ka*'s of Old Kingdom nobles may have stood well outside their personalities. Some of the Old Kingdom names suggest that a noble's *ka* may have been the pharaoh or a specific god, which is another way of saying that the noble's fortune in life and death was not intimately related to him personally but was dependent upon the favor of a god or of the god-king.

With regard to the masses, we have no direct evidence on the belief about their future existence. However, on the basis of what has been said, we may make a generalizing hypothesis: The future life of each class of society was treated as an advance over this life. The pharaohs had been gods on earth and became greater gods in the next world. The nobles had been servants of the god-king on earth and became more happily and successfully his servants in the next world. The peasants had been servants of the nobles on earth and became more happily and successfully their servants in the next world. Thus the hope of eternal life would be an advance within one's own rank.

Such a system has its own seeds of change. The hope and expectation of reward and promotion in the next life left the possibility that the next life might even bring change in rank. If our theory of consubstantiality be correct—the view that the ancient Egyptian saw the phenomena of his existence as being of a single substance, banded in one continuous spectrum of blending hues—then there would be no flat interdict against change of rank following death. We shall see that such change actually took place for the noble in the following period, when he assumed the formerly exclusive prerogatives of the king and became a god after death. That was a factor of the breakdown of centralization around the king, a process with which we still have to deal. In the earlier period, when centralization was still strong, it was the pharaoh alone who expected to have the fullest life in the future, for he was a god who would continue to be a god; the immortality of nobles and peasants and the success of their future lives were, however, dependent in each case upon their relationship to their masters and their continued service of their masters in another existence.

13. H. Ranke, in *ZÄS*, LXXV (1939), 133.

The sudden and brilliant maturing of Egyptian culture in the first four dynasties called forth the highest abilities of individual Egyptians. The nation was moving forward politically, economically, materially, artistically, and intellectually. This was a group movement, personalized within the figure of the pharaoh and at first redounding to his greater power and glory; but it demanded the individual efforts of every person of ability, intelligence, and ambition. As the state became more powerful and effective, it had to have a larger number of able and trustworthy servants. As government offices elaborated in number and scope of activity, officials had to carry out the commission of the king with increasingly independent judgment. Thus the centripetal forces supporting the absolutism of the king were actually building toward a centrifugal counteraction of individualism apart from the king. As men were called upon to undertake new tasks and discovered thus their own personal powers, their arbitrary dependence upon the pharaoh would be gradually replaced by individual voluntarism. This process was effective throughout the Old Kingdom, but in a slow and evolutionary way, never with the sharp break of a social and political revolution. It would be the breakdown of the state in the First Intermediate Period following the Old Kingdom that would give recognition to the process of decentralization, with Egypt reconstructed into a feudal state and with a "democratization" of the afterlife. Even so, the process would be relative to the original absolutism and would never be a trend to full democracy, while the dogma of the pharaoh's supremacy, because of his divine nature, would be reiterated without regard to changes in this life and the next. However, we still have to study the process of decentralization and to document our claim that nobles came to recognize their own independent powers.

For one thing, the political absolutism of the king was successfully challenged by another god, the sun-god Re. The rebellion of Re against the pharaoh was effective at the beginning of the Fifth Dynasty. One may use the pyramids to present an argument in material terms. In the Fourth Dynasty, the Great Pyramid soared up over 480 feet high, dominating everything around it. It was accompanied by a "sun-boat," dug out of the rock pavement, so that the deceased pharaoh might accompany the sun-god Re in daily journeyings around the earth. However, the sun-boat was of modest size in contrast to the pyramid, the symbol of the pharaoh himself, and for the Great Pyramid there is known no obelisk, the symbol of Re. Let us contrast the situation in the Fifth Dynasty. The pyramid of Ne-user-Re was 165 feet high, but the accompanying sun-obelisk was 5 feet higher. Ne-user-Re's pyramid was 250 feet on a side, but the accompanying temple of the sun-god was 250 by 330 feet. In the Fourth Dynasty the pharaoh had dominated Re; in the Fifth Dynasty Re dominated the pharaoh.

The names of the pharaohs are added evidence. Prior to the Fifth Dynasty, a minority of pharaohs had names which incorporated the name of the sun-god Re; we see such names as Udi-mu, Nefer-ka-Sokar, Djoser, Snefru, and Khufu. Early in the Fourth Dynasty, Re came into greater prominence in the names of the pharaohs, and, from the Fifth Dynasty on, it was the regular practice that the king's royal name related him to Re—Khaf-Re, Sahu-Re, Ne-user-Re, and so on. Further, the Fifth Dynasty first affirmed the pharaoh's filial relation to the sun-god in a formal title, "the Son of Re," which took over the king's personal name, given to him at birth, and stated clearly and emphatically that the pharaoh had been born as the physical son of Re, thus giving him legitimate title to rule over Egypt.

Egyptian legend also records that the Fifth Dynasty diminished the absolutism of pharaoh and asserted the increased importance of the priesthood of Re of Heliopolis. A certain papyrus tells how a prophecy was uttered in the Fourth Dynasty that the royal succession would pass to sons of the sun-god Re, miraculously born to the wife of a priest of Re, and that the eldest of these boys would pass from the high priesthood of the Temple of Heliopolis into the kingship. "It is the wife of a priest of Re ... who has conceived three children to Re. ... And he has said of them that they are to fill this beneficent office (of king) in this entire land and that the eldest of them is to be High Priest in Heliopolis." This is an explicit memory in legend of the passage of power from the king alone to the king in co-operative relationship to the priesthood of Heliopolis.[14]

Success usually brings a weakening of effort. The pharaoh's success in setting up and justifying a state which was incorporated in his person seemed to be complete by the Fourth Dynasty. The dogma of absolutism was an accomplishment; it was possible to relax the pressure and to enjoy the inherited acceptance of his position as a god on earth. The pharaoh's keenest abilities would no longer be summoned to the task of kingship, and his power would make demands instead of seeking new order and prosperity. Specifically, the demands went into noneconomic services for the god-king. It was one thing to authorize the digging of an irrigation canal or the dispatch of a commercial expedition, both enterprises which would promote the prosperity of the land; it was

14. Erman, *LAE*, pp. 36 ff.

another thing for each generation of kings to build an ever larger personal tomb. We do not suppose that there was a revolutionary protest against such arrogation of the national resources, unless it might be in the abrupt assertion of power by the priesthood of Re at Heliopolis. It is unlikely that the nobles who had to provide labor and taxes for the construction of the royal pyramids expressed any formal protest against the nonproductive enterprise. Yet the burden in duties and goods must have been as heavy in Egypt of the Pyramid Age as it was in Palestine when Solomon built his temple, and Solomon's pretensions split Israel open. As time went on, it may have been that the local provincial rulers who were required to send workers for the building of the royal tomb began to delay and evade this obligation and to try to keep their people for work in the home provinces. This would be related to the increasing self-confidence of local nobles in the later Old Kingdom.

The nobles had discovered their powers through the business of setting up and extending the Egyptian state and working out the various expressions of Egyptian culture. Their tomb biographies were scrupulous to express debt and fidelity to the pharaoh, and yet those biographies breathe an air of triumph at personal success, of satisfaction in a rise in rank through personal merit. We may follow the successful climbing of the political and social ladder on the part of career men. A certain Uni began his service modestly as the keeper of a government storehouse; later became the keeper of grounds for the royal pyramid, being responsible for the quarrying and delivery of stone for the pyramid; was the sole magistrate officiating at an important trial involving the royal harem; later was the general in charge of an Asiatic campaign; then became Governor of Upper Egypt, responsible for the movement of goods and taxes in half the kingdom; and ended, full of honors, as a courtier in the palace, apparently royal tutor and companion of the bedchamber.[15]

The autobiography of the architect Nekhebu (Fig. 8c) gives the pharaoh due credit:

His majesty found me a common builder. His majesty conferred upon me the (successive offices of) journeyman builder, master builder, and master of a craft. (Next) his majesty conferred upon me the (successive offices of) Royal Constructor and Builder, Royal Attaché, and Royal Constructor and Architect. . . . His majesty did all this because his majesty favored me so greatly.

Did Nekhebu win these promotions through the ranks of his craft by sedulous courting of the king, by inherited position, or by diligent

15. Breasted, ARE, I, §§ 294, 307 ff., 320 ff.

labor? Probably a combination of the three, but he tells us that he was not averse to beginning at the bottom and working upward.

> Now when I accompanied my brother, the Foreman of Construction Work ..., I acted as clerk, I carried the scribe's palette. When he was appointed journeyman builder, I carried his measuring-rod. When he was appointed master builder, I accompanied him. When he was appointed Royal Constructor and Builder, I ruled the (workmen's) city for him. I did everything thoroughly in it. ... As for everybody there with whom I had to negotiate, it was I who made them satisfied, and I never went to bed angry against anybody.[16]

That was an active, bustling, extroverted age. Success came through conformity to a pattern, which involved the expression of complete loyalty to the king and also hard work along one's chosen career. Conformity to the principle that the king was all-wise and all-present did not preclude individual striving toward greater wealth and position. As far as we can see, it was possible for an intelligent, alert, and active man to make himself indispensable and thus to attain practically independent authority, even though he was thoroughly loyal to his pharaoh. When one considers that the First Cataract was five hundred miles from the capital at Memphis and remembers that communications along the Nile must have been slow, it will be clear that the outlying royal officials and the outlying provincial rulers had to be accorded a generous measure of individual initiative. Such, for example, were the powerful nobles of the First Cataract, who held the southern frontier of Egypt and who led political and commercial caravans into the Sudan, bringing back cattle and luxury products. They were explorers and adventurers and accredited diplomatic agents. "Now when the (Nubian) Prince of Irtjet, Setju, and Wawat saw how powerful and numerous was the troop of (Nubians of) Yam which was going back with me to the capital, as well as the army which had been sent out with me, then this prince sent and gave me large and small cattle and pointed out to me the route on the highlands of Irtjet, because I had shown greater alertness than any courtier or caravan leader who had been sent to Yam previously. ... Further his majesty sent me to Yam a third time. I went forth from Hu(?) on the Oasis Road. I found that the ruler of Yam had just gone out to the land of the Tjemeh-Libyans, to thrash the Tjemeh as far as the western bend of heaven. I went out in pursuit of him to the land of Tjemeh. I pacified him until he praised all the gods for the sake of the Sovereign."[17] The word translated "pacified" may mean "subdued by force" or "bought off." In either case we have an extension of

16. D. Dunham in *JEA*, XXIV (1938), 1 ff.

17. Breasted, *ARE*, I, §§ 335 f.

the *pax aegyptiaca* by the energetic and independent action of a noble.

Egyptian literature of all periods contained books of instruction, characteristically addressed by a father to his son and carrying advice as to proper behavior and deportment in the affairs of this world. This was their closest approach to the concept of wisdom, and it is significant that the practical Egyptian glorified this kind of "teaching," precepts for personal guidance and adjustment. Such works were not religious in any formal sense or ethical in any abstract sense; they dealt directly with typical situations which might be faced by a junior official in his contacts with superiors, in the law court, in meeting unexpected setbacks, or in marrying and setting up a household. Modern counterparts might be the letters of Lord Chesterfield or the homely advice of *Poor Richard's Almanac*. We possess such books of instruction from different periods, and they are an invaluable aid to us in understanding the spirit of different times as applied to the affairs of every day. Since they are applications of the ancient Egyptian culture to mundane situations over approximately two thousand years and since that culture presents the paradox of suffering constant change and yet insisting upon its changelessness, it is no surprise to find that the wisdom literature maintained its general form and many of its specific applications over that long period of time. And yet the books of different periods differ very decidedly from one another, in true conformance with the changing times.[18] There is no better way of observing how the ancient Egyptian clung successfully to the main outlines of his cultural system by making constant adjustments within the system in order to resist the attacks of historical movement. It is a question, of course, how long one can continue to make changes in degree without effecting a change in kind, how long one can adjust and patch up the whole without having a system which is different in essence. The extraordinary phenomenon of ancient Egypt is her success in denying change by tacitly accepting change—in much the same way as she denied the flat fact of death by accepting death as renewed life. The Instruction of the Vizier Ptah-hotep was composed in the spirit of the Old Kingdom; the Instruction of the minor official Amen-em-Opet was composed in the spirit of the centuries following Egypt's world power. There is anywhere from fifteen hundred to two thousand years between them. Now there are passages in the later work, Amen-em-Opet, which are practically identical with passages in the earlier work, Ptah-

18. R. Anthes, *Lebensregeln und Lebensweisheit der alten Aegypter* ("Der Alte Orient," 32.2 [Leipzig, 1933]).

hotep, thus giving a first impression that practical wisdom and the application of the Egyptian ethos to everyday life were serenely unchanging and unchangeable. However, a closer study of the two texts shows how radically different they are. Placed side by side, Ptah-hotep appears areligious, extroverted, bustling, and assured, conforming to the self-confident forward movement of the Old Kingdom, whereas Amen-em-Opet appears pious, withdrawn, quiet, and undemanding, conforming to the pietistic resignation of late times. We could find no better indexes of the fiction of changelessness and the fact of change in Egypt.

The Instruction of Ptah-hotep may thus serve us for our argument about the development of individual voluntarism in the Old Kingdom as a factor of decentralization. Ptah-hotep urges upon his son constant effort to get ahead in the world. That is achieved by following the rules, but the rules themselves provide for individual initiative. Any ambitious man who fits himself into the established administrative and social systems and who meets the demands of those systems for industry and honesty will gain wealth, position, and recognition. The world order has provided a place for the initiative of the "wise" man, who is constantly set in contrast with the "ignorant" man. The goal is definite worldly advantage, with little regard to spiritual values or to the future life. The title of Ptah-hotep is: "the beginning of the expression of good speech . . . in instructing the ignorant about wisdom and about the rules for good speech, as of advantage to him who will obey them and of disadvantage to him who may neglect them."[19] "The wise man rises early in the morning in order to establish himself, but the fool rises early in the morning (only) to distract(?) himself." "If a son accepts what his father says, no plan of his miscarries . . . (and he) will stand well in the estimation of the officials. . . . As for the fool who does not listen, he can do nothing. He regards wisdom as ignorance and profit as loss. He does everything blameworthy, so that one finds fault with him every day."

The text combines an insistence upon obedience to the precepts of the past and an encouragement of personal endeavor, because the precepts of the past allow for a degree of individualism. Throughout, there is an emphasis on useful eloquence, on knowing how to speak effectively and to the point. "If thou art a man of consequence, one sitting in the counsels of his lord, summon thy heart for good. If thou art silent, it is better than teftef-flowers. (But) speak if thou knowest how to solve (difficulties). It is a (real) craftsman who can speak in counsel, for

19. Erman, *LAE*, pp. 54 ff.

speaking is more difficult than any (other) labor." "If thou art a man of intimacy, whom one great man sends to another, be thoroughly reliable when he sends thee. Carry out the errand for him as he has spoken. Do not be reserved about what is said to thee. . . . Grasp hold of the truth, and do not exceed it." In debate with an opponent, one should be properly respectful to one's superior and blandly tolerant of an inferior, but an equal should be faced with energy: "Show thyself: do not be silent when he speaks badly. (Then) the talk (of thee) will be great on the part of the listeners, and thy reputation will be good in the opinion of officials." However, one should never cease striving for improvement, because no man has developed his full skills. "Let not thy heart be puffed up because of thy knowledge; do not be overconfident because thou art a wise man. Take counsel with the ignorant as well as the wise. The (full) limits of craftsmanship cannot be attained, and there is no craftsman equipped to his (full) ability. Eloquence is more hidden than the emerald, yet it may be found with maidservants at the grindstone."

It is conformance to the principles of *ma·at*, "right dealing," "truth," or "justice," that brings the desired rewards of property and position. "If thou art a leader commanding the affairs of the multitude, seek out for thyself every beneficial deed, until thy business be free from wrong. *Ma·at* is great, and its effectiveness is lasting; it has not been disturbed since the time of him who made it, whereas there is punishment for him who passes over its laws. It is the (right) path before him who knows nothing. Wrongdoing has never brought its undertaking to port. It (may be that) fraud gains riches, but the strength of *ma·at* is that it lasts, and a man may say: 'It was the property of my father (before me).'" The interpretation of how *ma·at* was to be applied in the daily activities of the official is intensely practical. It is more important that the magistrate show a sympathetic face than that he take full and final action: "If thou art one to whom petition is made, be calm as thou listenest to what the petitioner has to say. Do not rebuff him before he has swept out his body or before he has said that for which he came. The petitioner likes attention to his words better than the fulfilling of that for which he came. . . . It is not (necessary) that everything about which he has petitioned should come to pass, (but) a good hearing is a soothing to the heart." A man should remember to take care of his dependents, because he may have need of their good-will in the future: "Satisfy thy clients with that which has accrued to thee, that which accrues to one whom god favors. . . . One does not know what may happen, so that he may understand the morrow. If misfortunes occur among those (now) favored, it is the clients who (still) say: 'Welcome!' " Greed never gains what one desires: "If thou desirest thy conduct to be good, to set thyself free from all that is evil, then beware of covetousness, which is a malady, diseaseful, incurable. Intimacy with it is impossible; it makes the sweet friend bitter, it alienates the trusted one from his master, it makes both father and mother bad, together with the brothers of the mother, and it divorces a man's wife. . . . Long-lived is the man whose rule of conduct is right and who goes in accordance with his (proper) course; he wins wealth thereby, but the covetous has no tomb." No; covetousness is an abomination. However, the common sense of the Egyptian would not permit him to be quixotic in giving up his own rights: "Be not covetous at a division; be not greedy—except for thy (own) portion."

The junior official, ambitious for advancement, is charged to be watchfully respectful of his superiors: "Bow thy back to thy superior, thy overseer from the palace. (Then) thy household will be firmly fixed in its property, and thy reward will be as it should be. Opposition to a superior is a difficulty, because one lives as long as he is mild." Such deference borders upon sycophancy: "If thou art one of those sitting at the table of one greater than thyself, take (only) what he may give, when it is set before thy nose. Thou shouldst gaze at what is before thee; do not pierce him with many stares, (for such) an aggression against him is an abomination to the *ka*. Let thy face be cast down until he addresses thee, and thou shouldst speak (only) when he addresses thee. Laugh after he laughs, and it will be pleasing to his heart and what thou mayest do will be pleasing to the heart."

In the emphasis on material gain and position, even the wife was looked upon as a valuable property for the production of children: "If thou art prosperous, thou shouldst found thy household and love thy wife as is fitting. Fill her belly; clothe her back; ointment is the prescription for her body. Make her heart glad as long as thou livest, for she is a profitable field for her lord."

Ptah-hotep ends his advice to his son with a respectful bow to the king and yet with complete self-assurance: "Mayest thou reach me (in the next world), with thy body sound and with the king satisfied with all that has been accomplished. Mayest thou attain (my) years of life. What I have done on earth is not inconsiderable. I attained one hundred and ten years of life which the king gave me, my honor being beyond (that of) the ancestors, through (my) doing right for the king up to the point of venerated (death)."

In our desire to show the personal aggressiveness of the age, we confess to being unfairly selective from the Instruction of Ptah-hotep. We could have selected passages which emphasize honesty and administrative probity, but we believe that they would still have demonstrated the Old Kingdom belief that honesty was a good practical policy, resulting in the favor of the king, the approval of one's fellows, and material wealth. It was not an age which looked timidly to the gods for restrictive guidance or which tried to work out abstract principles of ethics.

What were the results of the weakening of the kingship through priestly collaboration with the throne, through a relaxing of royal effort, and through the advance of the independent authority of the nobles? First, decentralization showed itself in a clear geographic way. Gradually the eager clustering of the tombs of nobles around the pyramid of their king was modified to a point where a majority of the nobles erected their tombs in their home provinces. In the Fourth Dynasty the provincial cemetery had been very exceptional; by the Sixth Dynasty it had become the rule. The high officials and provincial nobles had become confident that they had a good chance of eternal life on their own momentum and not through importunate clinging to the pharaoh. They continued to assert their undying loyalty, but they built for eternity hundreds of miles away from him.[20] Such cemeteries, lying at considerable distances from the capital, exhibit the weaknesses of provincialism. There was still high artistic quality in the tombs in the royal necropolis at Sakkarah near Memphis, even though there was some loss of the earlier hieratic dignity and repose. The provincial cemeteries, however, exhibited the effect of their distance from the best models at the capital and the discipline of the continuing tradition of the court. They lost in purity of line and in continuity of subject matter, thereby gaining in liveliness and variety.[21] This, then, was architectural and artistic decentralization, following up the political, social, and economic decentralization.

We have already remarked about the fragmentation of royal offices, whereby positions originally held by a single individual came to be claimed by several different persons at the same time. Whether this was by royal patent or by self-arrogation we do not know. At any rate, the

20. Contrast the Fourth Dynasty inscription of Debehni (Breasted, *ARE*, I, §§ 211 f.), who asked his entire burial from the pharaoh, with the Sixth Dynasty inscription of Djau (*ibid.*, §349), who arranged his own burial in his own home province: "I made this (tomb) in Abydos of Thinis . . . through love of the district in which I was born."

21. W. S. Smith, *op. cit.*, pp. 214 ff.

splitting-up of some of the highest and most responsible offices, such as that of the Governor of Upper Egypt, shows that the unique control of the pharaoh had ended and that authority—or the claim of authority—was more widely distributed over the land. We stand far away from the extreme centralization of the Third and Fourth Dynasties and are closer to the anarchic fragmentation of the First Intermediate Period or to the feudal organization of the early Middle Kingdom.[22]

As yet these provincial tombs did not exhibit the further step of democratization, in which the nobles usurped the mortuary privilege of pharaoh to be a god in the next world. That step would be undertaken when the Old Kingdom went to pieces politically in the First Intermediate Period, when the rule of Egypt was claimed by several competing pretenders, and when provincial governors carried on in local independence. Then those texts which served to beatify the deceased pharaoh, the Pyramid Texts, would be appropriated for the use of the nobles, who would thereby enjoy a decided advance by the prospect of becoming gods at death. However, some extension of the exclusive prerogatives of the pharaohs may be observed in the tombs of queens at the very end of the Sixth Dynasty. Since such tombs were inscribed with the Pyramid Texts, it would seem that godly being, scope, and authority had been extended to the queens and that the absolute monopoly of divinity, which we have assumed for the pharaohs, had already broken down in an extension to others.

The position of women and particularly of queens in the Old Kingdom is not very clear. We have mentioned how the Instruction of Ptahhotep advises a noble to cherish his wife as a valued and productive piece of property, and it could be argued that women were basically chattels, although perhaps the most valuable of chattels. However, the position of a queen as the daughter of a god, the wife of a god, and the mother of a god was one of rank recognized in the dogma of the state, and this privileged position may have extended downward its helpful analogy during this period of decentralization. The pharaoh's first wife was the consort of a god, who had to be accorded the exceptional privilege of physical contact with him. If she was also the daughter of a preceding pharaoh, she had been engendered by the godly body and must have had within her some of the divine being. Here we have some of the elements contributing to a strong matriarchal trend in the theory of royal succession in Egypt, that the legitimacy for rule was condi-

---

22. H. Kees, *Beiträge zur altägyptischen Provinzialverwaltung und der Geschichte des Feudalismus* (Gött. GN, 1932), pp. 85 ff.

tioned both by the royal descent of the mother and by that of the father. Pharaohs might have many wives, taken from many sources, but the purest line to carry on the seed of the sun-god Re would show a mother directly of the royal family. This was the reason for brother-sister marriages by some of the pharaohs, for the purpose of assuring the most divine strain and for the derivative purpose of cutting down on the number of pretenders to the throne.

We do not know precisely what the Egyptian of the Old Kingdom meant when he stated that the pharaoh was the physical son of Re, coming from the body of the sun-god. Perhaps the situation known from the Eighteenth Dynasty may be extended backward into the older times.[23] If so, we should understand that the dogma of the divine nature of the pharaoh claimed that the sun-god assumed the guise and body of the reigning king, thus entered in to lie with the great first wife, and engendered the divine seed which was to become the future pharaoh. Thus the miraculously divine birth will have been carried beyond the pharaoh himself to the supreme god, masquerading temporarily in the form of the pharaoh. Then the "Mother of the God" will have been exceptionally marked among women, hardly to be considered a mere harem property of her lord.

The Old Kingdom, even before those late tombs of queens who were privileged to use the Pyramid Texts, does indicate to us some exceptional consideration for and authority of queens. The ladies of the ruling family in the Fourth Dynasty were accorded considerable prominence in the royal cemetery of Gizeh. In the Sixth Dynasty, Pepi II succeeded to the throne as a boy, and his mother acted as regent and appeared importantly in his early inscriptions.[24] The most interesting case is tantalizingly elusive because it rests largely upon the legend of Greek and Roman times that Egypt was ruled by a blonde courtesan at the end of the Fourth Dynasty. This might seem mere romantic fiction except for two strains of corroborating evidence. The tomb of a Fourth Dynasty queen has shown that Khufu's daughter, Hetep-hires II, had blond hair. The extant colors on the tomb wall show her hair as yellow, with fine red lines, in contrast to the conventional black elsewhere in this tomb and the rest of the cemetery.[25] One assumes that such a blond strain was introduced into Egypt from the Tjemeh-Libyans lying to

23. Breasted, *ARE*, II, §§ 196 ff.

24. *Ibid.*, I, §§ 339 ff.

25. G. A. Reisner in *Bulletin of the Museum of Fine Arts, Boston*, XXV (October, 1927), 66 f.

the west of the Nile Valley, a people of European connections and apparently of considerable wealth in herds of cattle. Another strain of evidence comes from the examination of the so-called "fourth pyramid" of Gizeh, actually a benchlike tomb in the form of a huge sarcophagus. This last important structure of the Fourth Dynasty was built for Queen Khent-kaus, who carried the legitimate line from the Fourth to the Fifth Dynasty. Here we have the origin of the late legend that the courtesan Rhodopis, that is, "Rosy-cheeked," who was the "bravest and fairest of her day, fair-skinned and rosy-cheeked, built the third pyramid." The legend is romantically inexact, but it does carry a correct tradition about the exceptional position of queens in the Old Kingdom.[26] Although we doubt that that high consideration effectively ransomed the wives of nobles and commoners from their status as valued chattels, and specifically from their obligation to bear a long series of sons for their lords, the lower wives were soon going to have higher standing through the process of decentralization and democratization. In the Middle Kingdom both nobles and their wives were accorded the pharaonic privilege of becoming gods at death, so that that age made no distinction in essence between a man and his wife.

If the theory and dogma of the state so thoroughly protected the authority of the king and if the security and prosperity of Egypt gained so greatly through rule unified under the pharaoh, how did the Old Kingdom happen to collapse at the end of the Sixth Dynasty? We have already indicated two of the divisive factors—the burden of building noneconomic and huge structures for each new king, structures which were supposed to last for eternity but which had to be built again for each generation, and the increasing spirit of self-sufficiency and independence upon the part of the nobles. Three other factors might be cited: first, the burden of setting up perpetual endowments which were supposed to finance the eternal care of the tombs of kings, queens, and nobles, thus separating lands from normal economy and laying heavier burdens on other lands; second, the burden of purchasing the loyalty of outlying provincial powers in Egypt; and, third, a probable breakdown of the surplus coming in from foreign commerce. We should say something more about these factors.

For the whole Old Kingdom, but particularly for the very end of that period, a number of charters of immunity have come down to us, decrees promulgated by the pharaoh in order to confer an exceptional

26. H. Junker in *Mitteilungen des deutschen Instituts . . . in Kairo,* III (1932), 123 ff.

advantage upon some agency within Egypt. Characteristically, such decrees protected a temple from dues in labor—probably not from taxes in goods—or from arbitrary seizure of its goods or labor by an official. Protection from the arrogant power of self-assertive officials might well be viewed as a formal statement of civil rights and privileges. Exemption from forced labor, however, can only be seen as special privilege, extended by the pharaoh in order to purchase for himself the support of important temples or districts, at a time when his waning power was in need of such support. Further, the exemption of any agency powerful enough to be an effective support for the throne would inevitably throw a heavier burden of duties upon less fortunate agencies.

As an example of such charters of privilege, we give extracts from a decree of Pepi I of the Sixth Dynasty on behalf of his remote ancestor, Snefru of the Fourth Dynasty, and specifically to the benefit of two pyramid-towns, that is, agricultural villages which supplied personnel and income for the service of Snefru's two pyramids. "My majesty has commanded that these two pyramid-towns be exempt for him in the course of eternity from doing any work of the Palace, from doing any forced labor for any part of the Royal Residence in the course of eternity, or from doing any *corvée* at the word of anybody in the course of eternity." The decree then proceeds to give specific examples of the kind of exaction which might be demanded and of the persons, property, and service which would be protected from such exactions. He exempted them from any service to himself, his royal family, or his officials. By thus holding out of the productive economy of Egypt the lands and persons belonging to a king who had died 350 years before himself, Pepi I was confirming the weight of the dead hand which lay heavy upon the land.

Another example of such royal decrees comes from the sweeping immunities accorded to the temple of the god Min at Koptos in Upper Egypt. "The Chief Prophet and the Subordinate Prophet of Min in Koptos, . . . all the serfs of the activity of the House of Min, the acolytes, the Following and Watch of Min, the people of the workhouse, and the two architects of this temple—they who are there—my majesty does not permit that they be put upon any activities of the King, whether herds of cattle, herds of donkeys, (herds of) small cattle, . . . any time-labor, or any forced labor to be credited in the House of Min in the course of eternity. They are exempted for Min of Koptos today quite anew, by a decree on the part of the King of Upper and Lower

Egypt: (Pepi II), living forever and ever. As for a Governor of Upper Egypt who may effect their removal to an office of a House of Royal Documents or of a House of the Master of the Revision or of an Archives or of (a House) Having an (Official) Seal, in order to put them upon any work of the Palace—he is one cursed with the word 'treason'!"[27]

Thus, in an attempt to win the support of powerful priesthoods in Egypt and thereby to bulwark the sagging throne, the pharaohs were actually damaging the economy of the land and also raising up strong nonroyal elements which would have the independent wealth and power to challenge the rule of the king. The system was self-defeating.

The other force which aided to topple the Old Kingdom throne cannot be seen clearly but may be guessed at with moderate confidence. We have said that the Old Kingdom did not attempt an empire but was content to keep open channels of international commerce, so that goods would flow to Egypt because of her cultural superiority, her greater wealth, and the force of tradition. We have guessed that foreign commerce was a royal monopoly and was a strong economic support of the kingship. Toward the end of the Old Kingdom the texts give us an indication of troubles in those foreign countries with which Egypt had trade relations. Military action had to be undertaken in Upper Nubia and the Sudan. There a passive and stagnant native culture was being shaken by a high primitive culture, washing in from the Sahara Desert and probably related to those blond Tjemeh-Libyans whom we have mentioned.[28] At any rate, the peaceful trade of earlier times had become subject to disturbance.

A similar situation seems to have prevailed in Asia, into which a Sixth Dynasty pharaoh had to send repeated punitive expeditions.[29] New peoples were coming in from the desert, Josephs who knew not Pharaoh, rendering the *pax aegyptiaca* untenable. Apparently, most of Palestine-Syria was valuable to Egypt only as a traffic road for the passage of goods, a road which had to be kept open but which was not normally in need of garrisoning and colonizing. It was different, however, at the Phoenician port of Byblos, a shipping point for cedar and cedar products, perhaps also a transshipping point for the copper and tin of the Mediterranean islands, the silver of Asia Minor, the wine and

27. Cf. W. C. Hayes in *JEA*, XXXII (1946), 3 ff.

28. Breasted, *ARE*, I, §§ 358 f., 365 ff.; cf. W. Hölscher, *Libyer und Aegypter* (*Mün. AF*, IV [Glückstadt, 1937]).

29. Breasted, *ARE*, I, §§ 311 ff.; cf. also § 360.

olive oil of the eastern Mediterranean, and the obsidian and lapis lazuli of more easterly countries. There the Old Kingdom had a fair-sized merchant colony, large enough to justify a temple and gifts dispatched from pharaoh. Such inscribed and datable Egyptian objects came to an abrupt break under Pepi II at the end of the Sixth Dynasty. The Egyptian temple at Byblos was burned to the ground, and we assume that trade broke off sharply.[30] Apparently the pressure of new peoples from the desert effected a drastic change in the population and traditions of Hither Asia. When the main line of traffic between Egypt and Asia was broken, the pharaoh was bound to suffer politically and economically.

In this chapter and in the following one we shall be forced to use certain words which carry a coloration of emotion: "absolutism," "privilege," "materialism," "individualism," "democratization," "provincialism," etc. Not only does the modern reader record such words in terms of his own personal experiences and prejudices, but the modern writer sets them down with some of the same bias, with an overtone of approbation or of disapproval. Such subjectivity seems to be both inevitable and the privilege of the historian, who records what he sees in terms of his own philosophy of history. However, we do wish to stress at this point that our writing is not dryly objective, that we find it difficult to discuss tendencies away from centralized absolutism toward individual voluntarism and a concern for the common man without giving away to some emotion of approbation. We would accompany this warning with two observations: the centrifugal trend which we have been discussing was not an unmixed blessing and did bring a decided loss of quality in the cultural product, as well as intense social and economic distress, in which the "Egyptianness" of the national system suffered loss which it would never regain; and our statement of the historical tendencies is presented in the form of an argument, so that it proceeds in a series of arbitrary generalizations, whereas the actual course of history was relative. The term "democratization" brings to mind the term "democracy," and one must state flatly that Egypt never approached anything like the rule of the people. Such terms are used relative to the antecedent situation, and a brief period of centrifugal action in Egypt must not vitiate our knowledge that Egypt was normally and continuingly a nation of high centripetal force.

30. M. Dunand in *Syria*, IX (1928), 173 ff., esp. 181 f.; H. H. Nelson in *Berytus*, I (1934), 19 ff.

NOTE ON ROYAL NAMES AND TITLES

We have been guilty of an anachronism in using the term "pharaoh" for the king of Egypt before the Empire. In Egyptian "pharaoh" meant "Great House" and referred originally to the palace rather than the inhabitant of the palace. It was not until the late Eighteenth Dynasty that it became a respectful circumlocution for the king himself.

The developed dogma that the king of Egypt was a god presented a series of formal titles expressing that doctrine.[31] The full titulary of the king had five titles, each followed by a didactic epithet or a name. As a whole, this titulary carried the teaching of the king's divine right to rule both parts of Egypt as one, while the variety of epithets and names used at various stages of Egyptian history was the dogmatic expression of the changing politics of the land. (1) As "the Horus," the king was the current ruler of Egypt, the sky-god who was the legitimate successor to his father, who had become an "Osiris." (2) As "the Two Ladies," the king incorporated into himself the two goddesses of the two parts of the land, Nekhbet of Upper Egypt and Uto of Lower Egypt. (3) The title "Horus of Gold" expressed some kind of sweeping power or glory, but its application is still obscure.

The two final titles preceded the king's most commonly used names, which were inclosed in *eartouches* or name-rings: (4) As "He of the *Sut*-Plant and of the Bee," commonly rendered "King of Upper and Lower Egypt," the king again united within himself the two parts of Egypt, using the recognized symbols for Upper and Lower Egypt. A second title frequently followed this and carried out the same idea: "Lord of the Two Lands." These titles introduced the *prenomen* within a *cartouche*, and this was the throne name, assumed by the king at his coronation. It was therefore highly significant in its statement. After the Fourth Dynasty, the *prenomen* regularly paid honor to Re in its statement: for example, Neb-hepet-Re or Neb-maat-Re. (5) As "the Son of Re," the king expressed his divine affiliation to the sun-god. A second title frequently following this may mean "Lord of Appearances," that is, divine epiphanies.[32] Then, in a *cartouche*, came the *nomen*, which was normally the personal name of the king since his birth. Thus it was often a dynastic name, presenting the Amen-em-hets and Sen-Userts of the Twelfth Dynasty, the Amen-hoteps and Thut-

---

31. H. Müller, *Die formale Entwicklung der Titulatur* (*Mün. AF*, VII [1938]); H. Frankfort, *Kingship and the Gods* (Chicago, 1948), pp. 46 f.; A. H. Gardiner, *Egyptian Grammar* (Oxford, 1927), pp. 71 ff.

32. Or perhaps "Lord of Diadems."

mosids of the Eighteenth, or the Ramessides of the Nineteenth and Twentieth Dynasties.

The closest equivalent to our word "king" was a term which originally meant "He of the *Sut*-Plant." The ruler was also called "the Good God" and "the Lord." Direct mention of the sacred person could be avoided by reference to "the Great House," "the House of the King," "the Residence," or "the Protected Place." The word which we translate "majesty" is the same as a word for "servant" and may originally have expressed the king's activity on behalf of the gods. To the name or title of the king there was often attached a pious wish: "May he live, be prosperous and healthy!"

Three divine attributes of kingship were *hu*, "authoritative utterance" or "creative command," *sia*, "perception" or "understanding," and *maʿat*, "justice."[33]

33. Wilson in H. Frankfort *et al.*, *The Intellectual Adventure of Ancient Man*, pp. 57, 83 f.

V

THE FIRST ILLNESS

Dynasties 7–11 (about 2200–2050 B.C.)

U<small>NDER</small> the Old Kingdom, Egypt realized her highest material and intellectual powers. She was a new culture, with all the excitement of working out her form of national expression. In future ages she would have very great achievements to her credit, but her subsequent endeavors never had the same self-assured composure. The Old Kingdom had vigor, *savoir faire*, and confidence. In terms of what the ancients seemed to be trying to establish as a way of life, the Old Kingdom appeals as the most Egyptian of periods. A career as yet unthreatened by outside peril or inner conflict permitted that sense of security necessary for full cultural expression. A strong factor of that expression was pragmatism and materialism. In the arrogance of realized powers, the Egyptian felt himself strong enough to cope with the universe; he had no need for the constant support of the gods and no need for an abstract code of ethics; as far as his experience went, he was able to face and meet any situation himself. His materialism applied particularly to the great goal of eternal life. An imposing tomb, a large mortuary endowment, the momentum of earthly success, and the earned favor of the god-king were the goods with which he bought immortality. That such materialism was supported by religion, by magic, and by some insistence upon the principle of *maʿat* does not vitiate the generalization that the Old Kingdom values were chiefly earthly success and wealth. That was the world order which the gods had given. It provided simple and straightforward standards of conduct and the view that riches and worldly recognition would be good for all time.

Such a system may have promoted a degree of independence upon the part of individuals, but it rested upon a known and established order, in which the pharaoh was the crucial figure. Not only did the dogma of the state assert categorically that all was his, but the political, social, and economic structure of the state rested upon the assumption and tradition that his fortunes and those of his people were identical. If the keystone of the state, the divine kingship, were shattered or extracted, the whole proud edifice would crumble.

Tradition says that Pepi II of the Sixth Dynasty reigned for more than ninety years, and there is some evidence to support the tradition. Whether the forces of disintegration were already too strong for any pharaoh to combat or whether his long and feebly defensive reign hastened the collapse we cannot know; but the Old Kingdom ended almost immediately after his death, somewhere around 2180 B.C. Then came anarchy.

At Memphis the Seventh and Eighth Dynasties went on claiming the rule of the entire land, but their claim was ignored by other parts of Egypt. A late tradition asserts that the Seventh and Eighth Dynasties consisted of seventy kings in seventy days. This is an absurdity, but it is only a dramatic exaggeration of the weakness and confusion of the formerly stable state, for the two dynasties probably lasted only about twenty-five years, with a rapid turnover of feeble kings. For the most part the provincial rulers seem to have done their best to try to keep their own little localities in order, with a few of them striving for wider authority. From Koptos in Upper Egypt a family pretended to the throne of Egypt for perhaps two generations, although it is doubtful whether their authority extended in either direction for more than a day or two's sail on the Nile.

Two generations after the fall of the Old Kingdom the situation clarified itself to the extent of showing the major competing forces. For about a century from 2150 on, a powerful local family at Herakleopolis in the Faiyum ruled a stretch of Egypt running from some point in the Delta well south into Upper Egypt. The Ninth and Tenth Dynasties under this family gave Middle Egypt enough stability so that we can see the period as being the formative time of the classical Egyptian literature, with a productive literary movement of considerable vigor. When the Herakleopolitan rule came into conflict with the growing power of Thebes, the Herakleopolitans received valued support from a strong and independent family of princes at Assiut in Middle Egypt. It proved to be a losing battle, and Thebes finally won out.[1]

The situation in the Delta in this First Intermediate Period is doubtful. We have spoken about the new movements of peoples in Hither Asia, and this restlessness affected the Egyptian Delta when the central authority broke down. It would be wrong to think of this in terms of an armed and unified invasion; probably there was only a constant trickle of small tribes. However, in time the Asiatics in the Delta were numerous enough to constitute a police problem for the Herakleopolitan rulers. Perhaps a few of the Asiatics claimed pharaonic titles and power, just as the little Egyptian princelings were doing. However, it would be wrong to consider the Asiatic incursion into the Delta an important or even a contributory factor in the confusion of the times. Some of the Egyptian documents try to excuse the national weakness by laying blame upon the Asiatics, but this is an evasion of responsibility. The Asiatics did not come in conquest or in large numbers; they took advantage of existing disorder to make their homes on the fertile soil, and when the First Intermediate Period was over they had already become absorbed into Egypt or were easily ejected.

The final major competitor for rule was a provincial family at Thebes in Upper Egypt, who had attained sufficient strength by 2135 to assert themselves as little pharaohs. For nearly a century Thebes fought Herakleopolis and its ally, Assiut. Finally, about the middle of the twenty-first century, this Eleventh Dynasty at Thebes defeated the northern state and went on to extend her sway and to present to her successor, the Twelfth Dynasty, a relatively united land. As we shall see, this new state was at first very decentralized and has justly been called a "feudal" state. The tight control of the pharaohs of the early Old Kingdom could not be regained. The centrifugal forces had been far too powerful, and the spirit of the early Middle Kingdom was highly individualistic.

That is the briefest outline of the political turmoil of the First Intermediate Period.[2] There is much more to say about the social and spiritual turmoil.

The First Intermediate Period has left us a respectable body of literature voicing the bewilderment and despair with which Egyptians faced the overturn of their once stable world.[3] Our quotations will be drawn

1. H. Stock, *Die erste Zwischenzeit Aegyptens* (Rome, 1949), discusses some of the opposing forces in the period.

2. See also pp. 125–27 below.

3. In Erman, *LAE*, pp. 86 ff. (the suicide); 75 ff. (instruction for Meri-ka-Re); 132 ff. (song of the harper); 92 ff. (prophecy of Ipu-wer); and 110 ff. (prophecy of Nefer-rohu).

from the argument of the man whose weariness of life drew him toward suicide, from the instruction of a Herakleopolitan king to his son, from a song urging men to forget their cares in heedless pleasure, and from two "prophetic" works. These texts agree in their sense of shock and grief at the sorry state of the land, but they propose different activities to escape the troubles of the day: suicide, forgetful indulgence, or the return of good rule.

Even though the Old Kingdom had been a time of change and of the opportunity for men to alter their stations in life, it had had its known rules of order within which change had taken place. One went ahead by intelligence, industry, and the favor of the king. Now there came an age of violence, in which one sought advancement by the ruthless overturn of the old standards. The prophet Ipu-wer said: "Why really, the land spins around as does a potter's wheel. The robber is (now) the possessor of riches. . . . Why really, all maid-servants make free with their tongues. When their mistresses speak, it is burdensome to the servants. . . . Why really, the ways [are not] guarded roads. Men sit in the bushes until the benighted (traveler) comes, to take away his burden and steal what is upon him. He is presented with blows of a stick and slain wrongfully. . . . Ah, would that it were the end of men, no conception, no birth! Then the earth would cease from noise, without wrangling! . . . Why really, the children of nobles are dashed against the walls. The (once) prayed-for children are (now) laid out on the high ground. . . . Behold, noble ladies are (now) gleaners, and nobles are in the workhouse. (But) he who never slept on a plank is (now) the owner of a bed. . . . Behold, the owners of robes are (now) in rags. (But) he who never wove for himself is (now) the owner of fine linen. . . . If three men go along a road, they are found to be two men: it is the greater number that kills the lesser. . . . All these years are civil strife: a man may be slain on his (own) roof, while he is on the watch in his boundary house."

The prophet Nefer-rohu added his voice: "This land is helter-skelter, and no one knows the result. . . . I show thee the land topsy-turvy. That which never happened has happened. Men will take up weapons of warfare, so that the land lives in confusion. Men will make arrows of metal, beg for the bread of blood, and laugh with the laughter of sickness. . . . I show thee the son as a foe, the brother as an enemy, and a man killing his (own) father. Every mouth is full of 'Love me!', and everything good has disappeared. . . . Men take a man's property away from him, and it is given to him who is from outside. I show thee the possessor in need and the outsider satisfied. . . . I show thee the land topsy-turvy.... I show thee the undermost on top.... It is the paupers who eat the offering-bread, while the servants jubilate.... The land is completely perished, so that no remainder exists, not (even) the black of the nail survives from what was fated."

In the fateful language of these "prophets," not so much of the fertile Black Land survived as might be found under a fingernail. What do they mean?

For one thing, they are talking about the breakdown of that central government in which the god-king was accepted as all-powerful. That cherished mystery of the divine nature of the pharaoh had been cheapened through competition for rule. "Behold now," said Ipu-wer, "it has come to a point where the land is despoiled of the kingship by a few irresponsible men. Behold now, it has come to a point where (men) rebel against the (royal) uraeus, ... which made the Two Lands peaceful. Behold, the secret of the land, whose limits are unknow(able), is laid bare. The Royal Residence may be razed within an hour.... The secrets of the King of Upper and Lower Egypt are laid bare." This is still highly symbolic language, but Ipu-wer makes himself clearer: "Why really, Elephantine, the Thinite nome, and the [shrine] of Upper Egypt do not pay taxes because of [civil] war.... What is a treasury (good) for without its revenues?" Such taxes as are paid are raided by anybody from the government treasury: "The storehouse of the king is a (mere) come-and-get-it for everybody, and the entire palace is without its taxes." Nefer-rohu points out that fewer tax-paying sources mean a heavier burden on those who are left to the palace: "The land is diminished, (but) its administrators are many; bare, (but) its taxes are great; little in grain, (but) the (tax)-measure is large, and it is measured to overflowing."

That former surplus coming from foreign commerce had disappeared, leaving only a paltry trade from the poor little oases to the west. Ipu-wer states the case in terms of luxury products. "No one really sails north to [Byb]los today. What shall we do for cedar for our mummies? ... (Nobles) were embalmed with the oil thereof as far away as Keftiu, (but) they come no longer. Gold is lacking.... How important it (now) seems when the oasis-people come carrying" mats and plants and birds!

In the sacred state, government offices had been treated as though they were divine inclosures. With the collapse of responsible government, "why really, the writings of the august inclosure are read. The place of the secrets which were is (now) laid bare.... Why really, (public) offices are open, and their reports are read. . . . Why really, the writings of the scribes of the mat have been removed. . . . Why really, the laws of the inclosure are put out-of-doors, men actually walk on them in the highways, and poor men tear them up in the streets."

This contempt for past law and order and for past property extended to the property of the dead, even the pharaoh himself. The pyramids had been robbed. "Behold now, something has been done which never happened for a long time; the king has been taken away by poor men. Behold, he who was buried as a (divine) falcon is (now) on a (mere) bier; what the pyramid hid has become empty." Men raided the crumbling tombs of their ancestors for the stones with which to build their own tombs; a Herakleopolitan king advised his son Meri-ka-Re: "Do not injure the monument of another; thou shouldst quarry stone in Troia. Do not build thy tomb out of the ruins." As kings' tombs were despoiled and neglected, so were those of nobles. The harper sang in melancholy voice: "The gods who lived formerly rested in their pyramids; the beatified dead also, buried in their pyramids, and they who built houses—their places are no more. See what has been made of them! I have heard the words of Ii-em-hotep and Hor-dedef, with whose discourses men speak so much—(but) what are their places (now)? Their walls are broken apart, and their places are no more—as though they had never been!" Not only were the old tombs broken down and abandoned by the mortuary priests, the endowments for their perpetual maintenance swept away in the general anarchy, but the present dead received none of the traditional care. Ipu-wer states it wildly: "Why really, many dead are buried in the River. The stream is a tomb, and the embalming-place has really become the stream." This includes suicide, with its despairing abandonment of the cherished values of tomb and mortuary services: "Why really, the crocodiles [sink] down because of what they have carried off, for men go to them of their own accord." Is it any wonder that the man who was weary of life pondered suicide in his loneliness: "To whom can I speak today? I am laden with wretchedness for lack of an intimate friend. To whom can I speak today? The sin which treads the earth, it has no end."

The pharaohs of Egypt in their desire to build up and extend the state had fostered individualism and self-confidence in their nobles, and now they had to lean on the support of many. The Herakleopolitan king said to his son: "Advance thy great men, so that they may carry out thy laws. . . . The poor man does not speak according to what is right for him, . . . (but) he is partial to him who has rewards for him. Great is a great man when his great men are great; valiant is the king possessed of courtiers; august is he who is rich in his nobles." Individual ability was still prized. "Do not distinguish the son of a (noble)man from a poor man, (but) take to thyself a man because of the work of his hands." Such a fostering of initiative and ability on the part of the king, no matter where he might find these talents, was laudable, but it was a centrifugal force, setting up potential and real opposition to the single authority of the pharaoh. Its logical extension was stated by the man who was considering suicide: "Hearts are rapacious. Every man seizes his fellow's goods."

Here we digress for a subjective moral criticism. The high achievements of the Old Kingdom were attained by an amoral people, or rather by a people whose morals were pragmatic and materialistic. They found the good life in successful activity—successful politically, socially, and economically. There was little piety toward the gods—other than the pharaoh; there was little emphasis upon abstract *ma'at* as the basis for conduct; and there had been no occasion for humility. The really great physical successes of the Old Kingdom had seemed to promise that energy and intelligence were all that man needed. When kings weakened and nobles became stronger, fracturing the solidity of the state, when the economy of the state became distorted by the dead hand of mortuary endowments and charters of immunity, and when the movements of new foreigners into other countries cut off the special advantages of foreign trade, that world of material success crashed suddenly and tremendously into anarchy and chaos. It is natural that the first reactions were bewildered despair. Like the pyramids, the world of the Old Kingdom had seemed to be based on eternity. It would take time and effort to work out new values for life. It was the genius of the Egyptian that his still basic optimism did survive and enable him to state the good life in new terms.

Except for the one contributing factor of the movement of foreign peoples in neighboring countries, all the elements which led to the downfall of the Old Kingdom seem to have been internal. This was a systemic illness and not an infection or injury dealt by others. The Egyptian body was not healthy enough to take the excesses of unrelieved materialism. Now the Egyptian texts of the period linger bitterly on the presence of foreigners within the boundaries of the state, and there is no doubt that Asiatics took up residence in the Delta. Not only is the literary evidence strong and circumstantial, but archeology has also shown Asiatic elements intruding into Egypt at this time, notably a distinctive type of button seal.[4] This, however, does not mean that an invasion of Asiatics was responsible for the overthrow of the Old Kingdom and for the new elements which arose within the First Intermediate Period.[5] Such an argument confuses cause and effect. There were disturbances and displacements in Asia, but no conquering horde crossed the Sinai wilderness, invaded Egypt, and overthrew the state. Rather, the state collapsed from internal strains, the frontiers were left undefended, and a steady trickle of displaced Asiatics seeped into the Egyptian Delta. Within a few generations they were numerous enough to hold some independent rule, so that the Herakleopolitan kings had to take military action against them. However, they were not the major factor of chaos in Egypt. They served as a convenient whipping-boy for the Egyptians in their time of distress: it was a satisfaction to ignore those divisive forces which were domestic and to lay the blame upon the Asiatics for the time of troubles. The texts therefore accord them a space disproportionate to their real influence. They were never powerful enough to end the Egyptian sense of normal security behind strong frontiers or the Egyptian sense of god-given superiority over other peoples. Thus the Asiatics in the Delta under the First Intermediate Period form a decided contrast to the Asiatics in the Delta under the Second Intermediate Period, the Hyksos, who were conquerors and dominators and thereby broke down the old Egyptian feeling of security, isolation, and special election. At the present time, these Asiatics were only one of many factors of chaos.

The Herakleopolitan king explained to his son that it was civil war within Egypt that permitted these foreigners to enter the land and advised stronger protection against them: "When thy frontier is endangered toward the [southern] region, it means that the [northern] bowmen will take on the girdle (of war). Build structures in the Northland." The prophet Nefer-rohu declared that the lack of security policing permitted the Asiatic entry: "Foes have arisen in the east, and the Asiatics have come down into Egypt.... No protector will listen.... The wild beasts of the desert will drink at the rivers of Egypt and be at their ease on their banks for lack of someone to scare them away(?)."

4. H. Frankfort in *JEA*, XII (1926), 80 ff.

5. The attempt of Flinders Petrie, *The Making of Egypt* (London, 1939), to derive practically every new epoch in Egyptian history from the influences of intrusive or invading foreigners ignores the physical isolation of Egypt, ignores the possibility of major internal changes, and begs the question on changes by simply shifting the cause of change abroad.

The prophet Ipu-wer stated the case in a way characteristically Egyptian. In their feeling of special election and special providence, the Egyptians called themselves "the people" in contrast to foreigners. Now the presence of foreigners in Egypt had blurred that distinction between "the people" and all outsiders: "[Why] really, the desert is (spread) throughout the land; the nomes are destroyed; barbarians from outside have come to Egypt. . . . There are really no people anywhere. . . . A man of character goes in mourning because of what has happened in the land. . . . Foreigners have become people everywhere. . . . Why really, the entire Delta marshland will no longer be hidden; the confidence of the Northland is (now) a beaten path. . . . Behold, it is in the hands of those who did not know it, as well as those who knew it: foreigners are (now) skilled in the work of the Delta." These words state to us the process of intrusion, confusion, and then amalgamation and absorption. The Asiatics became Egyptians in the course of time and took up the work of normal Delta dwellers.

It was therefore possible for the Egyptian to retain his superior feeling over foreigners, and the instruction for Meri-ka-Re characterized the Asiatics and their homeland with lofty scorn. "Lo, the wretched Asiatic—it goes ill with the place where he is, afflicted with water, difficult from many trees, the ways thereof painful because of the mountains. He does not dwell in a single place, (but) his legs are made to go astray (?). He has been fighting (ever) since the time of Horus, (but) he does not conquer, nor yet can he be conquered. . . . Do not trouble thyself about him: he is (only) an Asiatic, one despised (?) on his (own) coast. He may rob a single person, (but) he does not lead against a town of many citizens." Such a paltry person could not have overthrown the Egyptian state. The causes were internal, and the solution had to be found within Egypt itself.

How did Egypt react to the staggering blow that her world was not stable and eternal? The responses were varied, because the first shock was too violent to permit a calm adjustment. We have already indicated the sense of despair that led some to seek an end in suicide, certainly the very last resort for the Egyptian, who normally clung happily to life and invested death with an elaborate ceremonial. One literary document is given over to this theme, the argument between a desperate man and his own soul about seeking his death. The *ba* or "soul" was that element of a man's personality which had effective play after death, particularly in maintaining contact between the man's *akh* or "effective being" in another world and his corpse, tomb, and survivors in this world. The question at issue was whether this *ba* could remain with and serve a man who found his end by suicide in fire. The *ba* tried to dissuade the man from a death which would cut him off from a proper burial and normal mortuary service, then tried to persuade him to forget his cares in the pursuit of sensual pleasure, but finally agreed to stand by the man even in violent self-death. The man won over his *ba* by a series of poetical arguments, that his following the *ba*'s invitation to heedless pleasure would give him a bad name, that he had not a friend in this world of greedy violence, that death was itself a pleasure because it was a release from pain and care, and that the dead had high privileges.[6]

It should be clear that this text is thoroughly un-Egyptian in spirit—in its abandonment of life and embracing of death, in its giving up the customary funerary ceremony and psychology, and in the liberty which it accorded the individual to question the existing order and to work out his own solution of one of the weightiest problems. Yet there is no excuse for seeking outside Egyptian literature for a foreign prototype. The language used and the nature of the *ba* are purely Egyptian, and the document belongs essentially to the spirit of the age of pessimism we are discussing. It was un-Egyptian because a time of material and spiritual letdown was un-Egyptian. It may be an accident of survival, or it may be significant that this text of gentle pessimism was not copied by later generations, which worked out other answers for themselves.

A second reaction to the chaotic times was agnosticism and a call to hedonistic indulgence. The minstrel with the harp who entertained nobles with a melancholy chant, while they sat heavily and sleepily after a banquet, pointed out that neglect and ruin attended the tombs of the ancestors, so that that old elaborate funerary care could not keep the memory of the dead alive. How, then, can we know? Is there anything useful to do? "There is none who comes back from (over) there, that he may tell their state, that he may tell their needs, that he may still our hearts, until we (too) may travel to the place where they have gone. (Therefore) let thy desire flourish, in order to let thy heart forget the (funerary) beatifications for thee, and follow thy desire as long as thou shalt live. . . . Fulfil thy needs upon earth, after the command of thy heart. . . . Wailing saves not the heart of a man from the underworld. . . . Make holiday, and weary not therein! Behold, it is not given

6. Erman, *LAE*, pp. 86 ff.

to a man to take his property with him. Behold, there is not one who departs who comes back again!" This was an altered statement of materialism: since we cannot know about the unknowable, let us make the most of our life in this world, giving ourselves over to the pleasures of the senses.

However, despondency and cynicism were not the only answers which this age gave to its problem of suffering, nor were they by any means the most effective answers in terms of continuance. What makes the First Intermediate Period and the early Middle Kingdom glorious in the history of human endeavor is the discovery of higher moral values to take the place of the shattered materialistic values.[7] To their bewilderment, they found that the things which are seen—tombs, endowment, court position—are temporal. Gropingly and inadequately, they discovered that the things which are unseen may be eternal; and eternity was always their great goal. If they had been able to make their discovery increasingly effective in everyday life, as leading to the greater welfare of greater numbers of the people, Egypt might have been the first country to recognize the values in the common man and to continue attempts to work out a good life for the many. Unfortunately, the discovery of the essential importance of man in general turned out to be short-lived in Egypt, applying only to the time of troubles and its immediate aftermath, and Egypt soon returned to its materialism and absolutism. Perhaps, instead of regretting that she fell short of realization of the sanctity of the individual and of social justice, we should give her full credit for coming so close to a higher moral code. Instead of deploring her failure to attain anything like democracy, we should applaud her realized tendencies toward wider good for greater numbers. Before 2000 B.C., many centuries before the prophets Amos and Hosea, Egypt came close to the realization that the individual man had personal rights to just treatment. If she fell short of realization of that great dream or if she soon abandoned her search for social justice, we may still recognize that the ancient Egyptian had the capacity to see a broader base for human good and can only regret that her discovery was too early in human history to gain any lasting root.

However, these subjective moralizings are premature, for we have

7. This has been eloquently argued by J. H. Breasted, in his *Development of Religion and Thought in Ancient Egypt* (New York, 1912) and *Dawn of Conscience* (New York, 1933). Our argument falls short of Breasted's: we believe that social conscience existed before this age but was differently articulated; and we believe that the social conscience which was developed in Egypt's time of troubles weakened rapidly under Middle Kingdom prosperity. Nevertheless, in the main we follow Breasted closely.

not yet stated the argument that ancient Egypt did discover social justice as one of the greatest values.

The first observation is that the decentralization of the Old Kingdom had leveled down the king and raised up the nobles, so that a concept of equality was theoretically possible. The First Intermediate Period was the only time in Egyptian history in which the divine king was presented as humanly fallible and errant or in which an ordinary commoner pointed a denunciatory finger at his sovereign. With a thoroughly exceptional humility, a Herakleopolitan king confessed to his son Meri-ka-Re that he had done wrong and deserved punishment from the gods: "Egypt fights (even) in the necropolis, by hacking up graves. . . . I did the same, and the same happened as is done to one who transgresses the way of (?) the god." "Behold, a misfortune happened in my time: the Thinite regions were hacked up. It really happened through what I had done, and I knew of it (only) after (it) was done. Behold, my recompense (came) out of what I had done."[8]

Equally extraordinary was the boldness of the prophet Ipu-wer in blaming the pharaoh of his day for the anarchy in Egypt. The king should be the herdsman of his people, keeping them alive and well, and yet—charged Ipu-wer, facing the god-king upon the throne—his rule only set a pattern of death. "Authority, perception, and justice are with thee, (but) it is confusion which thou wouldst set throughout the land, together with the noise of contention. Behold, one thrusts against another. Men conform to what thou hast commanded. If three men go along a road, they are found to be two men: it is the greater number that kills the lesser. Does then the herdsman love death? . . . This really means that thou hast acted (?) to bring such (a situation) into being, and thou hast spoken lies." Did the divine fury strike down Ipu-wer for his presumptuous blasphemy? Did the all-wise, all-powerful, and all-good pharaoh put the prophet in his place with a devastating counterargument? On the contrary, the king answered the denunciation with the plea that he had tried to protect his own people by holding off foreign raiders. Then Ipu-wer looked at his ruler with some compassion and said that the royal efforts had been rightly intended but had fallen short because of royal ignorance and incapacity: "To be ignorant of it is something pleasant to the heart. Thou hast done what is good in their hearts, for thou hast kept people alive thereby. (But still) they cover up their faces for fear of the morrow." The whole point of the story is that the mere meeting of emergency did not constitute good

8. Erman, *LAE*, pp. 79, 82.

rule, which demanded positive and tireless effort on the part of the ruler. And such an admonition, in the democratic spirit of the day, might be addressed by a commoner to the king.[9]

As the god-king was leveled down toward the plane of common mortals, so also the nobles—and with them other common people—were leveled up toward the plane of the divine ruler. This is particularly apparent when one considers mortuary beliefs and practices. The formerly exclusive privileges of the pharaoh toward the fullest eternal life were now extended toward the nobles, in what has been termed "the democratization of the hereafter." Under the Old Kingdom it had been the pharaoh only who would be a god in the next world, accepted within the company of the other gods and enjoying a blessed eternity by divine right. In the extension of this world into the next, the Old Kingdom nobles had been dependent upon royal favor for otherworldly happiness, and they had been denied the operation of the Pyramid Text beatifications which would have assured them godliness after death. In the First Intermediate Period the nobles were independent of the pharaoh, or dependent upon him only by their own choice, and this individual voluntarism moved on to capture the next world. The nobles seized the Pyramid Texts and had them inscribed upon their coffins.[10] Those texts had originally been drawn up for kings who were gods in this world and would be even more effectively gods in the next. Their seizure by lesser mortals meant that any man who was prominent enough and rich enough to afford an inscribed coffin and priestly services at his funeral had magic and religion working for his deification at death. He would become an Osiris upon entry into the next world; he would be one of the body of the gods; over yonder there would be no distinction in essence between him and his pharaoh.

Not only were the royal mortuary texts appropriated for the use of the nobles, but the funeral ritual of kings was also taken over for the use of any good man. For example, the tomb scenes show us that certain dances originally executed for kings were featured at the burial of nobles.[11] Eternal life was the greatest good for the ancient Egyptian. Previously, there had been a qualitative difference between the eternal life of the pharaoh and that of his people. From now on, pharaoh and

9. *Ibid.*, pp. 106 ff.

10. We classify a series of similar mortuary texts as the Pyramid Texts of the Old Kingdom, the Coffin Texts of the First and Second Intermediate Periods and Middle Kingdom, and the Book of the Dead of the Empire and later periods.

11. N. de G. Davies and A. H. Gardiner, *The Tomb of Amenemhēt* (*TTS*, I [1915]), pp. 55 f.

people were to enjoy the same unlimited scope after death. Quantitative differences might remain in the elaborateness of the burial of the king or in the insistent emphasis of prayers and magic spells and priestly reciters which the king could afford; but now the same texts, the same ritual, and the same magic made identical promises of beatitude to king and commoner.

Again we are somewhat uncertain how far down this extension of good may have penetrated. It is not clear whether divinity after death was accorded also to the artisan and the peasant, who could hardly afford elaborate mortuary services and inscribed coffins. Perhaps, as before, actual practice made the lower classes the property of their masters, who might have need and use for them in the next world.[12] However, there is some evidence that the democratic theory of this unusual period knew no class lines but extended down to the lowest peasant. It would be most unusual that he could afford to purchase the ritual and magic for his deification, but in theory the opportunity was open to him. We have already quoted the passage from the instruction for Meri-ka-Re that men should not be distinguished by birth but by ability. We shall shortly discuss a story which tells of the triumphs of an ordinary peasant. We might also cite the claim of King Amen-em-het: "I gave to the destitute and brought up the orphan. I caused him who was nothing to reach (his goal), like him who was (somebody)."[13] The passage upon which we should like to dwell is one in which the creator-god states that he has made all men equal in opportunity and that, if there be any violation of this equality, the fault is man's.

"I did four good deeds within the portal of the horizon. I made the four winds that every man might breathe thereof like his fellow in his time. That is (the first) deed thereof. I made the great inundation that the poor man might have rights therein like the great man. That is (the second) deed thereof. I made every man like his fellow. I did not command that they do evil, (but) it was their hearts that violated what I had said. That is (the third) deed thereof. I made their hearts to cease from

12. From a later period we may cite a difference of the mortuary treatment of the well-to-do from that of the poor. In the Eighteenth Dynasty, there is evidence of a long and elaborate activity for the dead between death and burial: "A good burial has arrived in peace, (after) thy seventy days are completed in the place of embalming" (N. de G. Davies, in *Studies Presented to F. Ll. Griffith* [London, 1932], p. 289). A poor woman of the Nineteenth or Twentieth Dynasty received no such attention. Cairo ostracon 25554 runs: "Year 6, second month of the first season, day 15: Ta-heni died. She was buried on day 17" (J. Černý, *Ostraca Hiératiques* [*Cairo Cat.*, Vols. 87 ff. (1935)], p. 21, Pls. 42*, XXV).

13. Erman, *LAE*, p. 72.

forgetting the West, in order that divine offerings might be given to the gods of the nomes. That is (the fourth) deed thereof."[14] This extraordinary statement of human rights occurs in six copies in this period and, as far as we have found, did not survive into the mortuary texts after the Middle Kingdom. It is significant that so sweeping a statement of the ultimate opportunity of every man is known only from that period which came closest to democratic realization.

One must admit that the Coffin Texts, the mortuary inscriptions of the time, are otherwise disappointing in their statement of social conscience. Apart from the text just quoted and apart from the fact of their extension from kings to commoners, they are the same old hodge-podge of ritual, hymns, prayers, and magic spells as were the Pyramid Texts. It is possible to make some favorable contrast between the Coffin Texts and their successors, the Book of the Dead. Certain sentences in the Coffin Texts, as they stand, can be taken as statements of moral uprightness on the part of the deceased, while the Book of the Dead has added explanatory glosses which make these statements avowals of ritualistic action rather than of personal integrity. Thus, where the Coffin Texts were content with saying: "My sin is dispelled; my error is wiped away," the Book of the Dead added a gloss explaining that this meant the cutting of a baby's navel cord; the Coffin Texts' "The deceit which was with me is driven away" was explained as referring to the washing of a newborn babe, not to an afterworld judgment and vindication; and the Coffin Texts' "I go on the way which I have learned upon the Island of the Righteous" was made to refer to a pilgrimage to Abydos, the city of the god of the dead.[15]

Unfortunately, we cannot be sure that the glosses in the Book of the Dead, which established the text as being purely ritualistic and non-moral, were actually deliberate distortions of the text away from an original moral tone. For all we know, the original brief statement in the Coffin Texts may have been an avowal of correct ritual activity, not yet made specific in an explanatory gloss. Since the bulk of the Coffin Texts carries so much of magic and ritual, we do not dare isolate a few passages consisting of brief sentences and declare them to be purely moral.

Happily, however, we have evidence outside the Coffin Texts that moral probity was a prerequisite to eternal happiness and that material

14. A spell from the Coffin Texts, not yet published by A. de Buck. Dr. T. George Allen states that the passage comes from a spell "temp. 269," and is known from six coffins: B1Bo, B1C, B1L, B3C, B6C, and B9C.

15. From the 17th chapter of the Book of the Dead: H. Grapow, *Religiöse Urkunden* (*Urk.*, V [Leipzig, 1915-17]), pp. 22 ff.

goods were not so important as character. This period provided for a mortuary judgment by the gods before entry into paradise was granted. In later times the god Osiris was to become the judge of the dead, presiding over the weighing of a man's heart—the seat of his mind and will—against the symbol for ma'at. At the present time the divine tribunal was under the presidency of the sun-god Re, and the weighing was called "counting up character." There is reference to "that balance of Re, in which he weighs ma'at." It was recognized that a man would come to the point of death with faults as well as virtues; the "counting up character" on the scales would take the faults into the reckoning. If the virtues were in excess, the faults would be canceled out, and the deceased would be permitted to join the gods. "He shall reach the council of the gods, the place where the gods are, his ka being with him and his offerings being in front of him, and his voice shall be justified in the counting up of the surplus. Though he may tell his faults, they will be expelled for him by all that he may say." "Thy faults will be expelled and thy guilt will be wiped out by the weighings of the scales on the day of counting up character, and (then) it will be permitted that thou join with those who are in the barque (of the sun-god)."[16] From this time forward, the deceased were called "justified of voice" or "triumphant," meaning that they had been adjudged righteous by the court of the dead.

Ma'at, "truth, justice, righteousness, right dealing, order," had thus become critically important for the supreme prize of eternal happiness. Meri-ka-Re was advised by his father to "do ma'at whilst thou endurest upon earth." Why? The text goes on to relate royal justice upon earth to the judgment at death: "The council which judges the deficient, thou knowest that they are not lenient on that day of judging the miserable, the hour of doing (their) duty.... Do not trust in length of years, for they regard a lifetime as (but) an hour. A man remains over after death, and his deeds are placed beside him in heaps. However, existence yonder is for eternity.... He who reaches it without wrongdoing shall exist yonder like a god, stepping out freely like the lords of eternity." Whereas those of earlier times had tried to purchase their immortality by huge tombs and elaborate endowments for perpetual offerings, the new emphasis on character shifted the focus from goods to good. The instruction for Meri-ka-Re expressed this nonmaterialism in

---

16. Frankfort *et al.*, *The Intellectual Adventure of Ancient Man*, p. 108. A different treatment of the subject in J. Spiegel, *Die Idee vom Totengericht in der ägyptischen Religion* (*Leip. AS*, II [Glückstadt, 1935]).

three passages: "Be not evil; patience is good. Make thy memorial to last through the love of thee," with a contrast to a memorial of stone. "Give the love of thyself to the whole world; a good character is a remembrance." The most striking passage states flatly that the gods prefer uprightness to propitiatory offerings: "More acceptable is the character of one upright of heart than the ox of the evildoer."

The age of distress and the new sense that one had to answer to the gods for one's deeds brought in a piety which had been lacking in the Old Kingdom. Much of this was ritualistic piety, and King Meri-ka-Re was advised that serving as priest, visiting the god in the temple, and increasing the offerings was "of advantage to his soul." However, he was also advised simply to "revere the god," and the passage that we have cited about character as preferable to offerings is highly significant. Ipu-wer also called into fond memory the many little things which one should do in a temple or at a feast, but immediately followed with a description of the good ruler as a conscientious shepherd who looked after his flocks with loving care: "It shall come to pass that he brings coolness to the heart. Men shall say: 'He is the herdsman of all men. Evil is not in his heart. Though his herds may be small, still he has spent the day caring for them.'" The concept of the good shepherd rather than the distant and lordly owner of the flocks shifted the idea of kingship from possession as a right to responsibility as a duty. Property itself had rights, and the possessor was obliged to exert himself to the point of pain in protecting and nurturing his flocks.

The text which brings out most clearly the new approach to social equality and the new responsibilities to render *maʿat* to one's fellows, rather than simply to the gods, is the story of the eloquent peasant.[17] In the time of the Herakleopolitan kings, an ordinary peasant was robbed of his goods by a man who enjoyed court connections. The peasant went to lodge a complaint with this man's superior, the Chief Steward of the Palace. Because the peasant proved to be vigorous and elegant of speech, the Chief Steward did not answer his petitions but kept him talking through nine appeals. What the peasant wanted was the return of his goods; he demanded as his right *maʿat* from one who was placed to be a dispenser of *maʿat*. The long text gives us the clear argument that *maʿat*-justice was not a neutral maintenance of past order or a negative repair of breaches of order but a positive search for new good.

There is a certain crescendo in the appeals of the peasant. As he finds

17. Erman, *LAE*, pp. 116 ff.

no response to his claims for justice, he is emboldened to attack the Chief Steward with bitter denunciation. At first he argues that a magistrate who is appointed to dispense *maᶜat* and to curb its opposite, "falsehood," will find a reward in meeting human distress. "If thou embarkest upon the lake of *maᶜat*, mayest thou sail on it with a fair breeze! A squall(?) shall not tear away thy sail, and thy boat shall not lag. . . . (Even) the timid(?) fish shall come to thee, and thou shalt attain some of the fattest fowl—because thou art the father of the orphan, the husband of the widow, the brother of the divorcee, and the apron of him that is motherless, . . . a leader free from covetousness, a great man free from wrongdoing, one who destroys falsehood and brings *maᶜat* into being, and who comes at the cry of him who gives voice. When I speak mayest thou hear!" Again, the peasant argues that the dispenser of *maᶜat* must be as impartial, scrupulous, and exact as the scales or the grain-measure or Thoth, the god of just measure: "Doing *maᶜat* is the (very) breath of the nose. Carry out punishment against him who should be punished, and none shall equal thy scrupulousness. Do the hand-scales err? Does the stand-balance incline to the side? Is even Thoth indulgent? Then mayest thou (also) work mischief. When thou makest thyself the companion of these three, if the three are indulgent, then mayest thou (also) be indulgent." "Cheating diminishes *maᶜat*. (But) good full (measure)—*maᶜat* neither falls short nor overflows."

However, in the progression of his argument, the peasant does not stop with the concept of a blindfolded justice holding a sword and a pair of scales. Proper *maᶜat* cannot stop at the repair and punishment of "falsehood" or at the coldly impersonal leveling-off by the scales; proper *maᶜat* includes the positive seeking-out of justice. The dispenser of *maᶜat* must look for cases demanding his attention and not wait until cases come to him. *Maᶜat* involves the golden rule of doing unto others to cause them to do for us. "Now this is the command: 'Do to the doer to cause that he do.' That is thanking him for what he may do. That is parrying something before (it is) shot. That is ordering something from him who (already) has business. . . . If thou veilest thy face against violence, who then will punish meanness?"

In this period of social equality, the prophet Ipu-wer was able to denounce the pharaoh with immunity, and the humble peasant dared to hurl bitter taunts at a Chief Steward who was indifferent to a positive concept of *maᶜat*. He likened such an official to a businessman without charity, one whose sole interest was profit: "Behold, thou art a wretch of a washerman, covetous in injuring a friend, abandoning his partner(?) for the sake of his client. . . . Behold, thou art a ferryman who ferries over (only) him that has a fare, a straight-dealer whose straight-dealing is clipped short. . . . Behold, thou art a butler whose delight is butchering, the mutilation of which (does) not (fall) upon him." A negative rule which does not actively seek out good is no rule at all: "Behold, thou art a town which has no mayor, like a company which has no chief, like a ship in which there is no pilot, a confederacy which has no leader. . . . Thou wert appointed to be a dam for the sufferer, guarding lest he drown, (but) behold, thou art his (over)flowing lake!"

The peasant also argues that "falsehood" may win riches but is of short advantage, whereas *ma⸳at* belongs to eternity, an argument which always appealed to the Egyptian: "If falsehood walk about, it goes astray. It cannot cross over in the ferry; [it] does not advance(?). As for him who grows rich thereby, he has no children, he has no heirs upon earth. . . . Now *ma⸳at* lasts unto eternity; it goes down into the necropolis with him who does it. When he is buried and interred, his name is not wiped out upon earth, (but) he is remembered for good-ness. That is a principle of the word of god." *Ma⸳at* in the texts of this age did not carry its customary connotation of static order; it was not a matter of the pharaoh offering *ma⸳at* to the gods in token of the fact that the god-given order was stable and unchanging. *Ma⸳at* here was the positive force of social justice, of man's humanity to man. It was a magistrate who could be likened to the ferryman who carried over the poor widow without exacting a fare. It was a king who could be likened to a herdsman who wearied himself on behalf of his flock. In this near-democratic age, the emphasis was not upon the rights of the ruler but upon the rights of the ruled.

In that spirit we may note that the eloquent peasant not only received his stolen goods back and saw his robber punished but was even re-warded by the generous patronage of that Chief Steward whom he had denounced. The point of the tale is that even the humblest of men may rise up and demand his rights. It may be significant that the story en-joyed some popularity through the Middle Kingdom and thereafter dropped out of currency, as ideas about social justice changed.

There is one further observation about the period, and that has to do with the concept of speech or silence. We have seen in the instruction of the Vizier Ptah-hotep that eloquence was highly prized and might be found even in the humble maidservants at their grindstones. The story of the eloquent peasant carried on that view that even the lowliest of Egyptians may be able to speak out with telling effect. His eloquence was so admired that he was kept talking on and on, for the enjoyment of the court, finally receiving his just deserts only when he ran down. Similarly, Meri-ka-Re was advised: "Be a craftsman in speech, so that thou mayest be strong, for the tongue is a sword to [a man], and speech is more valorous than any fighting. No one can circumvent the skilful of heart. . . . *Ma'at* comes to him (fully) brewed, in accordance with the sayings of the ancestors." We wish to emphasize the high value which the period put upon speaking out on one's own behalf. We shall see in chapter xi that the final collapse of the Egyptian spirit brought an age of "silence," when men were denied the right to speak out in their own interests. No such blanket against personal protest lay over the First Intermediate Period.

This was ancient Egypt's democratic age. It is necessary that we clarify that statement, for "democracy" is a term of more than one meaning, and it is a term which has high emotional coloring today. By "democracy" in our context we do not mean a form of government in which the sovereign power resided or was thought to reside with the people at large; we are using, rather, the secondary but common meaning of social equalitarianism, the disregard of political or economic barriers in the belief that all men have equal rights and opportunities— or should have such. It seems clear from the texts which we have cited that there was a belief in social justice for everybody at this time and that even the poorest man had rights to the gifts of the gods because the creator-god "made every man like his fellow." However, social equalitarianism did not mean political democracy, with the rule of the many. The creator-god had given all men equal access to the winds and the waters—and to good rule by the god-king or by his delegates. *Ma'at* still belonged to the gods, was one of the divine attributes of kingship, and was worshiped as a goddess. But this age insisted that *ma'at* reached down to embrace the lowliest Egyptian and that he had a right to insist upon such a democratic coverage from his rulers.

The spiritual strength of the Egyptian culture at this time is shown by the fact that the state survived her first severe illness and came forth again, leaner, more sober, but with an upward-looking vision. That gay and lively world of material and social success under the Old Kingdom, a world which had seemed as stable as the pyramids, had crashed with violence, leaving confusion in its ruins. It was necessary for the Egyptians to rethink their code of values. It is to their glory that they came out with something positive and optimistic, the right of every man to greater good. Without abandoning their strong sense of national destiny or their expectation of a happy eternity, without sacrificing all their pragmatism and materialism, without surrendering the central dogma of the state, that rule belongs to the god-king, they added the concepts of social equality and humanitarian justice. When we consider that they stood more than a thousand years ahead of similar thinking by the Hebrews and the Greeks, we must give them all credit for a sublime vision.

It would be pleasant if we could say that Egypt, having discovered the inherent value of the individual man, went on to try to give that concept greater validity and more effective force within the state. We cannot do so. The coming chapters will show that this vision was born out of national distress and could not survive national prosperity and the renewal of materialism. When, under the national perils of the Second Intermediate Period and the aggressive nationalism of the Empire, the disciplined unity of the state became more important than the rights and opportunities of individuals, the concept of equality and social justice was finally swallowed up. This is the story of a people who once caught a clear but distant view of the Promised Land but who ended up wandering in the Wilderness.

VI

THE KING AS THE GOOD SHEPHERD

Dynasties 11–12 (about 2050–1800 B.C.)

E GYPT was reunited by force of arms. For about a century there had been intermittent warfare between the northern kings at Herakleopolis in the Faiyum and a vigorous family at Thebes in Upper Egypt. At first the advantages seem to have been on the side of Herakleopolis, which enjoyed the support of Assiut in Middle Egypt and of Hierakonpolis and Edfu to the south of Thebes. The previously unknown and unimportant nome of Thebes was thus invested and kept in check at the beginning of the war, perhaps about 2130 B.C. However, by 2050 Thebes had defeated the enemy coalition, ended the rule of Herakleopolis, and set up its claim to the entire state of Egypt. We do not know how this victory was won. From the standpoint of economic productivity and manpower Thebes was much weaker than the Faiyum region, particularly if the latter enjoyed the support of Lower and Middle Egypt. In modern times the Assiut area and the southern Delta are the most fertile regions of Egypt and have a greater concentration of population than Upper Egypt. Probably these factors were relatively the same in ancient times. Furthermore, as a theoretical consideration, we should consider Herakleopolis a more advantageous capital than Thebes. It was centrally located, pivotal between Lower and Upper Egypt, and more favorably situated for the commerce of Asia and the Mediterranean. Thebes was a little provincial town—many days' sailing from the Delta—and enjoyed no remarkable trade advantages. The trickle of commerce from the Red Sea through the Wadi Hammamat would be paltry compared to the trade movements in the

Faiyum area. Further, Herakleopolis seems to have shown an admirable cultural vigor if we may judge from the sole witness of its powerful literary movement. The instruction for King Meri-ka-Re and the story of the eloquent peasant would alone give us a feeling of cultural integrity and persuasiveness. These are very subjective impressions, to be sure, but no such cultural achievements are known for Thebes at the same time. In fact, Thebes and Amon, the god who shortly emerged into prominence in Thebes and from there went on ultimately to universal dominion, had scarcely been known before this time. It is legitimate to think of Herakleopolis as a central capital city, which could easily inherit the former rule of Memphis, carrying on that tradition which was so dear to the Egyptian, whereas Thebes was a rustic *parvenu*, offering little within herself or out of tradition to claim the allegiance of Egypt.

Nevertheless, it was Thebes which won out and reunited the Two Lands under a single rule. The period is too little documented for any assurance, and we can only guess at three factors. This was a period of high individualism and independent rule, and the spirit of separatism may have been stronger in the more cultured north than in the provincial south; the allies of Herakleopolis may have been grudging and undependable. The south was relatively poor and had more to gain by a conquest of the north; a certain ruthless greed and ambition may have given greater striking force to Theban arms. Further, this was a feudal period, in which the local rulers not only exercised a considerable local autonomy but even arrogated to themselves royal titles, epithets, and prerogatives. In such a time, they may have been unwilling to see the re-establishment of Old Kingdom rule, restoring a tradition of highly centralized government and absolute fealty to the pharaoh. They may, however, have been willing to accord—grudgingly, tentatively, and watchfully—leadership to the most powerful and ambitious feudal baron of their number. Such an allegiance would theoretically be of their own election, the Theban ruler would be recognized as *primus inter pares*, and the state would be set up as a kind of mutual protective association under the presidency of the most energetic of the members. This analysis is admittedly an absurdity in its thrusting of modern terms back into the ancient scene. The visible form of the Middle Kingdom rule was that the Theban dynasts were accepted as gods, sons of Re, and absolute rulers through the perpetuation of the traditional dogma. If, however, our claims of high individual voluntarism and social equality are valid, it should be clear that the continuing dogma of divine absolutism of the pharaoh was merely the surface aspect of the early Middle Kingdom, under which there was a high degree of separatism. As long as the mutual protective association worked, the provincial rulers were willing to support it. In practice it turned out to be so effective that separatist tendencies lasted only a generation or two into the Twelfth Dynasty and then a centripetal trend set in for the greater power of the throne.

This book is not concerned with the successive stages of the war between Herakleopolis and Thebes.[1] In the end, it was the little provincial town of the south which won out, and apparently it won out rather abruptly and conclusively, because the generation of the conqueror, Neb-hepet-Re Mentu-hotep, saw about forty years of peace and the resumption of normal conditions. To be sure, civil disorder was to break out again in the reigns of his two successors, and the smoldering of rebellion was to continue through the reign of Amen-em-het I, the first pharaoh of the Twelfth Dynasty. However, the Eleventh Dynasty king, Neb-hepet-Re Mentu-hotep, came to the throne with Egypt divided. Within nine or ten years he had conquered and reunited the entire land, and the remaining forty-odd years of his reign were devoted to peace. Either he was a remarkable organizer and ruler, or the land was weary of internal bickerings. For a time there was quiet.

This quiet permitted vigorous attempts to restore the conditions of the Old Kingdom. At Deir el-Bahri in western Thebes, this pharaoh built a large mortuary temple, terraced into the hillside and revolutionary in design compared to the older temples of the Memphis area. Commerce and the exploitation of mines and quarries were pushed once more. Across the Wadi Hammamat from Koptos on the Nile to Kosseir on the Red Sea went a detachment officially listed as three thousand men, each equipped with a water-skin and a carrying pole, with two jars of water and twenty loaves of bread allotted to each man for the four- or five-day trek across the mountain desert. In order to make the barren hundred-mile stretch easier for future caravans, the expedition dug out or reopened a dozen wells in the desert, presumably the same wells which one now sees in the Wadi Hammamat. At the Red Sea town, a "Byblos ship," that is, a seagoing vessel, was constructed and launched for a journey to the fabulous land of Punt, the region of fresh myrrh on the Arabian and African coasts south of the Red Sea. After dispatching this ship—perhaps the first agent of a resumed royal monop-

---

1. Well outlined, on the basis of existing evidence, in H. E. Winlock, *The Rise and Fall of the Middle Kingdom in Thebes* (New York, 1947), pp. 10 ff.

oly on foreign commerce—the expedition returned to the Nile Valley, with a pause in the mountain quarries to secure hard building stone.[2]

Another expedition pushed south into Lower Nubia seeking that firm stone which had been the pride of the pyramid age. The Bedouin of the desert sought to interfere with the quarrying, and a military expedition protected the pharaoh's rights.[3]

Sinai also was visited and we have the record of a Theban official who opened up the old mine shafts again, bringing back to Egypt copper, turquoise, lapis lazuli, and ores of strange and unknown names. This exploitation also was a military operation. "I held back the Asiatics in their foreign countries." And here we begin again to get that old adulatory credit to the pharaoh. "It was the fear of him that inspired the awe of me, his influence that inspired the terror of me . . . it was the love of him that enamored the Two Lands to him."[4] Conditions were rapidly returning to normal.

Our chief witness to the restoration of peaceful life and safe communications within Egypt under the Eleventh Dynasty lies in a series of private letters found at Thebes.[5] A crotchety old man named Heka-nakht lived at Thebes but had estates in the Memphis area and in the Delta. He spent a considerable portion of each year in the northern estates, writing peremptory and gossipy letters to his family in Thebes about his affairs. The possibility of ownership in north and south at the same time and the ability of a small landlord to travel about freely are in sharp contrast to the chaotic conditions bewailed by the "prophets" of the preceding century and show the success of the Theban conquest and reorganization of the land.

The Heka-nakht letters give us an extraordinarily vivid picture of the family life and concerns of a small landowner. No detail of land rental, the harvest, kitchen gossip, or the intrigues of his relatives was too small to escape the sharp eye of Heka-nakht. The letters provide a clear view into the life of the Egyptian two thousand years ago, and they may be illustrated by the life of the *fellah* in the fields of Egypt today.

Heka-nakht drove his eldest son, whom he had left in responsible

2. Breasted, *ARE*, I, §§428 ff.; J. Couyat and P. Montet, *Les inscriptions hiéro-glyphiques et hiératiques du Ouâdi Hammâmât (MIFAO*, XXXIV [1912]), pp. 81–84.

3. G. Roeder, *Debod bis Bab Kalabsche*, I (Cairo, 1911), 104 f.

4. A. H. Gardiner in *JEA*, IV (1917), 35 f.

5. Summarized, on the basis of preliminary translations by B. Gunn, by H. E. Winlock in *BMMA*, XVII (1922), Part II, 37 ff. As the hieratic text has not yet been published, the translations are those of that publication and not our own.

charge in Thebes, with a tight rein and a prodding whip. "As to any flooding on our land, it is thou who art cultivating it. Woe to all my people with thee! I shall hold thee responsible for it. Be very active in cultivating, and be very careful. Guard the produce of my grain—guard everything of mine, for I shall hold thee responsible for it." He permitted his son no discretion and was constantly in fear that the young man might be too generous with his father's property. "You must give these victuals to my people only while they are doing work. Mind this! Make the most of all my land; strive to the uttermost; dig the ground with your noses in the work. See, if you are industrious one will praise God for you. Lucky that I can support you. And any one of the women or men who may spurn the victuals, let him come to me here and stay with me and live as I live (here in the north)—not that there is anyone who will come hither to me! ... Why, they have begun to eat men and women here! There are none anywhere else to whom such victuals are given." We may guess that the tight-fisted old man was exaggerating his own plight in the north, in order to make his serfs and tenants satisfied with their little pay.

Heka-nakht intervened in every transaction of his household, with shrewd advice about bargaining or payment. "Have Heti son of Nakht go down at once with Sinebnut to Perhaa to cultivate two fields of land on lease. They will take its rental from the cloth that has been woven here. 'Excellent' thou wilt exclaim about the fabric. Let them get it, and when it has been sold in Nebesyt, let them rent the land with its proceeds. Find land—but do not rush on to just anybody's land. ... And with regard to whatever Heti son of Nakht may do in Perhaa, see, I did not credit him with victuals. The allowance for one month is 5 bushels of barley. ... See, if thou disobeyest this I shall make it up from thee by deduction. And as to what I have told thee—'give him 5 bushels of barley per month'—thou must give him only 4 bushels of barley per month; mind this!"

Heka-nakht worked his eldest son hard, but nothing was too good for his spoiled youngest son, Sneferu, or for his concubine Iut-en-hab. "See, if Sneferu has no allowance in the house with thee, do not fail to write about it. I have been told that he is discontented. Take great care of him and give him victuals. And salute him from (me here in) Khentekh a thousand times, a million times. Take great care of him and thou must send him off to me directly after thou hast cultivated." When the pampered lad refused to join his father, Heka-nakht wrote: "And if Sneferu should want to look after the bulls, then put him to looking after them, for he doesn't want to be running up and down cultivating with thee nor does he want to come hither with me. Indeed whatever he wants thou must let him enjoy it."

When his third son Si-Hathor and a maid servant started to cause trouble for his concubine Iut-en-hab, the old man wrote in wrath: "And have the housemaid Senen turned out of my house at once, and be very careful every day that Si-Hathor visits thee. Behold, if Senen spends a single day in the house, thou wilt be to blame if thou lettest her do harm to my concubine. What am I supporting thee for and what can my concubine do to you, you five boys? ... And as to doing any harm to my concubine, take warning! Thou art not associated with me as a partner. If thou wouldst keep quiet it would be a very good thing."

Ancient Egypt may have had many homesick and fussy little land-owners squatting down by the public letter writer and dictating a stream of self-important words about household affairs. By the accident of chance only this little bundle of letters has come down to us, to permit us to open the door of a private house and look in on the family.

The stable conditions of the reign of Neb-hepet-Re Mentu-hotep lasted only a short time after his long rule, and then there was a stretch of about seven years troubled by a resumption of civil war. We do not know the details of these wars. When they were over, a new Theban dynasty had emerged, the Twelfth Dynasty of the Amen-em-hets and Sen-Userts. Amen-em-het I had been a vizier under the last of the Eleventh Dynasty pharaohs. Just how he won the throne is not known, but his reign brought into prominence a god who had been practically unknown before this time, or, at any rate, had been no political force in Egypt. This was the god Amon, after whom Amen-em-het took his name.[6]

Amon was a force which could easily be extended toward wider dominion—ultimately to universal dominion. The name Amon meant "Hidden," so that Amon was an unseen being, a god who might be immanent everywhere. According to one old theological system, Amon, as invisibility, was one of the eight gods of precreation chaos. Thus he might be unseen and formless or the god of the air. At any rate, as a cosmic being he could easily be transplanted from one theological system to another as a god of far-reaching scope. He came to supersede the gods who had formerly stood for Thebes and to function as the god

6. For this emergence of Amon, see Winlock, *The Rise and Fall of the Middle Kingdom in Thebes*, p. 90.

of the nation. In this capacity he was grafted onto the sun-god Re, as "Amon-Re, King of the Gods." As the god of the Egyptian nation, he was to become the great imperial god under the Empire and thus to assume a universal nature. Over two thousand years the most massive temple of all time was constructed for him, Karnak, with its acres of structures built from the Middle Kingdom down to Roman times. Toward the end of the Empire he came to be the wealthiest force in the world, and the power of his high priest rivaled that of the pharaoh. Now, at the beginning of the Twelfth Dynasty, he was being dragged out of cosmic obscurity to begin this tremendous career.[7]

It was no easy task to be pharaoh under the Middle Kingdom, a loosely gathered feudal state, in which the local governors asserted their own retained sovereignty. For example, official dates in a province asserted the year of reign of the pharaoh and also of the local ruler, as if of equal importance.[8] The Twelfth Dynasty came out of civil war, and there was a palace conspiracy under the very first ruler. In fact Amen-em-het I himself told his son of the treacherous attack. This immediately poses a problem, for the words of this statement indicate that the conspiracy was successful in killing the pharaoh. Thus the "instruction" to his son and successor was voiced by a king already dead, advising the new ruler not to place complete trust in anybody. Is this document therefore a mere piece of literature, an unhistorical forgery? To our minds it is so, but we should not therefore discount it from the standpoint of the ancient Egyptian. To him the voice of the dead king was to be taken just as seriously as though a living king had affixed his seal to the document.[9] From a story of the period we have corroboratory evidence of a conspiracy at the end of Amen-em-het's reign, so that there is reason for crediting our literary text with a central strain of historical truth.

The dead king said to his son: "Hold thyself apart from those subordinate to (thee), lest that should happen to whose terrors no attention has been given. Approach them not in thy loneliness. Fill not thy heart with a brother, nor know a friend. . . . When thou sleepest, guard thy heart thyself, because no man has adherents on the day of distress.

7. K. Sethe, *Amun und die acht Urgötter von Hermopolis* (Berlin *Abh.*, 1929).

8. Breasted, *ARE*, I, §518.

9. For the argument that the "instruction" was composed in the name of Amen-em-het I after his death, see A. de Buck in *Mélanges Maspero*, I (*MIFAO*, LXVI [1935–38]), 847 ff.; B. Gunn in *JEA*, XXVII (1941), 2 ff. For the particular regard held for the dead and the expectation that the dead might intervene in affairs of this world, see A. H. Gardiner and K. Sethe, *Egyptian Letters to the Dead* (London, 1928).

I gave to the destitute and brought up the orphan, I caused him who was nothing to reach (his goal), like him who was (somebody), (but) it was he who ate my food that raised troops (against me), and he to whom I had given my hands that created terror thereby. . . . It was after supper, when evening had come. I had taken an hour of rest, lying upon my bed, for I had become weary. My heart began to follow after slumber for me. Then the weapons which should have been solicitous(?) for me were brandished(?), and I was like one crumbled, crumbled to dust, a snake of the desert. I awoke at the fighting, being by myself, and I found that it was a hand-to-hand conflict of the guard. If I had made haste with weapons in my hand, I should have made the cowards retreat helter-skelter(?). However, there is no one valiant at night, and there is no fighting alone. . . . I had not prepared for it, I had not (even) thought of it, my heart had not accepted (the idea of) the slackness of servants."[10]

In these words the dead pharaoh not only admits that he was unsuccessful in repelling the attack on himself, but he confesses that he was vulnerable because he had had no prior intimation of trouble. This is a long distance from the Old Kingdom conception of a sublime being, all-wise and all-powerful, far beyond the reach of ordinary man. This is the sorrowful plea of a fallible human. It emphasizes the loneliness and heavy burden of kingship and the necessity for being constantly alert. That same sleepless watchfulness appears in the lines graven on the faces of the portrait statues of these kings. Deep creases at the corners of the mouths and hollows under the eyes make these statues very moving pieces of "realism," a long artistic distance from the serene majesty of the portraits of Fourth Dynasty pharaohs. Yet perhaps we are discussing portraits of an age, rather than portraits of individuals. That is, the dogma of sublimated divinity of the pharaoh was a characteristic of the Fourth Dynasty and therefore appeared in the representations of the kings of that age; under the Middle Kingdom, the idea of the king as a watchful shepherd or as the lonely being whose conscience looked after the nation was a characteristic, and this responsibility lined the faces of the pharaohs of that age. In a culture which had recently insisted upon the rights of every individual and in which independent voluntarism was still strong, the pharaoh had to exhibit conscience and had to be wakefully alert. The apparent realism of these

10. Erman, *LAE*, pp. 72 ff.

royal heads is thus actually a different expression of the idealized ruler.[11]

Royal names in Egypt are often instructive, and we have seen how the two names Amon and Amen-em-het emerged into prominence together. One of the names which Amen-em-het I took for himself was "the Repeating of Births" or "Renaissance," indicating his consciousness that he was inaugurating a new era, which brought back to Egypt some of its past glories. Running through the names of the Twelfth Dynasty there is frequent repetition of the term *ma'at*, "truth" or "justice," or *ma'a*, "true" or "just." Amen-em-het II took the names "He Who Takes Pleasure in Justice" and "the Just of Voice." Sen-Usert II was "He Who Makes Justice Appear." Amen-em-het III was "Justice Belongs to Re," and Amen-em-het IV was "Just of Voice is Re." We are again finding something which was a characteristic of the age. The First Intermediate Period had insisted upon social justice for all men and had demanded of the ruler the quality of *ma'at*. The rulers responded by taking formal throne names which expressed their desire and obligation to render *ma'at* to men and gods. This was another formulation of the concept of the good shepherd.

The Twelfth Dynasty gave to Egypt good rulers. They continued to assert their interest in Thebes with building projects but moved the capital of the nation to the Faiyum, to a place called Lisht near the balance point of the Two Lands. In that fertile region they established extensive irrigation projects to promote the prosperity of Egypt as a whole. They built in the Faiyum a huge embankment to create a great catch basin for the fast-moving waters of the Nile inundation, thus opening up a larger area for cultivation. It has been estimated that these pharaohs added about twenty-seven thousand acres to the arable land in and near the Faiyum. Egypt is essentially an agricultural country, and a major extension of the cultivable land was for the welfare of the people.

Conservation and proper use of the Nile waters demands a knowledge of the timing and volume of the annual inundation, and the Twelfth Dynasty pharaohs took careful measures to use the water wisely. Far south of Egypt at the Second Cataract Egyptian officials noted the annual heights of the Nile on the rocky sides of the cataract. Word of an exceptionally high or low or early or retarded Nile could

11. H. G. Evers, *Staat aus dem Stein* (Munich, 1929); Pls. 78–92, 101–4, 111–16, 121–33; C. Ricketts in *JEA*, IV (1917), 71 ff. Our Figs. 12*a* and 12*b*.

be sent ahead to Egypt, so that the state might take measures to insure maximum production. These pharaohs were watchful and conscientious.[12]

Bronze, using a proper proportion of tin to copper, had finally been accepted as a basic metal for Egypt, and these pharaohs exploited the Sinai mines industriously, leaving us abundant evidence of their activity there. We assume that the commerce with foreign countries may still have been a royal monopoly, and the Twelfth Dynasty was assiduous in courting neighbors abroad. In Asia they attempted no political empire by sending out armies to conquer and hold, with resident Egyptian commissioners in the conquered territory. We know of only one military excursion into Palestine during the dynasty, and this may have been a punitive raid to secure the great commercial road through that land rather than a conquest for possession and rule.[13] The period seems to have been one of Egyptian commercial and cultural imperialism. It was somewhat prior to the period of Hammurabi in Mesopotamia, and the cultural supremacy of Egypt along the eastern Mediterranean was probably a strong force. The historian who is also a philologist must confess at this point that he may be influenced by the fact that this was the classical period of Egyptian literature and that he may be moved by aesthetic subjectivity in speaking of cultural supremacy. However, on the basis of the visible evidence, Egyptian material and intellectual leadership over neighboring Asiatic lands seems highly probable. Gifts from the pharaoh, from members of his family, or from members of his court to princelings of Syria were relatively frequent in this period and were probably flattering enough to win some friendship in the little city-states of Asia.[14]

After one has listed the Egyptian monuments found in Palestine and Syria and has accounted for them as royal gifts or as records of the residence of a commercial agent or a tutor, the chief Egyptian document about Asia is a literary piece, the story of Si-nuhe. Si-nuhe was a court official who apparently belonged to the wrong political party at the death of Amen-em-het I. Probably he was not one of those conspirators who attacked the king by night and brought about his death, or he would never have won an ultimate pardon, but he may not have

12. J. H. Breasted in *AJSL*, XXV (1908), 106; S. Clarke in *JEA*, III (1916), 174 ff.

13. Breasted, *ARE*, I, §§ 676 ff. The added example, proposed by A. M. Blackman in *JEA*, II (1915), 13 f., is unfortunately susceptible of other translation. Instead of his "... cattle of Retenu during the counting(?)," it may be translated "... cattle at every assignment(?)."

14. J. A. Wilson in *AJSL*, LVIII (1941), 235. See our Fig. 14*b*.

been wholeheartedly of the party of the crown prince and coregent
Sen-Usert I. Si-nuhe's alarm at the news of the old king's death was
enough to take him in sudden and furtive flight out of Egypt and up
into Asia, where he found a place of exile out of the reach of the new
pharaoh. This was somewhere in the highland of Palestine-Syria, a
land of figs, grapes, olive trees, barley and emmer wheat, and herds of
cattle, but close enough to the desert for hunting. Other Egyptians
were in the land, perhaps exiles like Si-nuhe. Although he was safe there
from punishment by the pharaoh, he entertained Egyptian couriers
going to and from the Egyptian capital. His land may have been close
to the great road running between the Lebanon and Anti-Lebanon.
The Asiatic sheikh who had offered Si-nuhe hospitality made the Egyptian commander of the local army. "When the Asiatics become so bold
as to oppose the rulers of foreign countries, I counseled their movements." These words may mean what they seem to say—the rulers of
other foreign countries—or they may apply to a new and specific peril
to the Near East, the incoming of a mongrel horde of restless peoples
of northern and eastern affinities, later to be known as the Hyksos. The
Egyptian words *hikau khasut*, "rulers of foreign countries," are the
etymological source of the term Hyksos, and the indication in our story
of attacks on the settled Asiatics suggests that these invaders were already rolling southward through Syria and Palestine.

Si-nuhe settled down in this "good land" and grew old, rich, and
famous there. But he was not happy in exile. A strong element of nostal-
gia runs through his story; to every Egyptian there was but one land
which was the center and summit of the universe, and no other home
was satisfactory. When Si-nuhe grew old, he was troubled by the fact
that he had not made the usual provision for death. How could one who
died and was buried in a foreign country be assured of eternal happiness? Finally he received an amnesty from the pharaoh and an invitation to return to the Egyptian court. His majesty blandly stated that
there were no charges against Si-nuhe, who must have run away on
some whim, and reminded the exile of the delights of proper Egyptian
burial. "For today, surely, thou hast begun to grow old; thou hast lost
virility. Recall thou the day of burial, the passing to a revered state,
when the evening is set aside for thee with ointments and wrappings
from the hands of the (goddess) Tait. A funeral procession is made for
thee on the day of interment, a mummy case of gold, with head of lapis
lazuli, with the heaven above thee, as thou art placed upon a sledge,
oxen dragging thee and singers in front of thee, when the dance of the

muu is performed at the door of thy tomb, when the requirements of the offering table are summoned for thee and there is sacrifice beside thy offering stones, thy pillars being hewn of white stone in the midst of (the tombs of) the royal children. It should not be that thou diest in a foreign country. Asiatics should not escort thee. Thou shouldst not be placed in a sheepskin when thy wall is made. This is too long to be roaming the earth. Give heed to sickness(?), that thou mayest return."

A generation had passed, and the threat against the throne had receded. Sen-Usert I was strong and assured in the kingship. Political exiles guilty of indiscretion rather than treason might be welcomed back to the court. Si-nuhe turned his Asiatic property over to his children, returned, and stretched himself out upon his belly in the presence of the pharaoh. Once more he became an Egyptian. "Years were made to pass away from my body. I was plucked, and my hair was combed. A load (of dirt) was given to the desert and my clothes (to) the Crossers of the Sands. I was clad in fine linen and anointed with prime oil. I slept upon a bed. I gave up the sand to them who are in it and wood oil to him who is anointed therewith." No, there was no land like this good Egypt. In wonder and delight Si-nuhe gave thanks to his majesty. "There is no poor man for whom the like has been done. (So) I was under the favor of the king's presence until the day of death came."[15]

Although the Egyptians of the Middle Kingdom made no attempt to conquer and hold Asia beyond Sinai, it was rather a different matter in Nubia and the lower Sudan. The policy to the south was aggressive and dominating. Pressure from Libya and the deeper south and a Nubian revival of culture had made conditions somewhat unstable above the First Cataract. As today, Egypt felt that the Nile Valley should be a unity, and so she pushed south to conquer and hold the land between the Second and First Cataracts. A string of fortresses was set up in Nubia,[16] and the effective Egyptian frontier was placed at the Second, rather than the First Cataract, holding against the northern pressure of the *Nehsiu*, as the Egyptians called the Hamites and Negroes to her south.

There are two boundary stelae set up by Set-Usert III at Semneh on the Second Cataract, to prevent any penetration of the *Nehsiu* north of that point, except for trading and business purposes. "Southern frontier made in the year 8 . . . in order not to permit any *Nehsi* to pass by it,

15. Erman, *LAE*, pp. 14 ff.

16. S. Clarke in *JEA*, III (1916), 155 ff.; A. H. Gardiner in *JEA*, III (1916), 184 ff., and in *Ancient Egyptian Onomastica* (London, 1947), I, 9 ff.

going north by land or with a ship, or any herds of the *Nehsiu*—except for a *Nehsi* who shall come to carry on trading in Iqen or on an (official) commission or anything which one may (otherwise) do well with them—without, however, permitting a ship of the *Nehsiu* ever to pass by Semneh going north!"

The second stela expresses for the southerners some of the same lofty scorn which the instruction for King Meri-ka-Re had shown for the Asiatic Bedouin.[17] Thus far, the Egyptians' dealings with their neighbors had only confirmed them in their proud sense that they were a distinctly superior people. "Year 16, third month of the second season: his majesty's making the southern frontier at Semneh. I have made my frontier by going further south than my fathers; I have increased what was bequeathed to me. . . . As for silence after being attacked, it emboldens the heart of the foe. To be aggressive is to be valiant; to retreat is to be a wretch. He is really unmanly who is pushed back at his (own) frontier, since the *Nehsi* hears (only) to fall down at a word. It is the (mere) answering him that makes him retreat. If one is aggressive against him, he turns his back. Retreat—and *he* begins to be aggressive. They are not really people (worthy) of respect; they are poor and broken of spirit. My majesty has seen them: it is not (said) in misrepresentation!"[18]

The frontier was held by Egyptian soldiers, re-enforced by Sudanese trackers, the *Medjai*. We have some of the frontier reports from the fortress named "Holding off the Land of *Medjai*" at the Second Cataract. "The patrol which went out to patrol the desert edge (near?) the Fortress 'Holding off the *Medjai*' in the Year 3, third month of the second season, last day, coming to report to me and saying: 'We have found the tracks of thirty-two men and three donkeys.' " This was in the burning month of June, as was the next. "Be informed, if you please, that two male and three female *Medjai* . . . came down from the desert in the Year 3, third month of the second season, day 27. They said: 'We have come to serve the Palace!' (They) were questioned about the state of the desert. They said: 'We have not heard anything, (but) the desert is dying from hunger'—so they said. Then this thy servant had them dismissed to their desert on this day."[19] The use of these Sudanese trackers and warriors, the *Medjai*, marked the beginning of the dependence of the Egyptians on foreign troops, as far as our visible evidence

17. See above, p. 112.
18. Breasted, *ARE*, I, §§ 652, 657.
19. P. C. Smither in *JEA*, XXXI (1945), 3 ff.

goes. To be sure, the Sixth Dynasty had employed Libyans and *Nehsiu* for raids upon Asiatic territory;[20] but the Sudanese *Medjai* were to continue in Egypt as shock troops and police. Indeed, the word *Medjai* came to be translatable as "police." The use of these Sudanese apparently continued right through the Second Intermediate Period, for the Seventeenth Dynasty used them as scouts in the war to expel the Hyksos.[21] The early Empire perhaps relied upon Egyptian troops for the conquest of foreign territory and used the *Medjai* as police at home, but the principle of foreign mercenaries was established and the Empire came increasingly to use slave troops and foreign mercenaries for its regular army. Whether the Egyptians did their own fighting or engaged others to do it may be an index either to the Egyptians' willingness to carry the burden of their own national expansion or to the prosperity of the land, so that outsiders could be employed to do the heavy and dangerous work.

The policed frontier of the Middle Kingdom lay at the Second Cataract, but Egyptian interests extended further to the south. The arable and habitable territory between the Second and Third Cataracts is narrow and inhospitable. South of the Third Cataract the Nile Valley widens out and affords greater possibility for cultivated fields and particularly for pasture lands. The Third Cataract itself is hazardous for navigation because of hidden rocks in the rapids, so that the promising area to the south is effectively disconnected from Egypt proper. Nevertheless, that area is worth commercial cultivation. Just south of the Third Cataract and its dangerous rapids lies the modern town of Kerma, possessing a modest agricultural and trading importance and serving as the northern limit of the good land to the south. Under the Middle Kingdom Kerma was an outlying trading post and transshipping point for vessels and land caravans; Egypt maintained a resident colony there for commercial and political advantage, with a fortified trading post known as "The Walls of Amen-em-het, the Justified." North of the Third Cataract the prevailing culture was a high, local primitive, affected by the Libyans and the Sahara Desert—generally a Hamitic culture. South of the Third Cataract there was a far higher proportion of Negroes, so that this post made contact with a people little known to the Egyptians.

The desert roads from Kerma were not bad. It was six easy days by donkey caravan to the Second Cataract and the resumption of safe

20. Breasted, *ARE*, I, §311.
21. Erman, *LAE*, p. 53.

shipping on the Nile. Or caravans could cut west to the Selimeh Oasis and then trek north along a well-marked desert road—the *Darb al-Arbain* of today—with wells almost every day, to reach the First Cataract region, the Abydos area, or the northern oases. From Kerma it was only two days by donkey caravan to the fertile area of the Fourth Cataract.

"The Walls of Amen-em-het, the Justified," was a large, fortified blockhouse of brick, able to withstand raids from the desert or to keep its merchant colony in security. The post was important enough to be placed under the charge of high Egyptian officials, the most interesting of whom was a certain Djefa-Hapi from Assiut in Middle Egypt (cf. Fig. 12c). At Assiut Djefa-Hapi had built a large tomb, with seven rooms and an axis length of 145 feet, one of the most imposing private tombs of the Middle Kingdom. This is famous for its inscriptions, the mortuary contracts in which Djefa-Hapi laid down the specifications for the priestly and ritual activities to be carried on for him at Assiut after his death.[22] These texts give us a vivid picture of the torchlight processions of priests going on a feast night to do honor to the statue of Djefa-Hapi at his tomb. After all this preparation, entailing the income from the fields of Djefa-Hapi's local estate, the tomb was unfinished and Djefa-Hapi was never buried in it.

Instead he was buried 800 miles to the south, in a huge tumulus at Kerma, where he had served as pharaoh's "Chief Headman of the South," the political-commercial agent at the Third Cataract, with a status like that of Clive or Hastings in India or like that of an American Indian agent. The unused tomb at Assiut, with its sober and businesslike detail of mortuary contract, was typical for the Egyptian kind of burial, well-ordered and elaborately developed over the centuries. His actual burial in the tumulus at Kerma, surrounded by a fortified brick enclosure 275 feet in diameter, held the simple and terrible pomp of the barbarians. Let the discoverer, Professor Reisner, tell what happened when Djefa-Hapi was buried here.

"A great funerary feast was made at which over a thousand oxen were slaughtered and their skulls buried around the southern half of the circle outside. The body of the prince was then laid to rest in the vaulted chamber, with his offerings; and the wooden door was closed. The sacrificial victims, all local Nubians, either stupefied during the feast by a drug, or strangled, were brought in and laid out on the floor

22. Breasted, *ARE*, I, §§ 535 ff., where he is called Hepzefi; G. A. Reisner in *JEA*, V (1918), 79 ff.

of the corridor—from two to three hundred men, women, and children. With these Nubians were placed a few pots and pans, occasionally a sword, and often their personal adornments. Then the corridor was filled in with earth, forming a low, domed mound. The top was covered with a floor of mud-brick. A great quartzite pyramidion was set up on top, and I believe that a mud-brick chapel was built around the stone."[23]

The Egyptians had carried into the Middle Kingdom an emphasis on social justice and the rights of the common man, but they still thought the Egyptians were the only proper humans and that foreigners were akin to the animals. They did not carry their concern for individual rights with them into their colonies. In Egypt the only known analogy to the mass sacrifice of retainers and servants was in a tomb of a First Dynasty princess,[24] but thereafter the practice seems to have died out. At Kerma Djefa-Hapi expressed the Egyptian attitude to foreign peoples, and he probably carried out a local and primitive custom of sacrificial murder on a large and impressive scale. Even though local custom may have sanctioned such a practice, on the belief that personal retainers were a prince's property and thus might be taken with him into the next world, so sweeping an observation of local practice could hardly have endeared the Egyptian overlords to the local Sudanese. The outthrust of empire is rarely accompanied by the humanity which one tries to practice at home.

On other frontiers the Egyptians showed the same energetic watchfulness. A new foundation across the Suez frontier was "The Wall of the Ruler, made to oppose the Asiatics and to crush the Crossers of the Sands." A "Chief Hunter of the Desert and Commander of the Western Deserts, Kai son of Beshet" depicted himself on his stela with his five greyhounds and said with assurance: "I am a citizen of the attack, a leader of the army on the day of difficulty, whose activity his lord praises. I have reached the western oases, I have investigated all their roads, and I have brought back the fugitives whom I found in them. My army was sound and without loss; what was entrusted to me returned successfully."[25]

Into the Sinai mines in the almost unbearably hot months of June, July, and August went an expedition to satisfy the demand for copper and turquoise. Hor-ur-Re, the leader of the party, admitted that "it was not at all the proper season for coming to this mining area. . . . It was

23. *Bulletin of the Museum of Fine Arts, Boston*, XIII (1915), 72.
24. P. 64, above.
25. R. Anthes in *ZÄS*, LXV (1930), 108 ff.

difficult in my experience to find the (proper) skin for it, when the land was burning hot, the highland was in summer, and the mountains branded an (already) blistered(?) skin." However, he kept addressing his workers with words of encouragement, and "my entire army returned complete; no loss had ever occurred in it.... There was no (cry of): 'Oh for a good skin!', (but) eyes were in festivity(?). It was better than at its normal season."[26]

This was an energetic age, which still summoned the best resources of individuals. Egypt was felt to be a going concern, and the dedicated contribution of each Egyptian to the welfare of the whole nation was an important obligation. A strong sense of national destiny and of the special providence of the gods made Egypt a forward-moving unity.

Previous chapters have traced the course of decentralization in Egypt, the disintegration of the power of the pharaoh, the rise of individual initiative and independence, and the emergence of demands for social justice for all men. This centrifugal trend particularly characterized the First Intermediate Period and lasted into the Middle Kingdom. However, under the successful rule of the energetic and conscientious pharaohs of the Twelfth Dynasty, the trend reversed itself and became centripetal, for greater actual and acknowledged centralization in the person of the king. It is necessary that we now try to document that statement.

We saw that in the Old Kingdom the pyramids of the pharaohs declined in size and quality and the tombs of the nobles ceased to cluster around the royal pyramid and became independently located out in the provinces. A similar observation may be made about the Middle Kingdom. At the beginning of the Twelfth Dynasty the tombs of the nobles were relatively large and their inscriptions were brusquely independent. The nobles used royal titles and epithets, and inscriptions were dated, not only in the reign of the pharaoh, but also in the reign of the local prince. As the dynasty went on, the nobles' statements became more modest, their tombs became smaller and less assured, whereas the royal tombs became larger and more dominating.

We may set in contrast texts from the independent spirit of the First Intermediate Period and the more dependent spirit of the Middle Kingdom. Of the first type is a provincial stela of Middle Egypt with a definite assertion of self-competence, characteristic of the age. "I was a commoner of repute, who lived on his (own) property, plowed with

26. Breasted, *ARE*, I, §§ 733 ff.

his (own) oxen, and sailed in his (own) ship, and not through that which I had found in the possession of my father, the honored Uha."[27] Over against this assurance that the good life lay in self-sufficiency, we may set the text of a provincial ruler under Sen-Usert II. "My favor in the court was greater than (that of) any (other) sole companion. He (the pharaoh) distinguished me from among his dignitaries, when I was [placed] ahead of those who had been ahead of me. I joined the official staff of the palace, praise was given appropriately, I bowed appropriately, my favor which had come to pass in the Presence being at the Word of the King himself. The like had never happened to servants whose lords had praised them, for he knew the activity of my tongue and the modesty(?) of my being. (Thus) I was a revered man of the royal Presence, my honor was with his court, and my amiability before his companions."[28] The tide had turned, and the good life now lay in securing the advantages of royal favor, at the cost of self-sufficiency and independence.

When Si-nuhe fled into exile, his conscience was troubling him, and he feared that he might be suspected of disloyalty to the new pharaoh. When his Asiatic host asked him how Egypt would fare now that the old king was dead, Si-nuhe opened his mouth and tumbled out the most eager praise of the new king. "He is a god without his peer; there is no other who surpasses him. He is a master of understanding, effective in plans and beneficent of decrees. . . . He is, further, a mighty man, acting with his (own) arm, an energetic man, without any like unto him!" The phrase which we wish to pick up in that statement is "acting with his (own) arm." Under the individualism of the First Intermediate Period, a repeated boast of the "commoner of repute" (literally, "excellent little man") was that he was one who "spoke with his (own) mouth and acted with his (own) arm." This frequent statement of the commoner became very rare in the Twelfth Dynasty, except for one usage: it was picked up and used by the pharaohs about themselves.[29] Thus, the claim of individualism and independence became a boast of overriding authority. We have seen how the nobles had appropriated to themselves the royal prerogatives of an abundant life after death. In this appropriation by the pharaoh of a commoner's statement about his own worth we have the royal revenge. By sleepless efficiency

27. D. Dunham, *Naga-ed-Der Stelae of the First Intermediate Period* (London, 1937), Pl. XXXII, pp. 102–4. Our Fig. 11a.

28. Breasted, *ARE*, I, §631.

29. J. Polotsky, *Zu den Inschriften der 11. Dynastie* (*Untersuch.*, XI [1929]), pp. 34, 44 ff.

the pharaoh had stolen back from his people the prize of individualism which they had wrested out of chaos.

The outstanding example of the surrender of the nobles to the pharaoh appears in a text credited to a chief treasurer of Amen-em-het III. In one of those "instructions" by which the Egyptians summed up the practical wisdom of their day he advised his children about the good life.

"The beginning of the instruction which he made for his children. I tell something important and cause that ye hear (it); I cause that ye know a counsel of eternity and a manner of living aright and for passing a lifetime of peace: Worship King (Amen-em-het III), living forever, within your bodies and associate with his majesty in your hearts. He is Perception which is in (men's) hearts, and his eyes search out every body. He is (the sun-god) Re, by whose beams one sees; he is one who illumines the Two Lands more than the sun disc. . . . He gives food to them who are in his service, and he supplies them who tread his path. The King is a *ka*, and his mouth is increase. He who is to be is his creation, for he is (the god) Khnum of all bodies, the begetter who creates the people. . . . He is (the goddess) Sekhmet against him who transgresses his command, and he whom he hates will bear woes. Fight on behalf of his name, and be scrupulous in the oath to him, that ye may be free from a taint of disloyalty. He whom the king has loved will be a revered one, (but) there is no tomb for a rebel against his majesty and his corpse is cast into the water. If ye do this, your persons shall be unblemished—ye will find it (so) forever."[30] This was all that this father could advise his children: the pharaoh is a god of manifold nature and far-reaching power; seek the good life by clinging to him.

The Middle Kingdom brought back to Egypt the benefits of peace, prosperity, and world dominion, but the price of these precious gains was a loss in a great potential. Egypt had been hovering at the threshold of a tremendous discovery, the sanctity, value, and human rights of the individual. Perhaps it was too early in world history for any people to achieve full and effective recognition of that dream. Babylonia at the same time was trying to work out a system in which the rights of the individual were asserted and protected by law; Egypt's way was to seek for him justice. But justice, *ma‹at*, was of the gods and of the divine order; it was not easy for the goddess *Ma‹at* to find her home among ordinary men. When, through the success of the state, the Twelfth Dynasty pharaohs demonstrated their capacity to be gods, they became

30. Erman, *LAE*, pp. 84 f.

once more the arbiters and dispensers of *ma‹at*. To this the Egyptian people were assenting. They were well-fed and busy and aware of opportunities for advancement; this was a far better time than the anarchy of the First Intermediate Period. The concept that the creator-god had made every man like his brother and the insistence of the eloquent peasant that the poorest man had inherent rights became blurred and forgotten under national prosperity. Pharaoh no longer needed to be sleepless and hungry in the herding of his flocks; the flocks were too fat to stray far from his throne.

We have now seen enough of Egyptian civilization to attempt some kind of characterization. Even though we moderns can never crawl inside the skin of the ancient and think and feel as he did, even though we bring to any such attempt eyes which are myopic from a focus on the modern world, even though our generalizations will and must be altered by future scholarship, we must as historians make the attempt. We must satisfy our readers—and ourselves—that we have an adequate measure of understanding to support the interpretations which we have laid upon the data. We must define the degree to which we have a sympathetic knowledge of the individuals whom we are studying, and thus confess also the degree of ignorance which we have not yet overcome. Where the culture is as remote in time as ancient Egypt, where our basic data are so limited and so tendentious, and where the spiritual expression of the ancient culture is so different from ours, the effort to understand is self-conscious, but nevertheless imperative.

There is another reason for seeking for the Egyptian character at this point: our account is approaching the period where that character will be subject to strong modifying forces, and these forces will alter it radically. In our preceding account, we had discussed the formation of a culture, its vigorous expression under the Old Kingdom, its survival under the first great illness, and its modification under the Middle Kingdom. And yet in change it seemed to us essentially the same in spirit and in outward expression. The Egyptian ethos, formed by the Fourth Dynasty, was older but unchanged in the Twelfth Dynasty. In the time to come, that ethos, we believe, changed so greatly that it ultimately reversed itself. If our understanding be true, the Egyptian character gave forth the same expression in the Eighteenth Dynasty, but it was already altered in spirit; by the Twentieth Dynasty it was also different in outward expression, and then the inner essence of ancient Egyptian culture was finished. Thereafter the Egyptians groped blindly for what they had lost, groped for a thousand years, groped for what they knew had been a treasure, but groped in vain: the inner spirit was dead, and the outer expression could never recapture what was lost. What was that inner spirit?

An element in the Egyptian psychology which we have stressed was confidence, a sense of assurance and of special election, which promoted individual assertiveness, a relish of life as it was, and a tolerance for divergences from the most rigid application of the norm. The Egyptian was never introspective and never was rigidly demanding of himself or of others, because he was free from fear. As yet he had been the architect of his own destiny, had achieved a proud, rich, and successful culture, and had survived one period of inner turmoil with a return to the full, round life. This feeling of security and of unimpaired destiny may have been the product of geographic isolation; it may have had its roots in the fertile black soil; it may have been warmed by the good African sun; it may have been intensified by the contrast of the harsh and meager life in the deserts that bordered Egypt. Or its origins may be too subtle for us moderns to penetrate. Yet it was there, and it gave to Egyptian civilization its characteristic cheerful urbanity. The dogmatic expression of this special providence was the belief that Egypt alone was ruled by a god, that the physical child of the sun-god would govern and protect Egypt throughout eternity. What was there then to fear?

If we claim that the Egyptians were the most civilized of the ancient oriental peoples, we do not thereby insist that they were superior to the Babylonians or the Hebrews or the Persians. We do not even mean that they surpassed their contemporary neighbors in the arts and crafts and techniques of civilization. We mean that they emerged from their pre-civilized state rather abruptly and rather completely into an adjusted and harmonious way of life which they enjoyed with practiced ease. There was a refinement and a genial complexity to Egyptian civilization which was a product of their self-confidence and their *joie de vivre*. By the same token, there was an indolent elegance and a self-conceit which sometimes accompany the term "civilized." The very qualities which suggest the claim that Egypt was highly civilized suggest also that she lacked self-criticism, that she never achieved profundity, and that she never felt the burning inner urge to achieve new and daring conquests of mind and spirit. Spiritual balance, given by the gods at the beginning of time, to last unchanged for eternity, frees a people from fear but it also frees a people from the necessity of continually discovering the gods and the gods' purposes for man. Egypt's strength was such that she did not feel the need for renewed strength until it was too late.

The statement that the Egyptians were an easy-going, gay, and light-hearted people must be underlined because of their apparent preoccupation with death. As we have said, this was no morbid terror of death, but rather was a firm and optimistic affirmation of continued life. The Egyptians relished their life. They clung to life, not with the desperation that comes from a horror of death, but with a happy assurance that they had always been victorious and so would defeat mortal change itself. There may be some sense of unreality here, but there is no morbidity and no mysticism. To the ancient Egyptians the gay, active, extroverted, successful life they lived was the great reality, and they light-heartedly refused to accept any extinction of that life.

Perhaps the polished and civilized urbanity which colored the Egyptian character so strongly may best be illustrated by their ever present sense of humor. The whimsical twist to a literary passage—even in a religious text—or the light burlesque touch in a tomb scene was almost universal with them. For the most part, such humorous twists were slight and incidental; they provoked a fleeting smile rather than a loud laugh. Those artistic products which carried the broadest caricature and those literary products which carried the rudest satire are known to us from later periods of Egyptian history, from the middle of the Empire and following. Those later periods were times of greater emotional excitation and of the vulgarization of elements which had once been held sacred. In the earlier period the humorous touch was lighter and gentler. It was a light-hearted coloring to an otherwise serious passage rather than a consciously underlined joke in a context deliberately playful.

We shall give some examples from the Old and Middle Kingdoms, but we must first insist that a sense of humor is highly individual to a culture, and we can rarely be absolutely sure whether the passage was deliberately humorous and so appealed to the ancient or whether we moderns find some of the solemnities of the ancient amusingly peculiar and thus read humor into them. For example, in the Pyramid Texts there is a "cannibal hymn," in which the deceased pharaoh threatens to devour men and gods and thus to incorporate into himself their powers. Of the gods whom he may gobble up, it is said:

The biggest of them are for his breakfast,
Their middle-sized are for his lunch,
And the littlest of them are for his supper.
Their old males and females are (good only) for his kindling.[31]

We find this amusing, and it is possible that it evoked a grim smile in antiquity. But it would be safer to assume that it was fiercely serious in its original formulation of the concept of the deceased pharaoh as a ruthless conqueror. Certainly any modern ridicule of a solemn Egyptian ceremony, such as the "ritual dance" in which an elaborately equipped pharaoh paced vigorously around a field, is ignorant and condescending. However, after we make allowances for differences in culture, there remains a marked content of Egyptian art and literature which we can describe as deliberately humorous.

Let us take some of the scenes and texts from the tombs of the Egyptian nobles of the Old and Middle Kingdoms. Humor never lowered the dignity of the owner of the tomb or of his family; they were always presented in respectful and hieratic stereotypes. However, the setting of the dignitaries' continued life was one of abundance, and that abundance included recreation and contrast. The slowly pacing noble might be shown as accompanied by a bustling little dwarf, whose pompous assertiveness provided an effective foil to the calm assurance of his master. Or the vigorous and tumultuous games of children (Fig. 10a) might be shown in close juxtaposition to the eternally poised figure of the noble receiving mortuary offerings. Such contrasts had the purpose of enhancing the dignity of the noble, but this artistic trick employed a mild humor for emphasis.

The dozing field-laborer, the obstinate donkey, and the mischievous monkey were common devices in the tomb scenes. Sometimes the humor is more boisterous, as when an ape seizes the leg of a servant to upset him. More often the effect is gained by strong contrast, like the emaciated herdsman with unkempt and matted hair, leaning feebly on his staff, but bringing in fat and sleek cattle for his master, or like the vigorous young boat-builder whose work is impeded by the idle gossip of a fat and slouching old man.[32] Belonging to the same tradition from the earlier Eighteenth Dynasty are two scenes from the Theban tombs. In one the golden opulence of a harvest scene is punctuated by a vignette of two girl gleaners entangled in a hair-pulling fight over their

31. R. O. Faulkner in *JEA*, X (1924), 98.

32. A. M. Blackman, *The Rock Tombs of Meir*, II (*Arch. Surv.*, XXIII [1915]), Pls. IV, VI, XXVI, XXX. Our Figs. 15a and 15b.

competitive snatchings. In the other the aged "Chief Bird-Catcher Ptah-mose" is depicted with a flock of pelicans. His bald head, rounded belly, and hand pocketed over his mouth form a delightful caricature to the fat pomposity of the pelicans, and there can be little doubt of the artist's satirical intent.[33]

The tomb scenes which depict the daily life of the Egyptians are commonly accompanied by brief texts describing the activity shown or giving the words of the workers. These words are often very lively, as in the shouts of the butchers felling an ox. Sometimes they are amusing to us and probably called forth the same smile from the ancient at the homely incidents in the scenes. Two craftsmen are shown drilling out stone vessels. One of them says smugly to his mate: "This jar is very beautiful." The answer is a dash of cold water: "Oh, get on with it!"[34] In another scene a patient is squatted on the ground receiving a pedicure. As his foot is grasped by the doctor, the patient nervously exclaims: "Don't let this hurt me!" The doctor's answer is sarcastically submissive: "I shall do your pleasure, O my sovereign!"[35] Again, we see the shepherd who has led his flocks in from the western desert margin to tread the newly sown grain into the oozing mud near the River. As his ankles sink into the moisture, he muses on his abrupt change of scene and sings an ironic little song.

> The shepherd is in the water, along with the fish;
> He talks with the shad
> And passes the time of day with the oxyrhynchus-fish.
> O west, where is the shepherd (now),
> The shepherd of the west?[36]

The same lightness of touch which was normal and at home in the solemn tombs crops up continually in Egyptian literature. The Middle Kingdom story of Si-nuhe tells how this political exile was received back into the Egyptian court in his old age and entered Pharaoh's presence dressed in Asiatic garb. We smile as we read of the sly solemnity of his reception, and there is good reason to believe that the ancient Egyptian enjoyed the passage. "Then the royal children were ushered in, and his majesty said to the Queen: 'Here is Si-nuhe, come as a Bedouin, (in) the dress of the Asiatics.' She gave a great scream, and

33. N. M. Davies and A. H. Gardiner, *Ancient Egyptian Paintings* (Chicago, 1936), Vol. I, Pls. LI, XLI. Our Fig. 16b.

34. The Sakkarah Expedition, *The Mastaba of Mereruka* (*OIP*, Vol. XXXI [Chicago, 1938]), Vol. I, Pl. 30.

35. J. Capart, *Une Rue de tombeaux à Saqqarah* (Brussels, 1907), Pl. LXVII.

36. Sakkarah Expedition, Vol. II (*OIP*, Vol. XXXIX), Pls. 169–70.

the royal children all chattered together, and they said to his majesty: 'It is not really he, O Sovereign, my lord!' And his majesty said: 'It is really he!' " In the following passage, the princesses sing a song in celebration of the occasion and they pun on Si-nuhe's name as Si-mehit, "Son of the North Wind": "this sheikh Si-mehit, a foreigner born in Egypt." They had their fun with him, and Si-nuhe, eager to be forgiven for past political offenses, was humbly grateful for humor instead of cold formality.[37]

In the wisdom literature there is amused tolerance, not precisely humor but advice with a twinkle in the eye, when the elder instructs a young man how to get on with a drunkard: "If you are drinking with a tippler, you partake (also) and his heart will be content. Do not be bad-tempered about food when in the company of a greedy man, (but) take (whatever) he gives you, and do not reject it; then that will soothe (him)."[38]

A tale about the deeds of magicians acquaints us with a delightful character by the name of Djedi. "He is a commoner 110 years old, (but) he eats five hundred loaves of bread and a haunch of beef for meat and drinks a hundred jars of beer down to this day." When the king's son went out to seek this venerable prodigy, "he found him lying on a mat at the threshold of his house, with one servant beside him rubbing him (with oil) and another massaging his feet. Then the King's Son Hor-dedef said: 'Thy condition is like (that of) one living before becoming old: (even) in the face of old age, the time of death, the time of burial, the time of interment, sleeping until (broad) daylight, being free from sickness, without the hacking of a cough. That is the greeting (proper) to one who is (so) venerable!' "[39] This passage is intended to give the picture of an extraordinary sage, but it also has its indulgent humor in presenting a tremendous old man enjoying the sensual comforts of the flesh with all his physical and mental faculties very much alive.

If any body of texts should have been consistently serious, it should have been the mortuary texts, designed to promote the eternal beatification of the deceased. And yet the pervading light touch colored even the Pyramid Texts, not in belly-shaking jests but in pictures or turns of expression which cut athwart the grim purpose of rendering immortal

37. See above, pp. 134–36.

38. From the Instruction for Ka-gemni; cf. A. H. Gardiner in *JEA*, XXXII (1946), 71 ff.

39. Erman, *LAE*, p. 41.

power and happiness to the pharaoh among the gods. Sometimes the deceased king is depicted in awful and conquering majesty, so that his title to join the other gods could not be denied. At other times an appeal is made on his behalf because he needs the assistance of the other gods to gain his place in paradise. For example, it is argued to the celestial ferryman that King Meri-Re needs his services because the pharaoh has no boat and has had to swim thus far on his otherworld journey. Further, the ferryman should transport him to paradise because the supreme god is expecting the pharaoh to entertain him by performing the comic dances of a pygmy. "O thou that ferriest over the righteous man who has no boat, thou ferryman of the Field of Reeds, Meri-Re is a righteous man in heaven and earth, Meri-Re is a righteous man at this island of land, and he has swum and he has reached it. . . . He is the pygmy of the dances of the god, who entertains the heart of the god before his great throne."⁴⁰ Certainly this was no context which brought ridicule upon the deceased pharaoh; that would have been unthinkable in this setting and at this time. There is here some of that multiplicity of approach which suggested new and different means of achieving desired goals. Further, the pygmy dance was of ceremonial significance. And yet the idea of the squat little man swimming through the celestial waters in order to prance and pivot before the gods for their "entertainment" certainly must have called forth a twinkle in the eye and a more than respectful smile.

The Pyramid Texts often treat the advent of the deceased pharaoh in the other world as a cataclysmic phenomenon at which heaven and earth tremble since he is so mighty a force. It is pleasing to find a variant of this, in which the earth-god and the sky-goddess shake with laughter, because pharaoh's arrival has brought calm rather than disturbance. "Geb laughs and Nut chuckles before Nefer-ka-Re as he goes up to heaven; heaven shakes for him and earth trembles for him, because Nefer-ka-Re has driven away the storm clouds."⁴¹ If there could be laughter among the gods, there might no less be laughter among mortals.

Playfulness was a normal characteristic of the ancient Egyptian. He loved games, whether he sat at the draughtsboard or watched children at play or engaged a troupe of wrestlers to put on a contest for him. The same playfulness appeared in his art and in his literature. The picture writing provided constant opportunity for vivid little vignettes to en-

---

40. K. Sethe, *Die altägyptischen Pyramidentexte* (Leipzig, 1908–10), II, §§ 1188–89.
41. *Ibid.*, §§ 1149–50.

liven the context or for playfulness in manipulating the signs to form a secondary enigmatic writing. Similarly, the literature abounded in colorful figures of speech and in stylistic tricks. The frightfulness of the devouring pharaoh in the "cannibal hymn" of the Pyramid Texts was emphasized by the reiteration of harsh sounds: *Unis pi sekhem wer, sekhem em sekhemu; Unis pi ʿashem, ʿashem ʿashemu, wer:* "Unis is the great power, overpowering the powerful; Unis is a bird of prey, preying upon the birds of prey, the great one."[42] Similarly, one of the books of wisdom enlivens a father's solemn advice to his son by ringing the changes on the word "to hear," to the effect that the son who listens obediently to his elders will some day become a magistrate who hears cases. "Hearing is of advantage to a son who hears. If hearing enter within the hearer, the hearer becomes one who hears. Hearing is good, and speaking is good, (but) the hearer has an advantage, (because) hearing is of advantage to the hearer, (so that) hearing is better than anything (else)."[43] This sounds like a nonsensical waste of good literature to us, but we miss the little nuances inherent in any play on words and we lack the Egyptian's pervasive playfulness.

This sportiveness with words was not merely whimsical but also had its religious-magical efficacy in relating similars, as in puns. Egyptian religious literature is loaded with puns, some of them rather far-fetched, and such similarities in sound were solemnly used for religious identification. When the deceased king was presented with two bowls of Buto (*imti*) wine, the priest said: "Take thou the maiden who is in (*imit*) the Eye of Horus," or two bowls of Mareotis (*hamu*) wine: "Take thou the Eye of Horus which he caught (*ham*)," or two bowls of Pelusium (*senu*) wine: "Take thou the Eye of Horus; it does not separate (*senu*) from thee."[44] There was no humorous intent in such offering puns, but there was still a kind of skillful game, in which one played tricks with language to the entertainment of men and gods.

This playfulness, this non-caustic humor, and this flickering smile are important in an understanding of what was strong and what was weak in the Egyptian system. This was a lightness of touch and a tolerance which lent flexibility to the system. Through the stress of changing times and conditions Egypt was to retain an essential sameness for many centuries—let us say, from the beginning of the Fourth Dynasty, around 2650 B.C., to the latter part of the Eighteenth Dynasty, around

42. *Ibid.*, I, § 407.
43. Erman, *LAE*, p. 64.
44. Sethe, *op. cit.*, I, §§ 93–94.

1400 B.C. The Egyptians never took themselves so seriously that their universe crashed in chaos if there were deviations from the norm. They took seriously the dogma that the pharaoh was a god, but they had tolerance for a pharaoh who showed mortal weakness, and their dogma was not upset by a time of competing god-kings. They had a firm faith in the happy destiny of Egypt. They did experience a brief period of doubt and disillusion in the First Intermediate Period, when that happy destiny suffered hurt, but they survived these troubles and emerged with a restored faith built on slightly different principles. A cheerful refusal to be absolutely dogmatic and rigorous gave the Egyptian way of life lasting qualities which would have been lacking if this people had been as serious and consistent as their Asiatic neighbors.

If we describe the same qualities as easygoing or as lacking in thoroughness, we see the reverse of the picture, and we see the weakness in an ancient civilization which achieved such great physical results and which lasted so long. Particularly, if we contrast the Egyptians with the Hebrews, we are aware of the tragedy of great gifts taken so lightly. Each of these cultures felt itself to be the Chosen People. The Hebrews were a little people, buffeted by their neighbors and ultimately dispersed to distant lands. For them God's choosing came to mean a demand for rigorous responsibility on the part of the group and of the individual. The Egyptians were a rich people, set apart from outside peril. For them the election by the gods meant the privileges of civilized life, including a tolerance of minor divergences within the system. Further, their special election was in their mythology a part of the original creation, so that effort or incentive toward change, what we call "progress," was out of the question. The only thing necessary was to get back again to original principles whenever the system went out of adjustment, that is, to restore the *ma'at* of the beginning.

This will explain why the only really creative period was at the beginning of Egyptian history, at the end of the predynastic and in the early dynastic. When the culture was formative, the Egyptians were trying to discover what it might be that the gods had given to them. One might say that they were then trying to write their mythology. So the earliest dynasties showed the most exacting technology, the closest approach to a scientific attitude, and the closest approach to a philosophy of being. By the time that the culture was formed—by the Fourth Dynasty—the governing mythology was known, and further experimentation or change was proscribed. The system had been set for eternity. But it already had that lightness of attitude, that gentle humor, which gave it the flexibility for long life.

In the following chapters we give a subjective analysis of the changes which came over that system when Egypt was exposed to the outer world and when her former isolated security was broken for all time. Here we wish to note one aspect of that change to come. The earlier humor seems more kindly, a humor of contrast or incongruity. The humor which developed in Egypt's later cosmopolitanism seems more biting and sarcastic, a humor of ridicule. If this be a true understanding, the later humor did not have the tolerance of the earlier, and instead of giving flexibility to the system, tended to undermine some of the supporting posts of the nation. But the evidence for any such claim is still to come.

VII

THE GREAT HUMILIATION

Dynasties 13–17 (about 1800–1550 B.C.)

IF THE Middle Kingdom possessed such admirable qualities and if the Egyptian system had such flexibility, how did it happen that the state collapsed so suddenly shortly after 1800 B.C.? We wish that we knew the answer. A number of suggestions may be offered, which cumulatively may be of some significance, but the abrupt disintegration of a going system must still remain a mystery.

Probably the Middle Kingdom had an inner structural weakness in that it began as a feudal state and retained many elements of local independence. If the pharaoh was accepted as the head of a mutual protective association, he would be so accepted as long as he was powerful, alert, and vigilant. Most of the Twelfth Dynasty pharaohs had such qualities, but we know less about the rulers at the end of the dynasty, either because they were already losing power under external forces or because they lacked the necessary abilities. If they were weak kings, the latent individualism of the local princes might quickly reassert itself so that the state would be fractured. We have noted that that individualism was pretty well subordinated to group solidarity within the state, so that this factor probably was not the initial or strongest element in the Middle Kingdom collapse. There must have been other factors at first, promoting the latent spirit of separatism.

We shall consider below a series of execration texts, by which the enemies of the state were ceremonially cursed. It will then appear that there may have been a serious problem of loyalty within the royal family itself, so that it is possible that the throne was disastrously weakened by inner competition.

External factors may also have weakened the Egyptian state. We have guessed that Egypt did not have a political empire in Asia during the Middle Kingdom but enjoyed the spiritual and economic rewards of cultural and commercial imperialism. That is, she dominated the land and water trade of the eastern Mediterranean area and reaped a satisfactory economic surplus through that dominance. In addition to the goods which she had to offer—perhaps grain and copper and gold—she had won over the Asiatic and Aegean lands by organized and patrolled commercial services in caravans and fleets, and also by the blandishments of a superior and attractive culture. The neighboring Asiatic and Mediterranean states had been small and disorganized; their spiritual and economic advantages had lain in good relations with their Egyptian partner. The organization and maintenance of these trade advantages would be a function of the central Egyptian government. As long as the trade flowed smoothly, the profit and the power would come to the pharaoh.

However, trade relations were set up with regard to known factors, and the incursion of new and unknown forces into Asia or Africa would interrupt those relations. There is evidence that restless movements were penetrating both regions to upset the orderly prosperity of the past. In Africa this was the slow and filtered northward pressure of Negroes.[1] In Asia the force was more rapid, large, and powerful. The movements in Asia were destined to disturb the order of the entire Near East, throwing a people known as the Kassites into Mesopotamia and a people known as the Hyksos into Egypt.[2] Ultimately the source of this great movement of peoples came from the north and northeast, possibly across the Caucasus, but there is still a great deal to learn about their origins. Slowly, over a few centuries, they moved down into the Fertile Crescent and conquered or dislodged the sedentary people there. When, in the 18th century B.C., they penetrated Egypt as conquerors, we call them the Hyksos, and this name is extended by archeologists back into the recognizably new culture in Palestine and Syria. They brought a number of new elements of power into the Near East, the most notable being the horse and chariot. For the moment, our con-

1. H. Junker in *JEA*, VII (1921), 121 ff. Junker's arguments based on racial types as found by excavation are supported by G. A. Reisner, *Excavations at Kerma, IV–V* ("Harvard African Studies," Vol. VI [Cambridge, 1923]), p. 556.

2. W. F. Albright, "The Role of the Canaanites in the History of Civilization," in *Studies in the History of Culture* (1942), pp. 11 ff. This has a convenient summary of material, although the author's treatment of the Hyksos is thrown out of balance by his focus upon the importance of the Canaanites.

cern with them is that they were disturbing Asia while the Middle Kingdom was still in power, and this external upset may have been one of the factors which weakened the Twelfth Dynasty. We shall consider the Hyksos culture shortly.

A very interesting series of documents shows the enemies of the Egyptian state around the end of the Middle Kingdom. These are the execration texts, by which the pharaoh ceremonially and magically cursed his actual and his potential foes. In date they cannot be earlier than the middle of the Twelfth Dynasty and may come from the Thirteenth.[3] In form they are of two kinds: red pottery bowls or rough human figures of clay (Fig. 17c), in each case inscribed with specific cursings and then ceremonially smashed, as all opposition to pharaoh must be smashed.[4]

The ceremony of naming and destroying enemies by a curse apparently goes back to the Old Kingdom, since one of the titles for a magic spell in the Pyramid Texts is "breaking the red jars."[5] These two Middle Kingdom lots, the red bowls from Thebes and the human figurines from Sakkarah, happen to be our chief documents for the ceremony.

The formula used in condemning pharaoh's enemies was comprehensive, including not only the known peril but also the potential. The full formula for each cursed foe may be illustrated by the example of a Nubian prince: "Bakuait, called Tjai, the ruler of Ubates, the son of Ihaasi and Unkat, and all the retainers(?) who are with him, and their mighty men, their swift runners, their allies, and their associates, who may rebel, who may plot, who may fight, who may think of fighting, or who may think of rebelling—in this entire land!" Thus a specifically named foreign prince, with all his real or potential adherents who might be hostile to the king of Egypt or who might only think of hostility, was magically thwarted by the breaking of this bowl or figurine.

To be sure, it was difficult to name every possible foe, so that the texts had certain general sections to cover all contingencies:

"All men, all people, all folk, all males, all eunuchs, all females, and all nobles, who may rebel, who may plot, who may fight, who may think of fighting, or who may think of rebelling, and every rebel who thinks of rebelling—in this entire land!

---

3. W. F. Edgerton in *Journal of American Oriental Society*, LX (1940), 492, n. 44.

4. K. Sethe, *Die Aechtung feindlicher Fürsten* . . . (*Berlin Abh.*, 1926); G. Posener, *Princes et pays d'Asie et de Nubie* (Brussels, 1940); Posener in *Chronique d'Égypte*, No. 27 (1939), pp. 39 ff.

5. K. Sethe, *Die altägyptischen Pyramidentexte*, I, § 249. See also the Old Kingdom inscribed tablets published by H. Junker, *Gîza*, VIII (Vienna, 1947), 30 ff.

"Every evil word, every evil speech, every evil slander, every evil thought, every evil plot, every evil fight, every evil quarrel, every evil plan, every evil thing, every evil dream, and all evil slumber."

Turning first to the cursed foreigners, we see that the texts dispose rather briefly of the Libyans to the west, and we may assume that they constituted no great peril at the time. To the south of Egypt, several named rulers were condemned, and, insofar as we know any of the geographic localities, it would seem that they were Sudanese rather than Nubians, as the few names which can be located lie south of the Second Cataract. This may have been the *Nehsi* peril against which Sen-Usert III had policed the Second Cataract, a peril arising from the pressure of Negroes to the south.

The Asiatic lists are the most interesting and tantalizing. There are place names about which we may be certain: Byblos, Ascalon, and Achshaph; and a number of names which are highly probable: Uzu opposite Tyre, Jarmuth, Elteqon, Yeshanah, and—most interesting—an Aushamem, which must be Jerusalem. The personal names of the Asiatic rulers in the disguise of Egyptian writing are also tantalizing. When we find that Jerusalem had two rulers, Yaqar-Ammu and Setjanu, we can spot the first as a Semitic name, but we are in doubt about the second. Why should a town have two rulers, and could one of them be Semitic and the other non-Semitic? In the personal names of the rulers of other places, there is a fair proportion of Semitic; the gods Shamash, Hadad, El, and Ammu appear. Other names, however, fail to fall easily into that pattern and probably show the presence of many non-Semites among the rulers of Asiatic city-states. The pattern of Palestine and Syria was already spotted with strange peoples.

In addition to the foreign enemies, the execration texts list eight Egyptians specifically by name and title. The formula in these cases states flatly that these proscribed Egyptians shall die:

"Ameni, born to Hetep and son of Sen-Usert, shall die!"

"Sen-Usert the Younger, called Ketu, the Tutor of Sit-Ipi, (who is the daughter of) Sit-Hat-Hor, and Tutor of Sit-Ipi, (who is the daughter of) Sit-Ameni, and Chancellor of Ii-menet, (who is the daughter of) Sit-Hat-Hor, shall die!"

Of the eight listed Egyptians, four are called tutors or chancellors of Egyptian women. Further, the listed names are those of the Egyptian royal family in the late Twelfth and the Thirteenth Dynasties: Sen-Usert, Amen-em-het, Sehetep-ib, Sebek-hotep, and Sit-Hat-Hor. It seems clear that we have here a record of dissension connected with the royal harem, where fond mothers so often cherished high hopes for their princely sons and where idle chancellors intrigued for advantage in some future government. We know of other harem conspiracies in ancient Egypt, and it may be pure coincidence that they occur at a time when a government is declining: toward the end of the Sixth Dynasty and in the Twentieth Dynasty. Apparently the same dissatisfaction and internal plotting were present at the end of the Middle Kingdom.

If these texts must be later than 1850 B.C., on the basis of the Egyptian names and the handwriting, they must also be earlier than 1730 B.C., when the invading Hyksos established themselves in the Delta. The lists are very comprehensive for the Asiatics, but all these are in Asia, and there was as yet no necessity for cursing Asiatics within Egypt. They may be taken as documents showing the situation of the Middle Kingdom before its thorough collapse and the consequent opening of the frontier to the invading hordes.

The Egyptian state, then, disintegrated over a period of time—perhaps two generations—before the Hyksos invasion and conquest. It is not the function of this book to analyze the chronological complexities of the Second Intermediate Period. It will be sufficient to say that there were synchronous and competing dynasties, even though we cannot be precise about which dynasty was which or about the time limits of each. Some kind of rule continued at Thebes throughout the period, although for a time this rule was subordinated to that of the Hyksos. In addition, the beginning of the period may have seen a native Egyptian dynasty at Xois in the Delta competing with Thebes. Thus the pattern would be Theban dynasties throughout, perhaps a Xoite dynasty at the beginning, and Hyksos dynasties for the latter three-quarters of the period. The Theban rulers held on to Nubia, as evidenced by the presence of their monuments there, but probably lost the Third Cataract trading post at Kerma, since it was destroyed shortly after the Twelfth Dynasty. The Xoite dynasty, originally the expression of the internal breakup of the state, must have disappeared shortly after the Hyksos had established their authority in the Delta.

When we come to the Hyksos themselves, we face a baffling phenomenon: the absence of contemporary written records. If this conquest were as critical to the course of Egyptian culture as we claim, how could Egyptian writings have blanketed it with silence? The answer lies in the nature and purpose of Egyptian texts, which asserted the eternal and not the ephemeral and which presented for eternity those aspects of life which were felt to represent most truly the gods' purposes for Egypt. In that psychology, there was no impulse for writing down the record of a great national humiliation; that record would come when and as the Hyksos were successfully expelled.

There is material for the historian, however, in the later writings and in the physical remains of Hyksos rule.

Our first document is taken from a much later period, the Nineteenth Dynasty, and celebrated an anniversary at the city of Tanis in the northeastern Delta. This city was not only the Egyptian capital under the Nineteenth Dynasty, but it had also been the Hyksos capital in the Second Intermediate Period. Any Nineteenth Dynasty reviving of the place would have to ignore that fact or else make a virtue of it. They chose to do the latter in a characteristic kind of reconciliation, by celebrating the anniversary of the rule of the Egyptian god Seth, who was also recognized as a god of the Asiatics. A stela was erected, showing the king doing honor to Seth, who was garbed in a distinctively Asiatic dress, with a text which introduced the god as an Egyptian ruler: "Year 400, fourth month of the third season, day 4, of the King of Upper and Lower Egypt: Seth, the Great of Strength; the Son of Re: He-of-Ombos, beloved of Re-Har-akhti, so that he exists forever and ever." This stela may be dated to 1330 or 1325 B.C., so that it marked a Tanite beginning of the rule of the god Seth around 1730 or 1725 B.C. By this bland device, the later Egyptians recognized the founding of Tanis as an important city by the Hyksos, without giving the Hyksos themselves any credit for the act.[6]

In the late tradition as given by Josephus, the Hyksos were easterners of unknown race, who entered Egypt suddenly and unexpectedly and conquered the land without a battle; they ruled the land savagely from an armed capital and treated the Egyptian temples with disregard. Josephus writes that Avaris, their capital—the later Tanis—was a walled enclosure of ten square miles, held by a garrison of 240,000 warriors; that, when the Egyptians finally succeeded in driving the Hyksos out of the rest of Egypt, Avaris proved to be too strong for capture, so that there was a treaty by which the Hyksos marched peacefully out of Egypt and built the city of Jerusalem in Judea.[7] This account is tendentious, since Josephus wishes to equate the Hyksos and the Children of Israel; but, after we discount some of the specific elements, there is still a good tradition of conquering easterners of unknown race, build-

6. Sethe in ZÄS, LXV (1930), 85 ff.; Montet in Kêmi, IV (1933), 191 ff.

7. Josephus Contra Apionem, I, 14, in the Loeb Library translation (New York, 1926), I, 190–201.

ing walled camps from which to rule Egypt, setting themselves in opposition to Egyptian religion, and ultimately being forced to retire into Asia.

About a century after the expulsion of the Hyksos, Hat-shepsut gave the invaders passing mention in terms which confirm the tradition that they were rulers unsympathetic to Egyptian culture. "I have restored that which had been ruined. I have raised up (again) that which had formerly gone to pieces, since the Asiatics were in the midst of Avaris of the Delta, and vagabonds were in their midst, overthrowing what had been made, for they ruled without Re, and he did not act by divine command down to (the reign of) my majesty. . . . I have made distant those whom the gods abominate, and earth has carried off their foot (prints)."[8]

The only other document playing upon the Hyksos rule is a folk tale written down in the Nineteenth Dynasty and having its setting in the arrogant domination by the Hyksos king over the Theban ruler. "Distress was in the town of the Asiatics(?), for Prince Apophis was in Avaris, and the entire land was subject to him with their dues. . . . And King Apophis made him Seth as lord, and he would not serve any god who is in the land [except] Seth." The manuscript goes on to tell how this Hyksos king Apophis injured the dignity of the tributary pharaoh at Thebes by sending him an arrogant and insulting message that the noise from the hippopotamus pool in Thebes was disturbing to Apophis four hundred miles away in the Delta. Unfortunately the story breaks off in the middle of a sentence, so that we do not know how the Theban king extricated himself from this embarrassment. However, the tradition of an irreligious and overpowering foreign rule bears out what we know from other sources.[9]

The Asiatic penetration of the Delta at this time was not like that in the First Intermediate Period, a trickle of Bedouin and poorly equipped easterners, who were grateful for the opportunity to settle on fertile soil and who were quickly assimilated into Egyptian culture. It had been possible to brush aside that earlier infiltration. This, however, was an invasion in force for the purpose of rule, and it was not basically respectful of the higher Egyptian culture. This was barbarian domination. These invaders had conquered the Egyptians by superior force, they laid the subject land under an exacted tribute, they lived apart in fortified camps, they neglected the old temples of the gods,

8. A. H. Gardiner in *JEA*, XXXII (1946), 43 ff. The sentence about the "divine command" means that the god Re refused to rule Egypt until Hat-shepsut's time.

9. Erman, *LAE*, pp. 165 ff.

and they introduced a god of their own, one whom the Egyptians identified with their own semi-apostate god Seth. The Hyksos showed no tendency to reach out hungrily for Egyptian civilization; they let shadow pharaohs continue at Thebes instead of eliminating Egyptian rulers and taking over the entire divine rule at Avaris-Tanis. Their interest was regular tribute from the Egyptians rather than incorporation into the native culture. Arrogance of this kind was the more brutal to the once superior Egyptian.

On the physical side, we know a good deal about the Hyksos. Some of their fortified camps have survived in Egypt and Asia, great rectangular enclosures of beaten earth. The rectangle at Tell el-Yahudiyeh in the southern Delta is 400 yards on a side, with an embankment 15 to 20 yards high; that at Hazor in north Galilee is about 500 by 1,000 yards; and a magnificent camp at Qatna in northern Syria is about 1,000 yards on a side. Many smaller ones have been identified in Palestine and Syria, and the type of structure is said to be discernible in Iran and in the Caucasus.

In addition to the Hyksos camps and the horse and chariot, a number of other elements are associated with this people: certain kinds of pins and jewelry, weapons and body armor, a distinctive type of pottery, and certain elements of design.[10] On the basis of the physical evidence archeologists have distinguished an earlier and a later Hyksos type—the earlier more foreign in nature, the later having strong ties to the Hurrian culture in northern Mesopotamia. In any case, we may be sure that the conquering horde which invaded Egypt was not composed of pure strains from some original home beyond the Caucasus. The movement southward was undoubtedly slow and picked up many restless or displaced elements in hither Asia. By the time the Hyksos entered Egypt, they must have included few of the original newcomers, but many Hurrians and Semites and other displaced persons from Syria and Palestine. The result was that their culture and those Hyksos names known to us show considerable mixture of various ethnic elements.

It would be unfair to leave the impression that the Hyksos were

10. In H. E. Winlock's *The Rise and Fall of the Middle Kingdom at Thebes* (New York, 1947), the author devotes his final chapter to "Hyksos importations into Egypt." One concedes readily the introduction of the elements of power, that is, the horse and chariot, body armor, many of the weapons, and an interest in metallurgy. When, however, the author suggests that the Hyksos may also have brought in the *shaduf* water sweep, the vertical loom, humped cattle, cattle branding, the lyre and the lute, etc., he ruins an otherwise good case by overstatement. Simply because we do not know the origin of some of the factors in the Egyptian culture we should not credit them to an invading people of unknown source or type and of an obviously warlike and unsettled aspect. What we knew about the Hyksos eleven years ago was summarized by R. M. Engberg, *The Hyksos Reconsidered* (SAOC, 18 [Chicago, 1939]).

uncouth savages, totally unresponsive to the civilizations of the countries of their conquest. If they formed a composite of various peoples through whose countries they had driven their chariots, they must have included many who had had contacts with Egyptian and Mesopotamian cultures. They did not scorn all the ways of Egypt, nor were they hopelessly out of place in their new setting. Commerce was not completely halted. A type of jar associated with the Hyksos appears as far south as the Third Cataract and as far north as Cyprus. The name of one of the Hyksos kings, Khayan, has been found on monuments at Gebelein in southern Egypt, at Gezer in Palestine, on a granite lion which turned up in Baghdad, on an alabaster jar lid found at Knossos in Crete, and on a cylinder seal in Athens. These monuments are all properly inscribed in Egyptian hieroglyphic. Indeed, there may have been a strong commercial element among the later Hyksos: in the Second Intermediate Period a basic standard weight disappears in Egypt, to be replaced by another weight standard, with probable Mesopotamian connections.[11] Nor did the arts suffer an eclipse in this period, as some of the important scientific documents were carefully copied while the Hyksos were in the land.[12]

However, the essential factors in the Hyksos rule of Egypt were that this land was for the first time conquered and dominated by foreigners and that these foreigners appeared to the Egyptians to be impious and unsympathetic barbarians, who "ruled without Re." That happy sense of security from attack which had been the cornerstone of the Egyptian system had been fractured; Egypt was not so isolated that she could afford to be tolerant and carefree. The distresses of the First Intermediate Period had arisen out of internal factors and could be remedied without altering the essential optimism. The present distresses struck a vital blow into the native self-confidence, the faith that the gods had given Egypt—and Egypt alone—the good life unto eternity. If foreign barbarians who cared nothing for the gods of the land could so humiliate Egypt, what secure foundation did life still offer?

11. A. S. Hemmy in *JEA*, XXIII (1937), 56.

12. We omit here discussion of the Hyksos in Palestine and Syria, although this note might point out that there were important changes as a result of their incursion. The archeology of Palestine for this period shows destruction, rebuilding, and some shifting of concentration. For example, the Judean hills had been sparsely populated in earlier times; the Hyksos placed towns of respectable size in the hills. At the southwest corner of Palestine the town of "old Gaza" at Tell el-Ajjul came into prominence; south of the Sea of Galilee the town of Khirbet Kerak was destroyed. In Phoenicia, Byblos suffered a severe slump, while Ugarit shifted its intimate relations from Egypt to Cyprus and the Mycenean area. Wherever we can control the evidence it is clear that the Hyksos thoroughly upset former conditions in Syria-Palestine.

Frustrated power also produces long-lasting hatred, and the Hyksos had a number of fighting advantages over the Egyptians. The speed and striking power of the horse and chariot gave them the most obvious superiority, but their concentration in fortified camps made them practically invulnerable to an attacker with lesser weapons. It has been estimated that their enclosure at Tell el-Yahudiyeh could maintain ten thousand men with their horses and chariots, and this would be a very large force for that day. If we concede to the Hyksos the further advantages of body armor and of new types of sword and dagger, their sudden success becomes the more credible. Perhaps as important as the horse and chariot was the introduction of the composite bow, built up of layers of wood, sinew, and horn glued together. This would have a far greater striking distance and penetration than the simple little bows in Egypt before this time. The proud superiority of Egypt over all her previous opponents was very rudely dashed to the ground, with important consequences to the Egyptian spirit.

Driven by a new chauvinism for liberation and revenge, the Egyptians paid their tribute to their Hyksos masters but also acquired and learned to use the new weapons. Probably this took about a century, down to about 1600 B.C. Finally they felt able to test their powers against their overlords. The war for liberation started from the old capital at Thebes, where a dynasty had been permitted to exist tributary to the Hyksos. It is possible that Thebes made an alliance with the important town of Hermopolis in Middle Egypt. At least, such an assumption would explain the presence in the names of the Theban royal family in the Seventeenth and Eighteenth Dynasties of the elements Thut- and Ah-, since Hermopolis was the center of the moon-cult (Ah) and the moon-god (Thoth).

The earliest document on the war for liberation may be the mummy of a King Seqnen-Re of the Seventeenth Dynasty, who clearly died violently and perhaps in battle. The head of this mummy shows wounds from arrows, from a sword or dagger, and a crushing blow from a mace. The temptation to ascribe his death to defeat in a battle against the Hyksos is obvious, although proof is completely lacking.[13]

At the very end of this period a Theban ruler by the name of Kamose rebelled against the truce which divided Egypt between him and the Hyksos king and which made him the tribute-paying partner in the

13. J. H. Breasted, *The Edwin Smith Surgical Papyrus* (*OIP*, Vol. III [Chicago, 1930]), Vol. I, Fig. 5.

alliance. Our chief text on this outbreak of fighting comes from a schoolboy's copy of a royal inscription, and the poor boy was not a skilled copyist.[14] The inscription uses a literary device characteristic of the Empire texts: a conference at the Egyptian court, in which the divine wisdom and daring of Pharaoh are set in contrast to the uninspired caution of his followers. Despite this propagandizing twist, the document must be treated with respect as a historical source.

"His majesty spoke in his palace to the council of nobles who were in his retinue: 'Let me understand what this strength of mine is for! (One) prince is in Avaris, another is in Ethiopia, and (here) I sit associated with an Asiatic and a Negro! Each man has his slice of this Egypt, dividing up the land with me. . . . No man can settle down, when despoiled by the taxes of the Asiatics. I will grapple with him, that I may rip open his belly! My wish is to save Egypt and to smite(?) the Asiatics!'"

But the nobles urged that the situation was not so bad: the Hyksos lines were overextended, whereas "we are at ease in our (part of) Egypt." Under the truce, the people of Upper Egypt were permitted to pasture their cattle in the Delta, to plow fields in the north, and to secure emmer wheat for pig fodder. Pharaoh should fight only if attacked: "He holds the land of the Asiatics; we hold Egypt. Should some one come and act (against us?), then we shall act against him."

Ka-mose indignantly rejected this timid advice, apparently asking—the context is broken—why he should respect the Asiatics and announcing his intention of sailing north to launch the attack as "the protector of Egypt." Carrying "the command of Amon," he engaged a Hyksos vassal in Middle Egypt, just north of Hermopolis. "I broke down his walls, I killed his people, and I made his wife come down to the riverbank. My soldiers were as lions with their loot, having serfs, cattle, milk, fat, and honey, dividing up their property, their hearts gay." The war for revenge was successfully launched. The text is broken off abruptly, and we must assume that the victories over the invaders were gained only in Middle Egypt, perhaps only against Egyptian vassal princes under the Hyksos. Nevertheless, the first taste of triumph with the new weapons must have been sweet. Complete victory was soon to come.

It is an ironical twist of history that we have no official source on the expulsion of the Hyksos from Egypt and that our best document is the

14. Carnarvon Tablet I; Erman, *LAE*, pp. 52 ff. Fragments of the original stela have been found at Karnak; cf. P. Lacau in *ASAE*, XXXIX (1939), 245 ff.

elliptical autobiography of a modest participant in the war, a ship's captain. A citizen of el-Kab in Upper Egypt, Ah-mose, the son of the woman Eben, tells of a series of campaigns in Egypt and then, after the fall of Avaris, of the follow-up into Palestine. After three campaigns Avaris fell. The war then shifted into Asia, and the town of Sharuhen in southwestern Palestine was besieged in three successive years before it fell. Apparently the central core of Hyksos had fallen back to this base in the part of Asia nearest Egypt. The ship's captain was rewarded with "the gold of valor," with something like seventy acres of land in his own home district, and with nineteen slaves.[15]

At last Egypt was free of the arrogant invader. Might she not resume the old easygoing life?

15. Breasted, *ARE*, II, §§ 1 ff. Ah-mose lists his nineteen "male and female slaves of the loot." Most of the names are good Egyptian, but there appear a Pa-Aam, "the Asiatic," and two Semites, Ishtar-ummi, "Ishtar Is My Mother," and Tꜥamutj, a feminine name similar to Amos.

VIII

FAR FRONTIERS

Earlier Dynasty 18 (about 1550–1375 B.C.)

IT TOOK about a century of the Eighteenth Dynasty before the Egyptians themselves answered the question as to whether they would return to the fat and cheerful isolation of earlier times. Perhaps they were not clearly aware that the question was posed to them, although, as we shall see, there was a strong difference of opinion about policy around 1500 B.C. In official terms, however, Egypt never changed to the new; she always reverted to the *maʿat* which had been given by the gods at the beginning. Any national policy which was different was presented as if belonging to that order which had controlled Egypt from the creation.

In the external manifestations of culture, the Eighteenth Dynasty resumed where the Twelfth had left off—or perhaps one should say that there had been no cultural break in the Second Intermediate Period. Architecture and art repeated the forms and themes of earlier times. The small peripteral chapel was derived from earlier models, and Hatshepsut's terraced temple was adapted from the neighboring temple of Mentu-hotep of the Eleventh Dynasty (Fig. 19*b*). The eye detects no major differences between sculptured scenes of the Twelfth Dynasty and those of the early Eighteenth. In literature a slight vulgarization is felt in the inscription of Ka-mose which we have just mentioned, but most of the texts were in good "Middle Egyptian," following the classical models faithfully and with success. The tombs of the nobles resumed the theme of the good, gay life and its extension into the next world. In these aspects no change of essential is visible.

We can, however, see one new factor from the beginning of the Eighteenth Dynasty. The old placid introspection and concentration on matters within the Nile Valley had been replaced by a vision of effective frontiers far away in Asia and Africa. It was no longer enough to exhibit to foreign countries the superiority of Egyptian culture and thus to harvest a favorable trade. Those foreigners were no longer subjects to be patronized for their own good and for the good of Egypt; they had shown themselves to be "rebellious." Pharaoh must take the time to teach them effective lessons of discipline in their own lands.

Ah-mose I drove the Hyksos out of Egypt. In a quarry there is an inscription dated in his twenty-second year, with a scene showing a large block of stone being dragged by six humped oxen. The text says: "The stone was dragged by cattle which his [majesty?] carried off [from] throughout the lands of the Fenkhu," who were probably Phoenicians.[1] Raids into Palestine alone were no longer sufficient, although they were vigorous enough there. Tell el-Ajjul, Beth-Shemesh, Shiloh, and Beth-Zur all suffered destruction in the sixteenth century B.C. But the "rebels" were not only in Palestine. They stretched as far north as Naharin, the region around the great bend of the Euphrates in northern Syria. Well before 1500 B.C., the pharaoh Thut-mose I campaigned up to Naharin and set up a stela of triumph on the banks of the Euphrates River.[2] Egypt's eyes were now effectively turned abroad.

There is a minor but significant phenomenon in the texts of the Eighteenth Dynasty. At other periods the military forces were called "the army of his majesty" or "the army division of (the god) Amon" or similar names, a concession of authority to a divine leader. Only in this first stretch of concerted vigor do the Egyptian texts speak of "our army," with a sense of sharing in a common national adventure.[3] The desire for revenge, the triumph of liberation, the lust for loot, and the discovery of power combined to make the period uniquely nationalistic and patriotic. This was not simply pharaoh's war; every active citizen of Egypt shared in this common enterprise.

Against whom? We cannot be sure that the Asiatics whom they attacked in Palestine and Syria were demonstrably the same as those who had conquered and humiliated Egypt. But the texts give some indication that the revenge motif lasted for a long time. On Thut-mose III's obelisk which now stands in Central Park, New York, a monument

1. Breasted, *ARE*, II, § 27.
2. *Ibid.*, II, §§ 73, 478.
3. *Ibid.*, II, § 39, n. *d*, to which add the instance in *ibid.*, II, § 427.

erected more than a century after the expulsion of the Hyksos, pharaoh describes himself as "the smiter of the rulers of foreign countries who had attacked him."[4] In discussing the story of Si-nuhe we saw that the phrase, "rulers of foreign countries," *hikau khasut*, was the etymological source of the term Hyksos.[5] In like manner, Amen-hotep II boasted that "no one could draw his bow among his own army, among the *hikau khasut*, or among the princes of Retenu (Palestine-Syria)."[6] Why should he make a distinction between two kinds of Asiatics, unless one of them embraced those old conquerors of Egypt who had themselves introduced the composite bow into the Near East?

When, somewhere around 1470 B.C., under Thut-mose III, a consistent series of military campaigns was inaugurated to establish and hold the Egyptian Empire in Asia, the focus of hostility was directed against the town of Kadesh on the Orontes, as the leader of opposition to pharaoh. Where the central plain between the Lebanon and Anti-Lebanon debouches into the broad stretches of north Syria, Kadesh stood in command. It had a Hyksos earthen fortification wall. Close by it was Tell es-Sufinet Nuh, with an even greater Hyksos camp, and only 35 miles away was Qatna, with the greatest camp of all. There is evidence that the Egyptians were not content to drive the Hyksos out of Egypt but felt compelled to pursue them with vindictive fury for more than a century. If so, the easy-going isolationism was ended.[7]

However, Egypt did not plunge directly into the full career of empire building. It took three full generations to effect the work of reconstruction after the Hyksos were expelled. The military campaigns into Asia under Ah-mose I, Amen-hotep I, Thut-mose I and II were in the nature of punitive raids, rather than conquering campaigns, on no regular or systematic pattern; there was as yet no attempt to organize Asia into a controlled province. The military activity into Nubia and the Sudan may have been more consistent, since the Middle Kingdom had held that territory and reconstruction would involve rewinning the area for southern commerce and for the gold mines. Thut-mose I penetrated south of the Third Cataract, and we may properly speak of an African empire before the Asiatic empire was organized under Thut-mose III.[8]

4. *Ibid.*, II, § 636.

5. P. 135, above.   6. Breasted, *ARE*, II, § 792.

7. This we believe, although we are unable to accept Sethe's restoration (*ZAS*, XLVII [1910], 74 ff.) of the beginning of Thut-mose III's annals as referring specifically to the Hyksos rule in Egypt, later continued as a "revolt" in Asia. All the critical elements for Sethe's argument lie in the lacunae of the text.

8. Breasted, *ARE*, II, §§ 67 ff.

Undoubtedly the main effort of the state had to be internal at first. Under the Hyksos the Theban ruler had been a tributary prince holding only the southern part of the land. Now a full government for the Two Lands had to be reinstituted, offices and services re-established, and the government machinery with regard to agriculture, irrigation, taxes, shipping, foreign commerce, etc., brought back into play. A commercial fleet supported by (or doubling as) a navy had to make working contacts with Asiatic and Mediterranean towns which were ruled by strange new people. The civil and religious bureaucracy of Egypt had to be constructed and trained. Most important from the Egyptian point of view, the gods had to be propitiated by buildings and new services.

Of the Hyksos in Egypt, Hat-shepsut said: "They ruled without Re, and he did not act by divine command down to (the reign of) my majesty."[9] The direction of the affairs of the nation by the gods was a serious matter in Egypt. The relation was mutual: if the ruler failed to consult the god, the god would not give orders for the state. For this purpose of consultation, the pharaoh was the effective high priest of all the gods. As he himself was a god, he was the proper intermediary between gods and mortals. For the period before the Eighteenth Dynasty, we do not know the normal and accepted means by which pharaoh ascertained the will of the gods. It is possible that he sought spiritual communion with them in any way that a god might commune with other gods and then announced his divine word as being the gods' directive for the nation. Increasingly through the Empire we find recognized machinery for receiving the divine command. A god might speak in a dream, as when Thut-mose IV received the order to clear the Sphinx.[10] A god might volunteer his command by a visible miracle, as when Thut-mose III was picked out as the future pharaoh.[11] The most common means was consultation of the deity by the pharaoh, as the god was enshrined in his temple or went forth in his portable shrine and was graciously pleased to articulate his will by an oracle. Thus Amon-Re of Karnak spoke from his sanctum in the temple and directed Hat-shepsut to undertake the commercial exploration of the land of Punt. "The majesty of the palace made petition at the stairs of the Lord of the Gods. A command was heard from the Great Throne, an oracle of the god himself, to search out ways to Punt, to explore the roads to the terraces of myrrh." Then follows the speech of

9. Above, p. 160.
10. Breasted, *ARE*, II, § 815.   11. *Ibid.*, II, §§ 138 ff.

the god in direct quotation.[12] We moderns would like to know just what took place in the holy-of-holies when the pharaoh, perhaps attended only by the High Priest of Amon, received the god's command. Texts of the end of the Empire tell us of a visible sign by the god, a "nodding" for an affirmative response and lack of motion or a "recoiling" for a negative response.[13] Presumably, then, a yes-or-no proposition was addressed to the god's statue, or a series of propositions was laid before the figure, so that the god might give a visible sign of selection. The ancient did not have our agnostic curiosity; he was able to accept the miracle as the just means whereby the gods might indicate their pleasure.

The evidence is that, from the Eighteenth Dynasty on, the gods directed the affairs of Egypt more actively. It is possible that this evidence may be misleading, in that we lack the comparable material from earlier times. However, there is a physical phenomenon which corroborates our suggestion: the temples of the gods became larger and more important under the Empire, and this increased size began before the full tide of empire under Thut-mose III. The blow to national confidence resulting from the Hyksos domination may have brought an uncertainty, in which Egypt turned more directly to her gods to ask for guidance. If so, we have the answer to the greatly increased power of the gods and of their priesthoods.

Since the bulk of our evidence comes from Upper Egypt, we know more about the advance of Amon than any other god. However, this is not entirely misleading, since those texts which deal with the temples of Egypt as a whole show clearly the enormous dominance of Amon-Re of Karnak. When the Theban dynasty emerged from the Second Intermediate Period as the liberators of Egypt from impious oppression, the Theban god emerged as clearly the "King of the Gods." He was the "Hidden One" by name, the invisible god of air, who might be everywhere and thus easily became the god of far-flung empire and the universal deity when the fortunes of the Empire carried him abroad. With his temple looming up close to the palace, he was the most immediate partner of the pharaoh as a ruling god of Egypt. As time went on Amon's importance relative to the throne was to provoke extreme political problems of competition. In earthly terms, this would be a struggle for power between the High Priest of Amon and any of a

12. *Ibid.*, II, § 285.
13. J. Černý in *BIFAO*, XXXV (1935), 41 ff.

series of antagonists: high priests of other gods, the vizier, the head of the army—and ultimately the pharaoh himself.

In practice this struggle was not along clearly drawn lines because of the overlapping and interlocking of offices. It was certainly no competition for power between Church and State in modern terms. For the increasing problems of government in an expanding state, Egypt built up an elaborate officialdom and bureaucracy, in which the civil and ecclesiastical were joined together through the persons of the pharaoh and of the highest officials. This was a sacred state, in which the civil was unthinkable without the sanction of the ecclesiastical.

In a nation with a low literacy rate, where reading and writing are technical accomplishments of the civil or religious government, the resource of qualified functionaries is relatively small and normally will remain within certain families of the accepted aristocracy. Even when the state is expanding rapidly and there is a positive demand for more officials, experience at the top levels is a rare faculty, so that there will be a tendency to retain the highest positions within a relatively small group. This was so in the Egyptian Empire.

The highest officials of the land under the pharaoh were the High Priest of Amon of Karnak, the Vizier for Upper Egypt, the Vizier for Lower Egypt, and the "King's Son of Kush" or Viceroy for Ethiopia.[14] The last named position included three responsibilities: the delegated rule of the African Empire; the responsibility for gold mines of Nubia; and the command of the army in Africa, pharaoh having the responsible leadership for pushing the Empire into Asia. This viceroyship was often a training ground for the crown prince.

The retention of position within a few trusted families and the interlocking of the highest offices may be illustrated with two or three examples. Hat-shepsut's Vizier for Upper Egypt, Hapu-seneb, had been preceded in that office by his grandfather; but Hapu-seneb was also High Priest of Amon, as his great-grandfather had been before him. Rekh-mi-Re, Thut-mose III's Vizier for Upper Egypt, followed his paternal uncle and his grandfather in that office. A certain Thut-mose held the Vizierate for Lower Egypt, and his son Ptah-mose became High Priest of Ptah at Memphis.[15]

Sometimes we find an official who prefers to be a sort of Pooh-Bah,

14. A. Weil, *Die Veziere des Pharaonenreiches* (Strassburg, 1908); G. Lefebvre, *Histoire des Grands Prêtres d'Amon de Karnak jusqu'à la XXIe Dynastie* (Paris, 1929); G. A. Reisner in *JEA*, VI (1920), 28 ff., 73 ff.

15. R. Anthes in *ZÄS*, LXXII (1936), 60 ff.

the "Lord High Everything Else." Such a person was the favorite of Hat-shepsut, Sen-Mut (Fig. 19a), who gathered to himself extraordinary power, without holding one of the four highest offices. He was "Hereditary Prince and Count, Sealbearer of the King of Lower Egypt, Sole Companion, Steward of Amon"; Overseer of the Fields, the Garden, the Cows, the Serfs, the Peasant-Farmers, and the Granaries of Amon; Prophet of Amon; Prophet of Amon's sacred barque; Chief Prophet of Montu in Hermonthis; Spokesman of the Shrine of Geb; Headman in the House of the White Crown; Controller of the Broad Hall in the House of the Official; Steward of the King; Overseer of the Royal Residence; Controller of Every Divine Craft; Steward of the Princess Nefru-Re; Great Father-Tutor of the Princess Nefru-Re; Controller of All Construction Work of the King in Karnak, Hermonthis, Deir el-Bahri, the Temple of Mut at Karnak, and Luxor; and "a superior of superiors, an overseer of overseers of construction works."[16]

The dogma that the king alone was the state remained the formal expression, but the delegation of office to responsible officials was an absolute necessity in a state of such complexity. We know a good deal about the functions and authority of the Vizier for Upper Egypt from the texts of Rekh-mi-Re and of some of the other viziers of the period. We need not go into his duties and his powers here, beyond noting that he reported daily and directly to pharaoh, that he was the chief magistrate of the land, that he was responsible for taxes from Egypt and "tribute" from foreign countries, that he oversaw the public works and the crafts of the nation, etc.[17] Pharaoh rightly called him "the supporting post of the entire land." There is, however, one comment to be made in connection with his chief magistracy. As far as we have evidence, the law which he dispensed was not codified and written law, to which he could refer as the impersonal principle for the dispensing of justice. We have had to abandon the idea that forty scrolls of the law lay before the vizier in his hall of justice; it now appears that these were forty leather thongs which were the symbols of his disciplinary authority.[18] If so, we have no evidence of written codes of law for at least 750 more years in Egypt, until the time of Bak-en-renef of the Twenty-Fourth Dynasty. What the vizier dispensed was customary law, phrased as the commanding word of pharaoh and arising out of

16. K. Sethe, *Urkunden der 18. Dynastie* (*Urk.*, IV [Leipzig, 1906]), pp. 395–417; Breasted, *ARE*, II, §§ 345–68.

17. N. de G. Davies, *The Tomb of Rekh-mi-Re at Thebes* (New York, 1943), I, 88–94; Breasted, *ARE*, II, §§ 671 ff. Cf. our Fig. 21b.

18. Davies, *op. cit.*, pp. 31 f.

pharaoh's three divine qualities of *Hu*, *Sia*, and *Maʿat*, Authority, Perception, and Justice.[19] Of course there were royal ordinances to fit specific instances, and of course there were precedents out of past judication;[20] but there was nothing in Egypt corresponding to the Mesopotamian codes, detailed written law, publicly displayed as the symbol of impersonal justice. In Egypt, the law was personally derived from the god-king and was tailored as justice and equity to the individual appellant.

For that reason, a special charge was laid upon the vizier to be scrupulously fair in dispensing justice. "The abomination of the god is a show of partiality. So this is the instruction; thou shalt act accordingly: thou shalt look upon him whom thou knowest like him whom thou dost not know, upon him who is close to thy person like him who is distant from thy house. As for the official who acts thus, he will flourish here in this office."[21] The vizier might not expect to "show consideration for nobles and officials but make serfs out of all (the rest of) the people," because, "as for the official who is in public view, wind and water make report on all that he does, so that his acts cannot be unknown."[22] The authority of the vizier was very great, and he must inspire immediate and unquestioned respect—called "fear" in the texts —but his goal must be justice, rather than the search for arbitrary authority. "Inspire the fear of thyself, so that men may fear thee. The (real) official is an official of whom men are afraid, because the (proper) dread of the official is that he should do justice. But if a man (simply) inspires fear of himself a million times, there is something wrong with him in the opinion of the people, and they do not say: 'Well, he *is* a man!' "[23] What was needed for this very personal justice was the proper blend of authority and sympathy—what we call paternalism.

With such a delegation of authority within Egypt, the pharaoh was free to lead his armies out of Egypt and establish an empire. However, Egypt did not give herself up to empire-building and empire-holding without a contest to maintain the old isolationist complacency. The first generations of the Eighteenth Dynasty carried on the earlier tra-

19. H. Frankfort *et al.*, *The Intellectual Adventure of Ancient Man* (Chicago, 1946), pp. 83 f.

20. Davies, *op. cit.*, p. 88.

21. Davies, *op. cit.*, p. 87; Breasted, *ARE*, II, § 668.

22. Davies, *op. cit.*, p. 86; Breasted, *ARE*, II, § 667.

23. Davies, *op. cit.*, p. 87; Breasted, *ARE*, II, § 669.

dition of punitive raids into Asia rather than administrative incorporation of conquered territory. Then came a struggle of personalities,
which was also a struggle of principles and policies. The evidence on
the period known as "the feud of the Thutmosids" is complicated and
by no means clear, but perhaps we can be content with one phase of
the contest for power. Thut-mose III must have been quite young
when he succeeded to the throne at the death of his father. His later
career shows him as a man of energy and administrative ability. Yet for
the first twenty-two years of his reign he was in eclipse, and the rule
was usurped by his remarkable aunt and stepmother Hat-shepsut. She
gained such power that her monuments ceased designating her as the
"Great King's Wife" and gave her all the formal titles and attributes
of a king. The struggle for the rule of Egypt then centered in this
rivalry between Hat-shepsut and Thut-mose III, with the latter held
firmly in control until his abrupt emergence as the sole power at the
end of his twenty-second regnal year.[24]

The reigns of Hat-shepsut and of Thut-mose III contrast strongly
in the activities of the state. She records no military campaigns or conquests; he became the great conqueror and organizer of empire. Her
pride was in the internal development of Egypt and in commercial
enterprise; his pride was in the external expansion of Egypt and in military enterprise. This was a conflict between the older concept of the
Egyptian state, an isolated and superior culture, which needed to express no major concern about other countries because no other country presented an important challenge to Egypt, and the new concept
of the Egyptian state, a culture which felt obliged to assert its superiority by capturing and holding foreign territory. Through the time of
Hat-shepsut, the foreign contacts had been exploited through commercial and cultural penetration, to the material advantage of both
parties. Thut-mose III was to introduce a formal and consistent policy
of military and political imperialism, in order to gain security at home
by pushing Egypt's effective frontier far beyond her geographic borders and in order to control foreign commerce by her own army and
navy. The formal introduction of imperialism ended Egypt's formal
isolationism, had a profound effect upon Egyptian psychology, and
ultimately brought the characteristic Egyptian culture to an end.[25]

24. W. F. Edgerton, *The Thutmosid Succession* (*SAOC*, 8 [Chicago, 1933]), where
the antecedent literature, with divergent interpretation of the data, is cited.

25. There are major exceptions to the sharp policy line as here drawn. Egypt had
had military and political imperialism before this, to a lesser degree geographically and
functionally. The Sinai mines had been developed with the use of the military as early

Our theory then is that there was a choice to be made and that two different parties chose differently, Hat-shepsut's faction in terms of the lesser effort of earlier times and Thut-mose III's faction in terms of a new and major international venture. The three generations which had passed since the expulsion of the Hyksos had seen a great deal of military effort in Africa and in Asia, particularly in the raids of Ah-mose I and Thut-mose I, sporadic campaigns which served notice on the Asiatics and Africans that Egypt should be inviolable. Hat-shepsut seems to make a break with this somewhat spasmodic activity by eschewing military endeavor and concentrating on peaceful goals. Thut-mose III rejected the pattern of the past by making military activity regular and purposeful.

We do not have sufficient data to discuss the composition of the two parties. One assumes that the royal family was divided, with Hat-shepsut at first dominant over Thut-mose III, who was both young and born to a queen of lesser lineage, that the army—such as it was at this time—was in favor of the imperial effort, and that the civil service was in favor of Hat-shepsut's domestic program. The other important political factor in Egypt would be the great priesthoods. Thut-mose III tells us that he was chosen in his boyhood to be the future pharaoh by the god Amon himself,[26] so that the predisposition of that priesthood toward the future imperialist is probable. We know nothing of the sympathies of the priesthoods of other gods. However, it may be significant that Hat-shepsut was emphatic in her statement that she was the first to restore the Egyptian temples after the Hyksos[27] and that she built greatly to the glory of Amon. This must have been an effort on her part to win over the priesthoods to her party. It may also be significant that Hat-shepsut's vizier, Hapu-seneb, was also the High Priest of Amon, thereby holding together the civil bureaucracy and the priesthood.

Hat-shepsut gave Egypt internal glories instead of external victory. She built her beautiful Deir el-Bahri temple and its little valley temple, as well as small structures at Medinet Habu and at the Second Cataract.

---

as the First Dynasty. The Middle Kingdom had reached out for the western oases and for an African empire as far as the Third Cataract. There had been punitive raids into Asia at least as early as the Sixth Dynasty. None of these efforts attempted to organize and control as large and as populated a territory as that won by Thut-mose III. The difference in effort made this far more influential.

26. Breasted, *ARE,* II, §§ 131 ff.

27. In the inscription of the Speos Artemidos; A. H. *Gardiner* in *JEA,* XXXII (1946), 43 ff.

She brought huge obelisks from the Assuan quarries and erected them in the Temple of Amon at Karnak; she built Amon a shrine and the Eighth Pylon at Karnak. In the hills west of Thebes two tombs were cut for her. Such public works contrasted with the smaller amount of building before her day; she must have maintained a considerable draft of labor from the provinces. It is highly significant that her favorite minister, Sen-Mut, was her Minister of Public Works and architect.

In foreign affairs she repeated the traditional pattern from the past. Her building at the Second Cataract was in relation to the familiar desire for gold from the south, and she exploited the Sinai mines. The foreign enterprise of which she was proudest was a commercial expedition by sea to the land of Punt, the land of incense to the south, perhaps chiefly in the Somaliland area, but also Arabia Felix.[28] Her temple at Deir el-Bahri gives major space to the record of the five large vessels which sailed away with the manufactured products of civilized Egypt, jewelry, tools, and weapons, and which returned with small cattle, apes, incense trees, ivory, myrrh, and rare woods. The scene in the land of Punt is shown in forceful detail, with a nice touch of humor. The people of Punt are flatteringly amazed at the boldness of the Egyptian sailors: "How did you reach here, this country unknown to men? Did you come down on the ways of heaven, or did you travel by land or sea? How happy is God's Land (Punt), which you (now) tread like Re!" The Prince of Punt is accompanied by his wife, depicted as an enormous, fleshy creature, followed by a meek little donkey, over which is the laconic text: "the ass which carries his wife."[29]

There had been expeditions to Punt before this, and there would be such in the future. The unusual prominence given to this venture has meaning as an expression of policy, that Egypt should cultivate more intensively the friends she already had and let the unfriendly Asiatics suffer from their own stubborn hostility because Egypt would not deal with them. Hat-shepsut was demonstrating the feasibility of the old pacific and tolerant policy of the past.

Her end came abruptly, after she had been "king" for seventeen years. We do not know precisely what happened. Perhaps Hat-shepsut died a natural death, and her party collapsed when it was without her backing. Perhaps she was put out of the way by a coup d'état. At any rate, the evidence of the vindictive fury of Thut-mose III is clear. His

28. M. Hilzheimer in ZÄS, LXVIII (1932), 112 ff.

29. Breasted, ARE, II §§ 257-58; Breasted, Geschichte Aegyptens (Zürich, 1936), Figs. 223-24.

partisans, for example, marched into the Deir el-Bahri temple, knocked down the statues of Hat-shepsut, and sent them tumbling in bits into a near-by quarry (Fig. 18a). The favored architect Sen-Mut also disappeared from history. He had taken advantage of his position to smuggle figures of himself into Hat-shepsut's temple, reliefs of himself at prayer, which were so located as to be hidden behind opened doors. These were hacked out by the newly triumphant party. A tomb which Sen-Mut had skilfully inserted under the Deir el-Bahri temple was desecrated and blocked up. The disappearance of the party of peace was abrupt and violent.[30]

Almost immediately Thut-mose III set forth to defeat those rebellious to Egypt and to extend the frontiers of the land. If he seized sole power around the first of February, 1468 B.C., seventy-five days later, about the middle of April, he had assembled an army and was leading it out of Egypt along the Suez frontier. "His majesty made no delay in proceeding to the land of Djahi (Palestine-Syria), to kill the treacherous ones who were in it and to give things to those who were loyal to him."[31]

There was definitely a "rebellion" in Asia, from the Egyptian standpoint. We can only speculate as to whether Hat-shepsut's death was the occasion for Asiatic alliance against Egypt, whether this alliance was the cause of her downfall, or whether the timing was coincidental. At any rate, the Prince of Kadesh on the Orontes had come down to Megiddo in Palestine and had there gathered three hundred and thirty princelings, "every one of them having his own army," to hold the Megiddo pass against pharaoh.[32] The number of allied princes shows the extraordinary fragmentation of Palestine-Syria. These could be only rulers of little city-states, with "armies" consisting of little more than a guard. It would be impossible to deploy any very large army on the plain of Megiddo. As the outcome of the battle showed, the Asiatic alliance was not very effective, and we may guess that the "princes" were too independent to form a single, unified army.

The great commercial road which was the nerve center of Palestine-

30. H. E. Winlock, *Excavations at Deir el Bahri. 1911–1931* (New York, 1942), pp. 105–6, 142–53, 158–59.

31. R. Mond and O. H. Myers, *The Temples of Armant. A Preliminary Survey* (London, 1940), Pl. CIII, pp. 182 ff. On the chronology, cf. p. 183, n. *b*.

32. In addition to the Armant source of the last note, there are (*a*) the "Annals" of Thut-mose III in the Temple of Karnak—Breasted, *ARE*, II, §§ 391 ff.; H. H. Nelson, *The Battle of Megiddo* (Chicago, 1913); and R. Faulkner in *JEA*, XXVIII (1942), 2 ff.; and (*b*) the Gebel Barkal stela— G. A. and M. B. Reisner in *ZÄS*, LXIX (1933), 24 ff.

Syria entered the Fertile Crescent at Gaza in southwestern Palestine and moved north through the Philistine coastland and the Plain of Sharon, broke through the Carmel Range to emerge into the Plain of Esdraelon at Megiddo, and then forked for the Phoenician coast, the central valley of Syria, or the hinterland at Damascus. The Megiddo Pass was therefore of high military importance, as it continued to be throughout history and as the Book of Revelation would make it—there called Armageddon—in the apocalyptic battle at the end of the world.[33] The Prince of Kadesh had chosen his vantage point wisely. He had assembled a formidable coalition of city-states, with elegant little princelings driving up in "their great chariots of gold and silver, as well as those which were polished," and encamping in showy tents, outfitted with furniture of finely inlaid workmanship. At the final victory, Thut-mose III captured nearly a thousand chariots, a figure which is our chief index for the size of the Asiatic coalition.

Pharaoh's energy is shown by the fact that his army covered the 150 miles between the Egyptian frontier and Gaza in ten days. Military security and logistics thereafter slowed the progress, so that it took eleven more days to move the 80 miles to a town south of the Carmel Range. There Thut-mose III held a conference with his officers, which is reported with the familiar *cliché* of pharaoh's superhuman wisdom and daring. The courtiers wisely counseled against attempting to move through the narrow Megiddo Pass, where the army would be strung out in single file, and they pointed to two alternative passes, by which they might take the Asiatic army on the flank. But Thut-mose was a god, who might not be represented as humanly cautious. He took a mighty oath: "My majesty shall proceed upon this Aruna road! Let him of you who wishes go upon these (other) roads of which you speak, and let him of you who wishes come in the following of my majesty!" He would not permit "these enemies whom Re abominates" to ask: "Has his majesty set out on another road because he has become afraid of us?"

Kingship had responsibilities resulting from such divine assurance. Thut-mose had to guarantee his bold and direct scheme by riding at the head of his army, carrying an image of the god Amon-Re, who had promised the victory. And truly the god had worked for Egypt, because the enemy sat placidly secure at the northern end of the narrow pass, while the army of pharaoh threaded its way through the defile

33. Revelation 16:16.

(Fig. 20). This process took an entire day, and the stupidity of the Asiatics in permitting the dangerous passage is almost incredible.[34]

The two armies encamped for the night, and at dawn Thut-mose made an epiphany at the head of his forces, "in a chariot of fine gold, adorned with his accoutrements of combat, like Horus, the Mighty of Arm, a lord of action like Montu, the Theban, while his father Amon made strong his arms." At the Egyptian attack, the Asiatics broke and fled, abandoning their chariots and their rich camp. There is a nice touch of straight-faced humor in the observation that the people within Megiddo had locked the city gates, so that the routed enemy danced frantically below the wall until those in the city let down their clothes to hoist the panic-stricken warriors up into the town. And there is a word of severity at the looting greed of the Egyptian troops: "Now, if only his majesty's army had not given up their hearts to capturing the possessions of the enemy, they would [have captured] Megiddo at this time, while the wretched enemy of Kadesh and the wretched enemy of this town were being dragged (up) hastily(?) to get them into their town." When we are later told some of the Asiatic treasures which formed part of the loot we can understand the lack of discipline in this ancient army.

Megiddo was too strong a fortification for the siege weapons of the day. The city was invested with a moat and a fence, and the Egyptian army sat down to starve the enemy into subjection. They had arrived in Palestine at the season of the wheat harvest, and they took over that wheat, some 450,000 bushels, "apart from what was cut as forage by his majesty's army." For the rest, they sat and waited. Although the Asiatics were walled in, Thut-mose notes grimly that "there was no lack of runaways among them."[35] Finally, after seven months' siege, from May to December, the remaining Asiatics sent out their children carrying weapons to give them up to pharaoh, while the Asiatic warriors "were standing on their walls, giving praise to my majesty, seeking that the breath of life might be given to them."

Thut-mose III proved his wise magnanimity. Other pharaohs sometimes made a brutal example by ceremonially slaying the enemy princes, and perhaps the Prince of Megiddo had escaped. At any rate, Thut-mose shrewdly bid for their gratitude. He administered to them an oath of fealty for their lifetime. "Then my majesty gave them leave (to go) to their towns. They all went on donkey (back), so that I might

34. S. Yeivin in *JNES*, IX (1950), 101 ff.
35. K. Sethe, *Urkunden der 18. Dynastie* (*Urk.*, IV [Leipzig, 1907]), 767:9.

take their horses." By his restraint pharaoh laid the cornerstone of empire for a century.

We shall not detail the rich booty won by this victory, except to note that it shows that Palestine-Syria was a region of cosmopolitan elegance. The Asiatic princes slept in inlaid beds, traveled in inlaid sedan chairs, carried carved walking sticks, and had vessels of gold and silver. The enemy prince brought to the battle an ebony statue of himself, worked with gold, with a head of lapis lazuli. The captured cattle numbered two thousand or more, the goats two thousand, and the sheep twenty thousand. This was an agricultural and pastoral area, but it had a craftsmanship of high quality. That craftsmanship pouring into Egypt through the activity of empire was to have a profound influence upon the static calm of Egyptian art. The next century was to see more change in Egyptian artistic expression than the preceding ten centuries.[36]

For the next twenty years Thut-mose kept the power of Egypt alive in the Asiatic consciousness by parades of force almost annually. Sometimes he had only to march his army around and receive tribute; now and again he had to fight. However, he did not have to face a coalition of Asiatics again; he had effectively broken up united opposition. Thereafter his two main enemies were the Prince of Kadesh and the King of Mitanni in northwestern Mesopotamia. Palestine and Phoenicia—except for occasional restlessness—were his. The fighting frontier was to the north.

Thus, in the sixth campaign in his thirtieth year and again in a final campaign in his forty-second year, Thut-mose conquered Kadesh. It is instructive on the hyperbole of official language that this town was "destroyed" in the thirtieth year but had to be reconquered twelve years later, when one of the Egyptian officers tells us: "His majesty sent forth every valiant man of his army, to breach the new wall which Kadesh had made. I was the one who breached it, being the first of every valiant man, and no other did (it) before me."[37]

The most ambitious campaign was the eighth in Thut-mose's thirty-third year, directed against "that enemy of the wretched Naharin," the King of Mitanni. Naharin was the region of the great bend of the Euphrates, and Mitanni was a kingdom, of strong Indo-European coloring, based on the east of the Euphrates but with ambitions toward

36. P. Montet, *Les Reliques de l'Art Syrien dans l'Égypte du Nouvel Empire* (Paris, 1937), although he overrates the Asiatic influence on Egyptian art.

37. Breasted, *ARE*, II, § 590.

the country lying to the west of the River. The expanding Egyptian Empire naturally came into conflict with the expanding Mitannian Empire.[38] Thut-mose's energy and vision in undertaking an attack on an enemy who lay behind a body of water are shown in his preparations for the campaign. "I had many ships of cedar built on the mountains of God's Land near the Lady of Byblos. They were placed on carts, with cattle drawing (them), and they journeyed in [front of] my majesty, in order to cross that great river which lies between this foreign country and Naharin."[39] This was a king who left nothing to chance. He embarked upon the Euphrates and pursued the fleeing King of Mitanni by boat. It is not claimed that he captured the enemy, but pharaoh is emphatic in stating that he ravaged "that land of Naharin, which its lord abandoned because of fear." He then set up a stela of triumph on the eastern bank of the Euphrates, serving arrogant notice of his invasion. Egypt was to have trouble with Mitanni for two more generations, but we have no further record of a pitched battle between the two powers.

Much of the record is given over to the details of the administrative organization of the new empire. Sea power was particularly important as the army moved farther from Egypt and communications became difficult. The eastern Mediterranean cannot be held without an active, dominating navy.[40] Thut-mose gave great attention to the Phoenician harbors as he moved northward. "Now every port town which his majesty reached was supplied with good bread and with various (kinds of) bread, with olive oil, incense, wine, honey, and fruit." Or, in another statement, the harbors were organized and outfitted "according to their assessment and their yearly custom." Thut-mose further seized ships, in order to provide transport to and from Egypt.[41]

Thut-mose extended a military and political rule over Asia, with a high commissioner for the region and resident commissioners in important towns, supervising the Asiatic princes. Gaza in Palestine was the administrative center.[42] It had not revolted against Thut-mose III at the time of the Battle of Megiddo and was not listed among the towns which he defeated. Old Gaza had a fortress tower of the type which the Asiatics called a *migdol*, and it served as the control station at the begin-

38. On the campaign see R. Faulkner in *JEA*, XXXII (1946), 39 ff.; A. H. Gardiner, *Ancient Egyptian Onomastica* (London, 1947), I, 153* ff.

39. G. A. and M. B. Reisner, *op. cit.*, pp. 28 f.

40. D. G. Hogarth in *JEA*, I (1914), 9 ff.

41. T. Säve-Söderbergh, *The Navy of the Eighteenth Egyptian Dynasty* (Uppsala, 1946), pp. 34 f.

42. W. F. Albright in *AJSL*, LV (1938), 352, n. 41.

ning of the great road through Palestine-Syria. Along that road moved "the king's envoys to all foreign countries," a hardy and adventurous group of couriers, who drove their chariots through difficult and treacherous country, to serve as pharaoh's messengers and ambassadors. They carried clay tablets written in the diplomatic language of the day, Akkadian cuneiform, between Thebes and Boghaz Keui, between Tell el-Amarna and Byblos, performing the notable service of binding together an empire which had the most primitive communications. So well did Thut-mose III establish that empire that couriers could travel hundreds of miles away from Egypt with relative safety.[43]

During Thut-mose III's active career and the early years of his successor, Amen-hotep II, control was made effective by frequent parades of power through Asia by the Egyptian army. One hundred years later the memory of this strong vigilance led an Asiatic prince to cry out: "Who formerly colonized Tunip? Did not Manahbirya (Thut-mose III) colonize it?"[44] Another disciplinary factor was that the campaigning season came at a critical time of the year. The grain harvests in Egypt were in the earlier spring; thereafter pharaoh's army marched in Asia, to arrive at the time when the Asiatic harvests were ripening, so that the locals were most vulnerable. The Egyptian troops of course lived off the land and particularly enjoyed catching an enemy in harvest season. Of a campaign in Phoenicia the record runs: "Their orchards were filled with their fruit. Their wines were found lying in their vats, as water flows, and their grain was on the threshing floors, being ground. They were more plentiful than the sands of the shore. The army overflowed with its possessions. . . . Why, his majesty's army was as drunk and as anointed with oil every day as if at feasts in Egypt."[45]

As time went on and the tradition of pharaoh's lightning fury became fixed, the Asiatic empire could be held by little garrisons scattered throughout the various towns. It seems almost incredible that forces of five to twenty-five Egyptians could hold a city. But the Asiatic towns were small and always disunited. Behind the little garrison lay the vast power of pharaoh's army, so that the handful of troops could act as a local police and as an intelligence system. Until the shattering forces of the Amarna period crumbled the Empire, this resident force was enough.

43. For a somewhat exaggerated picture of the hardships and dangers of the courier's life cf. Erman, *LAE*, pp. 227 ff.

44. H. Ranke in *ZAS*, LVI (1920), 73.

45. Breasted, *ARE*, II, §§ 461–62.

After the Battle of Megiddo Thut-mose had imposed an oath of fealty and had let the Asiatic princes go back to their towns. In general, he was content to let them continue their rule under his commissioners and his garrisons. However, he added a practice which combined the advantages of holding hostages for the current princes and of egyptian-izing the future princes. In his sixth campaign this policy is stated. "Now the sons of the princes and their brothers were brought away to be hostages in Egypt. Then, whoever of these princes died, his majesty was accustomed to make his son go to stand in his place. List of the sons of princes carried off in this year: thirty-six men."[46] Thus, although the princes were confirmed in their rule, they had given important hostages for good behavior, and their heirs were educated in Egypt, so that they might become more at home at the Egyptian capital than in their own towns. The system seems to have worked well for Egypt, if one may judge from the continued loyalty—the almost fanatical loyalty—of some of these Asiatics in the troubled Amarna period.

The annals of Thut-mose III give us some incomplete indication of the wealth which poured into Egypt through empire. The evidence is clouded by the fact that the official propaganda listed as "tribute" whatever was wrested from a conquered district by force and whatever came to Egypt in the normal flow of international commerce or as gifts from powerful foreign kings. Thus, the "tribute" from Assyria, the Hittites, or Babylonia was not exacted from those distant powers, but was either the commerce of the royal monopoly or resulted from the exchange of royal gifts between the kings of those nations and pharaoh of Egypt. Such gifts do illustrate the power relations of the time. Mitanni is not recorded as participating in these gifts and was encircled by the Hittites and the Egyptian Empire to the west and by Assyria and Babylonia to the east. She would be squeezed until she sought the support of one or more other powers, and she later lined up with Egypt and then, perforce, with the Hittites.

The government monopoly of the coniferous woods of Asia, which we lump together in the translation "cedar," is shown by Thut-mose's words on his Barkal Stela. "Every year there is hewed [for me in] Djahi genuine cedar of Lebanon, which is brought to the court... without passing over the seasons thereof, each and every year. When my army which is the garrison in Ullaza comes, [they bring the trib-ute], which is the cedar of my majesty's victories. . . . I have not given (any) of it to the Asiatics, for it is a wood which (Amon-Re) loves."[47]

46. *Ibid.*, § 467.
47. G. A. and M. B. Reisner, *op. cit.*, pp. 34 f.

Amon-Re of Karnak benefited hugely from the foreign tribute. He had promised the victory, and his image accompanied the armies on the march; he received a lion's share of the loot. The purpose of Thut-mose III's "annals," carved in the Temple of Karnak and copied from an original leather scroll kept as a field journal, was to state that the pharaoh had fulfilled his share of the contract with the god. For example, Amon was the patron and the senior partner in the exploitation of the gold mines in Nubia and the Sudan. In Thut-mose III's thirty-fourth year, Amon received more than 700 Troy pounds of gold from these mines; in the thirty-eighth year about the same; and in the forty-first year somewhat over 800 pounds.[48] This was no slight amount in that day.

In the Temple of Amon Thut-mose had long lists carved giving the countries and city-states which he claimed to have captured. The names range from southern Palestine to northern Syria, and we can identify at least half of the sites. In general, it was the great arterial road and its branches which captured the Egyptian interest and not the higher country off that road: it was the Philistine and Sharon plains, the Megiddo Pass, the plain of Acre, the Plain of Esdraelon over to Beth-Shan and then on up to Damascus, the Hazor Pass in Galilee and then on up to Kadesh on the Orontes, and the north Syrian plain of Aleppo and the Euphrates. There are few certain sites in the highlands of Judea and Ephraim, and the cities of Phoenicia are rare, perhaps because they did not share in the Megiddo rebellion.[49]

A similar spotting of Egyptian influence may be seen by tracing the presence of objects bearing the names of the pharaohs and found in Palestine and Syria under the Empire. They lie in the Philistine plain and up into the hills as far as Lachish and Beth-Shemesh—but no farther —in the Plain of Esdraelon and across the Jordan on the way to Damascus, close to Capernaum in Galilee, on the Phoenician coast, and at Kadesh on the Orontes. Again the great road is the nerve center.[50]

One listing of the datable Egyptian objects found in Palestine and southern Syria is an index to the weight of Egyptian interest in Asia. The Middle Kingdom showed about one hundred and fifty, the Empire close to five hundred, with a very sharp falling off—to seventy-five—in the post-Empire period.[51] Even though the accidents of survival

48. Breasted, *ARE*, II, §§ 494–95, 514–15, 526–27.

49. J. Simons, *Handbook for the Study of Egyptian Topographical Lists Relating to Western Asia* (Leyden, 1937).

50. W. F. Albright and A. Rowe in *JEA*, XIV (1928), 286 f.

51. A. Rowe, *A Catalogue of Egyptian Scarabs . . . in the Palestine Archaeological Museum* (Cairo, 1936), pp. xiii–xlvii and graph in the end papers.

affect the figures, the proportions are marked enough to be significant.

What we are chiefly interested in is the effect of this intensified activity of empire-building on the Egyptian spirit. The initial impulse had been to drive out and punish the impious Hyksos. However, the old sense of security had been damaged beyond repair, and the imperial spirit relished the sense of power in victory. The ruling forces of Egypt, civil and religious, benefited materially by conquest and gained in personal authority. The sense of far-flung frontiers was perpetuated by the focusing of attention upon continued peril. The Hyksos peril was perpetuated by the Asiatic "rebellion" at Megiddo, which was succeeded by the competition of Mitanni, which was followed by rivalry with the Hittites, which gave way to the peril of the Sea Peoples and the Libyans. The Empire was always faced by some alarm or other, some of them very real because of an attempt to invade the land of Egypt itself, some of them quite remote, threatening only the distant reaches of the Asiatic empire. But they were all real enough to keep alive the sense of insecurity. They provided the excuse for continual military activity and alertness, so that the country remained on a basis of centralized authoritarian power. That this enriched the palace and the temple is of less importance than the fact that it changed the spirit of ancient Egypt drastically.

Success in winning empire was credited to two gods: the god-king who led the armies and the imperial god who gave his sanction to the wars. When Amon-Re graciously permitted a campaign against the Asiatics and lent his "sword" to the pharaoh, with the divine standard leading the way into battle, the god had to be repaid after victory with an extensive share of the booty from that specific venture and with a grateful increase of his regular offerings. As time went on, Amon grew greatly in wealth, with every victory adding to his resources, and—we must assume—no decrease in his assets as a result of defeat. This was a working relation between the imperial god and the nation which had no cynicism of a bargain but which represented divine participation in the affairs of a sacred state.

Other priesthoods, such as those of Re of Heliopolis, Ptah of Memphis, and Seth, the god of Asiatics (Fig. 17*b*), also shared in such pyramiding of wealth and power, although by no means to the extent of the priesthood of Amon of Karnak. The temples of the Old and Middle Kingdoms had been relatively small and localized; under the Empire the temples of the gods became huge and acquired vast estates. Grateful pharaohs executed charters exempting the temples and the temple staffs from duties which fell upon other citizens. Egypt became top-heavy with priests and specially privileged temple holdings. This meant that the clergy of Egypt had invested in empire, and it was important to them that the domination of the foreigners by Egypt be pushed at all times. Ultimately the burden of maintaining such an effort was too great, and the nation gave up its empire and retired within its own boundaries. Then the internal economy of Egypt was saddled with the vast temple estates, thoroughly disproportionate to the ability of Egypt to carry on in the same magnificence as in the days when revenues were rolling in from abroad. But this anticipates the story of Chapter X.

The great effort of building up and maintaining a new organism, such as an empire of remote frontiers, required national unity, and, in the first surge of vengeful patriotism after the Hyksos, that unity was formed out of the devoted fervor of all Egyptians. However, the burden of maintenance was of indefinite time, and the fruits of empire were not shared equally by all. Of course, the wealth pouring into Egypt affected everybody in some degree, but it also created and widened a gap between the governing class and those who were governed. Those who took the lead in the national adventure became increasingly powerful and wealthy. As time went on, they did not need to march with the armies but were tied down at home with their increasing investments and local concerns; they were able to hire functionaries to carry on the laborious jobs. And so we see an increasing number of professional factors, the major-domo of some domestic enterprise or the mercenary soldier. Such factors originally were hired servants and did not expect to succeed to positions of independent authority. However, toward the end of the Empire their continued responsibilities had built them into a powerful group of palace butlers or professional soldiers. Furthermore, the hired professional factor stood between the ruling, wealthy class and the ordinary mass of Egyptians; there was no longer that regular and easy contact between the master and his peasants. There was a class cleavage, and it was no longer possible—theoretically and exceptionally—to move upward in the social scale. That high value set upon the individual Egyptian, down to the ordinary peasant, in the early Middle Kingdom was a thing of the distant past. Under the Empire the peasant was only an indistinguishable element in the mass of Egyptians organized and restrained for national unified effort.

To be sure, expanding government demands new workers, and it had to draw upon the able resources in the land. However, the resources increasingly became foreign. As early as the Old Kingdom, Egypt had

drafted the people of Nubia and the Sudan for her army. Military successes under the Empire brought into Egypt thousands of captives,
taken in battle. They were quite willing to serve as Egyptian soldiers,
even against their own racial kinsfolk, because Egypt was at first the
land of great opportunity, with the promise of military loot and the
chance of rapid advancement. As the rulers of Egypt became fat and
wealthy, these able foreigners were an initial resource for activity, so
that *Nehsiu* and *Medjai* of the south, *Shasu* of the east, *Meshwesh* of
the west. and *Sherden* of the Sea Peoples were increasingly engaged
to serve in the army or to fill the factorial posts in the civil service or
great estates. Many of the foreigners were mere slaves of the palace,
of the domains of the nobles, or of the temple estates. However, slavery
was not then the sharply and legally delimited category which it was
in more modern times. The household slave was much better off than
the native Egyptian peasant. As the leg-man for a government bureau,
as the body-servant of a noble, as an attendant in the royal harem, or
as the sergeant in a mercenary detachment, the slave had greater opportunity to make himself indispensable and thus powerful. The end of
the Empire found foreigners in positions of independent authority as
royal butlers or chamberlains, messengers of government bureaus, or
officers in the army. The poorer native Egyptian sank to a lower social,
political, and economic level, in contrast to his native rulers and their
foreign factors. The great adventure of national unity turned into an
effective disunity, which could be welded together only by rigid discipline.

The civil and ecclesiastical bureaucracy and the army all developed
hierarchies, with definitely recognized classes. The army might serve
as the example of this hardening of system. In the lesser effort of earlier
times the body of the army had probably been amateur, based upon a
draft of able-bodied citizens, who served seasonally and then returned
to their homes. Only the police had been regular professionals, and
many of them were foreign mercenaries. Even the officers had been
high-placed civilians who led the troops only in their seasonal activities.
The Empire, however, could not rely upon seasonal amateurs; it had to
place professional soldiers in the garrisons of distant lands. So we see
regular and consistent organization in the army from the time of Thut-
mose III on. In the infantry the "soldier" might hope for a small command as a "standard bearer" or for a higher command as the "commander of archers." The chariotry formed a *corps d'élite*, socially
higher than the infantry. Field officers who had shown merit in combat

were rewarded with gifts of gold, land, or slaves, or were given easy jobs within the civil service. In particular, many of them became "chief stewards" of the royal estates.

On the staff side, there were important officers with the functions of supplies, accounts, records, communications, and operations, for all the business and bookkeeping services of a widespread army. At the top stood the "chief army commander," who in theory should have been the pharaoh himself and perhaps was so at the very beginning of the Empire. Very soon pharaoh delegated this supreme command to his son and successor, the Crown Prince. At the time of the Amarna Revolution, however, the post passed to a nonroyal individual, Har-em-hab, and it is significant that he was able to take the ultimate step from this generalcy to the kingship, just as the viziers who became Ramses I and Seti I were able to do after him and just as Heri-Hor did at a later time. The independent power and high standing of the army under the Empire was a normal product of empire but a break with the past.[52]

The great excitement of the Egyptian Empire was the spread of communications and contacts. Ships more insistently plied the Mediterranean between Delta ports and Asia or the Aegean area. Moving armies or royal couriers demanded better roads in the desert of Sinai or through the mountains of Asia, and we have some record of the maintenance of a military road between Egypt and Palestine.[53] Furthermore, greater numbers of Egyptians were regularly resident abroad or travelled abroad on the business of empire, while tens of thousands of foreigners were introduced into Egypt. Many of these foreign captives had been able and important in their homes, and brought into Egypt a sense of other values. This was an international era, with foreign ambassadors detailed to other countries, with a regular flow of communications between capitals carried on by couriers of education and ability. Under such constant contacts there came to be an appreciation of values other than Egyptian. If the frontiers of Egypt were effectively the Fourth Cataract to the south and the Euphrates River to the north, those added areas must be worth something in themselves. Their ways of life, their religious expression must command interest and respect. Of course, Egypt expressed this new, outgoing interest in terms of imperialism rather than internationalism: national dogma stretched the effective frontier out to include foreign areas. The gods of Egypt became gods of the universe, having an effective concern for

52. H. W. Helck, *Der Einfluss der Militärführer in der 18. ägyptischen Dynastie* (*Untersuch.*, XIV [Leipzig, 1939]).

53. A. H. Gardiner in *JEA*, VI (1920), 99 ff.

humans outside the valley of the Nile. The divine sanction for empire-building lay in the newly recognized universalism of native Egyptian gods. Since the most important Egyptian gods were to some degree cosmic forces—sun, air, earth, thunder—it was easy enough to see them abroad and to acknowledge their functional validity away from Egypt. However, we should like to underline the spiritual importance to Egypt of political, social, and economic internationalism and religious universalism. It brought to an effective end the old superior isolationism and its consequent static security. From now on changes were rapid.

The amount of movement to and fro in this period was quite extraordinary, particularly in contrast to previous ages. The number of foreigners who were resident in Egypt, whether voluntarily or by capture, was constantly increasing. For example, Thut-mose IV's mortuary temple enjoyed the services of a colony of Asiatics, whom he had captured at Gezer in Palestine and presented to the priesthood of this shrine.[54] Phoenician ships sailed into Egyptian harbors and unloaded their wares for Egyptian inspection.[55] An amusing example of cultural influence comes from Tell el-Amarna and is slightly later in time, but it nicely illustrates how the orthodoxy of Egypt was affected by contacts with strange peoples and customs. One of the simpler Amarna estates showed deviation from the stylized formality of Egyptian domestic architecture and landscape gardening. In its garden, instead of the orderly rows of trees planted in careful balance, there was a scattered grove of trees planted at random, as is known from Aegean frescoes. The stairs leading to the roof were not supported by a blank wall, as usually in Egypt, but by a square pier, as usually in Crete or in the Mycenean area. This house yielded to the excavator a Rhodian pilgrim bottle, a pottery face in Aegean shape, and a number of Mycenean sherds. It is the suggestion of the excavator that this was the residence of "the inevitable Greek grocer of his day."[56] All the evidence shows that the owner of the house was a free agent and a neighbor acceptable to the Egyptians, but that he did not feel bound to follow their formal ways of building or planting. Amarna also yielded a stone slab depicting a bearded Syrian soldier sitting with his Egyptian wife, while an Egyptian servant offers his Asiatic master a drinking tube for a wine jar.[57]

54. Breasted, *ARE*, II, § 821.

55. A. Erman and H. Ranke, *Aegypten und ägyptisches Leben im Altertum* (Tübingen, 1923), Pl. 40, 1.

56. J. D. S. Pendlebury, *Tell el-Amarna* (London, 1935), pp. 120 ff.

57. W. Spiegelberg and A. Erman in *ZÄS*, XXXVI (1898), 126 ff., Pl. XVII.

The scenes of foreign "tribute" in the tombs of the Eighteenth Dynasty are quite common, and it may be doubted whether they always represented an exacted obligation or merely an active flow of commerce. Undoubtedly there is a strong coloring of arrogant propaganda in scenes which show the Prince of Keftiu (the Aegean area), the Prince of the Hittites, the Prince of Tunip in north Syria, and the Prince of Kadesh kneeling and making offering—the ruler of Tunip offers his infant son.[58] In other tombs, the Asiatics or Africans or Mediterraneans bring their characteristic products into Egypt under conditions which suggest a normal commerce in "silver, gold, lapis lazuli, turquoise, every august costly stone," and other goods of less elegant sound.[59] There is no doubt that Egypt held an empire from which she exacted and collected tribute as her just due. In Africa this would include the Nile Valley to and including the region of the Fourth Cataract, as well as the western oases. In Asia it would include Palestine and a strip of territory on the eastern side of the Jordan, Phoenicia[60] and Coelesyria; beyond those limits the firm control becomes doubtful, even though the lists of conquered city-states include Damascus and Kadesh on the Orontes and the empire which was claimed extended to the Euphrates. It seems more likely that northern and eastern Syria was not held by Egyptian garrisons and resident commissioners, but was an area subjected to frequent raids, not so much to contain it within the Egyptian organism as to prevent its hostile action against that organism. Ancient frontiers seem not to have been delimited with the same precision as modern, so that there was a claimed zone of territory running beyond the effective zone permitted by logistics. In the scene mentioned above, the rulers of Keftiu and the Hittites were certainly not subject to Egyptian control, the rulers of Kadesh and Tunip perhaps only nominally so. In any event, the official dogma of Egypt

58. The tomb of Thut-mose III's High Priest of Amon, Men-kheper-Re-seneb: N. and N. de G. Davies, *The Tombs of Menkheperrasonb, Amenmose, and Another* (*TTS*, V [London, 1933]), Pls. IV, VII.

59. The tombs of Thut-mose III's Vizier, Rekh-mi-Re: N. de G. Davies, *The Tomb of Rekh-mi-Re at Thebes* (New York, 1943), II, Pls. XXI–XXIII; of an army officer under Thut-mose IV, Tjaneni: Sethe, *Urkunden der 18. Dynastie* (*Urk.*, IV [Leipzig, 1909]), 1007; of Hat-shepsut's chief architect, Sen-Mut: N. M. Davies and A. H. Gardiner, *Ancient Egyptian Paintings* (Chicago, 1936), Pl. XIV; and others.

60. Under Thut-mose III, there was an Egyptian garrison at Ullaza in north Phoenicia: G. A. and M. B. Reisner, *ibid.*, pp. 34 f. Under Amen-hotep II, it is highly probable that there was a garrison at Ugarit; a tentative translation of the Karnak stela of this pharaoh published by G. Legrain in *ASAE*, IV (1903), 126 ff., l. 11, would run: "Now his majesty heard that a few [of] the Asiatics [who] were in the town of Iket (read Ugarit?) were conspiring(?) to work out a plan for abandoning the garrison of his majesty."

lumped together the assessments enforced upon subject territory and
the free commerce from independent territory: "giving praise to the
Lord of the Two Lands, kissing the ground to the good god by the
princes of every land, as they extol the victories of his majesty, with
their tribute upon their backs, . . . seeking that there be given to them
the breath of life."[61]

Another example of active intercultural contact lies in the exploitation of the Sinai mines by the Egyptian state through the agency of
Asiatic slave workers. Some time within the range of the early fifteenth
century B.C., Canaanites were used as the miners for turquoise and
copper at Serabit el-Khadem in Sinai. Presumably they were captives,
held in the Delta and brought out seasonally, under armed escort, for
the mining. They used Egyptian pottery, carved statues imitating
Egyptian forms, and depicted their own Semitic gods in the form of
the Egyptian deities Ptah and Hat-Hor. However, their Semitic inscriptions pray to their own goddess Baalat. These were not the local
Bedouin of Sinai, but were Canaanites of some degree of sophistication.
We owe to them a great invention: they wrote their simple little texts
in a hieroglyphic alphabet. They rejected the cumbersome Egyptian
system of an indefinite series of picture-signs and took one sign for each
consonantal sound in their language: from the word *alif* "ox" they
used an ox-head for the Semitic sound called *alif*; from the word *bêt*
"house" they used the picture of a house for the *b* sound; and so on.
This *alif-bêt* series became the lineal ancestor of our own and other
modern alphabets. It is an ironic commentary on the ancient Egyptian
culture that its system of writing included signs which were essentially
alphabetic in character but which were never recognized as the only
necessary phonetic elements for writing, whereas one of their subject
peoples borrowed many of their pictures and used them in a simpler
system which ultimately would make writing an instrument within the
grasp of far greater numbers of people.[62]

Under Thut-mose III, the Chief Treasurer Sen-nefer was dispatched
to Byblos, to secure cedar logs. Before going up into the forest-pre-
serve to select the timber, he made offerings to the goddess of Byblos,
a local Baalat, whom the Egyptians identified with their Hat-Hor.[63]

61. N. and N. de G. Davies, *op. cit.*

62. For the most recent discussions, see W. F. Albright, in *Bulletin of the American
Schools of Oriental Research* (1948), No. 109, pp. 5 ff.; No. 110, pp. 6 ff. For evidence
of the Semites at the Egyptian mines in Sinai—although of the Middle Kingdom, rather
than the Empire—see J. Cerný in *Archiv Orientální*, VII (1935), 384 ff.

63. Sethe, *op. cit.*, pp. 531 ff. P. Montet, *Byblos et l'Égypte* (Paris, 1928), Texte, pp.
35 ff., Pl. XXVIII, 2.

This respect for the gods of foreign countries was not new for the Egyptians, and at Byblos it extended back into the early Old Kingdom. However, the Empire witnessed a far greater interchange of deities, including a domestication of Egyptian gods in Asia and of Asiatic gods in Egypt. In part this worked through identification: Hat-Hor was equated with Baalat, Seth with Baal or Teshub of the Hittites, Re with Shamash, and so on. In part, there was colonization in both directions. Ramses III built a temple of Amon in Canaan, and Ptah had a sanctuary at Ascalon.[64] Within Egypt, from the late Eighteenth Dynasty on, there were priests of Baal and Astarte.[65] The latter was recognized under the name "Astar of Syria" as a goddess of healing.[66] Egyptian literature used the Asiatic gods Baal and Reshpu (Fig. 28b) or goddesses Astarte, Anath, and Qedesh as metaphors of power or violence. The personal names of Egyptians accepted the Asiatic deities in the same terms as their own divine beings: Baal-khepeshef, "Baal-is-(Upon)-His-Sword," like the name Montu-her-khepeshef, "Montu-is-Upon-His-Sword," and Astart-em-heb, "Astarte-is-In-Festival," like the name Mut-em-heb, "Mut-is-In-Festival."

The Egyptians dispatched by the Empire to live abroad paid due regard to the deities in their new locations. At Beth-Shan in Palestine, the architect Amen-em-Opet and his son erected a stela addressing a perfectly normal Egyptian mortuary prayer to "Mekal, the god of Beth-Shan,"[67] and at Ugarit on the northern Phoenician coast, Memi, a scribe and steward of pharaoh's palace, directed his mortuary prayer to "Baal-Zaphon, the great god," a being with the Asiatic pointed beard and conical cap ending in streamers.[68] These foreign gods were treated in context indiscriminately with good Egyptian deities, as when a woman in Memphis appealed on behalf of her correspondent in a letter "to the Ennead which is in the House of Ptah, to Baalat, to Qedesh, to Meni(?), Baali-Zaphon, and to Sopdu."[69] In a sacred state, where the theological system is the formally recognized product of long centuries and has encysted itself as the vested protector of the

64. Breasted, ARE, IV, § 219; G. Loud, The Megiddo Ivories (OIP, Vol. LII [Chicago, 1939]), 11 ff.

65. A "Prophet of Baal" and "Prophet of Astarte" in Memphis at the end of the Dynasty: C. R. Lepsius, Denkmäler aus Aegypten und Aethiopien, Text (Leipzig, 1897), I, 16.

66. H. Ranke, in Studies Presented to F. Ll. Griffith (London, 1932), pp. 412 ff.

67. A. Rowe, The Topography and History of Beth-Shan (Philadelphia, 1930), I, Pl. 33.

68. C. F.-A. Schaeffer, Ugaritica I (Paris, 1939), pp. 39 ff.

69. A. H. Gardiner, Late-Egyptian Miscellanies (Bibl. Aeg., VII [1937]), p. 89.

land, the free intercultural exchange of deities is significant of the disintegration of the old canons and sanctions. This was truly a cosmopolitan period, within which the break-up of Egyptian culture as a
distinct phenomenon was rapid.

Every student of Egyptian art has read that the "Amarna Revolution" around 1375–50 B.C. produced an expression which was so
markedly different from the art of previous times in its liquid flow of
line and in its exaggerated naturalism as to mark a sharp break with
the past. On further examination it is clear that the antecedents of the
Amarna movement were present in Egypt thirty or forty years before
the formal revolution. Such an observation needs no highly refined
aesthetic sensitivity; it lies on the surface of the art. It is a thesis of this
book that the change from the older stylized and poised forms is sensible as early as the reign of Thut-mose III and that the monuments
of Hat-shepsut were the last consistently successful exponents of the
earlier tradition. That thesis cannot be proved, since it rests upon an
aesthetic impression which may be subjectively induced by the general
argument of the book. However, it seems certain that Hat-shepsut's
art belongs to the proper tradition of past centuries and that a change
was informally but strongly under way before the Amarna period.
The dividing line between the old and the new will be a matter of
individual opinion.

Clearly much of the new, loose naturalism had been accepted as
early as Thut-mose IV around 1415 B.C., and clearly the new liveliness
and antihieratic feeling in art owed much to foreign influence.[70] The
decoration of the chariot of Thut-mose IV is nearly as true an exponent of the new art as is the lively pavement of Amen-hotep III's
palace.[71] To a lesser degree, we feel that it is possible to discern the
new vulgarization in the artistic products of the reign of Thut-mose
III. For example, the same theme is shown in tombs of nobles under
Hat-shepsut and under Thut-mose III: Minoans and Aegeans bringing
gifts to Egypt.[72] In the earlier instance the figures and the composition
retain the squareness, rigidity, and balance of the older art, based on
cherished standards coming from the Third and Fourth Dynasties,
essentially unchanged for twelve hundred years. The Thut-mose III

70. H. Frankfort (ed.), *The Mural Painting of El-ʿAmarneh* (London, 1929), pp. 1–30.

71. H. Carter and P. E. Newberry, *The Tomb of Thoutmôsis IV* (*Cairo Cat.*, XV
[London, 1904]), Pls. IX–XII; R. de P. Tytus, *Preliminary Report on the Re-excavation
of the Palace Amenhotep III* (New York, 1903).

72. N. M. Davies and A. H. Gardiner, *Ancient Egyptian Paintings* (Chicago, 1936),
Vol. I, Pls. XIV, XXIII.

instance has made some small sacrifice of dignity in order to gain vivacity: the lines have not the same cubism or balance; there is more movement. The influence of cosmopolitan excitation is already visible in the blurring of the old sharp line under the first shadow of the forthcoming modernistic revolution.

It may be pure coincidence, but the royal sarcophagi of the Eighteenth Dynasty show an abrupt break, in material, form, and technique. At the beginning of the dynasty the coffins were made of wood, carrying out the boxlike pattern of the Middle Kingdom. Hat-shepsut introduced an innovation with a sarcophagus of stone, but it carried on the form of its wooden prototype, in shape and decoration. After Hat-shepsut the royal coffins were made of stone, treated as stone, and became anthropoid in shape. The influences for so marked a change are obscure, but the break with tradition is obvious.[73]

One who admires the unique quality of earlier Egyptian forms is rather impatient with the modernistic trends coming in at this time. Such admiration is a matter of taste, and it is obvious that the best of the new art is more immediately receptible by us moderns, because of its naturalism, than some of the austere idealism of earlier Egypt. Three considerations may be advanced in favor of the older tradition at its best: it had greater simplicity and economy of line; it carried a more exacting demand for accurate craftsmanship; and it was a truer expression of Egyptian culture alone. The newer art was more diffused and cluttered; it was produced in a haste which often made it cheap and insincere; and it was clearly under strong outside influences.

One may compare the little peripteral temples of Hat-shepsut and Amen-hotep III with the great Temple of Amon at Karnak or with the mortuary temple of Ramses III at Medinet Habu.[74] The peripteral temples were relatively small buildings, with simple lines and decora-

73. W. C. Hayes, *Royal Sarcophagi of the XVIII Dynasty* (Princeton, 1935). We have not attempted to catalogue a series of artistic or cultural expressions which show marked change in the Eighteenth Dynasty. However, two recent references might be added here. The crouching lion-sphinx of the Middle Kingdom, erect, rigid, and facing forward, was still used by Hat-shepsut, but when we next see this beast, under Amen-hotep III, it had relaxed, softened in line, and turned its head to the side: U. Schweitzer, *Löwe und Sphinx im alten Aegypten* (Mün. AF, XV [Glückstadt, 1948]), p. 47. The written Egyptian language (developed out of the spoken) which was formalized before the Middle Kingdom was becoming obsolete before the Eighteenth Dynasty and was clearly a dead language before 1350 B.C.: W. F. Edgerton in *JNES*, VI (1947), 1 ff. This was a very rapid change, when one considers the weight of tradition which tended to hold the official language rigid.

74. E. Baldwin Smith, *Egyptian Architecture as Cultural Expression* (New York, 1938), pp. 139 ff., 149 ff. 159 ff. To the peripteral temples compare the little chapel of Sen-Usert I, *Illustrated London News*, June 4, 1938, pp. 998 f.

tion, resting on the ground with unpretentious and unmaterial straight-
forwardness. The great pyloned temples of later times, with their peri-
style and hypostyle courts are towering, massive, and personify aggressive power, but are also definitely pretentious. The tremendous Great
Hypostyle Hall at Karnak, with its ordered forest of massive and soaring columns, can still fill one with a feeling of awe. Such lifting weight
has spiritual impressiveness, and no one would belittle the engineering
problems involved in raising such columns and in placing 60-ton archi-
trave blocks on top of columns 80 feet above the ground. However,
the architecture in this hall was not honest in the terms of the Great
Pyramid or of some of the earlier temples. These mighty columns
rested upon foundations of small, friable, and loosely laid stones, invisible to the eye under the ground. This was not a work of a conscientious craftsman. The wonderfully impressive show rested upon a
hasty and insecure base. The marvelous precision of the Great Pyramid shows a patient and honest architecture. The Temple of Karnak,
the Colossi of Memnon, or the temple of Abu Simbel in Nubia strained
after overpowering size but were not carefully built. There was haste,
and there was a show-off ostentation in these later monuments which
contrast sadly with the earlier.[75]

Such a blatantly imposing superstructure without honest foundations
is like the noisy claim of Ramses II that he defeated the Hittites at
Kadesh, a claim which he asserted in scenes and texts on many temples
of Egypt, whereas we know that he was badly taken by surprise in
that battle and returned to Egypt without achieving his objectives.
There was much in the later Empire which was noisily and insincerely
aggressive and which may have been a product of insecurity.

There is a minor but amusing aspect of the Empire, and that is the
emphasis on sports and athletics which appeared in this period of extending and policing the conquered territory. Akin both to the traditional Egyptian love of games and to the spurt of physical energy
that set up the empire, there was a brief period of glorifying the successful sportsman and athlete. It ran from Thut-mose III through
Amen-hotep III, with a revival under Tut-ankh-Amon, and with the
chief exponent of the outdoor life Amen-hotep II. The vigorous Thut-
mose III started the mode, telling us with relish how he hunted one
hundred and twenty elephants in northern Syria, how "he killed seven
lions by shooting in the completion of a moment and he captured a

75. S. Clarke and R. Engelbach, *Ancient Egyptian Masonry* (London, 1930), pp. 72 ff.

herd of twelve wild cattle within an hour, when breakfast time had taken place," how he drove an arrow nearly 9 inches out of the back of a copper target which was 2 inches thick and then deposited the evidence of this tremendous marksmanship in the Temple of Amon. "I speak to the fact(?) of what he did, without lying or protestation therein, in the face of his entire army, without a phrase of boasting therein. If he spent a moment of recreation in hunting in any desert, the amount of what he carried off is greater than the booty of the entire army."[76] Here was the king who gave visible evidence that no one could stand against his arms, because he personally had the power and prowess of a god in the disportments of men. He descended from his august throne to show his invincibility to his people and to the foreigners.

It was Amen-hotep II who left us the most engaging—and at the same time the most brutal—account of his muscular prowess. From his boyhood to his death he delighted in outdoor exercise and in his superiority over other competitors. In one of the Theban tombs the noble Min is shown with the young prince as he "gives the principles of lessons in archery. He says: 'Span your bows to your ears.'" The legend over the boy runs: "enjoying himself by learning about shooting in Pharaoh's Broad Hall of Thinis [by the Prince Amen-hotep]."[77] When he died at what must have been an advanced age, he took with him into his tomb his long-bow, a composite of wood and horn, corresponding to his reiterated boast that "there is no one who could draw his bow among his own army, among the rulers of foreign countries, or among the princes of Retenu, because his strength is so much greater than (that of) any king who has ever existed."[78]

One of the most engaging passages in Egyptian literature tells of the youthful Amen-hotep's delight in the open air. It occurs on a stela erected near the sphinx to honor that monument, because the prince had so enjoyed himself there before the cares of state descended upon him. "Now when he was a lad, he loved his horses, he delighted in them, he was persevering at exercising them and knowing their ways, skilled in training them, and penetrating in plans. When it was heard in the palace by his father (Thut-mose), the heart of his majesty was glad at the news, rejoicing at what was said about his eldest son, and he said to himself: 'This is one who will become lord of the whole land, with-

76. Mond and Myers, op. cit.

77. K. Sethe, Urkunden der 18. Dynastie (Urk., IV [1909]), pp. 976 f.

78. G. Daressy, Fouilles de la Vallée des Rois (Cairo Cat., III [1902]), p. 68, Pl. XIX; Breasted, ARE, II, § 792.

out an opponent. . . . He is still only a good, lovable boy, he is not yet mature, he is not yet at an age for doing the work of Montu, but he has turned his back on the desires of the body and loves strength. . . .' Then his majesty said to his retinue: 'Let there be given to him the very best horses of the stable of his majesty which is in Memphis. Tell him to take care of them, to make them obedient, and to give them (strong) treatment if they rebel against him.' Now after the King's Son had been instructed that he was to be privileged with horses of the Royal Stable, he acted on the instructions, while Reshpu and Astarte were rejoicing in him—doing everything which his heart desired. He trained horses without their like. They did not tire when he took the reins. They did not sweat (even) at a high gallop.

"He harnessed in Memphis . . . and came to a stop at the rest-temple of Harmakhis (the Sphinx). He spent some time there, going around and around it, looking at the charm of this rest-temple of Khufu and Khaf-Re, the deceased, and he longed to perpetuate their names. So he put it in his heart . . . to carry out what his father Re had ordered of him.

"After this, his majesty was crowned as king . . . and the land was in its normal state, peaceful under its lord, (Amen-hotep II). . . . Then his majesty remembered the place where he had enjoyed himself in the region of the pyramids of Harmakhis. A command was issued to erect a stela of limestone there and to carve it with the great name of (Amen-hotep II), the beloved of Harmakhis, given life forever."[79]

The young athlete had had so good a time around the monuments of Khufu and Khaf-Re that he wanted to honor those distant ancestors. This nicely illustrates the changing and the unchanging in ancient Egypt. The picture of the eager prince galloping his horses across the desert is typical of the physical energy of the Eighteenth Dynasty and is typical of the literary *genre* describing the pharaohs of that period; but it is utterly foreign to the spirit of the Fourth Dynasty, when Khufu and Khaf-Re sat remote from human pastimes in awful majesty. At the same time, both periods were describing a king who was a god, the Fourth Dynasty depicting him as a being who stood divinely above human activities and emotions, the Eighteenth Dynasty, as a being who superhumanly excelled all men in their disportments. The portrait of Amen-hotep II is undoubtedly based upon the fact of his interests and triumphs, but it is as much the portrait of an age as it is of an indi-

79. Selim Hassan in *ASAE*, XXXVII (1937), 129 ff.; G. Steindorff and K. C. Seele, *When Egypt Ruled the East* (Chicago, 1942), pp. 69 f.

vidual. Further, the stated dogma of invincibility could not be made up of whole cloth; it must have rested upon known achievement; but we are not entirely sure how far Amen-hotep's triumphs were the outcome of honest competition or how far they resulted from contrived flattery and the propagandistic advertising of the period. A true portrait of an individual has been exaggerated by the sweeping brush strokes which painted an age.

After Amen-hotep became pharaoh, he did not neglect demonstrations of his athletic invincibility. He claimed that he could drive an arrow through a copper target 3 inches thick, so that 9 inches of the arrow stuck out on the back of the target, or, in another record, so that seven-ninths of the arrow stuck out on the back. He seems to have left the latter target standing for the admiration of Egypt, with a reward for anyone who could duplicate his feat: "As for anybody who shall open this target and match the arrow of his majesty, he shall have these things."[80] One day he visited the armory and tested three hundred bows "in comparing the work of their artificers." He then went into a garden. "He found that they had set up for him four targets of Asiatic copper 3 inches thick, with 34 feet separating one post from the next. Then his majesty mounted his chariot like Montu in his strength. He took his bow and grasped four arrows at a time. Then he drove north, shooting at them like Montu in his regalia. His arrow (went through and) came out on the back of it. He (then) tackled the next post. It was really such a feat as had never (before) been accomplished nor heard of by report—shooting an arrow at a target of copper, the arrow coming out of it and falling to the ground—except for the king, mighty of achievement, (Amen-hotep II)."[81]

Further, this prodigy, at the age of eighteen, "knew every craft of (the war-god) Montu, with no one like him on the field of combat. He knew horses, with none like him in this great army. There was no one in it who could draw his bow. He could not be overtaken in running races. He was strong of arm, never tiring when pulling the oar. (One day) he was rowing as the stroke(?) of his falcon-boat in a crew of two hundred men. It had been cast off, and they had covered two-thirds of a mile of rowing. They were miserable; their bodies were weak; whereas his majesty was strong under his 34-foot oar. He fin-

80. H. Chevrier in *ASAE*, XXVIII (1928), 126; F. Bisson de la Roque and J. J. Clère, *Rapport sur les Fouilles de Médamoud (1927)* (Cairo, 1928), p. 146; H. Schäfer in *Orientalistische Literaturzeitung*, XXXII (1929), 233 ff.; XXXIV (1931), 89 ff. See our Fig. 21a.

81. Selim Hassan, *op. cit.*

ished and landed his falcon-boat after he had covered 4 miles of rowing, without making a pause in pulling. Faces were beautiful in watching him when he had done this."[82]

Even after one confesses to a skepticism about the precise figures given or about the honesty of the competition, or after one agrees that the record is generic, rather than individual, one still has the account of a single king who successfully typified his age and its delight in physical success. Thut-mose IV also left us record of his horsemanship and hunting, and the commemorative scarabs of Amen-hotep III list for us that king's hunting triumphs.[83] Further, the pharaohs set the pattern for commoners. The old soldier Amen-em-hab came to the attention of Amen-hotep II by his energy when rowing the royal barge and was rewarded by the pharaoh with a responsible office. "Then his majesty noted me rowing [in his state] barge [which] carried him. . . . When we had landed, I was brought up to the private quarters of the palace and made to stand before (Amen-hotep). . . . Then he said to me: 'I knew thy character when I was (still) in the nest, when thou wert following my father. I commission thee with an effective office, that thou shalt be army deputy . . . and shalt control the valiant men (of the personal bodyguard) of the king.' "[84]

It would be pleasant to pause here and leave the impression of an age which delighted in the out-of-doors and in sports. That, however, is only a part of the picture. Two factors must be recognized about the love of sports at this time: these were individual competitions and did not emphasize the subordination of the individual in the success of the team, because the focus of attention was upon the one mortal who was divine, and the competitive element in these sports was practical in the period, because it led to skill in warfare. Pharaoh was not simply the invincible athlete; he was demonstrably the invincible warrior, with his speed, his strength, and his accuracy with the chariot and with the bow. It was not incompatible with his prowess as a sportsman that Amen-hotep II was a ruthless warrior.

He had no scruples in telling us how he bashed to death seven Asiatic princes with his own mace and then hanged their bodies on the city wall.[85] This contributed to the building up of a legend to encourage his Egyptian followers and discourage any Asiatic rebels. When Kadesh on the Orontes surrendered to him, he first administered to the Asiatics an oath of fealty and then put on an exhibition for their entertainment.

82. *Ibid.*
83. Breasted, *ARE*, II, §§ 813–15; 863–65.

84. *Ibid.*, § 809.
85. *Ibid.*, § 797.

"His majesty shot at two targets of copper in hammered work(?), in their presence, on the south side of this town."[86] He deliberately took chances, with a relish in his independent power. When his army was crossing the Orontes, he guarded the rear and was attacked by Asiatics. He claimed that he put them to rout and captured eight men all by himself. "Not a single one was with his majesty, except for himself with his valiant arm." He drove to the Syrian town of Khashabu "alone, without a companion. He returned thence in a short moment, and he brought back sixteen living *maryanu*-warriors[87] on the two sides of his chariot, twenty (severed) hands (hanging) at the foreheads of his horses, and sixty cattle driven before him. Submission was made to his majesty by this town." His most foolhardy exploit was the personal guarding of more than three hundred Asiatic captives all night. "After his majesty saw the very abundant plunder, they were made into living prisoners, and two ditches were made around all of them(?). Then they were filled with fire, and his majesty kept watch over it until daybreak, while his battle-axe was in his right hand, alone, without a single one with him, while the army was far from him, far from hearing(?) the cry of Pharaoh."[88] This was sheer and unnecessary bravura, of the spectacular nature which would be widely reported in order to impress men with the futility of withstanding so superhuman a warrior. The feat may have been inspired. It came immediately after the god Amon had appeared to pharaoh in a dream "to give valor to his son" and to serve as "the magical protection of his person, guarding the ruler." After such oracular assurance, Pharaoh may have felt obliged to demonstrate his valor and his inviolability. But the feat was in character, in any case.

We have spent an inordinate amount of time on the emphasis of this period upon physical prowess, because it so clearly typifies the age, before imperial languor set in and it became easier to employ somebody else to toil and to meet danger. The initial setting up of empire was strictly an Egyptian task, and it called for the adventurous energies of the land, as symbolized in the person of the pharaoh. There were to be later examples of personal prowess—as in Ramses II's brave extrication of himself from an ambush at Kadesh—but these would be exceptional in an age which was ostentatiously magnificent and which

86. A. M. Badawi in *ASAE*, XLII (1943), 1 ff.

87. On the *maryanu* warrior aristocracy of Syria-Palestine, see W. F. Albright in *Archiv für Orientforschung*, VI (1930–31), 217 ff.

88. Badawi, *op. cit.*

could rely upon professional soldiers and hired mercenaries as shock troops. The athletic period was a fitting stage of energy before Egypt could enjoy the fruits of accomplished empire.

Before leaving the exploits of Amen-hotep II, we should mention the captives which he brought back to Egypt. Included in the captives of his seventh year were 270 women, "the favorites (or musicians?) of the princes of every foreign country . . . in addition to their paraphernalia for entertaining the heart, of silver and gold." The addition of these ladies and entertainers from Asia to the Egyptian harem is significant for the international character of the time. In his ninth year, pharaoh brought back no less than ninety thousand captives, including 127 Asiatic princes. As far as we can control the figures, the Bedouin of the south numbered about fifteen thousand, the settled inhabitants of Palestine-Syria, about thirty-six thousand, the settled inhabitants of north Syria, about fifteen thousand, and the ʿApiru numbered thirty-six hundred. These ʿApiru interest us, because the word is etymologically related to the word "Hebrew," although the present group cannot have come from the Children of Israel. The term here probably applies to nomadic peoples, perhaps from Transjordan. The large total of the captives means that so great a number of foreign slaves could be used successfully on Egyptian enterprises and that the growth of empire was already putting a demand upon the army to bring back slave troops.[89]

One of the effects of international consciousness was the new cosmopolitan character of the Egyptian court and the consequent breakdown of some of the older principles about the succession to the throne. A prince who had been born to a subordinate queen had formerly found it wise to have his legitimacy strengthened by marriage to a princess of the direct royal line, in order to validate his title to the throne. Thus Thut-mose III had been of inferior birth and had felt obliged to strengthen his position by marrying at least three princesses of full legitimacy. His son was thus of full blood and right. But the grandson, Thut-mose IV, was again the son of a subordinate queen, and now, with the Empire two generations under way, did not feel the old compulsion to strengthen his position. On the contrary, he took to wife the daughter of Artatama, the King of Mitanni, and she became the mother of the future Amen-hotep III. The latter was certainly not of the purest royal line, with such a father and such a mother—he was half-Mitannian. He showed no concern about the purity of his royal blood. He made an Egyptian commoner his Great King's Wife, the girl Tiy,

89. *Ibid.* On the ʿApiru, cf. J. A. Wilson in *AJSL*, XLIX (1933), 275 ff.

whose parents bore no titles of any consequence.[90] There was a grand, imperial sweep to this demonstration that the pharaoh of Egypt was beyond rules and beyond reproach, and Tiy was a woman of character and energy, who made an excellent queen. However, this rapid process of diluting the royal blood shows clearly how the former canons and traditions had broken down, how it was possible to ignore the old sacred proscriptions and the old isolations of Egypt and of the pharaoh.

The marriage of Thut-mose IV to a Mitannian princess witnessed the end of hostilities between Egypt and that country. It brought in a different alignment of power because of a new threat, the Hittites of Anatolia. Hittite pretensions imperiled both Mitanni and Egypt, so that those countries must have composed their rivalry in northern Syria and joined together to keep out the new competitor. The alliance lasted until Hatti finally overwhelmed Mitanni in the Amarna age. Before that, there were at least two further royal marriages, for one of which we possess the formal announcement on a commemorative scarab of Amen-hotep III: "Year 10 under Amen-hotep and the Great King's Wife Tiy, whose father's name is Yuya and whose mother's name is Tuya. Marvels brought to his majesty: Gilu-Khepa, daughter of the Prince of Mitanni, Shuttarna, and the chief of her harem-ladies, 317 women."[91] Even on the proclamation of this great marriage of state, the priority of the daughter of commoners, Tiy, was asserted. The coming of a foreign princess did not endanger her position as the first wife.

One feature of the imperial age of Egyptian history was the prominence of women. In one sense, this was not new. Egyptian queens had been important factors in the Old Kingdom, when Khent-kaus erected for herself a monument vying with the pyramids in size, and when the queen-mother of Pepi II served as regent during his infancy.[92] The Eighteenth Dynasty, however, surpassed previous ages in the acknowledged influence of women. Hat-shepsut took unto herself male titles and attributes and became a "king." Tiy and Nefert-iti were given unusual artistic prominence by their husbands, Amen-hotep III and Akh-en-Aton. In statue groups, Tiy may appear in colossal size, seated by her colossal husband, instead of modestly clinging to his leg as an individual of relative insignificance and thus of depicted smallness (Fig. 22a). Her husband delighted to announce that he was honoring her, by digging for her a pleasure lake, whereon the imperial couple might sail in the royal barge named "Aton Gleams."[93] The guarded privacy of the royal harem was infringed by such conspicuous display of a queen, and in the Amarna period there would be even more public demonstration of the secrets of the life of the royal family.

This acknowledged importance of women was not restricted to queens—who were, after all, daughters or wives or mothers of gods. It has been pointed out that the artistic convention of a married couple under the earlier periods gave priority to the husband and made the wife his attaché, whereas the Empire presented the couple as a balanced pair in equal prominence.[94] Further, such business documents as we possess from the Empire show that women had their own rights to property, to buying and selling, or to testifying in court. As we have been stressing, this was a highly developed society, meriting the term "civilized."

Fifty years after the conquests of Thut-mose III, thirty years after the muscular feats of Amen-hotep II, Egypt was able to indulge herself in imperial magnificence under Amen-hotep III and Queen Tiy. The empire seemed assured, so that a military parade of power was needed only rarely. Egypt appeared to be the very center of the known world, with material and spiritual tribute pouring into the land. There seemed to be an unending wealth for the rulers of the world. The effort had been great, but the fruits were rich. It was now time to sit and enjoy those fruits.

Amen-hotep III built extensively in Egypt, Nubia, and the Sudan. In sheer bulk the monuments attributed to him are impressive. His imperial magnificence was expressed in large public works, and he started that passion for the colossal which characterized the later Empire. The Cairo Museum has a tremendous seated group of Amen-hotep and Tiy, towering and impressive or bulky and coarse, according to one's taste.[95] In front of his mortuary temple in Thebes, the two soaring "Colossi of Memnon" symbolized his obsession with size. At the south end of the Theban necropolis he built an extensive palace, close to a great pleasure lake, which was a mile and a half long by two-thirds of a mile wide. The fragmentary remains of this palace show a sumptuous art, with a fluid and naturalistic line that foreshadows the forthcoming revolution of the Amarna period.

93. Breasted, *ARE*, II, § 869.

94. W. Spiegelberg in *JEA*, XV (1929), 199. See our Figs. 7c and 7d.

95. G. Jéquier, *L'Architecture et la Décoration dans l'ancienne Égypte. Les Temples Memphites et Thébains* (Paris, n.d.), Pl. 77.

To the court of Amen-hotep III came the world, bringing its "trib-ute" to the mighty emperor and hoping to carry away some of the gold of Nubia. The grovelling protestations of humble loyalty which we may read in the international correspondence of the time asserted the universal sway of Egypt, so that pharaoh might sit comfortably at home, assured that his throne was firmly planted on top of the world. He looked at his mortuary temple and felt confident that he would be imperially served throughout eternity: "Its workhouse is full of male and female slaves, of the children of the princes of all the countries which his majesty captured. Its storehouses contain (all) good things, whose numbers cannot be known. It is surrounded with the settlements of Syrians, colonized with the children of princes. Its cattle are like the sands of the shore; they make up millions." In gratitude, pharaoh turned to the imperial god who had guaranteed for him such wealth and "made other monuments for Amon, the like of which has never occurred."[96]

Thus Egypt, by extending her protective frontiers, had won new power and reputation and seemed to have gained a new security. She sat lazily content in her wealth and might. There is a stela depicting Amen-hotep III and Tiy which seems to symbolize the rather jaded and effete opulence of the period (Fig. 22b). The pharaoh is seated in a languid and weary position, old and fat and empty of new joys and excitements. The tremendous experiences of the past century had left no contentment in the serene and patient expectation of eternal life. Now a young king might throw himself violently into hunting or campaigning, but an old king had experienced so much adulation and novelty that even the after-life could offer nothing of great appeal. Where were the new worlds to conquer?[97]

In a very true sense, the period between Thut-mose III and Amen-hotep III—less than a century in length—was the transitional point in the Egyptian culture. More clearly than the late predynastic period it was an urban revolution which altered the simple agricultural and introverted society in the Nile Valley. Throughout the preceding cen-turies the maintenance of status had been a stronger force than the slow changes of time. Under the shock of empire changes became so rapid that the old sanctions of life could no longer hold the society within its distinct integrity.

Returning to the concept of the "folk society," which we examined

96. Breasted, *ARE*, II, §§ 878 ff.
97. The stela was published by F. Ll. Griffith in *JEA*, XII (1926), 1 f.

in Chapter II,[98] we saw that it was defined as relatively small, isolated from other influence, homogeneous, and strongly conscious of the group as a unit. The Empire struck the strongest blow against isolation and group solidarity, and it certainly expanded the recognized size indefinitely. In the folk society a ruling unit is the family or the clan; the old principles of hereditary legitimacy in the royal family were violated by the Empire. In the folk society the force of tradition governs behavior and the sacred governs the secular, but when the folk society changes to the urban society, there is cultural disorganization and the secular makes headway against the sacred. These elements of the loss of traditional behavior, the disintegration of the recognized culture, and increasing secularization were all products of the changes brought in by empire. In previous centuries Egypt had been an overgrown folk society; suddenly it had become a cosmopolitan and urbanized society, diffused and heterogeneous, breaking with tradition, and more strongly secularized. The effects of such change on the Egyptian spirit could not fail to be sweepingly influential.

98. Pp. 34–35 above.

IX

IRREPRESSIBLE CONFLICT

Later Dynasty 18 (about 1375–1325 B.C.)

WHEN the hard shell of long-established custom is placed under insistent pressure along a new plane, something is certain to crack. A sacred society which has always emphasized its unchanging status cannot easily accommodate itself to a new order, with the vulgarization and alienation of its basic forms of expression. In theory, one would expect a conflict between the traditionalists and the modernists as the agonizing crisis of the culture. Such a conflict may have been the main feature of the antagonism between Hat-shepsut and Thut-mose III. If so, its virulence must have been relieved by the immediate success, materially and spiritually, of empire. Conservatism could not easily withstand the sweeping glory of military victory and the sudden increase in wealth and power for the ruling forces of Egypt. Thus the vulgarization and alienation of the cherished Egyptian system are clearly visible in a period of prosperity and evident self-satisfaction, that century between the Battle of Megiddo, around 1468 B.C., and the death of Amen-hotep III, around 1375 B.C. We may not doubt that there were conservative grumblers at the rapid and subversive changes affecting the land, but their criticism made little impression in an unparalleled era of luxury and world acclaim.

When violent and irreconcilable conflict finally did break out, in the Amarna age, the antagonists did not line up simply as conservatives and modernists, as priestly isolationists and militaristic imperializers. That issue apparently was dead with Hat-shepsut. The pious retention of Egypt's aloof superiority to all other cultures was not recognized as being the burning issue in the new contest for power. Nor did the crisis bring forward any party which clearly and emphatically demanded a return to the simpler and purer ways of pre-Empire Egypt. The line-up of the protagonists in the struggle was more complicated than that, and what we are able to see is a contest for the essential power in the land, with modernism being a forceful expression of that contest.

The spotlight throws itself upon pharaoh and the priesthood of Amon as the prominent opponents in the contest for power, and this focus is correct. But the pharaoh Akh-en-Aton appeared as the champion of the new in religion—particularly universalism—in domestic manners and morals, in art, and in language and literature, although he was elaborately disinterested in the empire, which had provoked the new. Pharaoh showed no desire to return to the ways of Hat-shepsut and earlier ages, even though his formal retirement from the capital at Thebes to a new, rural capital at Tell el-Amarna was a withdrawal from a cosmopolitan center of modern excitement. By implication, the priesthood of Amon was fully committed to the aggressive maintenance of empire, which had so enriched their temple, but was elaborately disinterested in the new fads in manners and morals which had come in with empire. Each party was apparently grasping for the current power in this great state, without relation to the past or to ideologies deriving from the past.

In pharaoh's camp we see a swarm of parvenus, men who had descended from families of no previous importance but who rose to high position in this new movement. On the other hand, the old ruling families who had handed down the highest offices in the land from father to son dropped out of sight in the revolution. This means that the old civil bureaucracy, a landed and hereditary aristocracy, was on the side of the priesthood of Amon, and that pharaoh had been obliged to find new civil servants among those recently rich through empire but not conservative because of vested interests and traditions. Interestingly enough, the army seems to have been aligned on pharaoh's side, even though this cost them the advantages accruing through an aggressive maintenance of empire. Whether the adherence of the general Har-em-hab (Fig. 26a) to the revolutionary pharaohs resulted from the professional loyalty of a soldier to his sovereign or whether the army was seeking to gain a power triumph over the civil bureaucracy and the priesthood of Amon, we cannot know. In view of the army commander's success in taking over the throne under Har-em-hab and again under the

Twenty-First Dynasty, it would seem that a political struggle was an important factor.[1]

Another political factor may have been other priesthoods which were jealous of the sudden and overpowering prominence of Amon and his priesthood. We may only guess at this possibility, since the evidence is almost silent on the point. The particular priesthood which might well have opposed Amon was that of Re of Heliopolis, an ancient and once dominating shrine, which may have regarded Amon as a bumptious upstart. Re was the sun-god, and we shall see elements in the revolutionary sun-worship which showed some retention of Re's cult. However, there is no visible evidence that the priesthood at Heliopolis instigated the attack on Amon. They may merely have been complacent onlookers at his temporary eclipse, or they may even have suffered eclipse as he did, although to a lesser degree. If the old shrine at Heliopolis were a factor, it would have been the only element fully on the side of ancient tradition against the changes of empire; but we do not know enough to claim that it was so engaged.

To be sure, all of this is anticipatory, because we have not yet given the history of the Amarna revolution, but it is a necessary preliminary for the general setting of a struggle for power which the records have personalized for us. Most of our knowledge about the revolution comes from the monuments of the revolutionary pharaoh, Amen-hotep IV, who became Akh-en-Aton, from correspondence addressed to his court, or from passing hostile references to him in later ages, after the revolution had failed. Further, the broodingly introspective figures of this king, rendered in an extremely naturalistic art which contrasted sharply with the past, make him stand out from the other pharaohs with individual sharpness. One who is an iconoclast, revolutionary, modernist, and intellectual is always a subject of personal interest. The history of the Amarna revolution is inevitably written around the personality of Akh-en-Aton. That focus on the individual instead of "the cultural process" is justified because Akh-en-Aton was not an ordinary man, so that his high individuality in his position of power made him far more than a tool of the forces of his day; it is also justified because this pharaoh was the acknowledged leader of forces of the day. Certainly one admits that the tensions in Egypt were such that some violent crisis was inevitable, no matter who was pharaoh; but the peculiar trend of the crisis was very highly conditioned by the peculiar character of the

1. Helck, op. cit., pp. 71 ff.; K. Pflüger, Haremhab und die Amarnazeit (Zwickau, 1936).

pharaoh who came to the throne. We may state the theoretical background of the struggle and may line up the political parties, but thereafter we shall write the story in terms of the individual Akh-en-Aton.[2]

We have already devoted some attention to the background of the Amarna movement, in art, in language and literature, and in domestic manners. We have also noted that a product of empire was universalism in religion, whereby once localized gods came to be recognized as having cosmic sway. We need, however, to give some attention to the background of the new revolutionary religion, Atonism, in the days before Akh-en-Aton made his formal break with Amonism.

Sun-worship had been perennial in ancient Egypt, and the sun had various phases which were recognized as distinct gods or as aspects of the same god. Re of Heliopolis came to be the sun-god par excellence, thereby taking over Heliopolitan power from Atum, the creator god, who was merged with the newcomer as Re-Atum. Re also manifested himself with other aspects of the sun, for example, the god of the horizon, as Re-Har-akhti. As the supreme god, Re was amalgamated with other important gods, to become Amon-Re or Amon-Re-Har-akhti, Sobek-Re, Khnum-Re, and so on. This process of syncretism is important, for the merger of originally distinct gods into a single being of manifestations could, in its logical development, lead to monotheism, with all aspects of deity compounded into one supreme being. That never became the situation in Egypt, because this culture was never logically consistent in our modern terms, and because the blending of different beings into a single being for a functional purpose never destroyed the separate identities of those beings. Amon and Re remained separate gods of air and sun, despite their functional incorporation as the supreme god of the nation, Amon-Re. The increasing wealth and political power of Amon-Re, King of the Gods, at Karnak never permitted him to take over the temple of the sun-god Re at Heliopolis. It is important to remember that the ancient Egyptians did not think as we do, and that their pragmatic nature permitted them to see functional aspects of deity as discrete and topical for specific functional purpose, here overlapping and producing a single compound god for one purpose, there distinct and retaining separate gods for different purposes.

2. Cf. L. A. White, "Ikhnaton: the Great Man *vs.* the Culture Process," in *Journal of the American Oriental Society*, LXVIII (1948), 91 ff. ("the *general trend* of events would have been the same had Ikhnaton been but a sack of sawdust"); and the answering criticism by W. F. Edgerton, " 'The Great Man': a Note on Methods," *ibid.*, pp. 192 f.

Any claim that the Egyptians were habitual monotheists[3] rests upon a misunderstanding of Egyptian psychology, with its alternative ways of looking at phenomena under different conditions and with its deliberate retention of the old despite new combinations. The syncretism of the sun-god with other deities did not lead to sun-worship as monotheism. On the other hand, the topical nature of syncretism did permit the focus on a single divine being such as we shall see in the Amarna religion.

Now among the various sun-gods or aspects of a sun-god, there had been no Aton before the middle of the Eighteenth Dynasty. The word *aton* had meant the physical disk of the sun, a seat of the god, but not a god in itself. However, the life-giving and life-sustaining power of the sun-disk was deified before the time of Akh-en-Aton. We have already seen that Amen-hotep III and Tiy sailed out on their pleasure lake in a barge named "Aton Gleams." Indeed, we may push the divinity of the Aton back to the reign of Thut-mose IV, who issued a large commemorative scarab stating that the pharaoh fought, "with the Aton before him," and that he campaigned abroad "to make the foreigners to be like the (Egyptian) people, in order to serve the Aton forever."[4]

When we find, under Amen-hotep III, that a certain Ra-mose was both a priest of Amon and "Steward in the Temple of the Aton," and that an inscription asks this pharaoh to induce Amon-Re to give a mortuary offering to the "Scribe of the Treasury of the Temple of the Aton" named Pen-buy,[5] we see that the Aton was a god possessing a temple at Thebes before the Amarna revolution and that this new god was apparently in harmonious working relation with Amon. These texts even make it possible that Amen-hotep III built a shrine to the Aton in or near the great temple enclosure of Amon at Karnak. At any rate, it is clear that Akh-en-Aton did not invent the life-sustaining sun-disk as a philosophical concept, but found such a concept already to hand.

Similarly, the mortuary god Osiris had not been displaced by the Aton on a monument rendered in the new modernistic art and therefore close to the Amarna period, representing a deceased Egyptian worshipping the enthroned Osiris and praying that he might go forth

3. Such as that of E. A. W. Budge, *From Fetish to God in Ancient Egypt* (London, 1934), pp. 3 f.: The Egyptian "was a monotheist pure and simple as a sun-worshipper. It avails nothing to call his monotheism 'henotheism.'" Similarly, for the syncretistic hymns published by A. H. Gardiner as "monotheistic hymns," in *ZÄS*, XLII (1905), 12 ff., and in *Hieratic Papyri in the British Museum. Third Series* (London, 1935), I, 28 ff.

4. A. W. Shorter in *JEA* XVII (1931), 23 ff.; XVIII (1932), 110 f.; see also XXII (1936), 3 ff.

5. S. R. K. Glanville in *JEA*, XV (1929), 5 f.

from the tomb "as a living *ba*, in order to see the Aton upon earth." Perhaps this means only the physical disk of the sun, because the man says to Osiris: "Thou arisest like Re on the horizon; his disk (*aton*) is thy disk, his form is thy form, his dread is thy dread." In a time in which the Aton was already worshipped as a god this monument does show him in relation to deities whom he later attempted to obliterate.[6]

One of the important aspects of the Aton was to be its universal cherishing of all living things in all countries, a recognition of the value of beings outside of Egypt which was different from the expressed parochialism of religion in the Old and Middle Kingdoms. However, this universalism was also known before the Amarna revolution. Amon, as the invisible god of the air, had been seen as unlimited before this time: "Lord of the *Medjai* and ruler of Punt . . . the beautiful of face, who comes (from) God's Land (to the east). . . . Jubilation to thee for every foreign country—to the height of heaven, to the width of earth, to the depth of the Great Green Sea! . . . The solitary sole one, without his peer, . . . living on truth every day."[7]

Twin brothers named Seth and Horus were architects at Thebes in the reign of Amen-hotep III. They erected stelae praising Amon in universalist terms and in language markedly similar to that which Akh-en-Aton was going to use in his hymn to the Aton. "When thou crossest the sky, all faces behold thee, but when thou departest, thou art hidden from their faces. . . . When thou settest in the western mountain, then they sleep in the manner of death. . . . The fashioner of that which the soil produces, . . . a mother of profit to gods and men; a patient craftsman, greatly wearying (himself) as their maker, . . . valiant herdsman, driving his cattle, their refuge and the maker of their living. . . . The sole lord, who reaches the ends of the lands every day, as one who sees them that tread thereon. . . . Every land chatters at his rising every day, in order to praise him." In this hymn the two brothers give exclusive attention to Amon, a god of universal sway, whom they call the "sole lord." This, however, does not preclude their devotion to other deities. In the scenes and texts which surround the main inscription, the brothers give service to Osiris, Anubis, Amon-Re, Mut, Khonsu, Hat-Hor in two forms, Re-Har-akhti, Sokar, Isis, and the deified

6. É. Drioton in *ASAE*, XLIII (1943), 15 ff.

7. Erman, *LAE*, pp. 282 ff. This Papyrus Boulaq 17 is from the pre-Amarna Eighteenth Dynasty. It may be earlier—although not necessarily in its universalist aspects—as passages from the hymn have been found from the Second Intermediate Period: Selim Hassan, *Hymnes religieux du Moyen Empire* (Cairo, 1928), pp. 157 ff.

queen Ahmes Nefert-iri. The centering of their attention upon one god did not mean their disavowal of other gods.[8]

There is another factor of the Amarna revolution which was fore-shadowed in previous reigns, and that was the propagandistic emphasis upon ma‘at, "truth." Akh-en-Aton and his god, the Aton, "lived on truth," and this applied both to the open candor of the sun-disk and to the open candor of the pharaoh's life. We shall examine this claimed devotion to "truth" shortly. Here we may note briefly that Amen-hotep III had also expressed an exceptional relation to ma‘at. Two of his names were Neb-ma‘at-Re, "the Lord of Truth (is) Re," and Kha-em-ma‘at, "He Who Makes Appearance in Truth." One of Amen-hotep III's courtiers said: "I performed truth for the Lord of Truth (Amen-hotep III) at all times, knowing that he rejoices in it," and another said: "I performed truth [for Amon-]Re, knowing that he lives on it," thus in clear anticipation of the same statements in Amarna times.[9] Insofar as this "truth" may be related to the new naturalism in art, we have seen that a fluid line and a new subject matter of art were already present in Amen-hotep III's reign, particularly in his Theban palace.

Although Amen-hotep III in his older age may have become jaded and languid, he had been an energetic king in his youth, vigorous in the hunt or in furthering public works. His roundish, commonplace face suggests nothing of the intellectual or dreamer or doctrinaire. His son, who at first bore the same name, was of a very different physical type. His face was thin to the point of being haggard, with a drooping and in-drawn expression that betokens an introspective personality. His shoulders were narrow and sloping, and his hips and abdomen were disproportionately large. Perhaps from his youth he had suffered from some systemic ailment, which robbed him of the possibility of imitating the vigor and athletic prowess of his predecessors and doomed him to a life of intellectual prowess—and to the company of the ladies of the harem rather than the gentlemen of the hunt and of the campaign. Physiologists who have commented on his peculiar physique have not agreed on the nature of his illness. Certainly he was strangely formed, but he had a reasonable span of life, including at least seventeen years of reign. It may be argued that he was of abnormal appearance from his youth, because his rounded head, drooping jaw, sloping shoulders, and pot-belly became an artistic convention for all Egyptians under his

8. A. Varille in BIFAO, XLI (1942), 25 ff.; J. S. F. Garnot in JEA, XXXV (1949), 63 ff. J. H. Breasted, The Dawn of Conscience (New York, 1933), pp. 275 ff., had recognized the importance of the hymn.

9. Glanville, op. cit., pp. 4 f.

reign, which would indicate that his abnormality had always been normal to him, so that the flattery of his artists accepted it as the proper design for all men and surrounded him in pictures with men and women like himself. His slightness of frame may have come from his mother Tiy, but there is no evidence that his ideas were so derived.

In the course of time the young prince Amen-hotep married his gracious sister Nefert-iti and was associated with his father upon the throne as coregent. We know that the elder Amen-hotep had badly abscessed teeth, and he may have been willing to let his son share some of the cares and duties of rule. There is one curious element in the reign of young Amen-hotep IV which needs comment, even though the answer must be uncertain. Somewhere around his sixth year he celebrated the jubilee of himself and of the Aton, thus expressing the doctrine that he and his god had been ruling for the same length of time. An Egyptian royal jubilee was normally—there are exceptions—commemorative of thirty years of accomplished rule. If the thirty years have any meaning in this case, they may indicate that the worship of the Aton had been formally instituted thirty years earlier, in the temple to that god which has already been mentioned, and perhaps that the pharaoh had also been born in the same year. The one obvious conclusion is that Amen-hotep IV was claiming a close ruling relationship between the god and himself, by so making the two of them coeval in time.[10]

Amen-hotep IV and Nefert-iti had six daughters, who are depicted as infants in most of the scenes of the time. The couple was probably not very old when the prince became coregent. On the other hand, shortly after the king's twelfth year, his eldest daughter was mature enough to function at the court as her father's chief womanly representative. In the orient, where girls mature early, she may have been no more than a dozen years old. This does give us a hint as to the youth of Amen-hotep IV and his sister-wife Nefert-iti. The fact that the couple did produce six daughters—and, alas! no sons—tells us that the pharaoh was not so diseased as to prevent his generating offspring. The family life of the royal couple and their daughters surpassed that of Amen-hotep III and Tiy in visible and publicized devotion. The austere seclusion of former pharaohs and particularly of their harem ladies was so vigorously renounced that we seem to have something of an official policy. Certainly women had never before been displayed so prominently as participants in public life, nor had there been such candid

10. F. Ll. Griffith in *JEA*, V (1918), 61 ff.

depictions of pharaoh's affection for his wife and daughters. It was an age of strong feminism.

Around 1377 to 1375 B.C. the old king Amen-hotep III died, and the young king found himself sole ruler of the powerful Egyptian Empire. He was living at the capital city Thebes, and thus far his reign had been marked by those rapid changes in custom and expression which we have already noted but by no formal and overt break with the past. However, all the elements of revolutionary proclamation were present, and the tensions must have been strong. The young pharaoh had been building monuments in the Temple of Amon at Karnak. Recent excavation there has shown that his construction works were later torn down and used as the inner core blocks for the monuments of subsequent pharaohs. His reliefs were already in that characteristic and naturalistic art which we associate with his reign: the human figures rounded and boneless, with something of the distortion of the body which pharaoh himself showed. The most extraordinary pieces are some fascinatingly ugly colossal statues of Amen-hotep IV, found directly behind the great Temple of Amon (Fig. 24b). In their nightmarish distortion of emaciated face and bulbous hips, they show that the extreme expression of Amarna "naturalism" was current at the beginning of the reign, before the official break and the move away from Thebes. It is noteworthy that some of the most violent modernism came at the beginning of the movement, and some of the most nearly conventional pieces came later in the reign.[11]

The nobles of Amen-hotep IV's early years had a number of tombs carved in the Theban hillside. These also were executed in that artistic style which marked the revolution, and they emphasized an adulation of the pharaoh rather than the extension of this life into the next. Thus religion was already showing its deviation from the past in the content of tomb themes, before the break with Amon and the move to Tell el-Amarna.[12]

11. J. D. S. Pendlebury, *Tell el-Amarna* (London, 1935), pp. 129 f., 135, Pl. VI; H. Chevrier in *ASAE*, XXVI (1926), 126 f., Pl. II.

12. N. de G. Davies in *JEA*, IX (1923), 132 ff. Davies noted the background of the new art in Theban tombs as early as the reign of Thut-mose IV (*BMMA*, December, 1923, Part II, pp. 40 ff.). One of the tombs from that reign "shows the same precise and careful work" as in the past. "But there is a later group which is characterized by a departure from the cold regularity and precision of the prevailing mode, in favor of a freer, more involved, and sketchy style. . . . These tombs . . . reveal observation of nature and some faith in it, but a great falling off in self-discipline and in technique." Most of the tombs of the reign of Amen-hotep III retain the older style, "careful, exact, and decorative still, but now softened, refined, and enriched to a very high degree." Then the tombs of Amen-hotep IV's early years reveal "with dramatic force the amazing change that had been wrought in that brief space alike in art-forms and in religious tenets."

How or why the formal break came we do not know. We have emphasized the struggle for power, and it must finally have become necessary for pharaoh to take violent action. In his sixth year, he changed his name from Amen-hotep, "Amon-is-Satisfied-(with-this-Person)," to Akh-en-Aton, either "He-Who-is-Serviceable-to-the-Aton" or "It-Goes-Well-with-the-Aton." The disavowal of the old god and the embracing of the new were formal, because the name of the king was an expression of state policy. Akh-en-Aton also moved the capital of Egypt from Thebes, the "City of Amon," to a new site in Middle Egypt almost three hundred miles north of Thebes, modernly called Tell el-Amarna. Perhaps it was not entirely an untrodden settlement, because there is evidence that his grandfather, Thut-mose IV, had had some interest in the place,[13] but certainly it was a new capital city on a free and expansive scale. Its limits were over eight miles apart, the city-planning was spacious, comprehensive, and directed toward eternity. This was to be the new political and religious center, Akhet-Aton, "the Place of the Effective Glory of the Aton."

Here were built the royal palaces and the Temple of the Aton. This temple, like the little personal chapels throughout the city, was open to the air, so that the sun-disk might be worshipped in its full glory, in contrast to the covered mystery of older temples. The nobles and officials laid out great estates on a generous garden-city scale, contrasting to the cramped concentration of Thebes (Fig. 25). Even the workmen's villages were erected on well-ordered streets, with small but neat and uniform houses. The city was attractive and was planned to be close to nature, under the life-giving sun-disk.

Of course, those who accompanied Akh-en-Aton to Amarna had elected to follow the king, because their careers lay in loyalty or because they were partisans of the revolution. Thus pharaoh was surrounded by a devoted court of like-minded enthusiasts or fawning sycophants. There was no one here to challenge his revolutionary ideas. From his sixth to his twelfth years, he was free to abandon himself to his interpretation of *ma'at* in religion, art, social life, and so on. For those six years the successful forward movement of revolution was greater than the political and economic advantage of maintaining status.

Akh-en-Aton took repeated vows that he would never leave his new capital, and he stated the reason for its foundation in terms of his god. He dedicated the entire area, from horizon to horizon, whether land, people, cattle, fowl, or anything else, "to my father, the living Aton,

13. Shorter, *op. cit.*

for the Temple of the Aton in Akhet-Aton, forever and ever."[14] We may contrast this dedication with the restoration inscription of Tut-ankh-Amon, after the revolution had failed. He described the effects of heresy. "The temples of the gods and goddesses . . . had gone to pieces. Their shrines had become desolate and had become overgrown mounds. . . . The land was topsy-turvy, and the gods turned their backs upon this land. . . . If one prayed to a god to seek counsel from him, he would never come [at all]. If one made supplication to a goddess similarly, she would never come at all. Their very hearts were hurt(?), so that they destroyed that which had been made." What could this penitent, restoring pharaoh do? "He expelled deceit throughout the Two Lands, and *ma·at* was set up, and lying [was made?] an abomination of the land, as (in) its first time." Tut-ankh-Amon had to propitiate the indignant gods by restoring and adding to their property. The new gifts to the temples were "privileged and protected to (the benefit of) my fathers, all the gods, through a desire to satisfy them by doing what their *ka* wishes, so that they may protect Egypt."[15]

As we might expect in ancient Egypt, these two texts give the whole *raison d'être* of revolution as the service of the gods. The changes in art, literature, and social manners had been evolutionary over several generations; the changes in religion struck at the supporting dogma of the state, so that evolutionary compromise was finally impossible and revolution was necessary. The divine sanctions of the state were at issue, and the priesthood of Amon could not consent to relinquish Amon's oracular control of the pharaoh.

The pragmatic Egyptian was a wonderful reconciler; he was normally able to fit together two apparently conflicting concepts and treat them as different aspects of the same concept. Here, however, the traditional theory of pharaoh's independent authority had clashed too directly with the vested authority of Amon. There was not enough room for reconciliation. The conflict was not simply political in our modern terms; the religious theory of the state was central to the proper functioning of government. The most important question at issue was whether the pharaoh, as a god, was a free and responsible agent, whose divine word was the law of the land, or whether he was the chief interpreter of the gods to Egypt, so that his official word derived from the oracular guidance by gods whose function was to direct the nation and the empire. The older theory had made the pharaoh the state; that

---

14. Breasted, *ARE*, II, § 972; N. de G. Davies, *The Rock Tombs of El Amarna*, V (*Arch. Surv.*, XVII [1908]), 34.

15. J. Bennett in *JEA*, XXV (1939), 8 ff.

theory had been limited but had not been abrogated by the Re revolution at the beginning of the Fifth Dynasty.[16] The newer theory, arising out of the religious cleansing of the state after the Hyksos impiety and out of the emotional insecurity at the beginning of the Empire, was that the gods ruled the state by "divine command," giving their direction through dreams or oracular responses, and that the pharaoh was merely the channel through which that guidance came. The tremendous rise of Amon and his priesthood, as a product of the success of empire, had placed these two theories in opposition, and, whatever the line-up of factions may have been, the function of pharaoh as ruler was a crucial question.

To be sure, there was a dramatic contrast between Amon and the Aton. Amon was by name "the Hidden One," the unseen and all-pervasive force, although his chief representation was in anthropomorphic form (Fig. 23b). His shrine was the innermost and darkest part of the temple, and he could only be approached through the proper ritual by authorized persons. Even when in public procession, his portable shrine was wrapped in a protective covering. On the other hand, the Aton was the naked physical disk of the sun, which could not be shrouded from any man. His temples lay open to the skies, so that he might be worshipped in visible candor. His only anthropomorphism lay in the fact that the rays coming down from the sun-disk ended in hands, which extended the hieroglyph for "life" to the pharaoh and his family (Fig. 23a). Whether Akh-en-Aton deliberately emphasized the opposition between these two gods we cannot know, but the essential antipathy in concept was innate.

The royal family rode happily around Amarna, worshipping the new god, supervising construction works, holding public ceremonies, and receiving the adulation of the court. It was a time of the concentrated unity of new adventure and of freedom from old restraints. One of the extraordinary features of the period was the public informality of the god-king and his family. They permitted themselves to be depicted in the most candid ways: receiving courtiers when very scantily attired, gnawing at bones at meals, fondling or kissing each other both in the palace and in the open, or the pharaoh caressing a daughter as she sits upon his knee. The dramatic grief of the god-king at the death of his second daughter was a new acknowledgement of Egyptian art.[17] This certainly was "truth," expressed with fanatic fervor. It also was a hu-

16. Pp. 87-88 above.

17. U. Bouriant, G. Legrain, and G. Jéquier, *Monuments pour Servir à l'Étude du Culte d'Atonou en Égypte* (*MIFAO*, VIII [1903]), Pls. VI-IX.

manizing of the god-king to a degree which must have been damaging to Akh-en-Aton's attempt to rewin authority for the pharaoh.[18]

The propagandistic slogan of the revolution lay in *ma‘at*, which here must be translated "truth," rather than "justice." The candor of family life, the naturalism in art, the open equity of the sun-disk, and the colloquial coloring of the texts were all aspects of this new emphasis on *ma‘at*. In his official names, Akh-en-Aton styled himself "he who lives on *ma‘at*" as the food which gave him life. The Aton became officially "he who is satisfied with *ma‘at*," that is, who accepted *ma‘at* as the proper offering of the worshipper. We have seen that this emphasis on *ma‘at* had appeared in the reign of Akh-en-Aton's father. It is also noteworthy that the Twelfth Dynasty had expressed an interest in *ma‘at* (where we preferred the translation "justice") and that that dynasty had shown a kind of naturalism or realism in art, particularly in the careworn faces of the pharaohs.[19] That is a valid comparison, even though the *ma‘at* of the Twelfth Dynasty had been articulated as social justice, rather than as an intellectual revolt against the cloistered secrecy of the gods.

Amarna art has been much discussed, and we shall not analyze it in detail here. Two generalizations might be made: that it varies quite markedly in its modernism from the grotesque to the mildly unconventional, but that all of it must have been anathema to one who was rigidly conservative of the older dignity. We have mentioned above the terrifying colossi of Akh-en-Aton at Karnak, in contrast to more sedate representations of the pharaoh. Similarly, the famous painted bust of Nefert-iti is extreme in its sloping lines, elongated neck, and dreamy expression. There are more conventional representations of the queen, which make her less exotic.[20] However, our modern appreciation of the gracious and natural portraits of Nefert-iti should not blind us to the recognition that such works of art were decidedly non-Egyptian in their startlingly sloping lines and flowing surfaces and in their idealizing the current and temporary instead of the otherworldly and eternal. If we could ask ourselves what was normally good in Egyptian art over the long centuries, rather than what looks good to our modern eyes, we should see how violently abnormal and, therefore, how "bad" the Amarna art was. We shall use the term "naturalism" for it, with an

18. Pendlebury, *op. cit.*, pp. 18 ff., although the amused condescension of his description does scant justice to the solemn purposes which introduced these innovations.

19. Pp. 132–33 above.

20. Pendlebury, *op. cit.*, Pls. V–VI, and *JEA*, XIX (1933), opp. p. 113. Our Fig. 24c.

explanation that this does not involve photographic realism or fidelity, but rather an overreaching attempt to serve nature, sometimes attaining distortion or caricature. It contrasted with portraits in normal periods of Egyptian history, where the seen and known was overlaid with the idealized type which would best serve eternity. Eternity was of less consequence at Amarna than the current exciting adventure.

Egyptian art was always at its happiest in dealing with plants and animals, and Amarna art was no exception to that generalization. The strong love of nature may be illustrated by a fresco from one of the palaces showing marsh life. It includes a superb painting of a kingfisher caught at the very moment of its dive, the instant of arrested power before lightning-quick movement. In the background, the papyrus plants are permitted to grow naturally, cutting across each other easily, instead of forming a fanlike bouquet. This is one of the superb creations of ancient art.[21]

There was a great deal of experimentation by the artists of this period, taking advantage of their liberation from the old restraints. This means that there was a large amount of inferior work, but it also means that the art had a high content of emotion. Sculptors who were excited about the new subjects and techniques in art succeeded in imparting to their creations a sense of strain or brooding or liveliness. When the purpose of their art was removed from eternal and unchanging poise to a portrayal of today's aspects, there was a sudden recognition of time and space, which had formerly been absent. The result was that the subjects portrayed, like that kingfisher in the fresco, seem to be tensed for immediate action because of an inner emotional excitement. Some of them are actually depicted in unusual motion. We see at Amarna the Vizier, who would normally be depicted in stately dignity, running by the royal chariot with an obvious—but un-Egyptian—display of energy.[22] The flying speed with which pharaoh drove his horses around town gives some of the nervous ardor which must have characterized the revolutionary venture and which certainly inspired its artists.

The naturalism which was permitted to run over into exaggerated line had its temptations for the artists. It was very easy to move from depicting everybody with egg-shaped heads, drooping shoulders, and pot-bellies, thus honoring the pharaoh, on to a sly extravagance of

21. Davies and Gardiner, op. cit., II, Pl. LXXVI; Pendlebury, op. cit., Pl. VIII. Our Fig. 28a.

22. N. de G. Davies, The Rock Tombs of El Amarna, II (Arch. Surv., XIV [1905]), Pl. XIII; IV (1906), Pl. XX.

flattery which was purposely grotesque. We may even point to little sketches as deliberate caricatures of the person of the king. The excavator at Amarna mentions a sculptor's practice piece showing the pharaoh with a scrubby, unshaven chin. A child's toy is directly and probably intentionally reminiscent of the scenes of pharaoh driving his chariot, while one of the little princesses pokes the horses with a stick. This toy "shows a model chariot drawn by monkeys. In the chariot is another monkey urging along his steeds (his receding forehead is terribly like the King's), by him a monkey princess prods the rumps of the horse-monkeys which are jibbing and refusing to budge an inch."[23] Where now was the sacrosanct dignity of the god-king, if his subjects dared to caricaturize him? His zeal for truth had led him to a distorted naturalism, which went easily over into parody, and to a candor about his domestic life, which brought him down to the plane of ordinary mortals. In a revolution to rescue his godly autonomy from infringement, he was sacrificing that mystery which alone could maintain the dogma of his divinity. If even those who had followed him to Amarna did not always take him seriously, there would surely be skeptics who would doubt his right to independent authority.

Language and literature were also vulgarized or colloquialized. We have already seen that this process had started much earlier, with the speech of the day creeping gradually into the official writings, into the inscription of Ka-mose at the end of the Seventeenth Dynasty, or into the military annals of Thut-mose III. A strong foreign influence appeared in the language, with the introduction of words from Asiatic languages testifying to the writer's cosmopolitan learning: the *maryanu* chariot warrior, the *merkebet* chariot, the *migdol* fortress, the *akunu* jar, and so on. A new system for the writing of such foreign words and names was even worked out and maintained for some generations.[24] These tendencies had been current before the Amarna revolution. That movement let down the barriers even further. The more formal religious texts at Amarna make some effort to address the god in the old classical language, but even they have a liveliness which is new. Other texts permit the language of the day to enter in broad sweep. The homely little passages between common people in the tomb scenes render the speech of the day with some success, and Akh-en-Aton's

<hr/>

23. Pendlebury, *op. cit.*, pp. xv, 19; H. Frankfort and J. D. S. Pendlebury, *The City of Akhenaten*, II (*EES*, XL [1933]), Pl. XXXI, 4.

24. For the problems connected with the system of writing, cf. W. F. Albright, *The Vocalization of the Egyptian Syllabic Orthography* (New Haven, 1934), and W. F. Edgerton in *Journal of the American Oriental Society*, LX (1940), 473 ff.

boundary stelae have definite passages of the colloquial. This was a sweeping revolution, and one aspect of "truth" was the acknowledgement of everyday speech.

As for the new religion, it included an affirmation of the Aton and a formal disavowal of the older opposing gods. This disavowal consisted of a virulent and consistent attack upon the god Amon, with a somewhat sporadic drive against other gods. Agents were sent throughout Egypt and perhaps through the Empire—we know only about the African Empire—to hack the name of Amon out of the inscriptions and thus to end his power. Their further activities were less consistent. Apparently their eyes were focused upon the hated name of Amon, which they erased as the god's name, in personal names such as Amen-hotep, and even occasionally when it was only the word *amon*, "hidden." Yet in the same inscriptions they might ignore the names of all other gods, as not being the major enemy. They sometimes attacked a deity within his main shrine. For example, Nekhbet was the goddess at el-Kab, and her name was chipped out in her temple at that place.[25] In general, it was too laborious to read every inscription and expunge the names of all gods; the eyes of the hatchet-men searched for the three hieroglyphs which made up the name Amon and tried, by the magic of destroying his name, to end his effective existence.

There is one important exception in this activity. A few inscriptions show a hacking out of the words "the gods."[26] This makes an important contribution to the argument that the Amarna religion aimed at the destruction of Egypt's old polytheism.

With certain exceptions which we shall note, the Amarna texts omit mention of any gods except the Aton. We have seen above, in the passage from Tut-ankh-Amon's restoration inscription, that the temples were neglected, so that the gods "turned their backs upon this land." At the new capital itself, there was a formal elimination of the old deities. If some of the uninitiated workmen smuggled in little household amulets of Hat-Hor and Bes, these were entirely unofficial and were expressions of a continuing folk religion, unrecognized by the new state faith. A violent change was the suppression of the former mortuary religion, with all its elaborate formulation centering on the god Osiris. Mortuary prayers and formulas were not now addressed to Osiris or

25. C. R. Lepsius, *Denkmäler aus Aegypten und Aethiopien* (Berlin, 1849 ff.), III, Pl. 80; *Text* (Leipzig, 1901), IV, 41–44.

26. J. H. Breasted in *ZÄS*, XL (1902–3), 109 f.; N. de G. Davies, *The Tomb of the Vizier Ramose* ("Mond Excavations at Thebes," I [London, 1941]), p. 4.

Anubis, but directly to the pharaoh Akh-en-Aton or through him to the Aton. Those little servant figurines which we call *ushebtis* or *shawabtis*, placed in the tomb to work for the deceased in the next world, show the suppression of the Osirian faith. Instead of calling upon the "Osiris *ushebti*" to perform any work which may be demanded in the future life, they were abbreviated down to the name of the deceased, without any profession of mortuary belief.[27] They seem thus to have been a mere offering or memorial for the dead, a retention of the older form, despite the cutting off of previous doctrine.

The Aton was the round disk of the sun, the source and preserver of life, in man or beast, throughout the universe. He had no other form as a god, although his rays might be depicted as arms which carried life for his worshippers. However, there was a retention of older beliefs in the affirmation that the pharaoh was the son of the Aton, "who issued from his body," as former kings had been the physical sons of Re. The Aton was treated as a ruler, and his formal dogmatic name was written within a cartouche like the names of the pharaohs. These officially promulgated names are instructive, because they show the retention of older names and older gods within the doctrinal concept of the new god. At first the official name of the Aton ran: "Re-Har-akhti, rejoicing on the horizon in his name: 'Shu who is in the Aton sun-disk.' " From the ninth regnal year on, the name was changed to eliminate the sky-god Horus and the light-god Shu, but with the sun-god Re retained: "Re, ruler of the horizon, rejoicing on the horizon in his name of 'Re, the father who has come in the Aton sun-disk.' "[28] The old process of syncretism was still effective and permitted the incorporation of three gods in the earlier version and of Re in the later version.

We do not know whether the worship of Re of Heliopolis was authorized by the Amarna faith. Akh-en-Aton continued in his kingly titles to style himself the "Son of Re," and his throne name was Nefer-kheperu-Re Wa-en-Re, "Beautiful-is-the-Form-of-Re, the-Sole-One-of-Re." His young relative and favorite was named Ankh-kheperu-Re-Smenkh-ka-Re. Two of his daughters were Nefer-neferu-Re and Setep-en-Re. The title of the High Priest of the Aton was "the Chief of the Seers," which was identical with the title of the High Priest of Re at

27. An exception, with modification of the Osirian text to the Atonistic doctrine, published by É Drioton in *ASAE*, XLIII (1943), 15 ff. It should further be noted that *ushebtis* abbreviated down to the name and titles of the deceased were known as early as the reign of Thut-mose IV, which is another document on the prior history of Atonism: A. W. Shorter in *JEA*, XVII (1931), 24.

28. B. Gunn in *JEA*, IX (1923), 168 ff.

Heliopolis. There is no evidence that he functioned as high priest of each god at each shrine; it is more likely that Re was incorporated into the Aton and that full worship at Heliopolis was suspended in the Amarna period. However, we should recognize that Re was given preferential recognition by the new religion, in decided contrast to the persecution of Amon or to the ignoring of Osiris. It should further be recognized that the personification of forces as deities continued at Amarna. The revolution placed an emphasis on *ma‹at*, "truth," and Ma‹at was a goddess and was sometimes so treated by the Amarna texts. In one passage Akh-en-Aton was called the god Shay, "Fate," for his land. It is futile to claim that this was the language of poetical imagery; in ancient Egypt personification *was* deification and not a figure of speech.[29]

The most important observation about Amarna religion is that there were two gods central to the faith, and not one. Akh-en-Aton and his family worshipped the Aton, and everybody else worshipped Akh-en-Aton *as a god*. In addition to his formal names and titles, the pharaoh was referred to as "the good god," and he asserted that he was the physical son of the Aton. The abundant scenes in the Amarna tombs show him serving the living sun-disk, while all of his courtiers bow in adoration to him. Their prayers were not addressed to the Aton, but directly to Akh-en-Aton. The courtier Eye, who was later to become pharaoh, asked Akh-en-Aton for mortuary benefits: "Mayest thou grant to me a good old age as thy favorite; mayest thou grant to me a goodly burial by the command of thy *ka* in my house. . . . May (I) hear thy sweet voice in the sanctuary when thou performest that which pleases thy father, the living Aton."[30] Another noble did pray to the Aton, but prayed only on behalf of Akh-en-Aton, with his petition for himself addressed to the pharaoh: "Mayest thou make thy beloved son Akh-en-Aton to live with thee forever, [to do] what thy heart [wishes], and to behold what thou dost every day, for he rejoices in the sight of thy beauty. . . . Let him (remain) here, until the swan turns black, until the raven turns white, until the mountains stand up to walk, and until the sea runs up the river. And may I continue in service of the good god (Akh-en-Aton), until he assigns (to me) the burial that he gives."[31] This is a stated acknowledgement of the centrality of the pharaoh in the worship of the Aton and of the dependence of the noble upon his god-king.

29. For example, Davies, *op. cit.*, II (1905), Pl. VII, l. 14, pp. 29 f.; IV (1906), Pl. XXXII, l. 1.

30. Breasted, *ARE*, II, § 994; Davies, *op. cit.*, VI (1908), 29, Pl. XXV.

31. Erman, *LAE*, pp. 292 f.; Davies, *op. cit.*, III (1905), 31 f., Pl. XXIX.

Akh-en-Aton himself in his famous hymn to the Aton asserted that this was his personal god. The hymn is entitled "the worship of the Aton . . . by the King Akh-en-Aton and the Queen Nefert-iti," and pharaoh says explicitly: "Thou art in my heart, and there is no other that knows thee except thy son (Akh-en-Aton), whom thou hast initiated into thy plans and into thy power."[32] It must be emphasized that the Aton faith had no penetration below the level of the royal family as an effective religious expression; it was stated to be the exclusive faith of the god-king and his divine family, and the god-king welcomed and encouraged his subjects' worship of his divine being as the source of all the benefits which they might desire.

The self-centered nature of Akh-en-Aton's faith, the fact that only the royal family had a trained and reasoned loyalty to the Aton, and the fact that all of pharaoh's adherents were forced to give their entire devotion to him as a god-king explain why the new religion collapsed after Akh-en-Aton's death. Political and economic factors were also important, but the observation that the Amarna courtiers had contact with the Aton only through their worship of Akh-en-Aton shows the fleeting and superficial nature of the religion. We cannot believe that they cherished within their bosoms the teaching about a benevolent and sustaining sole god, the Aton, when all of their religious exercise was exhausted in worship of Akh-en-Aton. When that pharaoh died and the movement collapsed, they must have scrambled penitently back into the traditional faith, which they could understand and in which they were allowed wider devotion.

Two important questions face us. Was this monotheism? If so, was it the world's first ancestral monotheism, and did it come down to us through the Hebrews? Our own answer to each question is in the negative, even though such an answer may rest upon definitions of the terms, and such definitions must necessarily be those of modern distinctions.

Our modern Jewish, Christian, and Moslem faiths express the doctrine that there is one—and only one—God and that all ethical and religious values derive from that God. In the application of this definition to the Amarna religion, we see that there were at least two gods, that the Aton was concerned strictly with creating and maintaining life, and that ethics and religion derived from the pharaoh Akh-en-Aton.

It is true that the Amarna texts call the Aton the "sole god, like whom there is no other." This, however, was nothing new in Egyptian religious address. The form of expression was a fervid exaggeration or

32. Erman, *LAE*, pp. 288 ff.; Davies, *op. cit.*, VI (1908), 30 ff., Pl. XXVII.

concentration, which went back to the earliest religious literature, more than a thousand years before Akh-en-Aton's time. In the period before the Amarna revolution, Amon, Re, Atum, Har-akhti, and Min were severally called "the sole god." Sometimes this term recalled the creation, when the one existent god was going to bring other gods into being. Sometimes it was a flattering exaggeration meaning the only important god, *like whom* there was no other. Often it was a focusing of the worshipper's attention upon one god, to the exclusion of others—what is called henotheism or monolatry. In no sense does it imply the absolute unity carried by the Moslem: "There is no god but God."

In ancient times a man's name was a vital part of his being: the effacing of his name from his tomb destroyed his continued existence in the next world; the expunging of an official's name from the records ended that earthly success which was so important to his survival. The same psychology applies to Akh-en-Aton's attack upon Amon and topically upon other gods. If the philosophy of the new religion was that only the Aton was a god and that, therefore, Amon did not and could not exist, why was there so virulent an attack upon Amon, and why was his name systematically hacked out of the records? In those ancient terms he had still some kind of existence as long as his name was effectively a part of a single record.

We are conscious that we are arguing in modern terms and that Atonism was at one and the same time native to Egyptian religion and unique within that religion. It was native because the Egyptian state was built upon the dogma that pharaoh was a god and stood between the people and the other gods; thus the double relationship at Amarna retained the past essentials. It was unique because the gods other than pharaoh were made one god, by a process of exclusion rather than syncretism, if we ignore that limited syncretism present in the official names of the Aton. It is immaterial to that argument that there was still personification in the texts, by which the Aton was described as "satisfied with the goddess Ma‹at" and Akh-en-Aton was praised as being "the god Fate," because personification was also native to Egyptian thought. Much more important was the elimination of Osiris from the mortuary faith, with the ascription of all mortuary benefits to the pharaoh. One could say that it was the closest approach to monotheism possible within the thought of the day. That would still fall short of making it a belief in and worship of only one god.

The question as to whether Atonism was ancestral to Hebrew monotheism and thus to modern expressions of religion is also difficult. However, it may be stated flatly that the mechanism of transmission from the faith of Akh-en-Aton to the monotheism of Moses is not apparent. This was the personal religion of a pharaoh who later became a heretic within one generation. It was not accessible to Egyptians at large. Their subsequent reaction in a fervent return to the older forms, particularly the Osirian faith and the cherishing care of little personal gods, shows how little penetration Atonism had below the royal family. Even assuming that there were Israelite slave troops in Egypt in Amarna times, there was no way by which they could learn the teaching of Atonism, that there was a single, universal god, who made and continued life, toward whom the worshipper felt a warm sense of gratitude. Atonism taught that the pharaoh of Egypt was essential as the only intermediary between god and people.

There is another discontinuity between Atonism and Hebrew monotheism as the latter developed, and that is the marked lack of ethical content in the hymns directed to the Aton. Akh-en-Aton's faith was intellectual rather than ethical; its strong emotional content derived from the fervor of the discoverer and convert, who rejected past forms and preached new forms. The conviction of right and wrong was not ethical, but was a passionate reiteration that the new was right and the old was wrong. Aton's blessings were primarily physical; he made and sustained life. The worshipper was called upon to render gratitude for that life, but was in no text called upon to render to the god an upright and ethically correct life in his social relations or in his innermost heart. The universalism of the Aton could have carried the implication that all men are equal under the god and should be so treated, but such a logical conclusion is strikingly absent from the texts.

The one point of question against this description of Atonism as nature worship lies in the understanding of *ma'at* emphasized by this faith. Akh-en-Aton lived on *ma'at* as his food, and the Aton was satisfied with *ma'at* as his offering. If this meant "righteousness" or "justice," it would carry an ethical weight. When, however, we see in scenes and texts the emphasis on candid relations, on the open air, and on adoration of the sun-disk, we can only translate it as "truth" and understand it as the worship of the forces of nature, in contradistinction to the remote and artificial activity of the older gods. Nowhere do we find that rigorous insistence upon law which was central in Hebrew monotheism.

There is a more important consideration about the transmission of monotheism from one culture to another, and that is whether any great intellectual, spiritual, or ethical concept can be passed from one culture to quite a different culture. We have argued that the Egyptians were "civilized" in a sense of the word which has both strength and weakness. Much of the importance of the Hebrews to world history lies in the fact that they avoided some of the weakening and distracting phases of civilization. A concept which was imperfectly articulated and understood at pharaoh's court at Amarna would have been quite foreign to Asiatic tribes wandering in the desert. When the Children of Israel penetrated Canaan and settled down to work out a new way of life, their progressive religious steps were achieved through their own national religious experience as their own God-given discoveries, without derivation from any foreign source. Such precious and inner expressions of religion can never be borrowed, but must be experienced. When they have been experienced, the *forms* in which they are uttered may be borrowed from others, but never the innermost spirit.

This brings us to a main argument for the contact between Atonism and Hebrew religion: the extraordinary parallelism in thought and structure between Akh-en-Aton's hymn to the Aton and the 104th Psalm.[33] Three selected passages will illustrate the striking similarity.

The Aton Hymn	Psalm 104
When thou settest in the western horizon, The land is in darkness like death. . . .	Thou makest darkness and it is night,
Every lion comes forth from his den;	Wherein all the beasts of the forest creep forth.
All creeping things, they sting.	The young lions roar after their prey.
At daybreak, when thou arisest in the horizon . . . Thou drivest away the darkness . . . Men awake and stand upon their feet . . . All the world, they do their labor.	The sun ariseth, they get them away . . . Man goeth forth unto his work, And to his labor until the evening.
How manifold are thy works! They are hidden from man's sight. O sole god, like whom there is no other, Thou hast made the earth according to thy desire.	O Jahweh, how manifold are thy works! In wisdom hast thou made them all; The earth is full of thy riches.

It has been claimed that such correspondences must show derivative connection and that the Hebrew psalmists must have known the Egyp-

33. J. H. Breasted, *A History of Egypt* (New York, 1905), pp. 371 ff.

tian sun-hymn. Since the obliteration of Atonism was complete some six or seven centuries before the psalm was written, it is argued that the Aton hymn must have passed into Asia when Akh-en-Aton was still in power and escaped destruction by translation into some Semitic dialect.[34]

So ingenious a mechanism of transmission is not necessary. We have already seen that the several ideas and modes of expression visible in Atonism were present in Egypt before Atonism and independent of Atonism.[35] Since these were current forms in Egypt, not invented by the Amarna priests or scribes, it is not surprising to find them still in use after the fall of Atonism and without relation to the fact that the specific cult had been proclaimed a heresy.

A papyrus in Leyden dates from the Nineteenth Dynasty and has passages which have been called monotheistic, but which we, with a narrower definition, prefer to call syncretistic. These hymns treat the god Amon as the summation of all other important gods, without rejecting the separate existence of those other gods. "Mysterious of form, glistening of appearance, the marvelous god of many forms. All gods boast of him, to magnify themselves through his beauty, according as he is divine. Re himself is united with his body, and he is the great one who is in Heliopolis. He is called Ta-tenen (of Memphis) and Amon who came forth from Nun. . . . Another of his forms is the Eight (primeval gods of Hermopolis). . . . His soul, they say, is that which is in heaven, but it is he who is in the underworld and presides over the east. His soul is in heaven, his body is in the west, and his statue is in Hermonthis, heralding his appearances (to mankind). . . . One is Amon, hiding himself from them, concealing himself from (other) gods, so that his (very) color is unknown. He is far from heaven, he is absent from(?) the underworld, and no (other) god knows his true form. . . . All gods are three: Amon, Re, and Ptah, and there is no second to them. 'Hidden' is his name as Amon, he is Re in face, and his body is Ptah. . . . Only he is: Amon, with Re, [and with Ptah]—together three."[36]

Another set of hymns dating from the late Nineteenth or the Twentieth Dynasty treats Amon as a universal god, who again achieves unity by borrowing the forms of other gods. As the creator-god, he is Amon-Re-Atum-Har-akhti, four in one, or is Ptah, the fashioner of men. He

34. J. H. Breasted, *The Dawn of Conscience* (New York, 1933), pp. 367 f.

35. Pp. 210–12 above.

36. Erman, *LAE*, pp. 293 ff.; A. H. Gardiner in *ZÄS*, XLII (1905), 12 ff.

delights in assuming functional roles. "His love is (to play the role of) the moon, as a child to whom everybody dances. . . . His love is (to play the role of) Har-akhti shining in the horizon of heaven." He is both the son and father of *ma‹at*, the "truth" which destroys deceit: "Thy mother is Ma‹at, O Amon! She belongs uniquely to thee, and she came forth from thee (already) inclined to rage and burn up them that attack thee. Ma‹at is more unique, O Amon, than anyone that exists." He is the universal creator, "who spoke with his mouth and there came into existence all men, gods, large and small cattle in their entirety, and all that which flies and lights." He is the warmer and sustainer of all nature: "Green plants turn about in his direction, that they may be beautiful, and lotuses are gay because of him." He is the good shepherd: "Thou are valiant as a herdsman tending them forever and ever. . . . Their hearts turn about to thee, good at all times. Everybody lives through the sight of thee."[37]

We shall see that artistic forms and themes survived the condemnation of the Amarna movement, and it is equally true that religious concepts and forms of expression continued after Atonism had been made a heresy. This is an adequate explanation of the similarity between the Aton hymn and the 104th Psalm. Hymns of this kind were current long after the fall of Akh-en-Aton, so that when Hebrew religion had reached a point where it needed a certain mode of expression it could find in another literature phrases and thoughts which would meet the need.

The negative statement which we have made about the Aton religion has been argumentative and fails to do justice to the elements of supreme importance in that faith. To be sure, it was intellectual and lacking in full ethical value. At the same time, it expressed beautifully the concept of a god who was creative, nurturing, and kindly and who gave his gifts to all mankind and to all living things everywhere and not to the Egyptians alone. For such bounty the worshipper returned gratitude and devotion to the god. Atonism further brought religion out into the open and tried to end the remoteness and secrecy of the old cults of the powerful and wealthy gods. It was a major tragedy that a religion of such broad intellectual scope lacked the inner moral warmth to give it permanency. The fuller realization of the meaning of God's cherishing care was to be made by other and later peoples.

37. *Hieratic Papyri in the British Museum. Third Series. Chester Beatty Gift*, ed. A. H. Gardiner (London, 1935), I, 28 ff.

In describing the Aton faith, we have left the story of Akh-en-Aton's revolution at its peak of militant success. We must continue the account in terms of the political problem. This was the period of the Egyptian Empire in Asia and of collective security by an alliance between pharaoh and the King of Mitanni. In addition to the marriage of Amen-hotep III and Gilu-Khepa, a second marriage was arranged with Tadu-Khepa, the daughter of Tushratta of Mitanni, toward the end of Amen-hotep III's reign. It is doubtful whether the old king married her, and it seems more likely that she entered the harem of Akh-en-Aton.

The cuneiform correspondence known as the Amarna Letters tells us the story of the slow disintegration of the empire in Asia as a result of new forces in that area and of the indifference and preoccupation of pharaoh. Five stages in the rotting and falling away of the Asiatic branch of the empire may be discerned. Under Amen-hotep III, when the stability and continuity of Egyptian rule seemed to be taken for granted, a few local princes up in Syria experimented in separatism. This was the part of the empire which was most remote from Egypt and most insecurely attached to pharaoh. Individuals who were seeking for independent power used the desert nomads to help them carve out small states for themselves, protesting their continued fealty to pharaoh but actually competing with him in rule. The lofty indifference of Egypt permitted them to move on to the second stage, in which Abd-Ashirta and his son Aziru carved out a large part of north Syria as a separate state, working in an informal alliance with the King of the Hittites. All of these parties, including the Hittite king, were writing cordial letters to Egypt, but the northern part of the empire was lost to Egypt before the death of Amen-hotep III.

Akh-en-Aton's preoccupation in his intellectual revolution permitted the three remaining stages of disintegration. The Hittite King Suppilu-liumas moved south as a conqueror and gobbled up all of Syria. The separatism of the local princes led only to their becoming Hittite vassals. The important town Qatna was destroyed and never again was a power. Mitanni had to submit to Hittite domination. All of this seems to have been effected without an Egyptian sword raised in protest. With Syria lost, the disaffection rapidly spread to Phoenicia and Palestine. The Phoenician towns fell despite the fanatical loyalty to pharaoh of such a prince as Rib-Addi of Byblos. In Palestine, Labaya, a merchant prince who led caravans from further Asia into Egypt, combined with the Habiru of the desert and began seizing towns for his own rule.

Abdi-Khepa of Jerusalem wrote letters beseeching pharaoh for as few as fifty soldiers to hold the land. They were not sent. And so we see the final stage, in which the Egyptian garrisons were withdrawn from Asia and Palestine also was lost. Local rebels and desert nomads overran the vacated territory and destroyed Jericho and Tell Beit-Mirsim. The little Egyptian temple at Lachish was sacked. Most significantly, the *migdol* fortification at Old Gaza, which had been the center of Egyptian administration, was destroyed. Complacency, inertia, and internal distractions had lost to Egypt her vast and lucrative Asiatic Empire.

It is not so clear what happened in the African Empire. Akh-en-Aton's temple at Sesebi near the Third Cataract shows that he could be active so far away from home, but the structure may belong to his earlier years.[38] We know that he had a Viceroy for Ethiopia in the period when he was Amen-hotep IV, but we have no record of such an official when he was Akh-en-Aton. When there was dissension and disorder in Egypt, it could not have been easy to police the Nubian and Sudanese gold mines. If the mines were not in production, this may explain why the Asiatic princes wrote in vain asking for Egyptian gold. We may assume that the African Empire also was shaken.

Even in Egypt we do not know the facts. There is no record of rioting or rebellion against the crown. The army was on Akh-en-Aton's side and may have been successful in policing the land. However, the Edict of Har-em-hab, twenty or twenty-five years later, shows that there was a great deal of minor disorder, since it had to outlaw pillaging and peculation by officials. We may guess that the loss of empire was a serious blow to the old economy and that the overthrow of the temple estates led to unemployment and economic distress. We may further guess that the dispossessed priests and the landed gentry who had formed the old civil bureaucracy were aggrieved parties, who would be willing to see the revolutionary government encounter political and financial difficulties. Civil disturbance in small but insistent measure is nearly certain for Egypt, away from the capital city at Amarna.

Our only evidence that the revolution was running into difficulties lies in the history of the later years at Amarna.[39] Akh-en-Aton's twelfth year marked a crisis, followed by a recession from the extremes of revolution and the beginning of compromise. After the death of her husband, the dowager Queen Tiy had continued to live at Thebes. In the

38. J. H. Breasted in *AJSL*, XXV (1908), 51 ff.

39. See especially S. R. K. Glanville, "Amenophis III and His Successors in the XVIIIth Dynasty," in Winifred Brunton, *Great Ones of Ancient Egypt* (London and New York, 1930), pp. 105 ff., an article to which the present chapter owes much.

twelfth year, accompanied by a former official of Amen-hotep III, she paid a state visit to her royal children at Amarna. On the surface everything was amicable: Tiy joined the royal family in worshipping the Aton and sat for her portrait at the hands of an Amarna sculptor. However, it is a coincidence too strong to ignore that her visit came in the same year as a change in policy. If the state was already beginning to suffer from loss of revenue, particularly from foreign tribute, it is noteworthy that a record of foreigners bringing their gifts to pharaoh occurs only in the twelfth year. Tiy's face shows that she was an alert little pragmatist; she may have been the only one who could persuade Akh-en-Aton that his fiery zeal was leading directly toward political trouble and the loss of external and internal revenues.

From this time on, we see a change in direction, which was accompanied by a split in that family which had been so idyllically presented to the public. Queen Nefert-iti was exiled from the palace to the northern end of town. She was stripped of the throne name, Nefer-neferu-Aton, which Akh-en-Aton had conferred upon her when they moved to the new capital, and this name was given to pharaoh's new favorite, his younger brother Smenkh-ka-Re. Nefert-iti's name was erased from some of the monuments, and her eldest daughter Merit-Aton took over her mother's function as the first lady. Smenkh-ka-Re soon married Merit-Aton and was made coregent with Akh-en-Aton. Since we shall shortly see that the young coregent went back to Thebes and resumed relations with the god Amon, the implication is that his coregency was an instrument for some kind of compromise. Akh-en-Aton had sworn never to leave his new capital, and his illness may have progressed to the point where he was not fully capable. The young coregent might rescue the state.

A further implication of the split in the family is that Nefert-iti refused to abandon the ideals of the revolution and to compromise with the forces of reaction. In her exile in northern Amarna, she had her palace carved with the names of Akh-en-Aton and herself as though there had been no break. She asserted her loyalty to the revolutionary god by calling this place "the House of Aton." Her third daughter Enekhes-en-pa-Aton and her half-brother Tut-ankh-Aton shared her exile, if we may judge by the occurrence of their names in this part of town. This, we assume, was the unyielding party, still devoted to the "truth" movement, whereas Akh-en-Aton and Smenkh-ka-Re were already committed to conciliation.

There is evidence that Smenkh-ka-Re had returned to Thebes by his third regnal year, when Akh-en-Aton may still have been living. In an inscription dated in that year a Scribe of the Temple of Amon in the Temple of Smenkh-ka-Re at Thebes makes a prayer to the god Amon.[40] Apparently the younger pharaoh made definite efforts at conciliating Amon and restoring his worship, while the elder remained at Amarna and fulfilled his revolutionary vows.

Perhaps the tide of reaction was too strong. Both Akh-en-Aton and his young favorite Smenkh-ka-Re disappeared from the picture. The youthful Tut-ankh-Aton married Princess Enekhes-en-pa-Aton and became pharaoh, but was forced to make a full surrender. He announced his capitulation by changing his name to Tut-ankh-Amon and his wife's name to Enekhes-en-Amon, abandoned Amarna, and moved back to Thebes. The revolution was officially over in failure, although the taint of heresy would not be wiped out for some years.

Young Tut-ankh-Amon (Fig. 26b) was no personality strong enough to stand up against experienced priests and officials. His round, boyish face, his relish in sports, and the luxurious furniture of his tomb remind us much more of his father Amen-hotep III than of his father-in-law Akh-en-Aton. Willingly or unwillingly, he paid Amon's price. He built in Thebes, particularly in the colonnade of the Luxor temple. We have already seen how his restoration inscription stated his obligation to redress the damage to the temples of the gods.[41] Some of that inscription is rather pathetic in its desire to pay the penalty. "His majesty deliberated plans with his heart, searching for any beneficial deed, seeking out acts of service for his father Amon, and fashioning his august image of genuine gold. He surpassed what had been done previously: he fashioned his father Amon upon thirteen carrying-poles . . . whereas the majesty of this august god had formerly been upon eleven carrying-poles." The parvenus of the Amarna court were dropped and the old nobility was returned to office: "He inducted priests and prophets from the children of the nobles of their towns, (each) the son of a known man, whose (own) name was known." The temples were paid damages: "All the [property] of the temples has been doubled, tripled, and quadrupled in silver, [gold], lapis lazuli, turquoise," and so on. The temple personnel was increased at the cost of the royal purse: "Their work is charged against the palace and against the [estate(?)] of the Lord of the Two Lands." This was a thorough surrender. The attempt to rewin for pharaoh his former independent authority had failed. The

40. P. E. Newberry in *JEA*, XIV (1928), 3 ff.; A. H. Gardiner, *ibid.*, pp. 10 f.
41. P. 216 above.

personal rule of a god-king would never again be effective; pharaoh would be maintained as the head of a divine state but would be subject both to the priestly and official oligarchy and increasingly to impersonal law. The foundation stone of ancient Egypt had been cracked.

The tomb of Tut-ankh-Amon is well known and needs only passing comment here. It illustrates the extraordinary profusion of influences and furnishings which made the Empire so exciting a time. If such a wealth of treasure were packed into the tomb of a relatively minor king, what must have been the furnishings of an Amen-hotep III or of a Ramses II! The great unevenness in quality of furniture in this tomb, some of it maintaining the simplicity and balance of the older art, yet much of it gaudy, overdecorated, and exotic, illustrates admirably the florid, cosmopolitan, and highly civilized period. The age shows itself as precious, febrile, and sentimental. This was cultural disintegration packed into four small rooms.[42]

One notation about the tremendous furnishings is in place. The tomb contained a dagger with a superb blade of iron and two little iron amulets of Egyptian design. Such mined and smelted iron was quite new to the world in 1350 B.C., and it is interesting that there was no religious taboo against the use of a new metal for amulets and in a tomb. The iron probably came from the land of the Hittites as a royal gift.[43]

A cuneiform document must be introduced here, although it is uncertain whether it belongs after the death of Tut-ankh-Amon or after the death of another of the pharaohs in the Amarna period. Among the archives found at the Hittite capital was a letter from the king Mursilis III, telling about previous trouble between the Hittites and Egypt in north Syria. He then relates that the pharaoh of Egypt had died and that the widow wrote to Mursilis' father Suppiluliumas, stating that she had no sons and asking that the Hittite king send a son to marry her and hold the throne of Egypt. The Hittite king was naturally suspicious of such a request and sent a courier to Egypt to determine whether there was a trick lying behind her plea. The Egyptian queen answered that she did not easily humble herself and her country to beg for a Hittite prince, and Suppiluliumas permitted her to select one of his sons. As this prince was being escorted to Egypt, he was attacked and murdered by "the men and horses of Egypt," with the result that the Hittite army marched into Syria, captured the murderers, and led

42. H. Carter and A. C. Mace, *The Tomb of Tut.ankh.Amen*, I (London, 1923); H. Carter, *ibid.*, II (1927), and III (1933).

43. *Ibid.*, II, 109, 122, 135 f., Pls. LXXVII, LXXXII, LXXXVIII; III, 89 ff.; Pl. XXVII.

them to the Hittite capital to be tried and condemned in accordance with international law. The attempt to hold the throne for the Amarna family had failed.[44]

Very soon the throne was turned over to the Army Commander Har-em-hab, perhaps for the specific purpose of restoring order by vigorous police action. Har-em-hab's conventionality is indicated by the fact that the members of the Amarna family were officially branded as heretics under his reign, while he himself was recognized as the first legiti-mate pharaoh since the death of Amen-hotep III. The revolution was officially over.

The forces of reaction were in the saddle, and they wiped out every doctrinal trace of Atonism and excommunicated the memory of the heretic pharaohs Akh-en-Aton, Smenkh-ka-Re, Tut-ankh-Amon, and the short-reigned Eye. Further, by their victory, the reactionaries es-tablished the domination of the gods, particularly Amon-Re, over the pharaoh for the next four centuries. They were, however, either toler-ant of or ignorant of the significance of those modernistic forms of expression which had been in process before the Amarna movement and which were so visible a feature of that movement. The universalism and syncretism of the important gods continued in the texts. Classical Egyptian was a dead language, and colloquial speech increasingly pene-trated literature, very little into the religious texts which repeated old formulas, but quite sensibly into official texts of a secular character, and fully into texts of a consciously literary character. For the rest of the Empire, art did not recover its ancient hieratic dignity, but retained the fluid line, hasty drawing, and naturalism which were so strong at Amarna. All these were phases of life which could be detached from religious heresy and treated simply as modern forms of expression. They all showed the disintegration of the culture which Egypt had forged in the Old Kingdom. What we see from this time forward was a very different Egypt.

44. A. H. Sayce in *Ancient Egypt*, 1922, pp. 66 f.; *ibid.*, 1927, 33 ff.; *JEA*, XII (1926), 168 ff. Steindorff and Seele, *op. cit.*, pp. 222 f., assume that this was Akh-en-Aton's widow, rather than Tut-ankh-Amon's.

X

WHERE IS THE GLORY?

Dynasties 18–20 (about 1325–1100 B.C.)

I T TOOK a full generation for Egypt to recover internally from the
Amarna revolution. That is, she made no visible effort to re-estab-
lish her empire during Har-em-hab's thirty years of reign. He had
been a military man, and the tomb carved in his younger days indicates
an interest in Egypt's domination over foreigners. Yet we have no evidence that he was able to lead his armies on campaigns of military re-
covery. On the contrary, the evidence shows the need for energetic
measures to restore order and confidence within Egypt.

Such an understanding treats with skepticism the claim of the Army
Commander Har-em-hab, uttered in the tomb which was carved before
he became pharaoh, that he had accompanied a king "at the head of his
army to the countries of the north and the south" and that he was "by
the feet of his lord on the battlefield on that day of killing Asiatics."[1]
The only one of the Amarna pharaohs who made any protestation of
fighting the Asiatics was Tut-ankh-Amon, on the decorated box found
within his tomb, and we may treat this claim and that in the tomb of
Har-em-hab as the stylized reiterations of cherished old formulas,
rather than as records of fact. This may apply also to the lines which
describe Har-em-hab's police responsibilities for the relocation of foreign refugees, although here we may have a true reflection of the disorganization in Palestine during Amarna times. "Their countries are
starving, and they live like the beasts of the desert," and so the Army
Commander was charged: "Certain of the foreigners who do not know

1. Breasted, *ARE*, III, §§ 1 ff.

Fig. 17a.—Statue of a King Sebek-hotep of the Thirteenth Dynasty

Fig. 17b.—Empire Stela, Showing the Worship of the God Seth

Fig. 17c.—Inscribed Figurine Smashed at a Cursing Ceremonial

Fig. 18a.—Limestone Statue of Queen Hat-shepsut, Reconstructed
from Smashed Pieces

Fig. 18b.—Limestone Statue of Queen Ahmose Nefert-iri of
the Early Eighteenth Dynasty

Fig. 19b.—The Deir el-Bahri Bay, with Hat-shepsut's Temple in the Foreground and Mentu-hotep's in the Background

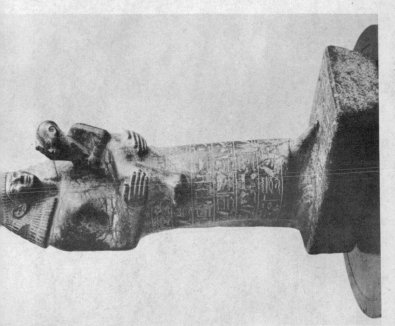

Fig. 19a.—Statuette of Sen-Mut as Tutor of the Royal Princess

Fig. 20.—*Looking North from the Pass through the Carmel Range toward the Mound of Megiddo in the Left Center*

Fig. 21a.—Amen-hotep II as an Archer

Fig. 21b.—Carved Plaque Carrying
the Title and Name of the
Vizier Rekh-mi-Re

Fig. 21c.—Rough Carving of Ramses II,
Overlying the Delicate Work
of Hat-shepsut

Fig. 22b.—Stela from Tell el-Amarna, Depicting Amen-hotep III and Tiy

Fig. 22a.—Colossal Group of Amen-hotep III and Tiy

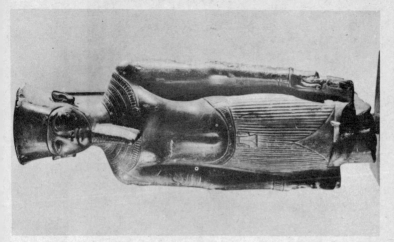

Fig. 23b.—Amon-Re, King of the Gods

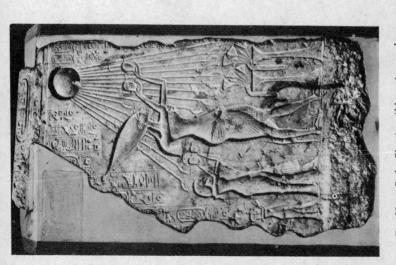

Fig. 23a.—Stela, Showing Akh-en-Aton and
His Family Worshiping the Sun-Disk

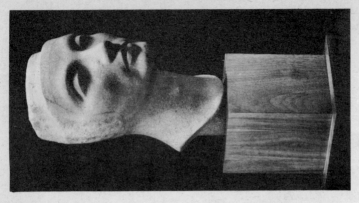

Fig. 24c.—Unfinished Head of Nefert-
iti from Tell el-Amarna

Fig. 24b.—Colossal Statue of Amen-hotep IV,
before the Full Revolution

Fig. 24a.—Trial Sketch of Akh-en-Aton from
Tell el-Amarna

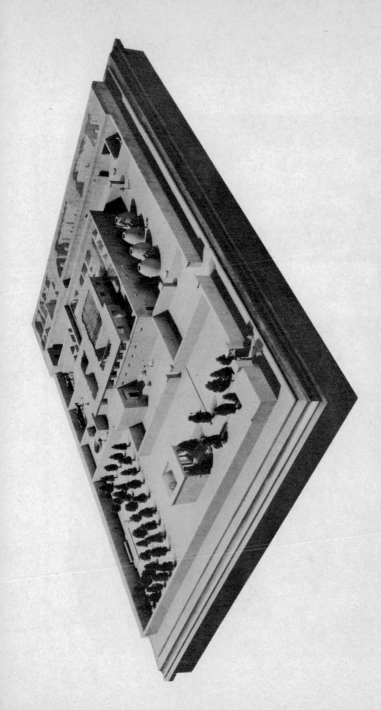

Fig. 25.—*Model of the Estate of a Tell el-Amarna Noble*

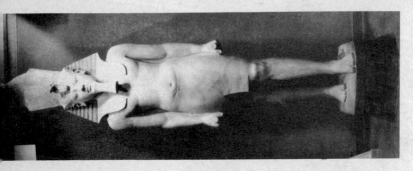

Fig. 26b.—Colossal Statue of
Tut-ankh-Amon

Fig. 26a.—Granite Statue of Har-em-hab as a Government Official

Fig. 27a.—*Ramses II Slaying an Asiatic Enemy in the Presence of the God Atum*

Fig. 27b.—*Ancient Copy of a Scene, Showing Ramses II Marrying a Hittite Princess*

Fig. 28a.—*Wall Painting from Tell-el-Amarna,*
Showing a Kingfisher in the Marshes

Fig. 28b.—*Stela of the Asiatic*
War-God Reshpu

Fig. 28c.—*Sculptor's Model Head of an Asiatic—Original on Left,*
Reconstructed Cast on Right

Fig. 29a.—The Ramesseum at Thebes, with the Shattered Colossus of Ramses II at the Right

Fig. 29b.—The High Priest of Amon, Amen-hotep, Being
Honored by Ramses IX

Fig. 30.—*Looking across the Nile to the Western Hillside, Where the Necropolis Workmen Lived*

Fig. 31b.—Painted Column Capital from
Megiddo in Palestine

a.—Composite Floral Column from
Excavations at Medinet Habu

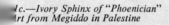
c.—Ivory Sphinx of "Phoenician"
rt from Megiddo in Palestine

Fig. 31d.—Stela, Showing a Nubian Soldier
Worshiping the God Osiris

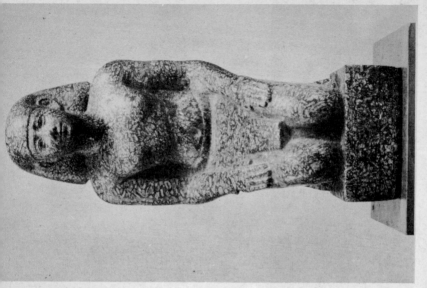

Fig. 32b.—A Priest of the Twenty-fifth or Twenty-sixth
Dynasty

Fig. 32a.—Tomb Relief of the Twenty-fifth Dynasty in the Tradition
of the Old Kingdom

how they may live have come [begging the breath of life(?)] of Pharaoh, after the manner of their fathers' fathers since the first times. . . .
So Pharaoh gives them into your hands to guard their boundaries." This
was the perennial attempt of the Asiatic to find a richer land in the
Egyptian delta; here it may have been also a search for refuge from
the invaders who were taking over Palestine.

The document from the reign of Har-em-hab which has the most
authentic ring is his edict correcting abuses and restoring order in the
land.[2] This was not a code of law, but rather a series of police regulations directed against specific malpractices and also a reorganization
of the administrative machinery in the land, in order to control future
abuses. There was no reference to the disorders as a product of the
Amarna period, and the expression of pharaoh's pleasure at executing
ma‹at and driving out deceit may be purely conventional. At the same
time, the whole tenor of the text shows that soldiers and officials had
been lawlessly using their power to enrich themselves at the expense of
common people and that the machinery of control was now being
turned over to the civil bureaucracy and the priests, two observations
which fit the revolution and counter-revolution rather well. Just as
Tut-ankh-Amon had restored the old conservative nobility to temple
position, so Har-em-hab put into the courts of law individuals of a
reactionary type. He tells us that he was at pains to seek out men "of
perfected speech and good character, able to distinguish the innermost
thoughts." These new appointees were "prophets of the temples, lay
officials of the Residence of this land, and ordinary priests of the gods.
. . . They shall judge the citizens of every town." If these are listed in
order of importance, the first were the higher temple priests, the second, those courtiers who held office by royal appointment, and the
third, the ordinary temple priests. The authority of the temples in the
civil courts is remarkable, since most of the cases involved administrative corruption. Pharaoh further made the courts of law free from any
tax of silver or gold, "in order to prevent an obligation of any kind
from being exacted from the courts of Upper and Lower Egypt." The
priesthoods had won their victory in the collapse of the Amarna revolution; they were now consolidating their authority and privileges, at
the expense of the king.

The abuses against which the edict was directed were the extortion
by officials or soldiers of property or labor from ordinary citizens, and
the diverting by the same authorities of goods and services from the

2. *Ibid.*, §§ 45 ff.; K. Pflüger in *JNES*, V (1946), 260 ff.

state. Apparently there had been an inordinate amount of graft in Egypt. Now the state asserted its legal rights to taxes and enforced labor, and acted also to protect the property of "poor people" from looting soldiers or thievish tax-collectors. The punishments meted out are very harsh for minor cases of plundering or corruption. The alarming spread of official dishonesty must have called forth an extreme severity of penalties. Only the firmest exhibition of legal power could restore ma'at to the land.

It must be said that, although the "poor man" may be the point of protection against extortion or looting, the edict does not show a primary concern for social welfare, but rather was intended to protect taxes at their source. Thus, the enactment forbids an official's requisitioning the boat with which a commoner is going to deliver his dues; it forbids the army's seizing hides which commoners are going to use to pay their taxes; it forbids the taking of certain dye plants and herbs which the commoners should turn over to the government; and it forbids certain tax-collectors—curiously called "the herdsmen of *kyky*-monkeys"—from falsifying the tax measure for their personal gain. The common people were not secured in the possession of their own property, except insofar as that property was to be rendered up to the state; the revenues of government offices were the primary concern of this reactionary edict.

The penalties seem harsh out of all proportion to the offenses. If any one takes away the boat which is used for the delivery of taxes, "the ordinance shall be carried out against him by cutting off his nose and putting him in Tjaru." Tjaru was a lonely, tightly disciplined, and unpopular place, the frontier fortress along the Suez border.[3] "[If] two detachments of the army which are in the field, one in the southern area and the other in the northern area, are taking away hides throughout the land . . . going from house to house, beating and squeezing(?) (the peasants)," and if the royal tax-collector therefore cannot collect the hides, "this too is a serious situation, and it shall be handled accordingly": with regard to the accused soldier, "beginning with today, the ordinance shall be carried out against him by beating him with one hundred blows and causing five open wounds, in addition to taking away from him the hide which he has seized as having been stolen."

Here we have a harsh and reactionary enactment, designed to check

3. Much later, Strabo records a similar use of another frontier fortress, modern el-Arish, as the place of exile of convicts, after their noses had been cut off. The town was therefore called Rhinokoloura: *The Geography of Strabo* (Loeb edition; London, 1930), Vol. VII, p. 279: 16.2.31.

the deplorable dishonesty of government people. It illustrates the breakdown of the older sanctions of the sacred state in which the generalized word of the king was topically applied for justice; now clearly specified and impersonal regulations were drafted to take over pharaoh's personal authority. The edict further shows remarkable control over the civil courts by the priests. Alone of the Amarna personalities, Har-em-hab was recognized as legitimate by later generations. He purchased that recognition by an abdication of the traditional supremacy of the pharaoh, surrendering much of his over-all authority to the priesthood and the civil courts.

In order to gain time and security for internal reconstruction, Har-em-hab abstained from any attempt to rewin the Asiatic empire. Perhaps he composed his difficulties with the Hittites, who had gobbled up Syria. From later references, it is clear that there was a formal treaty between Egypt and Hatti along about this time. At least, the treaty executed in the reign of Ramses II[4] refers to former treaties, going back several generations. The reign of the Hittite king Mursilis III coincided fairly well with that of Har-em-hab, and it may be that these two kings concluded the first Egyptian-Hittite treaty. Har-em-hab wanted the time and freedom to reconsolidate Egypt internally; the Hittites wanted to make their Syrian conquests effective, so that they might turn their attention to northern Mesopotamia. For a time there was peace between the two empire-building states.

At the death of Har-em-hab a new dynasty came into power. Ramses I and his son Seti I had been viziers of Upper Egypt and apparently stepped into the kingship without undue trouble. The new ruling dynasty showed a different orientation in its names: the Thut-moses and Amen-hoteps were replaced by the Ramseses and Setis and Mer-ne-Ptahs, the southern gods Thoth and Amon by the northern gods Re and Seth and Ptah. The name Seti meant "Seth's Man" and shows the same reverence for the god Seth as is visible in the stela commemorating the four-hundredth anniversary of the founding of Tanis.[5] This northern shift was effected by placing the working capital of Egypt at a Delta site, Tanis. For the international concerns of Egypt and for the rewinning of the empire, a capital near Asia and the Mediterranean was needed. Thebes remained a religious and a seasonal capital. The god Amon did not lose his power to Re, Ptah, and Seth; he continued to lead the state toward power, and he increased his own wealth and authority.

4. Pp. 248–50 below.
5. P. 159 above.

But the northern gods came into new prominence, and Seth, even though he was the enemy of the god of the dead, Osiris, and the enemy of Horus, received new recognition as the god of foreign countries and of storm.

There was a consciousness of a new era which would bring back Egypt's imperial glory. Seti I dated the years of his reign as a renaissance, for example: "Year 2 of the Repeating of Births of (Seti I)." "Repeating of Births" is literally Renaissance, and was used at other times to express the determination to go back again to older patterns.[6]

Seti I set out in his first year to recapture the Asiatic empire. He emphasized the maintenance and policing of the military road through the difficult Sinai wilderness, with relay posts and guarded waterholes. On a wall of the Temple of Amon at Karnak is carved a sort of military map of the Sinai desert between Tjaru, the Egyptian frontier fortress, and Raphia, the first village in Palestine.[7] Each pool or well along the way was guarded by a fortified *migdol* tower, with a resident patrol. The names of some of these oases show that they were new foundations or newly organized posts: "the *Migdol* of (Seti I)," "the Well of Seti Mer-ne-Ptah," and "the Town which His Majesty Founded Anew at the Well of *Heberet*." The Asiatic names show that these oases had existed before, but were now newly organized.

Just as in Thut-mose III's first campaign, the campaign of imperial conquest was based upon a claim of "rebellion" in Asia. The Karnak inscriptions solemnly aver that Seti I had received a report that the Bedouin of Palestine were "plotting rebellion. Their tribal chiefs are gathered in one place, waiting on the mountain ranges of Palestine. They have taken to clamoring and quarreling, one of them slaying his fellow, and they have no regard for the laws of the palace." It did not matter that these Asiatics had not been subject to "the laws of the palace" for two generations. This was the excuse to march again to glory; and "the heart of his majesty was glad at it." Seti led his army into "the Canaan," to rewin empire.[8]

In late May of his first year, Seti was in northern Palestine, when word came of an alliance of local princes along the upper Jordan. He acted with a vigor worthy of Egypt's past reputation. "His majesty sent the first division of Amon, 'the Mighty of Bows,' to the town of Hamath, the first division of Re, 'the Plentiful of Valor,' to the town of

6. For example, at the end of the Twentieth Dynasty. See J. Černý in ZÄS, LXV (1930), 129 f.; K. Sethe, *ibid.*, LXVI (1931), 1 ff.

7. A. H. Gardiner in *JEA*, VI (1920), 99 ff.

8. Breasted, *ARE*, III, § 101.

Beth-Shan, and the first division of Seth, 'the Strong of Bows,' to the town of Yanoam. When the space of a day had passed, (the rebels) were overthrown to the glory of his majesty."[9] With such energy and determination the power of Egypt might once more rewin a proud empire.

There is one significant element in the text just cited. Four of five towns named in this inscription cluster around the Jordan just south of the Sea of Galilee: Beth-Shan, Rehob, Hamath, and Pella. The fifth, Yanoam, was at a distance to the north, probably in Galilee somewhere north of Lake Huleh. Thus, in addition to quelling the local "rebellion," Seti sent one division north to throw a road-block against some more distant foe who might have interfered with the operation around Beth-Shan. That foe is likely to have been the Hittite army, since we shortly find pharaoh fighting against Hatti and attacking the town of Kadesh on the Orontes, where he was so successful that he was able to erect a monumental stela of triumph. The frontier of Egypt was again pushed into northern Syria.[10]

Seti I has left us a decree which shows the same brusque severity as the edict of Har-em-hab.[11] The new enactment was framed to protect a religious foundation at Abydos against the arbitrary seizure or use of its property by government officials. This again reflects the same lack of discipline within the state personnel as did the edict of Har-em-hab. The same rigorous penalties were invoked to give the decree force. For example, any official found guilty of shifting the boundaries of the fields belonging to this foundation was to be punished by cutting off his nose and ears and by his servitude as a peasant-farmer for the foundation. Anyone who arbitrarily and illegally took away one of the foundation's herdsmen, so that a loss of cattle resulted, was punished by two hundred blows and the exaction from him of the lost cattle at the rate of one hundred to one. Any herdsman who disposed of the foundation's cattle to his profit was impaled upon a stake, his wife, children, and all his property were confiscated by the foundation, and the cattle had to be returned by the purchaser at the rate of one hundred to one.

The severity of these punishments contrasts markedly with the penalties in earlier decrees. A Fifth Dynasty enactment protecting the priesthood of Abydos from forced labor provided that the guilty official should be removed from his office and put upon any kind of

9. A. Rowe, *The Topography and History of Beth-Shan* (Philadelphia, 1930), I, 24 ff.

10. Breasted, *ARE*, III, §§ 141 ff.; M. Pézard in *Syria*, III (1922), 108 ff.; G. Loukianoff in *Ancient Egypt*, 1924, 101 ff.

11. F. Ll. Griffith in *JEA*, XIII (1927), 193 ff.; W. F. Edgerton in *JNES*, VI (1947), 219 ff.

work, with his servants and property confiscated.[12] A Sixth Dynasty decree on behalf of the temple at Koptos provided only for removal from office.[13] A Sixteenth or Seventeenth Dynasty decree dealt with a very serious offense on the part of a priest of the Koptos temple, the "taking of enemies" or treason. The penalty was removal from office and the expunging of his name from official records, with the confiscation of his temple property. "Let him be ejected from the temple of my father Min; let him be barred from his temple office, from son to son and heir to heir, cast down upon the ground. Take away his income, his title-deed, and his priestly meat. Let his name not be remembered in this temple, as should be done to one like him, a rebel and an enemy of his god. His writings shall be removed from the temple of Min, from the treasury, and on every document likewise."[14]

Why are the decrees of Har-em-hab and Seti I so much harsher in punishment than these earlier enactments? Why do they add cruel physical abuse and the repayment of property in high proportion on top of the earlier removal from office and confiscation of property? It would seem that the word of the king no longer had the same effectiveness in maintaining order; pharaoh was no longer respected and feared as he had been in the more sacred state of earlier times. Now a harsh and impersonal law had to take the place of the older discipline which had been based upon the acceptance of the rule of a god-king. Further, Egypt had lost in security, self-confidence, and tolerance, had become nervously tense, arbitrary, and exacting. The individuals within the state no longer had the same element of freedom and voluntary expression but were more definitely bound to a disciplined service of the state. The Hyksos domination, the necessities of empire, and the Amarna heresy were all factors leading to a repressive authoritarianism—impersonally by the state rather than personally by the pharaoh.[15]

The decrees of Seti I show another interesting factor, the invocation of magic to support law. In the enactment on behalf of the Abydos foundation which we have cited, a magistrate who received an accusation but took no action toward justice was punished by removal from

12. K. Sethe, *Urkunden des alten Reichs* (*Urk.*, I [Leipzig, 1933]), I, 170 ff.

13. *Ibid.*, pp. 280 ff.

14. Breasted, *ARE*, I, § 778; for the date cf. H. E. Winlock, *The Rise and Fall of the Middle Kingdom in Thebes* (New York, 1947), pp. 108 ff.

15. How differently the same data may be interpreted may be seen in W. Wolf, *Individuum und Gemeinschaft in der ägyptischen Kultur* (Leip. *AS*, I [Glückstadt, 1935]). In sharp contrast to the thesis in the present book, Wolf sees no expression of individuality before the Empire.

office, servitude as a peasant-farmer, and beating with one hundred blows. Such an offense could be established by inquiry. But how could one find out about an ordinary person who might know of an offense without reporting it? Only the gods could control such furtive knowledge, and so the god Osiris "shall pursue him and his wife and his children, to wipe out his name, to destroy his *ba*, and to prevent his corpse from resting in the necropolis." Similarly, another decree summoned a family of gods to vengeful activity. "As for anyone who shall ignore this decree, Osiris shall pursue him, Isis shall pursue his wife, Horus shall pursue his children, and the great ones, the lords of the necropolis, shall make their reckoning with him." There was even a curse for future pharaohs who fail to conform to Seti's decree; they shall be responsible to the gods, who "shall be red like a flame of fire, and shall burn up the flesh of those who do not listen to me. They shall consume the violator of my plans and shall give him over to the execution place of the underworld."[16] It was no longer possible for pharaoh to issue his word, awfully potent because his divinity was unquestioned. Now he had to invoke the other gods by a curse to support his authority. The fear which had been his alone now had to be backed by magic.

Magic had been always an element of Egyptian life. Amulets are known from the earliest periods, and the Pyramid Texts are full of promotive or protective charms. This later period, however, showed an increased reliance upon various magical techniques and powers. Insecurity brought a longing for greater protection through some kind of external potency. Men turned to magic scrolls and images of prophylactic power; they went through elaborate rituals when they recited charms. They tried to counteract the new fatalistic cast of life by summoning the gods for magical support. Man was no longer strong enough in himself.

Although Seti I had some success in re-establishing the empire in Asia, his son and successor, Ramses II, ran into difficulties. The Egyptians were always trying to reassert the past in a world which would not stand still. Even though they were constantly forced to redefine the past in terms of more recent experience, their resolute ignoring of the present was ultimately destined to be fatal. At first it had been possible to take the valley of the Nile as the only essential, with the neighboring regions as inferior lands, which might be ignored or exploited. Under

16. Breasted, *ARE*, III, §§ 194, 180.

the Empire, Egypt had felt obliged to extend the essential to include the Fourth Cataract to the south and Syria to the north; the problems of competition had been acute in the area around Kadesh, with the chief competitor first Mitanni and then Hatti. It was still possible for Seti I to plan his campaigns with relation to Hatti, and Ramses II started off on the same basis but soon discovered that the Hittites alone did not focus his problem. The world had become much more complex than a bipolar contest between Egypt and Hatti.

The centuries from 1400 to 1100 B.C. saw some extraordinary readjustments in and around the eastern Mediterranean. This was an international age of new scope, not confined to Egyptians, Syrians, Hittites, and Mesopotamians, but bringing in peoples whose ultimate destinies were to be in Europe as Greeks and Latins. These new peoples were gradually streaming out of some northeastern Indo-European home and were slowly building up their challenging strength in the coastal regions of the eastern Mediterranean. The Egyptian texts called them "the northerners in their islands," and we shall call them the Sea Peoples. In their thrust for new homes they were to damage irreparably the balance in the ancient orient and were to bring new and significant forces into being in Europe. Much of Greek myth derived from the restless movements of this age: Jason and the Argonauts, Theseus and the Minotaur, and the siege of Troy.[17] At the beginning of the age, Egypt possessed her empire, and the Hittites were just looming up as the chief competitor. At the end of the age, the Egyptian and Hittite empires were destroyed, Assyria was moving to salvage the wreckage, the Children of Israel and the Philistines were in possession of the land of Canaan, the Phoenician city-states were moving to new maritime power, the Greeks could be discerned in their historical homes—and iron had replaced bronze as the basic metal.

The Sea Peoples appear to us under strange names in the hieroglyphic and cuneiform texts. Some of them, like the Philistines and Dardanians, can be identified. For others, like the Sherden and Shekelesh, we may postulate ultimate homes in Sardinia and Sicily. For others, like the Keshkesh and the Irwen, we must remain uncertain.[18] Within these limits, we may make a few tentative listings. About 1295 B.C.,

17. For an interesting but hazardous attempt to relate such myths to oriental records and archeological observation, see J. D. S. Pendlebury in *JEA*, XVI (1930), 75 ff.

18. The identifications have been much discussed. For a recent attempt, see G. Bonfante in *American Journal of Archaeology*, L (1946), 251 ff. See also G. A. Wainwright in *JEA*, XXV (1939), 148 ff.

Ramses II fought the Hittites at Kadesh. On his own side, he had the Sherden (Sardians or Sardinians) "of his majesty's capturing, whom he had taken by the victories of his arm." Hatti had gathered against him a coalition including the small states of northern Syria and Anatolia, the Dardanians, the Mysians, the Pedasians, the Lycians, and others. About 1230, Mer-ne-Ptah had to protect his western frontier against a Libyan invasion, which came in alliance with Achaeans, Tyrsenians, Lycians, Sardians or Sardinians, and Siculi or Sicilians. About 1190, Ramses III held his northeastern frontier against an invasion by land and sea on the part of Philistines, Teucrians, Siculi, Danuna, and others. The names are different within each of these groupings, but the relentless surge of wave after wave of Sea Peoples shows one great folk-wandering. In the slow course of centuries, such movements would forge the peoples of classical Europe, who would work out new cultures, radically different from those of the orient. Before that time Egypt and Hatti would sink to lesser importance, and the imperial leadership of the ancient orient would move east, away from the Mediterranean, to the Assyrians, the Babylonians, and the Persians. The Sea Peoples alone did not deal the vital blow to Egypt's proud position in the southeastern Mediterranean world, but they were one strong factor among many in sapping Egyptian power and shrivelling Egyptian spirit.

We know a great deal about Ramses II's major conflict with the Hittites at Kadesh on the Orontes in his fifth year. He was at pains to set on record his side of the adventure. It is not an account which invokes much admiration for his intelligence or foresight, even though his personal courage appears in a favorable light.[19] Baldly put, he walked into a Hittite ambush, and cut his way out, to save his skin and most of his army. Since his obvious purpose was to capture Kadesh and to drive the Hittite army back into Asia Minor, he sustained a definite setback. Yet there is no episode in Egyptian history which occupies so much carved wall space in Egyptian temples. Ramses returned to Egypt to celebrate a great and miraculous victory, claiming that "he had repelled all lands through terror of him, while the strength of his majesty had protected his army, so that all foreign countries were giving praise to his goodly countenance." The fact that he had walked into a trap and the fact that he had not routed the Hittites or taken Kadesh were drowned out by the ecstatic celebration of his super-human courage and prowess in cutting his way out of the ambush,

19. S. Yeivin in *JNES*, IX (1950), 101 ff.

"alone by himself, with no other with him." Four hundred miles away from Kadesh, it was possible to shout and shout again that there had been a glorious victory.

Ramses' claim was that he alone put to rout two waves of attackers. At the ambush he was surrounded by "twenty-five hundred spans (of chariotry) in his way out, consisting of every warrior of the Hittite enemy, together with the many foreign countries which were with them: of Arzawa, Mysia, Pedasia, Keshkesh, Irwen, Kizzuwadna, Aleppo, Ugarit, Kadesh, and Lycia; being three to a span, acting together." He prayed to Amon, and when that god came to his aid, "I found the twenty-five hundred spans of chariotry, in whose midst I was, becoming heaps of corpses before my horses." When the Hittite king saw this, he sent out a second attack, "the numerous princes, every one of whom had his spans, equipped with their weapons of warfare: the prince of Arzawa, him of Mysia, the prince of Irwen, him of Lycia, him of Dardania, him of Keshkesh, the prince of Carchemish, the prince of Cilicia, him of Aleppo, and the brothers of him of Hatti, united together. Their total was one thousand spans of chariotry." The Egyptian account makes a contrast between the glorious valor of Ramses II and the cowardly caution of the Hittite king Muwatallis, who did not join in either attack but "stood averted, shrinking, and afraid." Pharaoh charged into the foe six times and "made the plain of Kadesh turn white" with corpses, before the scattered Egyptian army was able to return to his side in the evening. It is obvious that we cannot accept with complete seriousness the miracle of one warrior routing a total of thirty-five hundred chariots, there being three northerners to each chariot. The basis of fact must be that there was a successful ambush, out of which the Egyptian troops cut their way with such credit that the Hittite coalition was unable to gain a resounding victory. Ramses was defeated, but Muwatallis was unable to press his advantage by sending the Egyptian army into chaotic flight. The small success which Ramses plucked out of the great failure could be magnified into a great personal triumph.[20]

Such an analysis of the accounts of the Battle of Kadesh does insufficient justice to the dogma of the Egyptian state, by which any accomplishment was unquestionably a product of the powers of the pharaoh, whose defeat or discomfiture was unthinkable. This was an essential

20. Ch. Kuentz, *La Bataille de Qadech* (*MIFAO*, LV [1928]); J. A. Wilson in *AJSL*, XLIII (1927), 266 ff.

part of the state mythology of Egypt, and there is no qualitative difference between these accounts of the discomfiture at Kadesh and the story of Thut-mose III's real victory at Megiddo.[21] In each case before battle the pharaoh held a conference with his officers, and therein exhibited his superior wisdom. In each case the victory was claimed to be personal, that of pharaoh supported by Amon. The myth of the divine king as the one and only incarnation of the state had produced a recognized literary form by which observed fact was rendered into a different kind of truth, the sincere and devout affirmation of the centrality of pharaoh.[22] However, there is a quantitative difference between Thut-mose III's report of the Battle of Megiddo and Ramses II's account of the Battle of Kadesh in emotional pleading. Ramses II doth protest too much; he spreads his protest large over the outer temple walls in Karnak, Luxor, western Thebes, Abydos, Abu Simbel, and probably the lost temples of the Delta, so that the sheer physical weight of his insistence distorts a setback into a stunning triumph. It is all too clear that he was a stupid and culpably inefficient general and that he failed to gain his objectives at Kadesh. It must also be true that he was personally courageous and that he succeeded in re-forming his army and in leading it back to Egypt in good order. We may sympathize with the desire to assert a moral victory out of these small triumphs, snatched from the jaws of utter rout. The fact remains that the arrogant bellowing of victory comes as an insincere ostentation similar to the bloated bulk of Ramses II's monuments or to his shameless appropriation of the monuments of his ancestors. Blatant advertising was used to cover up the failure to attain past glories.

This argument does not deny the personal bravery of Ramses II nor his continued attempt to rewin empire. In the years following the Battle of Kadesh he campaigned in Palestine and Syria, capturing Ascalon, "when it was wicked," and desolating Acre, so that "when the princes of Kadesh see him, the [terror(?)] of him is in their hearts." Against Tunip in northern Syria, a city held by "the fallen ones of the Hittites," he showed the same reckless bravado as at Kadesh, and he led the attack against the town for two hours before putting on his coat-of-mail. His fighting ranged all the way from southern Palestine to

21. See above, pp. 178–80.

22. A. de Buck, *Het typische en het individueele by de Egyptenaren* (Leyden, 1929). For fragments of a text honoring Thut-mose III in the grandiloquent style of Ramses II, see G. Botti in *Rendiconti. Atti della R. Accademia Nazionale dei Lincei,* XXXI (1923), 348 ff.

northern Syria, thus showing the difficulty of establishing and holding an effective frontier.[23]

Ultimately, both the Egyptians and the Hittites recognized the futility of expending against each other energies which had to be saved against the encroachments of the Sea Peoples. About 1280 B.C., in Ramses II's twenty-first year, Egypt and Hatti concluded a treaty of "good peace and brotherhood," providing for a defensive alliance. We are fortunate in possessing both the hieroglyphic and cuneiform versions of this compact.[24] According to the Egyptian version, the Hittite king Hattusilis sent envoys "to beg peace" from Ramses II, "the bull of rulers, who has made his frontier where he wished in every land." According to the Hittite version, Ramses took the initiative by approaching Hattusilis and suggesting a treaty of peace. Each side thus preserved for itself the dignity of assenting to the appeal of the other. The original document was written in Akkadian cuneiform, the language of international communication in that age. Probably the treaty was first formulated at the Hittite capital, with the aid of Egyptian ambassadors. This text was then carried to Egypt, inscribed upon a silver tablet. We may assume that Ramses II made some alterations in the interests of national prestige and that the text was newly engraved upon two silver tablets. One of these was carried back to Hatti and deposited "at the feet of" the Hittite storm-god; the other copy was laid "at the feet of" the god Re in Egypt. In each case the king took an oath before his god, so that the treaty was deposited with divine sanction and authority.

The treaty divides logically into five parts. The historical introduction recalls that there had been wars and previous treaties between Egypt and Hatti, asserts that the two present kings desire peace, and tells of the exchange of silver tablets carrying the text. Second, there is mutual assurance about non-aggression. "The Great Prince of Hatti shall not trespass against the land of Egypt forever, to take anything from it, and (Ramses II), the great ruler of Egypt, shall not trespass against the land [of Hatti, to take] from it forever." It is clear that they are not making promises about the land of Egypt within the Nile Valley and the land of Hatti in Anatolia, but rather the claimed empire in Palestine and Syria. That brings the modern reader to the extraordinary fact

23. Breasted, *ARE*, III, §§ 352 ff.; W. M. Müller, *Egyptological Researches* (Washington, 1906), II, Pls. 37-38, 44-45, 100-103; K. Sethe in *ZÄS*, XLIV (1907), 36 ff.

24. S. Langdon and A. H. Gardiner in *JEA*, VI (1920), 179 ff.

that the treaty defines no boundaries between the Hittite claims and the Egyptian claims. There must have been an acknowledged line somewhere or possibly a recognized no-man's-land between areas firmly held by each side. One would assume that Hatti laid claim to northern Syria, central Syria, and the northern Phoenician coast, that Egypt laid claim to the rest of Phoenicia and to Palestine up through the Galilean hills, but this must remain speculation.

The third part of the treaty provides for a defensive alliance against a major enemy, a third power attempting to challenge Egyptian or Hittite holdings, and against local rebellions in either of the empires. The fourth section deals with the extradition of political refugees, both those of high degree, "a great man," and ordinary citizens, "a man or two men, who are unknown." Interestingly, the deported refugee is to be treated humanely in the homelands to which he is returned: "they shall not raise any crime against him," and he may not be slain, mutilated, or deprived of his family or house. Apparently there was an accepted code of international law, which protected the person and property of such refugees, although not their former positions or privileges.

The final section of the treaty, like other ancient legal documents, listed the witnesses who attested to the compact, but in this case they were divine. "As for these words, a thousand gods of the male gods and of the female gods of them of Hatti, together with a thousand gods of the male gods and of the female gods of them of the land of Egypt, are with me as witnesses [hearing(?)] these words." Then follows an enumeration of specifically named gods, beginning with the sun and storm gods and ending with "the male gods, the female gods, the mountains, the rivers of the land of Egypt, the sky, the earth, the great sea, the winds, and the clouds." Since each king took his oath with this powerful band of witnesses, the breaking of the treaty would be the most serious offense possible.

The whole document is an instructive combination of the "modern" and the ancient. Its legal articles are clearly the product of a long period of international relationships, in which provisions for mutual military assistance and for political extradition had been worked out. It remains in statement a distinctly personal agreement between two kings, who— so they said—needed to consult only the gods, and the pervading element of divine approval shows the workings of a sacred state. The silver tablet which was retained in Egypt was carved with figures of the Hittite storm-god embracing Hattusilis and of a Hittite goddess embracing the Hittite queen Putu-Khepa. It carried the seals of the Hittite king and queen and of the Hittite storm and sun gods. The deities of each land lent their full authority to the treaty.

As far as we know, this compact between Egypt and Hatti was never abrogated. About fifty years later, Mer-ne-Ptah sent grain to the Hittites to rescue them from starvation, so that mutual aid was still in effect at that time.[25] In Ramses II's thirty-fourth year, about 1267 B.C., the good relations between the two countries were signalized by a great state marriage (Fig. 27b). This was of the same nature as the marriage alliance between Egypt and Mitanni in the Eighteenth Dynasty and was doubtless arranged through the appropriate diplomatic channels with the greatest ceremony. The Egyptian texts, however, pretend that Hattusilis was terrified because his land was despoiled by pharaoh's army. "So the Great Prince of Hatti sent and appeased his majesty year by year," but Ramses "never listened to them." Then, when Hatti was suffering from a drought, Hattusilis—in the Egyptian telling of the tale—realized that he would have to demonstrate his full surrender. He said to his court: " 'What is this? Our land is desolated; our lord Seth is angry with us, and the skies do not give water over against us. . . . Let us despoil ourselves of all our goods, with my eldest daughter at the head of them, and let us carry gifts of fealty to the good god, so that he may give us peace, that we may live!' . . . Then he caused to be brought [his] eldest daughter, with noble tribute before her: gold, silver, many great ores, horses without limit to them, cattle, goats, and sheep by the ten-thousands, without limit to the products of their [land]." Characteristically the Egyptian account makes the splendid dowry a humble offering of tribute.

Ramses II dispatched an official escort to meet the Hittite party in Asia, and, since it was early winter, he prayed to the storm-god Seth: "Mayest thou [delay] to make the rain, the cold wind, and the snow, until the marvels which thou hast assigned to me shall reach me!" Under such auspices, "the daughter of the Great Prince of Hatti marched to Egypt, while the infantry, chariotry, and officials of his majesty accompanied her, mingling with the infantry and chariotry of Hatti, for they were Hittite chariot-warriors like the troops of (Ramses II) and like his chariotry, all the people of Hatti mingling with those of Egypt. They ate and drank together, being of one heart like brothers, for peace and brotherhood were between them, after the manner of the god himself, (Ramses II)." Nor was the idyll confined to the comrade-

25. Breasted, *ARE*, III, § 580.

ship of the soldiers. When the Hittite princess was ushered into the presence of the middle-aged pharaoh, he "saw that she was fair of face [like] a goddess—indeed, a great, mysterious, marvellous, and fortunate affair. It was unknown, unheard of from mouth to mouth, not mentioned in the writings of the ancestors. . . . So she was beautiful in the heart of his majesty, and he loved her more than anything."

The end of this happy tale is stated as an era of peace and plenty. "And so it was that, if a man or a woman proceeded on their mission to Djahi (Phoenicia), they could reach the land of Hatti without fear around about their hearts because of the greatness of the victories of his majesty."[26]

Here, surely, was the old glory, dignity, and power of Egypt, successfully reasserted once more. Or was it? On the surface it seemed to be so. The great capital city at Tanis in the Delta, renamed Ramses in honor of the pharaoh, was a bustling place of vigorous commerce and cosmopolitan excitements. To it came luxury products and staples from the Mediterranean world and the lands of Asia. There the pharaoh built extensively, and the tradition that the Children of Israel were in bondage for the construction of Pithom and Raamses illustrates a famed period of activity there. In poetical compositions celebrating the grandeur of this new city, "the House of Ramses, the Great of Victories," its size and its bustle are given extravagant play. "His majesty has built himself a castle, the name of which is 'the Great of Victories.' It is between Djahi and Egypt,[27] and it is full of food and provisions. . . . The sun rises in its horizon and sets within it. All men have left their towns and are settled in its territory. Its west is the Temple of Amon, its south is the Temple of Seth, Astarte appears in its orient, and Uto in its north." "Its ships go out and come back to mooring, so that supplies and food are in it every day. One rejoices to dwell within it, and there is no one who expresses a lack to it. . . . The young men of 'the Great of Victories' are dressed up every day, with sweet oil upon their heads and newly dressed hair. They stand beside their doors, with their hands bowed down with flowers, greenery of the House of Hat-Hor and flax of the Her Canal(?), on the day when (Ramses II) enters in. . . . The ale of 'the Great of Victories' is sweet, . . . beer of Cilicia from the harbor and wine of the vineyards. . . . The singers of 'the Great of Vic-

26. Ch. Kuentz in *ASAE*, XXV (1925), 181 ff.; G. Lefebvre, *ibid.*, pp. 34 ff.

27. Figuratively between Phoenicia-Palestine and Egypt, actually in the northeastern Delta, most probably at Tanis: A. H. Gardiner in *JEA*, XIX (1933), 122 ff.; XXX (1944), 60.

tories' are sweet, having been instructed in Memphis. So dwell content of heart and free, without stirring from it, O (Ramses II), thou god!"[28]

In a sense, following the peace with Hatti, Ramses II did dwell content of heart, without stirring from the city of Ramses. If we guess that he was about twenty-two years old at the Battle of Kadesh, he would have been over fifty when he married the Hittite princess, but he was to reign on for another thirty years and more. In his length of rule, in the vast progeny which carried his divine seed, and in the massive bulk of monuments bearing his name, he left a tremendous shadow across Egyptian history, so that pharaohs named themselves after him for more than a century, and he passed into legend as the great conquering and imperial pharaoh.[29] His buildings attempted to impress by overpowering size, without concern for artistic quality. At Tanis rose a ninety-foot colossus. In the mortuary temple known as the Ramesseum there was another colossus, estimated at a thousand tons in weight. The tremendous cliff temple at Abu Simbel in Nubia is majestically impressive, but it is significantly a vast façade, with very little functional space behind. The mighty hypostyle hall at Karnak, completed by Ramses II, gives one of the great emotional experiences in Egypt, with its silent forest of sublimely lifting columns, and yet it was architecturally unsound and hastily built, with careless and crude carving. Not content with over-towering Egypt with his own tremendous buildings, Ramses II arrogantly used the monuments of his ancestors, both usurping previous buildings and statues by adding his name and also tearing down earlier structures for his own building stone. To be sure, he was not the first pharaoh to be so disrespectful to the memory of his predecessors, but his pious reverence for the honoring of a long list of past kings, as shown in the reliefs in his temples, is at variance with his bland ruthlessness in arrogating their stone memorials to his own glory (Fig. 21c).

So long a reign could hardly fail to leave a deep imprint on Egypt. It was a ceremonial custom in Egypt to celebrate the renewal of kingship by a jubilee, often after thirty years of reign and thereafter at shorter intervals. Ramses II duly held his first jubilee in his thirtieth regnal year, his second in his thirty-fourth, his third in his thirty-

28. Erman, LAE, pp. 270 f., 206 f.

29. Seventy-five years after Ramses II's death, Ramses IV prayed a god that he might be more faithful than was Ramses II "in his sixty-seven years," and that the god might reward him with the same length of life: Breasted, ARE, IV, § 471. On the legendary role of Ramses, cf. K. Sethe in Untersuch. (Leipzig, 1902), II, 3 ff.

seventh, and so on up to an eleventh in his sixty-first year.[30] The rejuvenation of the aged ruler must have attained something of the nature of a weary miracle when he was in his eighties. Over his years he produced a vast tribe of royal children—we know of more than one hundred sons—who became a new privileged class, bearing within them the seed of a god. It has been pointed out that the pharaoh may have found some difficulty in marrying off his many sons and daughters, since one prince is known to have taken the daughter of a Syrian ship captain to wife.[31] Ramses II lived on in voluptuous ease and adulation until it seemed that no other king on earth could match his glories. He is the fitting prototype for Shelley's "Ozymandias of Egypt":

> I met a traveller from an antique land
> Who said: Two vast and trunkless legs of stone
> Stand in the desert. Near them on the sand,
> Half sunk, a shatter'd visage lies . . .
> And on the pedestal these words appear:
> "My name is Ozymandias, king of kings:
> Look on my works, ye Mighty, and despair!"
> Nothing beside remains. Round the decay
> Of that colossal wreck, boundless and bare,
> The lone and level sands stretch far away.

So, in Ramses II's mortuary temple, there remain the pedestal and the fallen, battered head of a colossus of this king, whose other name was User-maat-Re or Ozymandias.[32] In his long and indolent ease he did not think to cope with the forces which were drowning out the ancient Egyptian culture. As far as he was concerned, Egypt was still at its heights of power and glory, and, if he had known how rapidly life was changing, he could have done little to stem the tide. Externally and internally the disintegrating pressure was playing upon Egypt.

When finally Ramses II departed this life and joined the gods in the other world, his twelve eldest sons had already died, and his successor was his thirteenth son, Mer-ne-Ptah, who must himself have been well advanced in years. Dutifully the poets hymned the opportunity of a new king to restore *maʿat* to the land, as each succeeding pharaoh did. "Be glad of heart, the entire land! The goodly times have come! A lord has been given in all lands, . . . the most serviceable of any king, Mer-ne-Ptah! . . . All ye righteous, come that you may see! *Maʿat* has banished

30. L. Borchardt in *ZÄS*, LXXII (1936), 52 ff. On the festival see H. Frankfort, *Kingship and the Gods* (Chicago, 1948), pp. 79 ff.

31. W. Spiegelberg in *Recueil de Travaux . . .*, XVI (1894), 64.

32. Cf. Diodorus Siculus, I, 47. See our Fig. 29a.

deceit. Evildoers have fallen upon their faces, and all the rapacious are ignored. The water stands and is not dried up; the inundation lifts high. Days are long, nights have hours, and the moon comes normally. The gods are satisfied and content of heart. [One] lives in laughter and wonder."[33] This does not mean, nor was it intended to mean that Ramses II's reign had ended in deceit, evildoing, and rapacity so great that the Nile would not flood, the days were cut short, and the moon was erratic. It was the proper salutation of the miracle of re-creation by a new pharaoh and was in no way invidious to his predecessor. In fact, Mer-ne-Ptah's reign was disturbed by the first serious attempt to invade Egypt since the Hyksos.

In the fifth regnal year, around 1230 B.C., a coalition of peoples attempted to penetrate Egypt from the west. The leader of this invasion was a Libyan prince, not of the desert Libyans who had long been in recognized relation to Egypt, but probably of the Cyrenaica region which looked out to the sea, for his allies were some of the restless Sea Peoples: Achaeans "of the countries of the sea," Tyrsenians, Lycians, Sardinians, and Sicilians. Mer-ne-Ptah met this attack at his western frontier and sent the Libyan prince fleeing "in the depth of the night, by himself. No plume was upon his head, his feet were unshod, ... and he had no water of the water skin to keep him alive." The size of the invading force is indicated by the fact that over six thousand of the allies were slain and more than nine thousand were taken captive. For a time Egypt was secure, so that "one walks with unhindered stride on the way, for there is no fear at all in the heart of the people. The forts are left to themselves, the wells (lie) open, accessible to the messengers. The battlements of the wall are calm in the sun until their watchers awake. . . . The cattle of the field are left as free to roam without herdsmen, even crossing the flood of the stream. . . . One goes and comes with singing, and there is no cry of people as when there is mourning, . . . for Re has turned himself around (again) to Egypt." The land had again demonstrated its physical superiority to foreigners, but the threat of invasion was coming nearer.[34]

A poetical composition celebrating this victory ends with a statement of Egypt's dominating power over all foreign regions, including the only reference to Israel in any Egyptian text:

---

33. Erman, *LAE*, pp. 278 f.

34. Breasted, *ARE*, III, §§ 569 ff. On the Libyans, see J. A. Wilson in *AJSL*, LI (1935), 73 ff.; W. Hölscher, *Libyer und Aegypter* (*Mün. AF*, IV [Glückstadt, 1937]).

The princes are prostrate, saying: "Mercy!"
  Not one raises his head among the Nine Bows.
Desolation is for Tehenu; Hatti is pacified;
  Plundered is the Canaan with every evil;
Carried off is Ascalon; seized upon is Gezer;
  Yanoam is made as that which does not exist;
Israel is laid waste, his seed is not;
  Palestine is become a widow for Egypt!
All lands together, they are pacified.
Everyone who was restless has been bound by (Mer-ne-Ptah).[35]

This paean of exultation corresponded to no reality. Mer-ne-Ptah was in good relations with Hatti, and, as far as we know, conducted no campaign into Asia. This is the customary magniloquent claim that the god-king was victorious over all opponents, whether he had met them in battle or not. The appearance of Israel in an Asiatic context is interesting, but has no meaning in terms of armed conflict against Egypt. It merely shows that an Egyptian scribe was conscious of a people known as Israel somewhere in Palestine or Transjordan. We do have a *terminus ante quem* for the Exodus of the Children of Israel from Egypt.

Because of our thesis that the Hebrews could have taken little from Egypt in Egypt's period of power, we should state our own views with regard to the Sojourn, Exodus, and Conquest of Canaan.[36] The story as set down in the Bible is a simple and honest attempt to tell the tale of Jahweh's preservation of His people and is given simplicity and directness for the purposes of national cohesion by making the climax the deliverance of the people from the mighty Egyptian nation. We Americans have simplified our early history in a similar way by accenting our relations with England, with emphasis on the Mayflower and the Revolution. Actually, in each case, the story is much more complicated. The individuals who ultimately made up the Hebrew nation and came to share a common history of Jahweh's gracious activity on their behalf derived from various strains, but had certain elements in common. In distant centuries, some of them had had an exodus from Egypt among the Hyksos. Most of them had been tributary subjects in Palestine under the Egyptian Empire; many of them were taken into Egypt as captive laborers. Some of them, as Habiru, had enjoyed a triumph over Egypt in crossing the Jordan and conquering Canaan in Amarna times. In the re-establishment of empire under Seti I and Ramses II, most of them

---

35. Breasted, *ARE*, III, § 617; Erman, *LAE*, pp. 274 ff.

36. For a discussion of some of these problems, see G. E. Wright, in *The Biblical Archaeologist*, III (1940), 25 ff.

had again been brought under the Egyptian yoke, and some of them must have been carried off to Egypt to work on the new mighty monuments.

Ultimately, a small group succeeded in making *the* Exodus from Egypt, in outwitting some pharaoh and escaping into the Sinai wilderness. This was the most egyptianized group, with a number of members whose names were Egyptian: Moses, Hophni, Phinehas, and Puti-El. This was the tribe of Levi, which entered Canaan late, as carriers of a new religion of a single mountain and desert god, who had delivered them out of Egyptian bondage. They were missionaries of a new cult, but a cult which struck a responsive chord in every heart which had suffered under Egyptian domination. Through their religious fervor, the diverse peoples of Canaan were given the unity necessary to make a single people, and that single people was able to build its varied experiences into one great experience of Jahweh's protecting favor.

None of these members was in any position to learn from Egypt her elegances of thought or her achievements in religion or philosophy. Slave troops on a government building project have no opportunity for discussion with priests and scribes. Their simple desert souls would see and shrink from some of the abominations of the effete civilization and long to escape dreary enslavement rather than admire the cultural triumphs of the land of bondage. What they finally brought into the land of Canaan was a god of desert simplicity, in no way related to the sophisticated concepts of Amon or Re or Horus. It would take several centuries of settled life in Canaan and of the testing of their religion by the vicissitudes of civilization before they would search for forms of expression similar to those used by the Egyptians. By the time the Hebrews were intellectually mature enough to seek for models of expression from neighbors, Egypt was a senile and repetitive culture, which had nothing dynamic to give. Egypt's past might give certain literary models and modes, but the spirit was lacking. Happily Israel did not lack spirit.

Our argument then is that there certainly were bondages and that there certainly was an exodus, but that neither of these experiences was an effective instrument for cultural transmission, but was rather a barrier to such transmission.

Mer-ne-Ptah was succeeded by four or five kings within the space of fifteen to twenty years, and then came a distressing interregnum, between the Nineteenth and Twentieth Dynasties. We know about it from a single document, which unfortunately may be translated in two different ways. After taking note of a kingless period, in which "the land of Egypt was (only) officials and rulers of towns," the text runs either: "Other times came afterwards in the empty years, and——, a Syrian with them, made himself prince," or "Other times came afterwards in the empty years, and Irsu, a Syrian, was with them as prince." Even though it is uncertain whether the name of the Syrian ("Horite") has dropped out or is to be read Irsu, the fact of an Asiatic ruler in years otherwise empty of kingship is clear. The text continues: "He set the entire land as tributary before him. One joined his companion so that their property might be plundered. They treated the gods like the people, and no offerings were presented in the temples. But when the gods reversed themselves to show mercy and to set the land right as was its normal state, they established their son, who had come forth from their body, to be ruler of every land, upon their great throne, (Set-nakht). . . . He brought to order the entire land, which had been rebellious. He slew the disaffected of heart who had been in Egypt. He cleansed the great throne of Egypt."[37]

That a Syrian should impiously seize the rule in Egypt is somewhat contradictory to our assertion that there was no effective mechanism for cultural transmission between Egypt and the Israelites. That contradiction is present, even though we may plead a difference between the enslaved Israelites, who escaped into the desert and who entered Canaan all innocent of Egyptian sophistication, and other Asiatics who rose to power and position in Egypt. The captive workers and laborers were present in large number. We have seen that Amen-hotep II brought back to Egypt from one campaign about ninety thousand, that Mer-ne-Ptah took more than nine thousand in his Libyan war, and that Ramses II led to Kadesh the Sardinians "of his majesty's capturing." Here and there we find figures on the numbers of foreign slaves held on some government activity. Under Ramses III, the estate of the Temple of Amon had 2,607 "Syrians and Negroes of his majesty's capturing," the estate of Re 2,093, and the estate of Ptah 205.[38] Ramses IV used eight hundred 'Apiru or Habiru on one of his quarrying enterprises.[39] In all there must have been tens of thousands of foreigners in bondage in the army, on government public works, in the temple workshops, and on the estates of the pharaoh and his nobles.

Of a different standing and a different opportunity were those foreign captives who were assigned to work of a personal, confidential, or re-

37. Breasted, *ARE*, IV, §§ 398–99.
38. *Ibid.*, §§ 225, 281, 338.
39. *Ibid.*, § 466.

sponsible nature. There were also some who came into Egypt as free-men, such as the attendants of the foreign princesses, that "Greek grocer" at Tell el-Amarna, or the daughter of the Syrian ship-captain Ben-Anath espoused to one of Ramses II's sons. Mer-ne-Ptah had in his court a chief herald named Ben-Ozen.[40] The presence of such foreign-ers in positions of responsibility in the royal palace is shown by a trial for conspiracy in the harem under the Twentieth Dynasty. One of the judges, a royal butler, bore the Semitic name Mahar-Baal. Another but-ler, Yenini, one of the criminals, was stated to be a Libyan, and another criminal, a butler and clerk of the treasury, was named "the Lycian."[41] The list could be multiplied. It is clear that there were foreigners who had cast their lot with Egypt, had become thoroughly egyptianized, and were normally accepted as members of the Egyptian community. It may have been one of these who seized the throne for a brief inter-regnum between the Nineteenth and Twentieth Dynasties. The indig-nant claim that he disregarded the gods of the land would be a propa-gandistic thrust after he had been overthrown.

Of a non-Egyptian nature were those slave-troops whose activities kept them under a heavy yoke or those Bedouin tribes who entered Egypt for the seasonal pasturing of their flocks in the Delta. Their longing was to return to their Asiatic homes. An Egyptian document of the period tells of the pursuit of two runaway slaves past the Suez frontier posts and out into the Sinai wilderness, on their way back to freedom.[42] In another text a frontier official reports that he has admitted "the Bedouin tribes of Edom" into the eastern Delta, "to keep them alive and to keep their cattle alive," and notes that there were specified days on which the frontier fortress might be passed for such purposes.[43] From all the evidence the Children of Israel were of such a nature, not egyptianized sophisticates, but simple Asiatic shepherds in nature and desire. Even the story of Moses indicates that he cast off his Egyptian teachings and reverted with fervor to the teachings and ways of his people. He was of the type which fled the "fleshpots of Egypt," rather than of the type which worked earnestly to become an acceptable Egyptian.

Those foreign troubles which Ramses II had averted by an alliance with Hatti and which Mer-ne-Ptah had checked by defeating the at-

---

40. A. Rowe in *ASAE*, XL (1940), 45 f.

41. Breasted, *ARE*, IV, §§ 423, 439 f.

42. Erman, *LAE*, pp. 198 f.   43. Breasted, *ARE*, III, §§ 636 ff.; cf. §§ 630 ff.

tempted invasion by Libyans and Sea Peoples assailed Ramses III insistently and finally brought the end of empire. Around 1190 to 1185 B.C., Ramses III fought off three attempted penetrations of the Egyptian Delta, all ultimately the product of the restlessness of the Sea Peoples, although only one of the wars was against that group and the other two were against Libyans. In his fifth and eleventh years the western Libyans attempted to settle in Egypt and were repulsed at the frontier. This was a real movement of peoples. In the second Libyan war more than two thousand captives were taken, of whom seven hundred were women and children, and the captured cattle numbered more than forty thousand, chiefly sheep and goats. The captives were made slave laborers in Egypt, and their egyptianization was speeded up by banning their own language and forcing them to speak Egyptian. We shall hear more about these western Libyans, whom the Egyptians called the Meshwesh.[44]

Ramses III still held his Asiatic empire in Palestine. His statue has been found at Beth-Shan, and there is record of him at Megiddo. He built for Amon a temple in Palestine, and the god owned nine towns in that country, as his dues-paying property.[45] The Egyptian frontier was in Djahi, somewhere along the coast of southern Phoenicia or northern Palestine.

Then there came south a great wave of Sea Peoples, moving by land and sea and clashing with the Egyptians in Ramses III's eighth year. They were Philistines, Teucrians, Sicilians, Danuna, and Weshesh in alliance. They overran Anatolia, Cilicia, Cyprus, and northern Syria, ending the Hittite empire, and set up a camp somewhere in the northern Syrian plain, preparatory to invading Egypt. Those on the sea had boats with an abruptly turned-up end and a sharp ramming point. Those on land moved in ox-drawn carts, which were loaded with their household goods and accompanied by their wives and children. "They laid their hands upon the countries as far as the circuit of the earth, their hearts confident and trusting: 'Our plans will succeed!' "

Ramses met the attack by land at his Asiatic frontier in Djahi and the attack by sea within the "river-mouths" of the Delta. He was successful in that none of the Sea Peoples was able to penetrate the land of Egypt,

44. Wilson, op. cit., pp. 76 ff.

45. A. Rowe, The Topography and History of Beth-Shan (Philadelphia, 1930), Pl. 51; G. Loud, The Megiddo Ivories (OIP, Vol. LII; Chicago, 1939), 11; Breasted, ARE, IV, §§ 219, 226, 384.

and it seems probable that he turned back their armies in Djahi. Temporarily the empire was saved, and Egypt continued to hold Palestine. Large numbers of captives were brought back to Egypt. "I settled them in strongholds, bound in my name. Their military classes were as numerous as hundred-thousands. I assigned portions for all of them with clothing and provisions from the treasuries and granaries every year."[46]

However, the victory lasted only for the lifetime of Ramses III. His is the last name of an Empire pharaoh to be found on Asiatic soil, and he was the last to record the holding of Asiatic territory. Immediately under his successors, Egypt withdrew from empire and contained herself within the Nile Valley. Ramses VI was the last pharaoh to exploit the Sinai mines.[47] Phoenicia and Palestine were left open to the invader. The glory was over.

Some of the Sea Peoples had been concerned far away from Egypt, in the siege of Troy and the consequent reshuffling of power in the Mycenean and Aegean world, but some of them were still waiting to take advantage of Egypt's sudden weakness. The Philistines and the Teucrians settled along the coastal plain of Palestine, bringing a distinctly new culture into that troubled land.[48] They ruled with small city-states, each under the Mycenean *sarens* or "tyrant." They had theaters and a building very much like the Greek *megaron*. They had at least two elements of physical superiority over the slowly forming Israelite power up in the highlands: the Philistines had chariots and they had iron. They declared a monopoly on iron and did their best to see that the Israelites did not learn how to forge this new metal.[49] Thus, in the period of the Judges, the Philistines exercised a definite material and cultural superiority over the Israelites, and it was not until the times of Saul and David that the weight was shifted to Israelite advantage. However, the contestants in Palestine did not have to concern themselves about pharaoh and his army. As a world power, Egypt was finished.

Before pronouncing the obsequies over a still restless corpse, we should like to go back and examine the culture which flourished in

46. Breasted, *ARE*, IV, § 403. On the war against the Sea Peoples, see *ibid.*, §§ 59 ff.; W. F. Edgerton and J. A. Wilson, *Historical Records of Ramses III* (*SAOC*, 12 [Chicago, 1936]), pp. 35 ff.

47. A. H. Gardiner and T. E. Peet, *The Inscriptions of Sinai*, I (*EES*, XXXVI [1917]), 15.

48. O. Eissfeldt, *Philister und Phönizier* ("Der alte Orient," XXXIV, 3 [Leipzig, 1936]).

49. I Sam. 13:19–20.

Egypt under the Empire, chiefly on the basis of the literature of the Nineteenth and Twentieth Dynasties. We shall find this a period of a very brisk and vivacious literary output. Before we characterize the efforts at *belles lettres*, we might look briefly at the art of the post-Amarna period. It definitely did not recover the earlier harmony, dignity, poise, and contrived stylization of pre-Amarna art; nor—with a few exceptions—did it recover the high quality of drawing and carving which characterized the temple of Hat-shepsut or the tombs of some of Amen-hotep III's nobles, for example. It was much more like the Amarna art, which in itself was a product of imperial excitation. It was fluid, naturalistic, lively, cluttered, and often badly drawn. The pre-Empire art of a smaller, more leisurely, and more composed Egypt had been able to hold eternity as the essential, and thus to make a composition with all patience and in terms of the everlasting ideal. The Empire was too nervously organized to keep its gaze fixed beyond the horizon; the here-and-now became much more important, and the old hieratic forms were abandoned in favor of a crowded and colorful vivacity. The Nineteenth and Twentieth Dynasty tombs show an interest in growth and movement and topical detail, which have nothing to do with eternity and which give the scenes a febrile and brittle quality far from the old serenity which we believe to have been truly and natively Egyptian.

The literature of the late Empire was deeply affected by two factors: new experiences and new contacts through the widening of Egypt's horizon, and the building up of a class of bureaucratic clerks to meet the needs of a larger government. The texts express an awareness of foreign countries as places where an Egyptian might live, rather than as regions of lonely exile. The stories of the Two Brothers, the Enchanted Prince, and Astarte and the Sea, as well as the long Satirical Letter all show an acclimatization to Syria as an essential of the text.[50] Many of the texts display a relish for foreign words and phrases, as exhibiting the cosmopolitan learning of the scribe. The writer who jeered that a coward had a reputation like that of "Qazardi, the Chief of Asher, when the bear found him in the balsam tree," was referring familiarly to some well-known episode of Canaanite folklore.[51] The free interplay of ideas had already broken down the sacred barriers around the Nile Valley.

The expanding empire needed more and more clerks, so that the scribal schools were very active. The schoolboys received a routine

50. Erman, *LAE*, pp. 150, 161, 169, 214 ff.   51. *Ibid.*, p. 230.

acquaintance with the classics, as they had to copy out some of the ancient texts, but the way in which they mangled their models shows that they had little understanding or appreciation of the older elegant literature.[52] Probably much more time was given to the professional needs of the expected career: clerk, paymaster, or letter writer. For such purposes the newly accepted colloquial language was used, much to the schoolboy's relief. Model letters showing the polite diction of address and the businesslike brevity of official messages were composed for every need. The schoolmasters played upon one theme over and over again: the life of a government clerk is preferable to any other career. They repeated that the soldier and the farmer and the baker— and even the priest and the knightly charioteer—had hard and discouraging tasks, but that the clerk was dressed in white linen, did not have to bend his back to hard labor, but bossed the work of others. The masters urged the boys not to frequent beerhalls or run after women, but to stick to their books so that they might become officials of high reputation. It is clear that youthful pleasures and the adventurous appeal of a soldier's life presented serious disciplinary problems to the teachers.[53]

In a reasoned text, it is argued that the learned man alone was assured of immortality. "Now then, if you do these things, you are skilled in the writings. As for those learned scribes from the time of those who lived after the gods, they who could foretell what was to come, their names have become everlasting, even though they themselves are gone, they completed their lives, and all their relatives are forgotten. They made themselves no pyramids of metal, with their tombstones of iron. Though they could not leave heirs in children, . . . pronouncing their names, they did make heirs for themselves in the writings and in the books of wisdom which they composed. . . . If doors and buildings were constructed, they are crumbled; their mortuary service is [done]; their tombstones are covered with dirt; and their graves are forgotten. But their names are still pronounced because of their books which they made, since they were good and the memory of them (lasts) to the limits of eternity. Be a scribe, and put it in your heart that your name may fare similarly." Then the names of some of the famous writers of antiquity were recalled, such as the two traditional sages, Hor-dedef

---

52. In particular, the Story of Si-nuhe (Erman, *LAE*, pp. 14 ff.), the Satire on the Trades (*ibid.*, pp. 67 ff.), the Instruction of Amen-em-het I (*ibid.*, pp. 72 ff.), and the Hymn to the Nile (*ibid.*, pp. 146 ff.). For a listing of Egyptian literary pieces see G. Posener, in *Revue d'Égyptologie*, VI (1949), 27 ff.

53. Erman, *LAE*, pp. 188 ff.

and Ii-em-hotep, Khety, to whom was credited the much-copied Satire on the Trades, and Ptah-hotep, whose Instructions were famous.
"Though they concealed their magic from everybody (else), it may
be read in a book of wisdom. Though they are gone and their names
are forgotten, it is writing that makes them remembered."[54] This glorification of "wisdom" or "teaching" was by no means new in Egypt;
it goes back to the Old Kingdom and the Instructions of Ptah-hotep
and for Ka-gemni. However, the older "wisdom" was the lore of the
father handed down to the son; under the Empire, the "wisdom" was
very often the curriculum of the scribal school.

If the schoolboy was sometimes happier on the streets than when
crouched over his practice writing, we may sympathize with him.
Many dull exercises were laid before him, like long and often disconnected catalogues of phenomena, registers of those things which a government clerk might have to write. A list of some six hundred such
words begins: "sky, sun-disk, moon, star, Orion, Big Dipper, . . ." continues later with "overseer of the army, clerk of the infantry, deputy
of the army, overseer of the treasury of silver and gold, royal messenger
to every foreign country . . ." or with "brewer, baker, moulder of incense . . ." or with "bin, storeroom, chest, storehouse, window . . ." or
with "wine of Egypt, wine of Palestine, wine of the oases . . ." and ends
with "fresh meat, cooked meat, sweetened meat." This dreary catalogue was no encyclopedia; it was merely a practice list "to teach the
ignorant to know everything that is."[55] Such pedantry was only partly
redeemed by being put into literary form, as in the poem on pharaoh's
war chariot, every single part of which was glorified by some punning
allusion.[56] This labored playfulness enters also into long hymns to the
gods, as in a composition celebrating Amon, in which the number of
each chapter is picked up by a pun in the first and last words of the
chapter.[57] These are tricks which the Egyptian always loved to play,
but never more than in this sophisticated period.

At its simplest the literature of the period is very appealing. The
stories of the Two Brothers and of the Enchanted Prince are artlessly
and naturally told in the newly sanctioned colloquial language, and
we have a sympathetic understanding of the tales of the Capture of

54. *Hieratic Papyri in the British Museum. Third Series. Chester Beatty Gift*, ed.
A. H. Gardiner (London, 1935), I, 38 ff.

55. A. H. Gardiner, *Ancient Egyptian Onomastica* (London, 1947), 3 vols.

56. Erman, *LAE*, pp. 280 f.

57. *Ibid.*, pp. 293 ff.

Joppa and of Seqnen-Re's difficulties with the Hyksos king Apophis.[58] Some products are more highly developed, like the allegory of the Blinding of Truth by Falsehood. In this tale, Falsehood succeeds, by telling a fantastic lie, in persuading the gods to blind and enslave Truth. The son of Truth grows up, avenges his father, and secures the punishment of Falsehood by telling an equally extravagant lie. We may be sure that the sophisticated Egyptian of the period relished the irony by which Truth was vindicated when his son outlied Falsehood himself.[59]

The period also gives us love songs which come very gratefully to our ears, despite the fact that the terms used for the lovers are "brother" and "sister." The theme is romantic, rather than erotic love: the longing for a beloved who may be unattainable. The expectation of a blissful union is implicit to the yearning, but the normal statement is that the lovers are not yet united. Another happy element in these love songs is the rejoicing in nature and the open air, themes which became strong in Egypt during the Empire. An example of eager longing is in the following:

> Would that thou wouldst come to the sister speedily,
>   Like a horse of the king,
> Picked from a thousand of all steeds,
>   The foremost of the stables! . . .
> When it hears the sound of the whip,
>   It knows no delay,
> And there is no chief charioteer
>   Who can stand before it.
> How well the sister's heart knows
>   That he is not far from the sister![60]

In another song the physical effects of romantic yearning are brought out in a way that would interest the modern physician.

> Seven (days) to yesterday I have not seen the sister,
>   And a sickness has invaded me;
> My body has become heavy,
>   (And I am) forgetful of my own self.
> If the chief physicians come to me,
>   My heart is not content with their remedies. . . .
> What will revive me is to say to me: "Here she is!"
>   Her name is what will lift me up. . . .
> The sister is more beneficial to me than any remedies;
>   She is more to me than the collected writings.
> My health is her coming in from outside:

58. Ibid., pp. 150, 161, 165, 167 ff.

59. *Hieratic Papyri in the British Museum. Third Series. Chester Beatty Gift*, ed. A. H. Gardiner (London, 1935), I, 2 ff.

60. A. H. Gardiner, *The Library of A. Chester Beatty* (London, 1931), p. 35.

When I see her, then I am well. . . .
When I embrace her, she drives evil away from me—
But she has gone from me for seven days![61]

One of the deeply colored strains of the day was a caustic sense of humor, which took satisfaction in the discomfiture of others. This was particularly directed against enemies of Egypt, as in the tumultuous battle scenes of the Empire. It appeared also in the historical texts. There is a grim pleasure in Thut-mose III's account of the Battle of Megiddo, when he describes how the routed enemy was locked out of the town and had to be hauled up onto the wall by lowered clothing, or how the enemy princes who had driven proudly to battle in chariots were sent home on donkeyback. In the scenes of Ramses II's Battle of Kadesh the enemy is depicted as driven into the waters of the Orontes River. The intensity of the composition is relieved by a picture of "the wretched Prince of Aleppo," held upside down by his soldiers to drain him of the water which he had swallowed.[62]

A similar mordant humor pervades the popular Satirical Letter, in which the scribe Hori bitingly attacks the official competence of the scribe Amen-em-Opet. After saluting Amen-em-Opet as "his friend, his excellent brother, . . . wise of understanding, whose like does not exist in any scribe," and after devoting much space to pious good wishes, Hori immediately remarks that his friend's letter to him was incompetent and incomprehensible. "I found that it was neither praises nor insults. Your statements mix up this with that; all your words are upside down; they are not connected. . . . Your letter is too inferior to permit one to listen to it. . . . If you had known beforehand that it was no good, you would not have sent it. . . . I answer you in like manner (but) in a letter which is original from the first page to the end." He then launches into a long and sarcastic attack upon Amen-em-Opet, ridiculing the poor fellow's learning and scribal ability, his competence as a paymaster on government projects, and his capacity to serve as a royal courier in Asia. At times he loftily pretends to forget Amen-em-Opet's name and calls him "Who's-This?" Constantly, in his sneers, he introduces venomous politeness: "O alert scribe, understanding of heart, who is not ignorant at all, a torch in the darkness at the head of the troops!"—you have no idea how to lead an army unit. We need not go into his many thrusts at his opponent. He concludes on a note of

---

61. *Ibid.*, p. 34. Other love songs in Erman, *LAE*, pp. 242 ff.

62. Ch. Kuentz, *La Bataille de Qadech* (*MIFAO*, LV [1928]), pp. 168, 179, Pls. XL, XLI; J. H. Breasted, *A History of Egypt* (New York, 1905), p. 434.

bland superiority. "Now how will this end? Should I withdraw? Why, I have (only just) started! You must submit! . . . I have shorn for you the (very) end of your letter, so that I might answer for you what you have said. Your speeches are gathered together on my tongue and remain upon my lips. They are confused when heard, and there is no interpreter who can unravel them. They are like the words of a man of the Delta marshes with a man of Elephantine. . . . You should not say: 'You have made my name stink before the rabble and everybody!' Why, I have (only) told you the nature of the courier, traversed for you the roads of foreign countries(?), and marshalled for you all foreign countries together and the towns according to their order(?). Please let yourself look at them calmly, so that you may find yourself able to repeat them and may become with us a [competent scribe(?)]."[63]

With so strong a satirical sense pervading scenes and texts it is no surprise to find a broad streak of irreverence directed against things once held sacred. The period provides us with caricatures, in which the proud figure of pharaoh charging against the enemy is degraded into a battle between cats and mice.[64] The gods did not escape such burlesquing: the story of the litigation between Horus and Seth for "the office" of Osiris is a broad and bawdy farce directed at the solemn conclave of the gods, who are depicted as knavish and childish. When the council of the gods shouted in favor of Horus, Re, the presiding magistrate, who favored Seth, taunted the infant Horus with the charge that the smell of his mother's milk was still stale in his mouth. Then the monkeyish god Baba rose in court and shouted at Re: "Your shrine is empty!" At this insult the president of the gods was so hurt that he left the court, went to his arbor, and lay upon his back sulking. So the gods sent Hat-Hor, goddess of love, to him, to cajole him out of his peevishness by exposing her charms to him. "Then the great god laughed at her, and he got up, and he sat down with the Great Ennead, and he said to Horus and Seth: 'Say your say!' " Later, Isis, the mother of Horus, became so insistent in court that the gods adjourned their sessions, went to Central Island for a picnic, and charged the ferryman not to transport any woman resembling Isis. Of course, Isis disguised herself and persuaded the ferryman, whose righteous indignation at her first, small bribe and complacence at the second, substantial bribe are told with succinct cynicism. When Horus and Seth agreed to an ordeal, whereby

63. Erman, *LAE*, pp. 214 ff.; A. H. Gardiner, *Egyptian Literary Texts. Series I* (Leipzig, 1911).

64. A. Erman and H. Ranke, *Aegypten und ägyptisches Leben im Altertum* (Tübingen, 1923), p. 620; G. Farina, *La Pittura Egiziana* (Milan, 1929), Pl. CCV.

they changed themselves into hippopotamuses and tried to see which could stay under water longer, Isis intervened to upset the ordeal with a harpoon, and then became confused as to whether she should attack her brother Seth for the sake of her son Horus. When, finally, the gods consulted Osiris, who dwelt in the underworld, that god of the dead fiercely demanded the rights of his son Horus with the threat: "The land in which I am is full of savage-faced messengers, and they are not afraid of any god or goddess! I can send them out, and they will bring back the heart of anyone who does wrong, and they will be here with me!" The gods then hastily reconvened and awarded the office to Horus, pacifying Seth by permitting him to be the thunder-god in the sky.[65]

On only a slightly more reverent plane is the myth of Re and Isis. Re had a secret name of power which he concealed from the other gods, but he was so old and feeble that he drooled at the mouth. Isis tricked him by kneading this spittle into a scorpion which stung him painfully. She refused to remove the poison until he communicated to her his secret name.[66] Or, in the myth of the destruction of mankind, Hat-Hor lusted in the slaughter of mortals, but Re repented of his anger and could halt the goddess only by tricking her into drunkenness.[67] The treatment of the gods as subject to human foibles and weaknesses was not new in Egypt, but the broadness of this treatment in the late Empire suggests that the sacred was no longer held in the same reverence. The supporting post of ancient Egyptian culture was showing visible cracks. If nothing could be taken with complete seriousness, what would hold society together?

The reign of Ramses III closed with two remarkable records. We have documents on a harem conspiracy, which apparently cost the pharaoh his life, and we have a long testamentary enactment, confirming the temples in their property and their annual dues despite the pharaoh's death.

The memoranda on the trial for conspiracy within the harem seem to indicate that Ramses III constituted the court of inquiry after his death, as he says that he is in the presence of Osiris. The posthumous authority and activity of the pharaohs were recognized factors in

65. A. H. Gardiner, *The Library of A. Chester Beatty* (London, 1931), pp. 8 ff.

66. *Hieratic Papyri in the British Museum. Third Series. Chester Beatty Gift*, ed. A. H. Gardiner (London, 1935), pp. 116 ff.

67. Erman, *LAE*, pp. 47 ff.

ancient Egypt, so that it was something more than a pious fraud when the new king issued orders in his father's name.[68] The king who had been a god in this world and was now a god in the other world had a responsibility to terminate his own affairs, and an oracle could transmit his commands, so that they might be accepted as emanating directly from him, not simply issued in his name.[69]

The deceased pharaoh charged the court to examine the case and specify the punishment of the criminals. However, he was careful to lay all responsibility for taking life or inflicting penalty upon the members of the court and thus to clear himself of any accountability as he stood before the gods. "As for all that they have done, it is they who have done it. Let all that they have done come upon their heads, whereas I am privileged and immune unto eternity, since I am among the righteous kings who are in the presence of Amon-Re, King of the Gods, and in the presence of Osiris, Ruler of Eternity." Although it is true that the deceased pharaoh wanted to carry no moral liability over into the other world, his disclaimer of responsibility and his specific fixing of the onus of impartial justice upon a court of civil officials, instead of leaving vengeance to his son and successor, illustrate the decline of the personal power and authority of the pharaoh. The law was fully delegated from the king to magistrates, who nominally acted in his name but were actually full arbiters of justice.

The chief criminal was a queen named Tiy, trying to seize the throne for her son. Various officials who had access to the harem were involved, either because they were active in inciting rebellion or because they concealed knowledge of the crime. Certain practitioners of magic were charged with collusion because they sold their black arts to the plotters. Some of the criminals were blanketed under pseudonyms which carried an indignant jibe: "the-Demon," "Wicked-in-Thebes," "Re-Hates-Him," and "Re-Will-Blind-Him." The guilty prince was referred to as "Pen-ta-Weret, who had that other name," avoiding reference to the throne name which the conspirators had tried to give him.

The court consisted of palace officials: butlers, clerks, the royal herald, army officers, and functionaries of the treasury. They were of the same official class as many of the criminals, and this turned out to be a serious danger, as it was subsequently discovered that two of the judges had been so indiscreet as to meet with some of the accused

---

68. Cf. the Instruction of Amen-em-het I, p. 131 above.
69. A. de Buck in *JEA*, XXIII (1937), 152 ff.; Breasted, ARE, IV, §§ 416 ff.

and "make a beer-hall" with them. Such undisciplined carousing reduced these two from judges to defendants, and "sentence was carried out by cutting off their noses and their ears because they had abandoned the good instructions given to them."

Some of the convicted plotters suffered the penalty for treason. "They examined them; they found them guilty; they caused their sentences to overtake them. Their crimes seized them." This was a delicate way of saying that they were executed. Criminals of higher standing, including the prince Pen-ta-Weret, were treated in conformance with a code of honor—condemned but not sentenced. "They found them guilty and left them in their (own) hands in the Place of Examination. They took their own lives; no penalty was carried out against them."

The plotters had resorted to witchcraft to further their schemes. Their magic was directed against the trusted officials of the palace, to "enfeeble their bodies," so that they could not detect or resist the conspiracy, and it was designed to give extraordinary powers to the traitors. One of the criminals tried to cast a charm over the harem guards, so that they might not notice the carrying of plotting messages: "he began to make human (figures) of wax, inscribed, so that they might be taken in by the Inspector (of the Harem), Irrem, harming one troop and bewitching the others, so that some words might be taken in and others brought out." One of the conspirators received from a magician a scroll endowing him with the terrible powers which should have been reserved for pharaoh alone. He said to the magician: " 'Give me a roll to endow me with strength and might.' And he gave him a magic roll of (Ramses III), the great god, and he began to work the magic powers of a god upon people." We should like to know what was inscribed upon this scroll, but it was surely a case of the most brazen lese majesty that a mere superintendent of royal herds should arrogate to himself the magic of a pharaoh. It is another of those symptoms of the breakdown of the sacred character of state and society in this period.

That great document by which the deceased Ramses III confirmed the temples of Egypt in their property gives an extraordinary picture of the ecclesiastical wealth at the end of the Empire. In his eleventh year the pharaoh had defeated the Meshwesh, the western Libyans, and taken more than forty thousand cattle by his victory. Two-thirds of these beasts were presented to Amon: 28,337 "animals which the mighty sword of Pharaoh carried off [from] the fallen ones of Meshwesh and which were made into herds which his majesty established anew [for] his father Amon-Re, King of the Gods."[70] The Great Papyrus Harris, his testamentary enactment on behalf of the temples, tells us that Amon had more than four hundred thousand large and small cattle and that one herd in the eastern Delta was tended by 971 Meshwesh.[71] This will illustrate how the gods' holdings had grown through the successes of empire.

We cannot go into detail in analyzing this document. The chief beneficiaries of pharaoh's devoted generosity were Amon of Thebes, Re of Heliopolis, and Ptah of Memphis; other gods were relatively poor. The long lists of property and income of each temple divide into three categories.[72] There is a statement of the regular income of the temples, deriving from legally established gifts by the pharaohs and from the endowments which supported the great feasts. There is a statement of the increase in the regularly held property of the temples by reason of the gifts of Ramses III in his thirty-one years of reign. This amazing record of royal generosity shows how the great shrines of Egypt, particularly the Temple of Amon-Re at Karnak, were squeezing the pharaoh to a point dangerous to the economy of the land. Finally, the summary of past ownings and recent gifts shows the temple estates as they stood at the time of Ramses III's death, in buildings, land, people owned as serfs, cattle, ships, and so on. This grand total was acknowledged by Ramses IV as the obligation which his father had left upon him.

The annual income which came to the temples through taxes was listed under two headings. Agricultural income was measured in units of grain, "the grain of the taxes of farmers," and all other income, whether goods or labor, was measured in units of silver, "silver, in property and in labor of people, given for the divine offerings." The preponderance of Amon's share will be seen by the fact that his temple received 86 per cent of the annual dues in silver, Re's temple 11 per cent, Ptah's temple 3 per cent, and the smaller temples none. In grain, Amon's portion was 62 per cent, Re's 15 per cent, Ptah's 8 per cent, and the smaller temples' 15 per cent. We have no idea how the temples' incomes compared with the revenues of the state, but an annual income of 1,000 lb. Troy of silver and of 1,100,000 bu. of grain must have

70. Edgerton and Wilson, op. cit., 67.

71. Breasted, ARE, IV, §§ 226, 224. Breasted's treatment of the papyrus begins with § 151.

72. The meaning of the lists is still in dispute, and our categories may be incorrect. Even so, the record of temple wealth will remain extraordinary. See H. D. Schaedel, Die Listen des grossen Papyrus Harris (Leip. AS, VI [Glückstadt, 1936]); A. H. Gardiner in JEA, XXVII (1941), 72 f.

bulked very large in the economy of the nation. In property the temples owned 169 towns, 9 of them in Syria, over 500 gardens, vineyards, and orchards, more than 50 shipyards and 88 ships, nearly half a million head of cattle, and so on.

Different interpretations of the lists will produce varying estimates on the temples' holdings in people and land relative to the population and extent of Egypt. The figure of 107,615 workingmen, exclusive of women, children, and the aged, would indicate a body of perhaps 450,000 persons belonging to the temples, and 1,100 square miles of land would be more than one-eighth of the arable territory of Egypt. But are these figures what Ramses III added to what was already present, or do they show the totals after his additions? Cautiously assuming that the figures give the final totals and guessing at a population of 4,500,000—we have no way of working out an approximation—we should arrive at the highly tentative conclusion that the temples of Egypt owned one person in every ten and one acre in every eight. The Temple of Amon alone would possess one person out of every fifteen and one acre out of every eleven. However, the guesses of others on the temple holdings have ranged from 2 per cent of the people and 15 per cent of the land to 15–20 per cent of the people and 30 per cent of the land.[73] We simply do not control the figures, so that the guesses might be regarded as futile, but they do tell something about the overwhelming power of the temples at this time.

The question whether these vast ecclesiastical properties were tax-free or not is still far from clear. We possess a large scroll from the Twentieth Dynasty, giving certain notations of the government tax-assessors on fields for about one hundred miles in Middle Egypt. Unfortunately, this mass of detail is not completely intelligible, because the system of notation is too abbreviated for us, so that we cannot tell whether the figures given are the measures of grain assessed per unit of land or are some kind of data which the assessor would later use to fix the tax. These are the government tax-collectors, and many of the lands are the stated property of the temples. The editor of this document notes that Herodotus and Diodorus, as well as Genesis 47:26, carry a tradition that the priests of Egypt were free from taxation and quotes a text of Persian times indicating that the temples were exceptionally forced to pay dues in a time of hardship, but then concludes that the temple privileges were partial only. He suggests that the priests themselves and the temple personnel were exempt from forced labor and

73. Breasted, *ARE*, IV, §§ 166–67; Schaedel, *op. cit.*, pp. 56 f.

that the charters of temple immunity forbade civil officials from violating this exemption, but that the temple lands were subject to government taxes. This is a decided amelioration of the situation, since tax-free lands running between 12 and 30 per cent of the arable acreage would have been a crushing burden. On the present evidence, the privilege of the temples was confined to an immunity from the *corvée* which burdened the rest of Egypt.[74]

In passing, we might note that the people who held and cultivated the fields which were recorded in this tax-assessors' scroll make an interesting cross section of Egyptian society. One block of neighbors included a slave, a woman, a Sardinian mercenary, a priest, the retainer of a Sardinian mercenary, a goatherd, a quartermaster, a stable-master, a tenant-farmer, and a soldier.[75] Elsewhere we find coppersmiths, embalmers, cattle-branders, beekeepers, sailors, scribes of the law-court, and various foreigners: Sea Peoples, Libyans, Syrians, and the *teher*-chariot-warriors, who may have been Hittites. It seems that a slave or a foreign mercenary might be the holder and cultivator of land on the same terms as a priest, army officer, or civil official—all of them under the general oversight of a high civil or religious administrator.

This document indicates an apparent flow of great resources to the coffers of the pharaohs in the middle Twentieth Dynasty. And yet these same pharaohs were forced to withdraw from empire and faced strikes by the workers in the government necropolis because of the state's inability to pay its laborers. How can we reconcile apparently high income with apparent bankruptcy? The editor of the papyrus believes that the answer may be that the pharaoh himself failed to receive the resources which were credited to him by the records and that these assets may have disappeared into the capacious maw of the god Amon. The effective grip of the High Priest of Amon upon the civil affairs and finances of the state may be shown by the distribution of offices within one family. Ramses-nakht was the High Priest of Amon under Ramses IV. His father Meri-Barset had been Chief Tax-master, and Ramses-nakht's sons were to hold two of the most potent offices in the land: Nes-Amon and Amen-hotep successively as High Priest of Amon, and User-maat-Re-nakht as Chief Tax-master and Manager of Pharaoh's Lands. Thus the priesthood of Amon could manage the finances of the state for its own benefit and withhold resources from the pharaoh as it desired. The divine king had become a prisoner of the

---

74. A. H. Gardiner, *The Wilbour Papyrus* (London, 1948), esp. II, 197 ff.
75. *Ibid.*, III, 26:35–27:10.

temple or of the little clan which held the highest temple offices. Ultimately the position of the pharaoh would be definitely limited by that clan, in the rule of Upper Egypt.[76]

That is not quite all of the story, as we shall see, for the control of the army and thus the policing of Egypt and of Nubia were important. Ramses-nakht was not commander of the army, but his grasp of the resources, powers, and authority of Upper Egypt was otherwise very sweeping. His son Amen-hotep, who held the High Priesthood of Amon from Ramses IV to Ramses XI, dared to sweep aside part of the pretense and violate one of the oldest canons of Egyptian art. The pharaoh had always been depicted in colossal size in proportion to all other Egyptians, who were only humans and not divine as he was.[77] In a scene in the Temple of Amon at Karnak, we see Ramses IX recognizing the services of the High Priest Amen-hotep with decorations. Pharaoh is shown in his customary heroic size in proportion to the two bustling little officials who carry out his instructions, but Amen-hotep had the arrogance to have his figure carved in the same scale as his king. Furthermore, the composition makes him the focus of attention instead of pharaoh. Nothing could illustrate more clearly that reality which the texts piously ignored: that the king was only an instrument of a ruling oligarchy.[78]

The Egyptian Empire had been able to exploit the gold mines of Nubia and the Sudan and the copper mines of Sinai. Egypt had no silver and relied upon her foreign trade to gain that metal, probably from the Hittite country. In the record of Ramses III's benefactions to the gods, there is a statement of the annual income of the chief temples, with the following amounts of metals, here converted to pounds Troy:

	Gold	Silver	Copper
Temple of Amon	139	2,675	6,422
Temple of Re		143	307
Temple of Ptah		24	
Annual totals	139	2,842	6,729[79]

76. *Ibid.*, II, 204. G. Lefebvre, *Histoire des Grands Prêtres d'Amon de Karnak* (Paris, 1929), pp. 264 ff.

77. H. Frankfort, *Kingship and the Gods* (Chicago, 1948), pp. 7 f.

78. J. H. Breasted, *A History of Egypt* (Scribner's, 1905), p. 509 and Fig. 177. Our Fig. 29*b*.

79. Breasted, *ARE*, IV, §§ 228, 283, 340. The value-ratio of gold to silver was about 2:1 (p. 289 below).

Thus Egypt was relying to a considerable degree upon metal from Asia for her economy. Early in the reign of Ramses III, the Hittite empire fell before the advance of the Sea Peoples, so that the established means for exchanging Egyptian grain and gold for Anatolian silver was placed in jeopardy. The same applied to iron, which had to come from the Hittite territory. By 1150 B.C., the bronze age was finished and the iron age was in play. Egypt's mines had provided her with the copper which was the base of bronze, but she had no iron. It is significant that the official exploitation of the Sinai copper mines stopped at this time. With the basic metal of power shifted from an ore which Egypt did possess to an ore which she had to purchase from abroad, her financial position became difficult. It is interesting that the period of Egypt's domination of the eastern Mediterranean world coincided rather closely with the times when copper was the essential and that she never enjoyed the same power in the iron age. The economic factor is not the only element in that coincidence, but it contributed to her sudden fall from power.

The adjustment of a national economy to a new basic metal must be painful, particularly when the nation has controlled production of the older metal but lacks the new. In Egypt's case, the severance of her relations with the Hittite empire made it difficult to procure iron, and it took time and suffering to make an adjustment. For forty or fifty years, from about 1160 B.C. on, we see an extraordinary inflation in the prices of grain in the Theban area, ending in a scale of prices notably higher than the earlier period.[80] The dynasty had started out with certain stable values, which were unchanged for about thirty years. The ratio happened to be 1:1—one sack of emmer wheat was worth one *deben* of copper.[81] Before the death of Ramses III, there was a slight increase in the cost of a sack of wheat, but this leveled off for another ten years. Then suddenly, about the middle of the twelfth century B.C., prices shot up in a dizzy fashion. Emmer wheat rose from 1½ *deben* per sack to 2, then to 4, and then to 5⅓ in the reign of Ramses IX. Barley similarly shot up, going to 8 *deben* per sack in the reign of Ramses VII. Finally, toward the end of the century, prices dropped and leveled off at 2 *deben* for a sack of emmer wheat or barley, just twice what they had been fifty or sixty years earlier. It is no wonder that this stretch of time saw the government in distress and confusion, with officials

80. J. Černý, "Fluctuations in Grain Prices during the Twentieth Egyptian Dynasty," in *Archiv Orientální,* VI (1933), 173 ff.

81. About 2¼ bu. of wheat for 91 grams (nearly 3 oz. Troy) of copper.

snatching advantage for themselves instead of working for the state. And what must the little man have suffered during the two generations of inflation?

One may guess at two factors which relieved the most acute distress of the inflation. The first would be the normal adjustment of an agricultural economy, which still had the basic productivity of its soil, to the successive blows of the incoming of the iron age and the loss of empire. The second factor was strongest at Thebes, from which most of our information on the inflation comes, although unquestionably a similar situation could prevail elsewhere. This was a new exploitation of the gold, silver, and other treasures which lay buried in the hills of western Thebes, that is, a large-scale and continued plundering of the tombs of pharaohs and nobles. We shall discuss that sad story shortly, but here we wish to point out that the gold and silver illegally and sacrilegeously mined from the tombs was put into active circulation by the robbers themselves, by their fences, and by conniving officials who received substantial bribes, and that this relieved the inflation. Thus we can understand why the tomb robberies persisted so long, despite solemn investigations and trials. The robbers were committing acts of sacrilege against the Egyptian state and its nominally cherished dead, but their nocturnal industry was bringing the overbalanced economy of the state back into some kind of equilibrium.

The period of the inflation was a time of acute distress for those commoners who were employed on state enterprises. The government workers who quarried, carved, decorated, and maintained the tombs of western Thebes (Fig. 30) were organized into two gangs under the immediate authority of three supervisors, who were the two gang foremen and the Clerk of the Necropolis. Over these three stood the Mayor of Western Thebes, who was responsible to the Vizier of Upper Egypt. The two gangs with their families were housed within the necropolis and apparently, as gangs, were held within certain walls, checked by gatekeepers and the police. In addition to the actual workers on the tombs, there were individuals detailed to make plaster, cut wood, construct buildings, wash clothes, raise vegetables, bring fish, and carry water. All the workers were paid in grain on a monthly basis.[82]

When inflation was just beginning in the latter years of Ramses III, this system of employment broke down because of the government's delay in delivering payment to the workers. A papyrus in Turin gives

82. T. E. Peet, *The Great Tomb-robberies of the Twentieth Egyptian Dynasty* (Oxford, 1930), I, 9 ff.

scattered notations on a workers' strike in a year which should be somewhere around 1170 B.C.[83] Through the hot summer months, the only
indication of trouble to come lay in the increase in the number of those
who performed services for the necropolis workers: twenty-four
water-carriers instead of the previous six, twenty fishermen instead of
four, two confectioners where there had been none, and so on. Perhaps
a slow-up in the delivery of rations from the government across the
River had necessitated an increase in local services, to keep the workers
reasonably content. If so, this action failed to meet the main trouble.

In the autumn the inundation receded, and the muddy fields crackled
with the first green promise of plenty, but the necropolis workers were
lean and hungry. They had received no grain to pay for the month
which would correspond roughly to our October. About the middle
of November they were two months in arrears on pay, and their pri-
vations drove them to an organized protest, the first strike about which
we have any information in history.

"Year 29, second month of the second season, day 10. On this day
(occurred) the crossing of the five walls of the necropolis by the gang,
saying: 'We are hungry!' . . . And they sat down at the back of the
Temple" of Thut-mose III, at the edge of the cultivated fields. The
three supervisors and their assistants came to urge them to return inside
the necropolis preserve, "and they took great oaths . . . : 'You may
come, for we have the word of Pharaoh!' " However, a promise in the
name of the king was not enough, for the strikers spent the day encamped against the rear wall of the temple, returning to their homes
inside the necropolis only at night.

They walked out again on the second day, and on the third day they
dared to invade the Ramesseum, the august enclosure around the mortuary temple of Ramses II. Then there was a great scurrying of pay-
masters, doorkeepers, and police. A chief of police promised to send
for the Mayor of Thebes, who had kept discreetly out of sight. The
mob was determined but orderly, and their invasion of the sacred
precinct seems to have been more effective than their previous sit-
down. The officials listened to their protest: "We have reached this
place because of hunger, because of thirst, without clothing, without
oil, without fish, without vegetables! Write to Pharaoh, our good lord,
about it, and write to the Vizier, our superior. Act so that we may live!"

83. A transcription into hieroglyphs in A. H. Gardiner, *Ramesside Administrative
Documents* (London, 1948), pp. xiv ff., 45 ff. There is no detailed analysis of the text
more recent than W. Spiegelberg, *Arbeiter und Arbeiterbewegung . . . unter den
Ramessiden* (Strassburg, 1895).

The royal treasury was opened, and rations for the preceding month were delivered to them.

The workers were mollified by this payment, but hard experience had made them determined not to be put off by partial satisfaction: they wanted their pay for this month also. On the next day they gathered at "the fortress of the necropolis," which must have been the police head-quarters. There the Chief of Police Montu-mose acknowledged the justice of their claim but asked them to maintain order: "Look, I give you my answer: Go up (to your homes) and gather your gear and lock your doors and take your wives and your children. And I will go ahead of you to the Temple of (Thut-mose III) and will let you sit there tomorrow." Finally, on the eighth day of the strike, the month's rations were delivered.

Two weeks later, when they were not paid on the first day of the new month, they walked out again. Now their grievance carried a veiled threat against their supervisors, that these were defrauding phar-aoh: "We will not come. So you tell your superiors, as they stand at the head of their companions, that we certainly did not cross over (the walls) because of our hunger (alone, but) we have an important accu-sation to make, that crimes are certainly being committed in this place of Pharaoh!" We are not told the result of this accusation, but the trouble dragged on. Two months later the Vizier was in Thebes on official business, but he was careful not to cross the River and face the strikers. Instead he sent a police officer to give bland promises to the three necropolis supervisors: "When something is lacking, I shall not fail to come to fetch it for you! Now about your saying: 'Don't take away our rations!'—why, I am the Vizier, who gives rather than takes away! . . . If it should happen that there is nothing in the granary itself, I shall give you what I may find!"

Eleven days later the gang again crossed the walls with the cry: "We are hungry!" As they sat encamped behind the Temple of Mer-ne-Ptah, the Mayor of Thebes passed by, and they shouted out to him. He prom-ised them relief: "Look, I will give you these fifty sacks of grain as a means of life until Pharaoh gives you rations." This looks like an act of official mercy, but in a few days we find an accusation lodged with the High Priest of Amon that the Mayor of Thebes was using the offerings of the Temple of Ramses II to feed the strikers; "this is a great crime which he is doing!" We are unable to gauge the relative weight of the forces behind governmental inactivity: lack of revenue, official dis-honesty, or petty politics. All three factors seem to have been present.

The document which we have been examining runs out into silence, so that we cannot tell whether that generation of workers and officials adjusted their difficulties. However, other texts tell us that the situation was not permanently corrected. From the reign of Ramses IX, more than forty years later, we have a journal of the necropolis work, kept by a paymaster clerk. The workers were idle for a long stretch of days, and then the clerk made a note that the rations of pay were already ninety-five days in arrears. Four years later, the gangs took advantage of an official visit to the necropolis to make their humble complaint: " 'We are weak and hungry, for we have not been given the dues which Pharaoh gave for us!' And the Vizier, the High Priest, the Butler, and the Chief Treasurer of Pharaoh said: 'The men of the necropolis gang are right!' " If any persons could have remedied the situation these officials could, but apparently they preferred to pay off the workers in righteous indignation rather than in sacks of barley and wheat.[84]

Let us take one final case, from the third year of Ramses X, nearly fifty years after that first strike. The gangs were idle and crossed the River to appeal to the highest officials. The High Priest of Amon argued that it would be technically incorrect for him to issue provisions against their hunger, since such rations should properly come to them from their immediate superiors. But the workers spent the night at the High Priest's office, to resume their petition in the morning. Then the high officials summoned the Secretary of the Vizier and a deputy governor of the royal granary and ordered them: "See the grain of the Vizier—give the men of the necropolis provisions from it." The grateful workers then presented two of the high officials with gifts: two boxes and a writing case. The terse statement does not explicitly connect the issue of emergency rations with the presents to the responsible officials, but the very terseness suggests that a poor man owed something to his patron.[85]

We have already seen that the collapse of empire and the incoming of the iron age were factors leading to a severe inflation. These were external causes of the government's failure to pay its workers. There were also internal and spiritual causes, which went back as far as the middle of the Empire, in the weakening of the central government and the loss of *esprit de corps* within the state: the humanization of the god-king, the Amarna heresy, the building of a tight ruling bureaucracy,

84. G. Botti and T. E. Peet, *Il Giornale della Necropoli di Tebe* (Turin, 1928——), 4:2—5:17; 25:6-10.

85. *Ibid.*, 55:24—56:4.

and the feuding between different parts of the government. At any rate, marked dishonesty was now visible in official circles. Let us illustrate this with examples.

Under Ramses XI, a certain Thut-mose was Clerk of the Great and August Necropolis. One of his functions was to travel around Upper Egypt collecting taxes in grain, part of which was allocated to the pay of the necropolis workers. A section of a letter of his runs: "Send your clerk and the Clerk of the Necropolis Yuf-en-Amon and the Doorkeeper Thut-mose or the Doorkeeper Khonsu-mose. Have them hurry to fetch the grain, so that the men will not starve and become idle in the business of Pharaoh's house and lay every word (of reproach) against you."[86] Was this humanitarian feeling? Another document gives us a hint of the shrinkage in the collected grain before it was deposited in Thebes. The Necropolis Clerk Thut-mose and his assistants went south to Esneh to collect the dues. What he received through the temple at that place amounted to 343.25 sacks.[87] However, 6.25 sacks were immediately surrendered at Esneh "for the expenses." When the boats arrived at Thebes, only 314 sacks were turned over to the Mayor of Western Thebes, Pa-wer-aa. Various deductions for "expenses" and "rations" were listed for different members of the expedition, but these accounts are so summarily made that they leave some of the grain still unaccounted for. It is quite clear that the reckoning has been falsified and that Thut-mose expected no punishment for his laxness.[88]

Government inefficiency and venality may have been latent throughout Egyptian history. In these records about the necropolis workers of the Twentieth Dynasty there is a frightening climax of laxness, indifference, avoidance of responsibility, and sheer dishonesty. Egypt had come a long way from the Middle Kingdom ideal of *ma‹at*. Social conscience, a sense of group interest, and official integrity were painfully absent.

Apart from the tomb robberies, which we shall examine presently, the most brazen example of long-continued dishonesty comes from the middle of the Dynasty, in a papyrus which is devoted to a detailed account of the improprieties and crimes of a priest of the Temple of Khnum at the First Cataract. One section of this document deals with annual dues for the temple. It was to receive annually 700 sacks of

86. J. Černý, *Late Ramesside Letters* (*Bibl. Aeg.*, IX [1939]), 69 f.; cf. A. H. Gardiner in *JEA*, XXVII (1941), 23.

87. About 775 bu.

88. Gardiner in *JEA*, XXVII (1941), 30–32.

grain[89] from certain fields in the Delta, and a ship captain had contracted to transport that grain each year. Near the end of the reign of
Ramses III, the responsible captain died and another was appointed by
the priesthood. For four years the new man delivered the 700 sacks in
full, "but in the year 1 of King (Ramses IV), the great god, he made
defaults in the grain." Here is the record of nine years of graft by the
Ship's Captain Khnum-nakht.

Year	Sacks Delivered	Deficit
1 of Ramses IV ..	100	600
2...............	130	570
3...............	"He brought none of it"	
4...............	20	680
5...............	20	680
6...............	"He did not bring it"	
1 of Ramses V ...	"He did not bring it"	
2...............	186	514
3...............	120	580

In other words, over a period of nine years, the temple received only
576 out of 6,300 sacks, slightly over 9 per cent. The ship captain could
not have engaged in such wholesale robbery without the knowledge
and participation of a host of agents, all the way up from the farmers
who delivered the grain to his boat in the Delta to the clerks who
registered it at the Temple of Khnum at the First Cataract. The sacks
which disappeared were recorded as the "total of the grain of the
Temple of Khnum, Lord of Elephantine, on which this ship captain
conspired with the clerks, administrators, and peasant-farmers of the
Temple of Khnum, and they looted it and made free with it for their
own purposes." Another charge against this Captain Khnum-nakht was
that he exacted fifty sacks of grain a year from each of two individuals—
a total of 1,000 sacks over ten years—"and he made free with it for his
own purposes; he brought none of it to the granary of Khnum."
Apparently the law finally caught up with the bold captain and his
fellow-grafters, but the fact that he was able to enrich himself on so
baronial a scale for ten years is a sad commentary on the discipline
within the Egyptian state at this time.[90]

This was a tragic age for Egypt, an age which might be characterized
by the haunting reference to "the year of hyenas, when men starved."[91]

89. About 1,575 bu.   90. Gardiner, op. cit., pp. 60–62.
91. T. E. Peet in JEA, XII (1926), 258.

Roving bands of foreigners terrorized the peaceful workers of the Nile Valley. The journals of the necropolis workers list many days when the men were idle "because of the foreigners." This became so common a situation under Ramses IX that the journal even noted days when there were no foreigners. In some of the contexts these roving and marauding bands are designated as Libyans (*Rebu*) or Meshwesh. It seems unlikely that they were desert nomads raiding the Nile Valley from the west; the necropolis police could have taken care of small bands of that nature. More probably they were mercenary soldiers, brought into Egypt by capture or enrollment and now idle because there was no military campaigning (Fig. 31*d*). Cut off from the looting of Egypt's enemies, perhaps unpaid like the necropolis workers, they were living by plundering from the people of Egypt.[92] The government would have difficulty in dealing with such bands. Insofar as possible the idle mercenaries, both the Libyans and the Sea Peoples, had been settled on the land as farmers. For example, Ramses III founded a settlement in Upper Egypt for "the Sardinian people and the royal army clerks."[93] Yet it must have taken several generations to curb the foreign mercenaries' restlessness and rapacity, particularly when their employing government was weak and financially straitened.

Probably under Ramses XI, there was a revolt against the High Priest of Amon, Amen-hotep. Our evidence comes only in allusions made at a later time, and it is not stated whether the rebels were rivals for his power or those whom he had held in subjection. A workman was testifying about the damage done to a piece of temple property, a portable chest, and said: "The foreigners had come and seized the Temple (of Medinet Habu), and I was driving some donkeys belonging to my father when Pa-hati, a foreigner, seized me and took me to the town of Ipip, at the time when Amen-hotep, who had been High Priest of Amon, had been attacked six months. Now it happened that I came back after nine full months of the attack on Amen-hotep, who had been High Priest of Amon, when this portable chest had already been damaged and set on fire. Then when order had been restored. . . ." Another witness also dated events to the same disturbances: "Now when the war against the High Priest took place, this man stole my father's property." It is probable that this revolt occurred somewhere between the twelfth and fifteenth years of Ramses XI, around 1105–1100 B.C., and it may be connected with other disturbances in Egypt, such as an "out-

92. E.g., Botti and Peet, *op. cit.*, 4:2 ff.
93. A. H. Gardiner in *JEA*, XXVII (1941), 41, and *The Wilbour Papyrus*, II, 80 f.

break in the northern area" and the "destruction" of a city in Middle Egypt by a certain Pa-Nehsi, who seems to have been the Viceroy for Ethiopia and Commander of the Army. A contest for power between the priestly ruling family at Thebes and the military is highly likely.[94]

Our greatest body of evidence on the stress and strain of the times comes from the records of the tomb robberies at the end of the Twentieth Dynasty.[95] A certain amount of looting from the richly piled tombs had always been endemic in Egypt. As far back as the Fourth Dynasty the tomb of Khufu's mother seems to have been plundered in his own lifetime.[96] The temptations were always great, but as long as the nation was busy and prosperous and as long as the government was strong, vigilant, and honest the tombs of the ancestors could be fairly well secured. The acute epidemic of tomb robbery in the Twentieth Dynasty broke out because the state was desperately ill. There in the western hillside of Thebes lay an amazing treasure of gold and silver and other rich furnishings in the tombs of kings and nobles. Poverty and hunger had followed the inflation. The police were unable to cope with the roving bands of foreigners. There were contests for power among the highest factions in the government. Most important of all, the recognized sanctions of the sacred state had weakened, so that there was no effective moral feeling against robbery within a government preserve and against the sacrilege of violating the eternal rest of gods and immortals. The papyrus records of the investigations and trials of the robbers show that ordinary workmen were engaged in mining the treasure from the hillside tombs, but the continuance of the looting for a full generation without effective check and the continuance in office of responsible officials throughout that period make it clear that highly placed persons were privy to the activity and probably were enriching themselves from the plundering. A strong and conscientious government would have halted the robbery or discharged the officials who were failing to check the depredations.

The most interesting records of government activity—and inactivity—in investigating the robberies come early in the series of documents, from the sixteenth year of Ramses IX, sometime before 1120 B.C. The month was July or August, when tempers are short because of the heat.

94. So H. Kees, *Herihor und die Aufrichtung des Gottesstaates* (*Gött. GN.*, 1936), pp. 4 ff. T. E. Peet in *JEA*, XII (1926), 254 ff., was inclined to date the outbreak between the thirteenth and seventeenth years of Ramses IX, twenty years earlier than Kees.

95. Peet, *The Great Tomb-robberies;* J. Capart, A. H. Gardiner, and B. van de Walle in *JEA*, XXII (1936), 169 ff.

96. G. A. Reisner in *Bulletin of the Museum of Fine Arts, Boston,* XXVI (1928), 76 ff.

The cast of characters included the Vizier Kha-em-Waset, acting on behalf of pharaoh, who remained in his northern capital most of the year, and the High Priest of Amon, Amen-hotep, who lent his authority to the investigations. The two important accused culprits were little men, the coppersmith Pai-Kharu and the stonemason Amon-pa-nefer. But the two chief antagonists were the government officials responsible to the Vizier for the rule and security of eastern and western Thebes. Pa-ser was Mayor of Thebes on the east bank, the capital city, while Pa-wer-aa was Mayor of Western Thebes, the necropolis area, and also Chief of Police in the west, thus directly responsible for the security of the tombs and temples in his district. Pa-ser was an informer and reformer, indignant at the robbing of the tombs, and his charges were thus ultimately directed against Pa-wer-aa, who should have kept his territory inviolate. We can never know whether the indignant Pa-ser was actually motivated by a burning desire for honesty and justice, whether he was a politician of a minority party working for advantage against the majority, or whether he was trying to work his way into the high-placed gang which was profiting from the robberies. On the face of it, he was the one figure crying out for justice and honesty, so that we may credit him as being a righteous informer surrounded by blandly cynical grafters. Unfortunately, he was isolated and inept, could be proved wrong on his specific charges, and thus was put officially in the wrong, no matter how right he may have been in his general accusations.

In his office on the east bank, Pa-ser received information about tomb robbery going on in Pa-wer-aa's territory on the west side. We now know that, for at least three preceding years, the gang of the stonemason Amon-pa-nefer had been systematically looting the tombs at night, "according to our regular practice." Pa-ser did not wait to check his information. He filed charges with the Vizier and other officials of pharaoh that ten tombs of kings, four tombs of queens, and many tombs of nobles had been broken into and robbed, and he specified by name the kings and queens whose burials had been violated. Thus he forced his rival Pa-wer-aa to demand an official investigation.

The Vizier named a commission of priests, clerks, and police officers, under the chairmanship of Pa-wer-aa himself, to go and find out the truth of the charges. On a hot summer day the commission toiled around the baking Theban necropolis, visiting the allegedly robbed tombs. Their findings were remarkable. Pa-ser had charged that ten tombs of pharaohs at the northern end of the necropolis had been broken into. Nine of these were found intact. Of the tomb of an Intef of the Seventeenth Dynasty they reported that thieves had started tunneling into it, but "it is uninjured; the robbers had not been able to enter it." Only one of the ten alleged robberies was confirmed. Of the tomb of Sebek-em-saf of the Seventeenth Dynasty, the commission reported: "It was found that the thieves had broken into it by mining through the lower chambers of its pyramid. . . . The royal burial-place was found empty of its lord, as well as the burial-place of the great queen Nub-khas, his queen, the thieves having laid their hands on them. The (commission) investigated it, and it was ascertained how the thieves had laid their hands upon this king and his queen." We shall hear more about this robbery. The commission then looked into the charges about robbed tombs in the Queens' Valley and in the hillside of the nobles' tombs. They then tabulated their results:

"Total of pyramid-tombs of former kings investigated today by the inspectors:

Found uninjured	9 pyramid-tombs
Found broken into	1
Total	10

"Tombs of the singing-women of the House of the Divine Votaress of Amon-Re, King of the Gods:

Found uninjured	2
Found broken into by the thieves	2
Total	4

"The tombs and chambers in which the beatified of old, the citizenesses and citizens, rest on the west of Thebes: it was found that the thieves had broken into all of them, had dragged their occupants from their coffins and sarcophagi, so that they were lying on the desert, and had stolen their funerary furniture, which had been given to them, as well as the gold, silver, and the fittings which were in their coffins."

Pa-ser was mathematically wrong. Only one out of ten kings' tombs, and only two out of four queens' tombs had been robbed. It seems to have been relatively unimportant that "all" of the tombs of nobles were reported as looted, with debris scattered all over the desert hillside. Pa-wer-aa felt vindicated on the specific situation but was obliged to offer up a sacrifice of unimportant, little men because of the general situation. "The Mayor of the West and Chief of Police of the Necropolis, Pa-wer-aa, gave the list of the thieves in writing to the Vizier, the nobles, and the butlers. They were arrested and imprisoned; they were examined and told what had happened."

Actually the examination was pitifully inadequate. On the following day a second commission, headed by no less a person than the Vizier himself, took a prisoner across the River to "tell what had happened." The miserable culprit was the coppersmith Pai-Kharu, who had confessed to some robbery in the Queens' Valley two years earlier. Now he was blindfolded, hustled along by police, questioned by the high dignitaries of the land. When his blindfold had been removed in the Queens' Valley, his memory could only identify two completely unimportant places in which he had been a robber: a tomb "in which no burial had ever been made and which had been left open," and the hut of a necropolis workman. Solemnly the coppersmith was placed under oath and "examined with a very severe examination," which means that he was trussed up, his hands and feet were twisted, he was beaten on his palms and soles with the *bastinado*, and he was threatened with having his nose and ears cut off and with being impaled upon the stake. But he insisted: "I don't know any (other) place here among these tombs, except this tomb which is open and this hut which I pointed out to you." The officials then examined the seals placed on the outer doors of the tombs and found them intact. Satisfied that charges of official negligence were greatly exaggerated, they returned across the River.

That evening there was an event of brazen callousness. The officials permitted the people of the west side of Thebes to make a parade of rejoicing over the whitewashing of their Mayor. "The high officials let the supervisors, the agents, the necropolis workmen, the chiefs of police, the police, and all the necropolis serf-laborers go around the west of Thebes in a great demonstration (reaching) as far as Thebes (across the River)." Very naturally the mob gave voice to its triumph over the puritanical kill-joy, Pa-ser, who had tried to upset the accepted order of things, and they came to his very door to express their exultation.[97] Pa-ser then lost his temper and accused the mob of spite. He pointed out that the investigators had discovered the robbery of the tomb of Pharaoh Sebek-em-saf. A workman in the mob broke in to say that the divine protection of pharaoh lay over the necropolis, so that all the kings, queens, princes, and princesses would be inviolate forever. When Pa-ser called the man a liar, the record neatly takes ad-

97. G. A. Wainwright in *JEA*, XXIV (1938), 59 ff., adduces some amusing parallels to modern demonstrations.

vantage of his irreverence to the doctrine of pharaoh's power by intoning piously: "Now really this was no light accusation which this Mayor of Thebes made." When his rival Pa-wer-aa heard that Pa-ser had promised five new accusations about tomb robbery, the Mayor of Western Thebes seized the initiative and asked the Vizier for a new investigation: "I have heard the words which this Mayor of Thebes spoke to the people of the great and august necropolis . . . and I report them to my lord, for it would be a crime for one in my position to hear something and conceal it. But I do not know the bearing of the very serious charges which the Mayor of Thebes says that (his informants) made to him. I really cannot understand them, but I report them to my lord, so that my lord may get to the bottom of these charges." Pa-wer-aa then put Pa-ser further in the wrong by pointing out that the latter had accepted information which ought to have gone directly to the Vizier.

The Vizier acted promptly on Pa-wer-aa's report. On the very next day a new commission of inquiry sat in the Temple of Amon. The Vizier himself presided, and the High Priest of Amon lent his dignity to the court. Among the officials on the bench was Pa-ser himself, sitting on the hearing on his charges. Three wretched prisoners were introduced, but before any testimony was heard, the Vizier made an opening statement which was so heavy with authoritative indignation that it choked off all debate: "This Mayor of Thebes (Pa-ser) made certain charges to the supervisors and necropolis workers (day before yesterday), in the presence of the Royal Butler and Secretary of Pharaoh, Nes-Amon, making statements about the great tombs which are in the Place of Beauty; even though, when I myself—the vizier of the land—was there with the Royal Butler and Secretary of Pharaoh, Nes-Amon, we inspected the tombs . . . and found them uninjured, so that all that he has said was found to be false. Now, see, the coppersmiths stand before you. Let them tell all that happened." Naturally, after so biased an opening statement, the coppersmiths felt no obligation to support Pa-ser's charges. "They were questioned, but the men were found to know no tomb in the Place of Pharaoh about which the Mayor had spoken the words. He was placed in the wrong about it. The great officials released the coppersmiths. . . . A report was drawn up; it is deposited in the Vizier's archives."

One can imagine Pa-ser sitting on the bench and hearing his charges swept aside by his superiors. He was completely outmaneuvered by those who wanted no disturbance of the evil status quo. The aftermath of the case is interesting. After this trial, we never hear another word about Pa-ser, the Mayor of Thebes. He drops out of the record. On the other hand, his wily rival, Pa-wer-aa, was still Mayor and Chief of Police in Western Thebes seventeen years later, seventeen years in which the tomb robberies in his district continued in crescendo. Fifteen months after this trial, one of the tombs in the Queens' Valley was found smashed to bits by robbers. In all the documents of investigation there was not a single defendant of high position. Only the little men, the stonemasons and coppersmiths and farmers, were caught. Why?

The deposition of the stonemason Amon-pa-nefer gives us the answer. He and his gang were the looters of the tomb of Sebek-em-saf. He described the tunneling into the tomb and the exciting first view of the jewel-laden "god lying at the rear of his burial-place." When the mummies of the pharaoh and of his queen had been stripped of the gold and silver and costly stones, the thieves set fire to the coffins. "And we made the gold which we had found on these two gods—from their mummies, amulets, ornaments, and coffins—into eight shares. And twenty *deben* of gold fell to each one of the eight of us, making 160 *deben* of gold, without dividing the rest of the furniture(?)." The total of gold from this tomb was nearly 40 lb. Troy, each robber taking 5 lb., which was no small amount for a peasant.

Amon-pa-nefer continued: "Then we crossed over to Thebes. And after some days, the agents of Thebes heard that we had been stealing in the west, so they arrested me and imprisoned me at the Mayor of Thebes' place. So I took the twenty *deben* of gold that had fallen to me as (my) share, and gave them to Kha-em-Opet, the District Clerk of the harbor at Thebes. He let me go, and I joined my companions, and they made up for me another share. And I, as well as the other robbers who are with me, have continued to this day in the practice of robbing the tombs of the nobles and people of the land who rest in the west of Thebes. And a large number of the men of the land rob them also."

Twenty *deben* of gold—nearly two kilograms or five Troy pounds—was a very large bribe. Not only did this stonemason walk out of imprisonment, but he was permitted to continue his robberies. What happened to the records of his arrest? Probably that District Clerk of the Theban harbor did not retain all of the twenty *deben*; the bribe went on up high enough to choke off any inquisitiveness about the failure of legal procedure. The long and sorry record of the tomb robberies of the Twentieth Dynasty is a story of higher officials evading their duties because they were gaining personal advantage out of such evasion. It was a cynical rejection of the content of *ma‹at* and a retention of so much of the form of *ma‹at* as would make an impressive documentary show. The unimportant little people who were threatened and beaten and tortured by examining magistrates were the sacrifices for the responsible officers who were examining them. Here the Egyptian spirit reached bottom.

A century after these tomb robberies had come to their climax the state finally took action to protect the sacred persons of those gods who had once been kings. Furtively they took the royal mummies to a secret pit in the necropolis and there stacked them up like cordwood: thirty in one room. Since they were already stripped of treasure they rested undisturbed for nearly three thousand years. But the damage had already been done when the priest-kings of the Twenty-first Dynasty gave them this inglorious reburial.

In the struggle for power in the Egyptian state, the pharaoh never regained the ground lost by the Amarna heresy. But it was not the High Priest of Amon nor the Vizier who won out. It was not a member of the family which held the high priesthood, Ramses-nakht and Amenhotep and their relatives, who took over the control of Upper Egypt. It was the army which snatched the power at the end of the Ramesside period. A certain Heri-Hor, of obscure parentage, served in the army and finally rose to the position of Viceroy of Nubia and Commander of the Army. Rather abruptly in the last years of Ramses XI, the final king of the Twentieth Dynasty, Heri-Hor appeared in Thebes as Vizier for Upper Egypt and High Priest of Amon. The implication is strong that there was an army coup to seize power from the ruling clique, and the ecclesiastical role of the new military dictator, Heri-Hor, was assumed by him in order to gather all the reins into his own hands.[98] Very soon the Ramesside pharaohs faded out of sight, unwept and unhonored, the last of a line of true claimants to the dignity of god-emperor. After an interval Heri-Hor took to himself the crown, passing the viziership and the high priesthood to his son, but he was also scrupulous to make his son Commander of the Army, because the control of the state lay in the exercise of police power. Heri-Hor did not attempt to rule all of Egypt. Merchant princes at the northern capital, Tanis, set up a dynasty of their own, so that the rule was divided between Upper and Lower Egypt. Never again was ancient Egypt to enjoy a firmly united land for any length of time. The inner dynamic power was dead in the organism.

98. H. Kees, *Herihor und die Aufrichtung des Gottesstaates* (Gött. GN [1936]).

XI

THE BROKEN REED

Late Empire and Post-Empire (1350 B.C. and After)

Somewhere around 1100 b.c., the last pharaoh of the Ramesside line was closing out his reign in shadowy neglect, while the effective rule of Egypt was divided between Heri-Hor, High Priest of Amon at Thebes, and Nesu-Ba-neb-Ded, the ruler at Tanis. In the spring of one of these years, a certain Wen-Amon, a functionary of the Temple of Amon-Re, set out from Thebes for Byblos in Phoenicia, to buy cedar wood for the divine boat of Amon-Re. The priesthood of the Temple gave him 5 *deben* of gold and 31 *deben* of silver for his expenses.[1] The amount was not very large, when one remembers that the stonemason Amon-pa-nefer had received 20 *deben* of gold as his share from the looting of one royal tomb and had handed that amount out as a bribe for his release. Seventy years earlier, Amon's annual income had been about 570 *deben* of gold and nearly 11,000 *deben* of silver.[2] Now the god's agent was sent off on a high official mission with a mere handful of value, without an escort, and faced with the necessity of finding any coastal vessel which would take him north. To be sure, he had a trump card to play in case of emergency: he carried with him a god, a portable idol named "Amon of the Road," the accredited divine emissary of the great Amon-Re, King of the Gods. Wen-Amon tells his tale

1. About 1¼ lb. Troy of gold and 7½ lb. Troy of silver. If a value ratio of gold to silver at 2:1 known for the Twentieth Dynasty holds (Peet, *The Great Tomb-robberies*, p. 101), this would amount to 20½ *deben* or about 5 lb. Troy in gold.

2. Above, p. 273. By the same ratio as in the last note, about 6,000 *deben* in gold.

with a mixture of naïveté and cunning that borders on the picaresque.[3]

At Tanis Wen-Amon trustingly surrendered his credentials to Nesu-Ba-neb-Ded, who found passage for him on an Asiatic ship. When this vessel put into the harbor of Dor in Palestine, a member of the crew ran off with Wen-Amon's gold and silver. The luckless Egyptian went to the Teucrian prince of Dor and demanded retribution, but that ruler politely declined responsibility for a theft from a foreign ship in his harbor. Sailing on toward Byblos, Wen-Amon found 30 *deben* of silver in a Teucrian ship and confiscated it against repayment of his own loss. He reached his goal, but he was without official credentials or adequate purchasing value. Zakar-Baal, the Prince of Byblos, not only refused to receive him, but even sent his harbor master every day with the curt order: "Get out of my harbor!" Egypt had fallen a long way from the days of Thut-mose III, when Amon-Re had so loved the cedar that he had given none of it to the Asiatics.[4] The forlorn emissary pitched his tent on the shore, hid "Amon of the Road," and sat down to wait.

He had waited twenty-nine days when a miracle intervened on his behalf. While Zakar-Baal was making a temple offering, one of the court pages had a prophetic seizure and was possessed by a god. The boy cried out: "Bring up [the] god! Bring up the messenger who is carrying him! Amon is the one who sent him out!" The Prince could not disobey the word of a god and invited Wen-Amon to attend him in his palace in the morning. The Egyptian gives us a vivid word picture of the Phoenician prince seated before a window overlooking the surf of the Mediterranean. "I found him sitting (in) his upper room, with his back turned to a window, so that the waves of the great Syrian sea broke against the back of his head."

Wen-Amon greeted the Prince politely, but the businesslike Phoenician dispensed with formality and began a series of caustic questions exposing the inadequacy of the Egyptian's mission. When Zakar-Baal suggested that Nesu-Ba-neb-Ded may have been guilty of trickery in sending Wen-Amon off in a foreign ship, when the ruler of Tanis had no less than twenty vessels in regular commercial relations with Byblos, the poor emissary "was silent in this great time." However, he regained his courage when asked about his business: "I have come after the woodwork for the great and august barque of Amon-Re, King of the Gods. Your father did (it), your grandfather did (it), and you will do it too!" Zakar-Baal was moved to sarcasm and pointed out that Egypt had formerly sent as many as six ships of merchandise to pay for cedar,

3. Erman, *LAE*, pp. 174 ff.; Breasted, *ARE*, IV, §§ 563 ff.
4. Above, p. 183.

"and he had the journal rolls of his fathers brought, and he had them read out in my presence, and they found 1,000 *deben* of silver and all kinds of things in his scrolls." The Phoenician Prince remarked that he was no subject of the ruler of Egypt and was under no obligation to release any cedar without payment. He was completely independent in his power: "If I cry out to the Lebanon, the heavens open up, and the logs are here lying (upon) the shore of the sea!"

Zakar-Baal is then credited with the remarkable statement that Amon was the universal god, the creator of all cultures, and that civilization once came from Egypt to Phoenicia, a far cry from Wen-Amon's piti-ful mission. "Now Amon has founded all lands. He founded them, but he founded first the land of Egypt, from which you come; for skill came out of it, to reach the place where I am, and learning came out of it, to reach the place where I am. What (then) are these silly trips which they have had you make?"

These words might well serve as the epitaph of Egypt's glory and its cultural leadership over western Asia, particularly over this port of Byblos, which had been so closely tied to Egypt. Zakar-Baal is antici-pating the Assyrian taunt that Egypt has become a "broken reed." And yet he stood only a generation away from the time when his father had cheerfully accepted the business of Amon-Re.

Wen-Amon summoned his resources and produced three effective arguments: he was on no "silly trip," because Amon-Re, King of Gods and owner of the universe, had sent him forth and had even sent "Amon of the Road" with him; Zakar-Baal should not ask for silver and gold, because Amon-Re could repay him with life and health; nevertheless, if Zakar-Baal would send his secretary to Egypt, the debt would be repaid. The remarkable result of this ingenious argument is that the hard-headed Prince not only dispatched his secretary to bring back payment, but even sent off seven cedar timbers in advance of payment.

After some weeks, the secretary returned with goods which must have been typical of Egyptian exports at that time: jars of gold and silver, fine linen, five hundred rolls of commercial papyrus, ox-hides, ropes, sacks of lentils, and baskets of fish. So the timber was felled and spent four months seasoning on the ground.

We shall not continue the detail of this remarkable document.[5] It suf-

5. Later passages show that Zakar-Baal had an Egyptian singing woman at his court and probably an Egyptian butler, judging from the name Pen-Amon. When Teucrian ships came to arrest Wen-Amon for his theft of their silver, Zakar-Baal refused to arrest the messenger of Amon and sent him off in a ship to take his own chance of escape. The end of the papyrus is unfortunately lacking.

ficiently illustrates the breakdown of the prestige of Egypt in Asia. Of all places, Byblos might have been most receptive to an envoy from Thebes. Instead, when the voluble Wen-Amon expressed the hope that Amon might give Zakar-Baal fifty years of life over and above his fate, the hard-headed Prince uttered a grim irony which should have been crushing: "What you have said to me is a great affirmation of words!"

Except for sporadic bursts of energy, which faded almost as quickly as they appeared, Egypt was no longer a nation but was broken into smaller states, which were independent of each other but loosely related by trade relationships. The Twenty-First Dynasty rule was divided by common consent between the merchant princes of Tanis in the Delta and the Heri-Hor dynasty at Thebes, those army commanders who had moved through the high priesthood of Amon into the kingship. This period saw the flowering of a new power, a family of Libyan descent from the Faiyum. Toward the end of the Twentieth Dynasty a Libyan bearing some such outlandish name as Buyuwawa or Beywaw had settled down at Herakleopolis in the Faiyum. The following five generations served as high priests of the local god Harsaphes, but continued to cling proudly to a hereditary title, "Great Chief of the Me," that is, the Meshwesh tribes of western Libyans. Perhaps they had originally been mercenary soldiers, settled upon the land when Egypt withdrew from empire. Around 950 B.C. one of these princes held sway as far south as Abydos and was so powerful that the last king of the Twenty-First Dynasty invited him "to participate in the festivals of his majesty. jointly receiving victory." It was well to be respectful to this Libyan-Egyptian Sheshonk because in a few years he seized the throne of Egypt and started the Twenty-Second Dynasty.[6]

The Libyan dynasty had an initial spurt of triumphant energy, marked by a military raid into Palestine,[7] but later lapsed into relative stagnation, punctuated by civil war and with increasing local separatism. Around 720 B.C. came the first successful invasion of Egypt for a thousand years, this time from the south. From a capital at the Fourth Cataract, Pi-ankhi, an Ethiopian, ruled the Sudan and Nubia. His culture was a provincial imitation of earlier Egypt, fanatical in its retention of religious form. Pi-ankhi had become powerful enough to covet the throne of Egypt, and seized upon the report that a little Delta

6. A. M. Blackman in *JEA*, XXVII (1941), 83 ff.; Breasted, *ARE*, IV, § 792.

7. I Kings 14:25-26; Breasted, *ARE*, IV, §§ 709 ff.; R. S. Lamon and G. M. Shipton, *Megiddo I* (*OIP*, Vol. XLII [Chicago, 1939]), 60 f.

Prince, a descendant from the Meshwesh, was conquering cities of Lower and Middle Egypt. The story of Pi-ankhi's conquest of Egypt is an extraordinarily interesting human document, particularly in the contrast between this backwater puritan and the effete and sophisticated Egyptians. His chivalry in battle, his austere avoidance of captured princesses, his delight in horses, his scrupulous performance of religious ritual, and his refusal to deal with conquered princes who were ceremonially unclean—"they were uncircumcised and eaters of fish"—are told in elegant Egyptian with solemn gusto. Having laid the foundations for Ethiopian rule over Egypt for sixty years to come, Pi-ankhi loaded his ships with treasure and sailed back to the Fourth Cataract.[8]

The Ethiopian capital was a long and weary distance from Egypt and from the oracular support of Amon. Pi-ankhi accepted a practice of preceding pharaohs, by placing in Thebes a loyal agent who would not be a rival. The High Priest of Amon had been too powerful an individual in the past, so that his position had been subordinated to that of a priestess, "the Divine Votaress of Amon," and this important office had been filled by a daughter of the pharaoh. Pi-ankhi appreciated the advantages of a viceregent who could control Egypt, particularly through the oracle of Amon, and who would still not covet the throne. He forced the current "Divine Votaress of Amon" to adopt his sister as her own daughter and successor. Thus Egypt fell under the nominal rule of an Ethiopian from the despised provinces and under the effectual rule of a woman.[9]

In the later centuries came the superiority of the Assyrians and Babylonians, including invasion and defeat, the conquest by the Persians and finally by the Macedonians. Even when Egypt gave some show of independence, as under the Twenty-Sixth or Thirtieth Dynasties, it was a loose and temporary independence at such times as the Assyrians or Persians were preoccupied elsewhere. The pharaohs of the Twenty-Sixth Dynasty were business men, who tried valiantly to restore Egypt's position by promoting the commercial success of the land, particularly in their busy Delta area. Upper Egypt became the agricultural granary, producing the goods which Lower Egypt sold. Upper Egypt was held in subjection by the same formula of the pharaoh's daughter as "Divine Votaress of Amon." The lower Delta was

8. Breasted, *ARE*, IV, §§ 816 ff. On the Ethiopian rulers, see M. F. L. Macadam, *The Temples of Kawa*, I (London, 1949), 119 ff.; D. Dunham in *American Journal of Archaeology*, L (1946), 378 ff.

9. Breasted, *op. cit.*, § 940.

settled by colonies of Greek and Ionian merchants, and the security of the state lay in the pharaoh's bodyguard of Ionian mercenaries. From Naukratis and Daphnae in the Delta, Greek merchants industriously traded the barley and wheat of Egypt and the wool of Libya for the oil and wine of the Aegean area. Herodotus and Diodorus preserve a tradition that the Twenty-Sixth Dynasty pharaohs overfavored their Ionian, Carian, and Lydian mercenary soldiers, so that the native Egyptian troops finally became jealous and marched south into Ethiopia, to join the rival ruler there.[10] This may not be true in detail, but it undoubtedly corresponds to the feeling about special privileges accorded to Greeks and Ionians by a pharaoh who had originally been set in power by an Assyrian emperor. The native spirit of Egypt would still be thwarted and helpless.

This was the nation which tried to intrigue in Asia against the Assyrian conquerors without itself giving any effective support, the nation about which the Assyrian commander taunted the people of Jerusalem: "Thou trustest upon the staff of this broken reed, even upon Egypt, whereon if a man lean, it will go into his hand and pierce it; so is Pharaoh, king of Egypt, unto all that trust on him."[11] When they finally did try, under Necho, to reconquer some part of Asia, the Babylonians defeated them and marched easily to the Delta frontier. Within a generation or two, the Persians invaded Egypt and took over the land without much effort. Cambyses was not content to place the land under an Egyptian deputy, as the Assyrians had done. He had himself acknowledged by the Egyptian gods as their legitimate son, the pharaoh.[12] There was no cohesion in the land of the Nile, and the rich land had become a dependency of other powers.

In considering the Empire following the Amarna period, we saw that art and literature remained vulgarized by the retention of modernistic forms, corresponding to the changing times and the non-Egyptian stimuli of the age.[13] A marked reaction appeared in the age following 720 B.C., with a deliberate archaism manifesting itself chiefly in art. The spiritual emptiness of the day sought compensation by seeking out ancient models and copying them faithfully (Fig. 32a). For the most

10. Herodotus, II, 30; Diodorus Siculus, I, 67.

11. II Kings 18:21; Isaiah 36:6.

12. G. Posener, *La Première Domination Perse en Égypte* ("Bibliothèque d'Étude," XI [Cairo, 1936]).

13. Above, pp. 235, 260–67.

part, the artists avoided the Empire and went back to the Old and Middle Kingdoms for their inspiration, back to the ages when the Egyptian spirit had been most vigorous and most native. At its best this copying was remarkably successful, so that it is often difficult to distinguish a statue of the Twenty-Fifth or early Twenty-Sixth Dynasty from a statue of the Sixth or Twelfth Dynasty. For some reason, the earlier stages of this renaissance were more effective, with a successful capture of form and vitality. When, however, the movement settled down to mere slavish copying, any attempt at creative recapture was lost, and the work became dull and lifeless.[14] We find much that is only mechanical antiquarianism. The outer brick wall of the tomb of Pe-di-Amen-Opet at Thebes used the same recessed paneling which had been typical of the mastaba-tombs at the very beginning of history, a style which had been discarded in the Third and Fourth Dynasties.[15] The walls of many tombs were filled with slavish copies of those Pyramid Texts which had been inscribed in royal tombs seventeen hundred years earlier. A Twenty-Sixth Dynasty official by the name of Ibi went to extraordinary pains in his antiquarian zeal. Somehow he discovered that his name and some of his titles were the same as those of a Sixth Dynasty official, who had been buried at Deir el-Gebrawi, two hundred miles north of Thebes. He sent draftsmen to Deir el-Gebrawi to copy scenes and inscriptions from the tomb of that Ibi of sixteen hundred years earlier. These were rearranged and amplified in his own tomb at Thebes, but the reproduction was so faithful that we may restore and correct elements in the older tomb from the later, and vice versa. The copied scenes were flat and uninspired, without that balance and strength which was possible to the older, creative artists. There were even barbarisms resulting from the mechanical imitation of elements which were no longer comprehensible around 625 B.C. After all, the model came from the revered past, so that it might have magical value, even though it no longer had meaning.[16]

An enfeebled and weary old age sought its compensation in the blind and ritualistic worship of a past of strength and accomplishment. This

---

14. H. Frankfort in W. Brunton, *Great Ones of Ancient Egypt* (London and New York, 1930), p. 177, draws a contrast between the work of the Twenty-Fifth Dynasty, which had a "happy blend of energy, reverence for the past, and realism of outlook," and that of the Twenty-Sixth Dynasty, "where a long array of empty and uniform faces appears fixed in a childish smile of contentment with a past, in the contemplation of which the ignominy of the present could almost be forgotten."

15. A. Lansing in *BMMA* (July, 1920, Part II), 15.

16. N. de G. Davies, *The Rock Tombs of Deir el Gebrâwi*, I (*Arch. Surv.*, XI [1902]), 36 ff.; Pls. XXIV f.

attempt to escape an inglorious present was not confined to Egypt. Over in Babylonia, Nabonidus, a contemporary of the Twenty-Sixth Dynasty, was deeply and reverently absorbed in the antiquity of his country, studying ancient records and attempting to restore temples with fidelity to the old plan. When the present was circumscribed and the future offered no hope of improvement, a culture sought its justification in the dreamy glorification of its past.

In order to understand the impoverishment of the Egyptian spirit, we must go back and examine certain artistic and literary forms from the time of Thut-mose III on. For example, there was a sudden and sweeping change in the decoration of Egyptian tombs beginning in the Nineteenth and Twentieth Dynasties. For fourteen hundred years, from the Fourth Dynasty on, the tomb scenes had emphasized a gay and rich life. The essential theme was the denial of death by the affirmation of the happy and successful phases of life. There was no more fear of death than the fear of walking in a familiar place in the dark: one had reassurance in the knowledge that the place was familiar and friendly by daylight. So the lusty and confident scenes had concentrated on pictures of fields golden with an abundant harvest, of ships pressing forward with a favoring breeze, of the exciting hunt in the desert, and of children shouting happily at their games. To be sure, the *purpose* of all scenes was mortuary: success and prosperity over here gave the momentum for eternal blessedness over there; scenes of the harvest or of herding animals were magically effective in feeding the dead noble in the next world; scenes of shipping gave him greater freedom of movement over there; scenes of his earthly wealth and success gave him high standing in paradise; and so on. The essential point is that all tombs from the Fourth to the Nineteenth Dynasty put their emphasis on life and denied the validity of death. That is what gave the tomb scenes their wonderful vigor, *joi de vivre*, and optimism.[17]

Most of the Empire tombs show the same lust for life. A typical Eighteenth Dynasty tomb crowded its walls with scenes of agriculture, viticulture, fishing, fowling, hunting in the desert, the work of the artisans, banquets, foreign tribute, and rewards from the pharaoh.[18] Gradually, however, a new sobriety was creeping in, to increase the

17. L. Klebs, *Die Reliefs des alten Reiches* (Heidelberg, 1915), *Die Reliefs und Malereien des mittleren Reiches* (1922), *Die Reliefs und Malereien des neuen Reiches* (1934).

18. N. de G. Davies, *The Tomb of Nakht at Thebes* (*Tytus*, I [1917]), 30 f.

emphasis or the quantity of scenes applying to death. In the late Eighteenth Dynasty the judgment of the deceased before Osiris, the procession to the grave, and the mourning widow were depicted anew or more prominently. Yet the Nineteenth Dynasty still focused on the pleasures of this world: the pleasant garden with its water-sweep, the treading out of grapes, trading in the market place, or rewards from pharaoh. The proportion of space devoted to scenes of life as against strictly mortuary scenes may have gone down from three to one to an approximate one to one, but certainly the basic expression was still the love of life.[19]

Suddenly, about the end of the Nineteenth Dynasty, we become aware of a drastic change. Within the space of two or three generations, the tomb had discarded its devotion to this world and dedicated all of its wall space to death and the next world. The shadow of an uncertain eternity had dropped over the sunny gaiety of Egypt. We see only the funerary procession approaching the western hillside, the judgment of the dead before Osiris, the feeding of the dead by the sycamore goddess, the preparation of the mummy, the gods and fearful demons of the next world, and a "farrago of wild mythology and amuletic defense."[20] The texts had abandoned autobiography and concentrated on hymns, rituals, and long religious texts for magical protection or for advancement in the next world. In scenes and texts, life had suddenly been discarded, and death had been embraced as an inevitable. The perennial joy of Egypt was gone; the next life was now presented as a release from this life and as a reward for humble patience in this life.

One can see this new resignation appearing in the names which are new at this period. Along with the confidently affirmative names which had become traditional in Egypt, there came in names expressing fear or dependency: "The Rescued," "The Humble Endures," "The Blind," "The Slave of Amon," "Re Says that He Will Live," and even "No Use!" The confident nomination of children toward success and power gave way to a naming which was timid or prayerful.

The discipline which the state had demanded, first to eject the Hyksos and then to extend and maintain the Empire, had killed the old, easygoing tolerance and pragmatism, with their acceptance of individual voluntarism. The individual had become strictly circumscribed by determinism for the advantage of the group, dogmatically for the service

---

19. E.g., N. de G. Davies, *Two Ramesside Tombs at Thebes* (*Tytus*, V [1927]).

20. Davies, *The Tomb of Nakht*, pp. 23 f.; G. Steindorff and W. Wolf, *Die thebanische Gräberwelt* (Leip. AS, IV [Glückstadt, 1936]), 64 f.

of the gods who ruled the land, including the pharaoh, but practically for the ruling oligarchy. As the highest nobility grew more powerful, the lower nobility, the middle class, and the masses became poorer and less powerful. Theology then advised them that this was their predestined fate and that they must submit to it with quietude, in the hope of a reward in paradise. The concept of Fate and Fortune as controlling deities was first visible in the Amarna period, when the Aton was praised as "he who made the god Fate and brought into being the goddess Fortune," and when Akh-en-Aton was called "the god Fate, who gives life."[21] A later hymn praising Amon as the creator-god, says: "Fate and Fortune are with him for everybody."[22] In scenes of the judgment of the dead, the god Fate may stand beside the scales in which a man's heart is weighed, with the goddesses Fortune and Birth-Destiny in close attendance, to prevent any eccentric individualism.[23] A man was hemmed in by an alarming bodyguard of regulating forces, which cut down on his freedom: "his ka, his stela belonging to this tomb which is in the necropolis, his Fate, his time of life, his Birth-Destiny, his Fortune, and his Khnum (the shaping god)."[24] To be sure, this predestination was not considered to be absolute and inflexible, within those general rules for behavior which society had set up. A wisdom text of the Empire advised the young man to follow his father's words for the guidance of his conduct. If he does so, "great is he in favor . . . , and his fate will not take place." There was still an element of voluntarism for him who would conform to the precepts of the past: "All these things are within a lifetime, outside of the goddess Fortune, without setting up a Birth-Destiny for it, except for giving breath to his nostrils."[25] Furthermore, a merciful god might rescue a man from Fate if the god so desired.[26] Nevertheless, these Empire texts contrast with an earlier theology in making the deities Fate and Fortune normally repressive, in place of the older theology's emphasis on a man's own ka, which may have stood outside of him but which was his alone and

21. N. de G. Davies, The Rock Tombs of El Amarna, II (Arch. Surv., XIV [1905]), Pls. VII f.; III (1905), Pl. XIX; Aegyptische Inschriften aus den königlichen Museen zu Berlin, II (Leipzig, 1924), 127.

22. Erman, LAE, p. 301.

23. The Book of the Dead. Facsimile of the Papyrus of Ani in the British Museum (London, 1894), Pl. 3.

24. N. de G. Davies and A. H. Gardiner, The Tomb of Amenemhēt (TTS, I [1915]), 99.

25. Ch. Kuentz, in Comptes rendus. Académie des Inscriptions et Belles-Lettres (Paris, 1931), pp. 321 ff.

26. Erman, LAE, p. 297.

therefore was more interested in his welfare than would have been one all-controlling god.[27]

It was inevitable that this new sense of personal inadequacy should be accompanied by a sense of sin.[28] This was not the self-righteous denial of ritual and moral wrongdoing such as appears in the Book of the Dead, particularly in the long protestation of guiltlessness of a whole series of possible shortcomings.[29] This was a humble acknowledgement that mankind was naturally inclined to error and failure and that he could find his salvation only through the gods. This humble attitude has led Breasted to call the late Empire "the age of personal piety,"[30] while the abasement of the penitent sinner has led Gunn to refer to the texts of confession as documents of "the religion of the poor."[31] Although it is true that the typical expressions of sinfulness came from humble workers in the Theban necropolis—draftsmen, sculptors, clerks, and priests,[32]—it is quite clear that they were sufficiently prosperous to afford well-carved monuments and that they were voicing the theology of their day, a theology which was accepted by all men on up to the High Priest of Amon himself.[33] This was a time of national defeat and withdrawal, and the gods asked all men to be "poor in spirit."

As evidences of this new humility, we see a number of monuments erected in petition to the gods.[34] For example, the son of the outline draftsman Neb-Re somehow had acted impiously with regard to a cow belonging to Amon-Re. Perhaps it was as simple an act as taking milk

27. A very late Book of the Dead alternates the *ka* in the traditional passage with Fate in the more modern version; hieratic: "Give sweet breath to his nostrils every day, doing what his *ka* wishes;" demotic: "Give sweet breath to his nostrils every day—that is what his Fate wishes": G. Möller, *Die beiden Totenpapyrus Rhind* (Leipzig, 1913), p. 48.

28. For exceptional confessions of shortcoming on the part of a pharaoh, see above, p. 115.

29. The so-called "Negative Confession." Ch. Maystre, *Les Déclarations d'Innocence* (*Livre des Morts, Chapitre 125*), (Cairo, 1937).

30. *Development of Religion and Thought* (New York, 1912), pp. 344 ff.; *Dawn of Conscience* (New York, 1933), pp. 312 ff.

31. In *JEA*, III (1916), 81 ff.

32. For a mountain-side shrine of these workers to their local deities, see N. de G. Davies, in *Mélanges Maspero, I* (*MIFAO*, LXVI [1934]), 241 ff.

33. A Vizier and High Priest of Amon under Amen-hotep III said: "I have reached this (state) by silence and coolness": A. Varille in *BIFAO*, XXX (1930), 504. A High Priest of Amon under Ramses II said: "I was a servant valuable to his lord, properly and truly silent": T. Devéria, *Memoires et Fragments* ("Bibliothèque Égyptologique," IV [Paris, 1896]), p. 279; cf. 281. On "silence" as meaning submissiveness, see below.

34. Breasted, *op. cit.*; Gunn, *op. cit.* The earliest text of this *genre* may come from the end of the Amarna period: A. H. Gardiner in *JEA*, XIV (1928), 10 f.

from the cow. At any rate, the son thereupon fell ill. The father acknowledged his son's ritual sin, the young man recovered, and the father dedicated a hymn of humble gratitude to Amon-Re, "who hears the prayer, who comes at the cry of the poor and distressed, who gives breath (to) him who is weak." Of Amon, the hymn says:

"Beware of him! Repeat him to son and daughter, to great and small; relate him to generations of generations who have not yet come into being; relate him to fishes in the deep, to birds in the heaven; repeat him to him who does not know him and to him who knows him: Beware of him!

"Thou art Amon, the lord of the silent man, who comes at the cry of the poor man. If I call to thee when I am distressed, thou comest and rescuest me. Thou givest breath (to) him who is weak; thou rescuest him who is imprisoned." Neb-Re recalls that he prayed to Amon on behalf of his son, "when he was lying ill and in a state of death, when he was (under) the power of Amon because of his cow. I found the Lord of the Gods coming as the north wind, with sweet breezes before him, and he rescued" the son from illness.

"Though it may be that the servant is normal in doing wrong, yet the Lord is normal in being merciful.[35] The Lord of Thebes does not spend an entire day angry. As for his anger—in the completion of a moment there is no remnant. . . . As thy *ka* endures! thou wilt be merciful, and we shall not repeat that which has been turned away!"

In another case, one of the minor dignitaries of the Theban necropolis was guilty of perjury in the name of Ptah and suffered blindness. Penitently confessing his sin, he called out to the god for mercy. "I am a man who swore falsely by Ptah, Lord of Truth, so that he caused me to see darkness by day. . . . Beware of Ptah, Lord of Truth! See, he will not overlook the deed of any man. Guard yourself against speaking the name of Ptah falsely. See, he who speaks it falsely, why, he falls down! He made me like the dogs of the street, while I was in his hand. He made men and gods to mark me as a man who has committed an abomination against his Lord. Ptah, Lord of Truth, was righteous toward me when he punished me. Be merciful to me! Look upon me and be merciful!"

This same man had also offended a local goddess called "the Peak of the West" and thereby suffered illness. In his introductory words he protests that he was "a righteous man on earth," and yet he was "an

35. A different formulation of man's normal sinfulness below (p. 305): "God is (always) in his success, whereas man is in his failure."

ignorant and witless man." In this period, a man might be as righteous
as he could be, and still his human ignorance made him subject to sin.
All he could do was to throw himself upon the mercy of his god.

"I knew not good or evil. When I did the act of transgression against
the Peak, she punished me, and I was in her hand by night as well as day.
I sat upon the (birth)-bricks like the pregnant woman. I called out to
the wind, but it would not come to me. . . . Beware of the Peak! for a
lion is in the Peak, and she smites with the smiting of a savage lion. She
pursues him who transgresses against her.

"But when I called to my mistress, I found her coming to me with
sweet breezes. After she had made me see her hand, she showed mercy
to me; she turned about to me in mercy; she made me forget the sickness which had been upon me. See, the Peak of the West is merciful,
when one calls upon her!"

In a final example of these penitential hymns, the offending man was
guilty only of a failure to be "silent" or submissive, and so felt the need
of his god.

"Come to me, O Re-Har-akhti, that thou mayest look after me!
Thou art he who does, and there is no one who acts without thee, unless it be that thou actest with him. . . . Do not punish me for my many
sins, for I am one who does not know himself, I am a man without sense.
I spend the day following after my own mouth, like a cow after grass.
. . . Come to me, . . . thou who protectest millions and rescuest hundreds
of thousands, the protector of the one who cries out to him!"[36]

The quality which this new age prized most highly was "silence,"
meaning patience, humility, submissiveness, and even resignation.
Before the Empire, silence had not been a characteristic which was
held in high esteem by the light-hearted and garrulous Egyptian.[37]

36. Erman, LAE, p. 307. Cf. ibid., p. 308, for a prayer that Amon may help the poor
man in the law court, since he was unable to win the favor of the court attendants
by bribes.

37. The only exception to this statement which we have been able to find lies in the
Instruction for Ka-gemni (Erman, LAE, pp. 66 f.; A. H. Gardiner in JEA, XXXII
[1946], 71 ff.): "May the fearful man prosper, the normal man be praised, may the
tent of the silent man be open, may the place of the contented man be wide. . . . Let
thy reputation go forth, while thou art silent with thy mouth, so that thou mayest be
summoned (to higher position)." This clearly shows a respect for modesty at an early
period, but the passage seems to be isolated, and it is at variance with the high value
put upon eloquence by the presumably contemporaneous Instruction of Ptah-hotep.
The passage in the Instruction of Ptah-hotep numbered 166 is corrupt and has defied
satisfactory translation. Although the Empire version may praise silence, with some
such translation as "Guard thy mouth beside thy dependents, so that there may be
made respect for the silent man," this connects poorly with the preceding advice to be
liberal with goods. The older version may advise against secretive greed with one's

On the contrary, the ability to speak eloquently and to one's advantage had been the prized quality. When the Vizier Ptah-hotep asked the pharaoh for permission to instruct his son so that the latter might take his place, the king responded: "Teach him first about speaking," and the title of the resultant instructions was: "the beginning of the expression of good speech . . . in instructing the ignorant about wisdom and about the rules for good speech, as of advantage to him who will listen and of disadvantage to him who may neglect them."[38] The essential theme of the story of the Eloquent Peasant is that effective and bold speech may be found in a man of low degree, and the poor peasant was kept talking simply because of the pharaoh's delight in his discourse.[39] This corresponds with Ptah-hotep's remark that "good speech is more hidden than the emerald, but it may be found with maidservants at the grindstones."[40] The wretched Khe-kheper-Re-seneb groaned that it was painful to keep silent about his miseries.[41] Nor did the earlier theology make a rigid cult of quiet submissiveness. When an attempt was made to shut the mouth of the Eloquent Peasant by reminding him that he was close to a shrine of Osiris, "the Lord of Silence," he seized upon the opportunity to bawl out an appeal to the god: "O Lord of Silence, give me back my goods!"[42] In the First Intermediate Period, the Instruction for King Meri-ka-Re put a high value upon eloquence: "Be a craftsman in speech, so that thou mayest be strong, for the tongue is a sword to [a man], and speech is more valorous than any fighting."[43] Indeed, the independent spirit of that age put a premium on the ability of a commoner to speak and act on his own behalf: "a valiant little man, speaking with his own mouth and acting with his own arm."[44]

Such a high appreciation of free and effective speech could be afforded by a culture which was successful and confident. But the Empire—and particularly the late Empire and post-Empire period—could not tolerate such individualism. The cultural expression com-

property: "Do not satisfy thy mouth beside thy dependents, for great is that which the dread of silence may achieve." The word here used for "dread" means aversion from, rather than respect for.

38. Erman, *LAE*, pp. 55 f. The same document advises clear and confident speech, and only thereafter a firm silence (*ibid.*, p. 59, no. 15) or silence only if one did not have the artistry to speak well (*ibid.*, p. 61, no. 24).

39. *Ibid.*, p. 120. In his attack on the high steward, the peasant urges him not to answer a petitioner "with the greeting of a silent man" (*ibid.*, p. 129).

40. *Ibid.*, p. 56.   41. *Ibid.*, p. 110.

42. *Ibid.*, p. 118.   43. *Ibid.*, pp. 75 f.

44. J. Polotsky, *Zu den Inschriften der 11. Dynastie* (*Untersuch.*, XI [1929]), pp. 34, 44 ff.

pletely reversed itself, the liberty to speak was abrogated, and a disciplined and resigned "silence" became the highest good. Where the title and purpose of the Instruction of Ptah-hotep had emphasized proud position gained through eloquence, the title and purpose of the late Instruction of Amen-em-Opet emphasized the humble quality of Amen-em-Opet, "the truly silent one in Abydos," who said to "his son, the least of his children, the littlest of his adherents": "Give your ears, hear what is said. . . . At a time when there is a whirlwind of words, they will be a mooring-stake for your tongue."[45] Whereas Ptah-hotep had urged a bold attack against an opponent in debate: "Do not keep silence when he speaks evil," Amen-em-Opet advised withdrawal: "Do not join in argument with the hot-mouthed, nor irritate him with words. . . . Spend a night before speaking. . . . The heated man in his hour—withdraw yourself from him and leave him to himself. God will know how to return (answer) to him."[46] Whereas Ptah-hotep had instructed his son to keep a wife "far from gaining control," the late Instruction of Ani was more restrained: "You should not supervise your wife in her house when you know that she is efficient. . . . Let your eye have regard, while you are silent, so that you may recognize her abilities."[47]

Whereas the earlier expression of individual initiative and self-sufficiency had been: "The reputation of a man will not be smaller through what he has achieved,"[48] the new expression advised passivity and the surrender of responsibility to the god: Do not combat those hostile to you, but "sit down at the hands of the god, and your silence will overthrow them."[49] Theology insisted that the gods now set the highest value upon humble submissiveness: "Beware of loudness of voice in his house, for god loves silence," and the god is one "loving the silent man more than him who is loud of voice."[50] The classic ex-

45. F. Ll. Griffith in JEA, XII (1926), 191 ff. On the relation between the Instruction of Amen-em-Opet and the Hebrew Book of Proverbs, particularly Prov. 22:17–24:22, see D. C. Simpson in JEA, XII (1926), 232 ff. In contrast to our attitude on the Aton hymn and the 104th Psalm (pp. 227–28 above), we believe that there is a direct connection between these two pieces of wisdom literature, and that Amen-em-Opet was the ancestor text. The secondary nature of the Hebrew seems established. Both texts may be as late as the seventh or sixth century B.C. and the relationship was a factor of free intercultural communication.

46. Griffith, op. cit., p. 201.   47. Erman, LAE, p. 240.
48. Ibid., p. 81; cf. B. Gunn in JEA, XII (1926), 283.

49. Griffith, op. cit., pp. 219 f. Let an old man "beat you, with your hand in your bosom; let him curse you, while you are silent. In the morning, if you come before him, he will give you food freely" (ibid., p. 223).

50. Hieratic Papyri in the British Museum. Third Series. Chester Beatty Gift, ed. by A. H. Gardiner (London, 1935), I, 42, 30.

ample of this new quality set a contrast between the "truly silent man" and the excitable and garrulous "heated man," who would come to an early end:

> As for the heated man of a temple,
>   He is like a tree growing in the open.
> In the completion of a moment (comes) its loss of foliage,
>   And its end is reached in the shipyards;
> Or it is floated far from its place,
>   And the flame is its burial-shroud.
>
> But the truly silent man holds himself apart.
>   He is like a tree growing in a garden.
> It flourishes and doubles its yield;
>   It (stands) before its lord.
> Its fruit is sweet, its shade is pleasant,
>   And its end is reached in the garden.[51]

The classic Egyptian system had been able to afford a remarkable amount of free play to the individual. In the common adventure of a rich and powerful culture, there had been plenty of room for the independent judgment and initiative of the ordinary Egyptian. This had reached a high point in the vigorous career-seeking of the Old Kingdom, the personal assertiveness of the First Intermediate Period and the early Middle Kingdom, and the development of a searching social conscience in the same age. The intrusion of a continuing sense of insecurity through the Hyksos conquest and the necessities of Empire had choked off that spirit and had brought in group determinism, restraining every individual in the name of the gods. Egypt had at last reached a stage of unquestioning discipline such as had characterized Mesopotamia—a less secure land geographically—from the beginning.[52] Man now had to be submissively obedient, for he was told firmly that he was nothing in himself, nothing without his gods. As the penitential hymn had declared that man was normally sinful, whereas the god was

51. Griffith, op. cit., p. 202. Cf. the virtues of "the silent man in the temple" (ibid., p. 203) and the passage from the Instruction of Ani: "Do not talk a lot, be silent, and you will be happy. Do not be garrulous. The dwelling of god—its abomination is clamor. Pray with a loving heart, all the words of which are hidden, and he will do what you need" (Erman, LAE, p. 236). The contrast between the "silent" and the "heated" also in a prayer to Thoth: the well of refreshment for the thirsting "is sealed up to him who has discovered his mouth, but it is open to the silent. When the silent comes, he finds the well, but (for) the heated, thou art choked up" (ibid., pp. 305 f.).

52. T. Jacobsen in H. Frankfort et al., The Intellectual Adventure of Ancient Man (Chicago, 1946), pp. 202 ff.: "In a civilization which sees the whole universe as a state, obedience must necessarily stand out as a prime virtue. . . . In Mesopotamia the 'good life' was the 'obedient life.' "

normally merciful,[53] so the late books of wisdom asserted that man without god was impotent and doomed from the start. "God is (always) in his success, whereas man is in his failure. One thing is that which men say, another is that which the god does." "For man is (but) clay and straw, and the god is his builder, and he is tearing down or building up every day. He makes a thousand poor men as he wishes, or he makes a thousand men as overseers(?)."[54]

Such discipline took all the joy out of life. That tumbling light-heart-edness and lust for life disappeared from the texts, as it had disappeared from the tomb scenes. Now death was a release from the spiritual empti-ness of this world. Amen-em-Opet said, with a sigh: "How joyful is he who reaches the West, when he is safe in the hand of the god."[55]

With such a hardening of the arteries, Egypt resorted increasingly to form, for the replacement of spirit. There came a devotion to ritualistic performance as the continued and familiar activity of hands and mouths which had been denied creative freedom of their own. Witchcraft, forms of protective magic, demonology, recourse to omens, and appeal to oracles appeared in greater prominence in the late Empire and per-sisted in the post-Empire period. By keeping busy at set forms, the Egyptians were able to forget that they were banned from any indi-vidual self-expression. If the outside of the cup could be kept clean, perhaps its emptiness could be ignored.

The picture of Egyptian culture given by the classical writers is a curious one. The Greeks saw the Egyptians with eyes which could never quite comprehend, because their own culture was essentially dif-ferent in its outlook and because Egypt had already encysted itself in a fraudulent past. The Greek writers made many misstatements and fre-quently misinterpreted what they actually saw. Yet, in general, they gave an accurate impression of a petrified culture, a culture which itself misinterpreted some of its cherished fossils. For example, the worship of animals was no feature of the earlier Egyptian religion. The term "worship" should not properly be applied before the first millennium B.C., by which time the characteristic faith had perished, leaving only its empty shell. In earlier Egypt animals had not been sacred in them-selves, as an entire species. Instead, a single beast had been selected *to be a place of manifestation* for a god, like his statue, which presented only a convenient place for his functional appearance and had no sanc-tity apart from his presence. The animal devoted to a god was to be

53. Above, p. 300.
54. Griffith, *op. cit.*, pp. 216, 221.   55. *Ibid.*, p. 221.

cherished and respected just as much as the physical structure of a temple and no more. Later Egypt confused the form with the substance and began so strict and so detailed a cult of the sacred animal that the term "animal-worship" was then justified and, in its generalities, was correctly reported by the Greeks.

On the other hand, the classical writers wrongly attributed to the Egyptians a belief in the transmigration of human spirits after death into other living forms, such as animals.[56] This was a misunderstanding of mortuary tenets about the scope and powers of the deceased. At death an Egyptian became an *akh*, that is, an "effective personality." Part of his effectiveness after death lay in his ability to assume any form which he might desire, for freedom of movement, for revisiting the earth, or for sheer pleasure: a lotus or a falcon or any other living thing. Thus the Book of the Dead provided magic spells for making transformations into these various forms, but this was topical and temporary and was at the volition of the deceased.[57] It was by no means a doctrine of metempsychosis whereby the spirit of a dead person immediately passed into a single animal, to remain there for the lifetime of that animal. The Egyptian belief in voluntary form for temporary purpose was so foreign to the Greeks that it is not surprising that the latter reported wrongly, but this will serve as a warning against our crediting their statements as being based on accurate personal observation.

Although we thus must exercise some caution in using the observations of the Greek writers, who thought so differently from the Egyptians that they were never quite able to gain full comprehension and who took their particulars from Egyptian informants who had long ago lost an appreciation of their own earlier culture, there is still something important to be won from the classical reporters. That is their overwhelming impression of a people wholly devoted to form. The emphasis which Herodotus gives to rites and rituals, to omens and oracles, agrees thoroughly with that stress on ceremonial and magical practice which we have seen in later Egypt.[58] The formation of society into rigid classes, with priests and warriors constituting castes of special privilege, and the punctilious application of written and codified law were phenomena unknown in Egypt before the late Empire but

56. Herodotus, II, 123; Diodorus Siculus, I, 98; Plutarch, *De Iside*, 72.

57. Especially chapters 76–88 of the Book of the Dead. For example, chapter 76 is headed: "The spell for making transformations into any form in which (one) desires to appear." Cf. A. Erman, *Die Religion der Aegypter* (Berlin, 1934), p. 223.

58. Herodotus, II, 37 ff., 58, 77, 83 f.

looming more and more important from that time on.[59] In such generalizations we may check the statements of the classical writers and give
them credit for conscientious accuracy.

Consider, then, the terrifying emptiness of Herodotus' picture of the
Egyptians as the most "god-fearing" of peoples: "They are beyond
measure religious, more than any other nation; and these are among
their customs: They drink from cups of bronze, which they cleanse out
daily; this is done not by some but by all. They are especially careful
ever to wear newly-washed linen raiment. They practise circumcision
for cleanliness' sake; for they set cleanness above seemliness. . . . The
Egyptians hold solemn assemblies not once in the year, but often. . . .
They keep the ordinances of their fathers, and add none others to
them."[60] Here we have a description of brightly polished automatons
unceasingly performing solemn gestures but utterly empty of mind or
heart. It is a true picture of the spiritual vacuum of late Egypt, which
left the land exposed to invasion by otherworldliness, monasticism, or
apocalyptic expectation.

There is a similar spiritual void in Diodorus' picture of the pharaohs
of the last Egyptian dynasties. We may recall the ancient dogma of the
god-king who was the state incarnate, whose word was law and who
stood divinely above all written prescriptions. We may remember how
severe a blow the Amarna heresy and the subsequent contests for power
dealt to this concept of the absolute ruler and how the pharaoh increasingly became the prisoner of the ruling oligarchy. Then read what
Diodorus Siculus derived from "the written records of the priests of
Egypt":

"In the first place, then, the life which the kings of the Egyptians
lived was not like that of other men who enjoy autocratic power and
do in all matters exactly as they please without being held to account,
but all their acts were regulated by prescriptions set forth in laws, not
only for their administrative acts, but also those that had to do with
the way in which they spent their time from day to day, and with the
food which they ate. . . . And the hours of both the day and night were
laid out according to a plan, and at the specified hours it was absolutely
required of the king that he should do what the laws stipulated and not
what he thought best. . . . For there was a set time not only for his

59. Herodotus, II, 164 ff.; Diodorus Siculus, I, 73 ff.

60. Herodotus, II, 37, 59, 79, following the translation by A. D. Godley, *Herodotus*
(Loeb Classical Library, New York, 1931), I, 319, 345 ff., 365.

holding audiences or rendering judgments, but even for his taking a walk, bathing, and sleeping with his wife, and, in a word, for every act of his life. . . . And in following the dictates of custom in these matters, so far were they from being indignant or taking offence in their souls, that, on the contrary, they actually held that they led a most happy life; for they believed that all other men, in thoughtlessly following their natural passions, commit many acts which bring them injuries and perils . . . , while they, on the other hand, by virtue of their having cultivated a manner of life which had been chosen before all others by the most prudent of all men, fell into the fewest mistakes."[61] What a distance the pharaoh had fallen from the supernal majesty of the Old Kingdom, from the Middle Kingdom responsibility to be the good shepherd, or from the superhuman wisdom and daring of the Empire! In a state where the dogma continued its monotonous reaffirmation of pharaoh's divinity, those "most prudent of all men," the priests, had been careful to see that there was no exercise of divine volition.

Our argument has undoubtedly carried moral tones, implying our approval of the older system as "good" and the later as "bad." That is a sincere subjectivity on our part, which may be justified. Ancient Egypt had many spiritual triumphs at a very early stage in human history: the technical and intellectual successes of the earliest dynasties, a great nation built around the concept of a divine ruler, the faith which dared to deny death, the high value placed upon the individual, the victory over disillusionment in the First Intermediate Period, the conception of social justice for all men, a culture which was civilized in the full sense of the word, the organization of the first great empire, the belief in the sustaining power of a universal god, and the discovery—by some —of god's forgiving mercy. All of these triumphs except the last belonged to the period of Egypt's power, from 3000 to 1250 B.C.; not a single comparable achievement arose in Egypt's long petrifaction after 1100 B.C. Indeed, throughout her history, she successively lost one high capacity after another; the process was not cumulative, so that she might add one spiritual or intellectual advance to another. She had ceased to be technically and scientifically creative by the time she pondered social justice. She had discarded an appreciation of the worth of the individual by the time she discovered god's universalism. The result was that when she ceased to attain any new heights she had no effective memory of any past heights; she cherished only a jealous insistence that

61. Diodorus, I, 70 f., following the translation by C. H. Oldfather, *Diodorus of Sicily* (Loeb Classical Library, New York, 1933), I, 241 ff.

the past had, somehow or other, been lofty and should be given ritual commemoration. In these terms, it seems fair to give high moral appreciation to the older times and to regret the spiritual poverty of later days.

There is another valid reason for holding the earlier times in high regard and for considering the later ages as failure, and that arises out of our attempt to discover what was "good" to the ancient Egyptian. The way of life which he had worked out by the Third and Fourth Dynasties was his own, scarcely affected by any other culture. It was a way of life which was so successful that he tried to continue it unchanged through eternity. In this attempt he had a remarkable success, as may be seen in the forms of art and literature, which were essentially the same and yet were charged with creative power from 2650 to 1450 B.C. This was the Egyptian system, and it was obviously what was "good" to him. What emerged out of the Empire was not a pure Egyptian culture but borrowed freely from the knowledge of a larger world with many different ways of life. Thereby it modified the visible forms of the older system in art, literature, religion, government, and society. When national success turned to national frustration, the reaction was one of retreat, any creative impulse was stifled, and the mere empty shell of form was enshrined as if it were the essence. What was left was non-Egyptian in the old sense. It may be studied for its own inherent values of struggle and adjustment to a different world, but if it be studied in contrast to the earlier system, one must condemn it as a tragic paralysis of former strength.

What can one say about the importance of ancient Egypt in world history or about the significance of this culture to us today? May we regard her as our direct spiritual ancestor, the creator of impulses which have come straight down to our times? If this was one of the earliest manifestations of civilization, that complex organization of individuals and institutions bound together by a common way of life, marked by a certain maturity of outlook, interdependent and yet encouraging the individual to some self-expression, then is there not an unbroken line from Egypt to us, a line which implies our material, intellectual, and spiritual debt to this ancient culture? Our social, economic, and political institutions are generally the same as those of Egypt and Mesopotamia; until the industrial revolution and the discovery of new sources of power, our way of life was like theirs. Ancient Egyptian history covered a life-span of three thousand years from the First Dynasty to

Roman domination. Even if one limits the fullest expression of the Egyptian culture to the period from 2650 to 1450 B.C., one must admit that twelve hundred years of stability constitute a very weighty achievement. Toynbee speaks respectfully of "the immortality" which Egyptian culture "sought and found in stone. It seems probable that the Pyramids, which have already borne inanimate witness to the existence of their creators for nearly five thousand years, will survive for hundreds of thousands of years to come. It is not inconceivable that they may outlast man himself and that, in a world where there are no longer human minds to read their message, they will continue to testify: 'Before Abraham was, I am.' "[62] Of what importance to us is such a civilization, which was so long-lived and so immortal in its physical expression?

One's answer will be highly subjective and even somewhat equivocal; namely, that we owe many institutions and forms to such ancient cultures as Egypt, but that there is a marked disjunction between their way of life and ours. Egypt worked out for herself, chiefly from her own dynamism, a culture of distinctive character, which was so well suited to the time and the place that it lasted successfully for an extraordinary period. Further, the Egyptians and the Babylonians anticipated the Hebrews and the Greeks in every formal expression of life: social, economic, political, esthetic, philosophical, and moral, and in each case the later culture built upon or modified its inheritance from the earlier. In view of our acknowledged debt to the Hebrews and the Greeks, should we not extend the debt back to the Egyptian and Mesopotamian cultures, as the inventors of the civilization which we try to enjoy?

In order to answer that question we must ask a series of relevant questions. Of what nature were the cultural achievements of the ancient Egyptians? Did they, in their long history, show a real understanding and cherishing of such triumphs? Is a process of formal transmission visible, either through the eagerness of the Egyptians to spread the gospel of their way of life or the eagerness of the later cultures to build their way of life upon the Egyptian? Which elements can we say were definitely transmitted, and which elements were independently worked out by the later culture? And, finally, how far can any independent and dynamic culture inherit from its predecessors and how far must it work out its own basic expression? It will be seen that such questions prejudice the answers toward the conclusion that forms and techniques may be inherited but that attitudes, ideas, and beliefs are

62. *A Study of History* (one-volume edition, Oxford Press, 1947), p. 30.

distinctive and must be worked out independently. Let us consider some Egyptian expressions in art and architecture, science and history, social ethics, and religion. These should be divergent enough to give a rounded picture.

The successful use of mass in stone architecture, in pyramids, tombs, and temples, was so distinctively Egyptian that we may call it an invention of theirs. The essential factor of mass was promoted by the desire to build for eternity, but it rested upon the easy availability of excellent local stone and upon the adaptation of form to environment. The structures imitated the solid mass of the desert cliffs and mountains, the flat wall surfaces denied the penetration of the blinding sun, and the open courts were able to ignore the possibility of rain in a rainless country. Structural elements of the buildings, such as the pylon towers, the torus moulding at the corners, and the several different orders of columns, derived from native materials and forms. Egypt was a country poor in timber, so that the primitive supporting post had been a bundle of reeds, tied together at top and bottom and liberally smeared with mud to give rigidity. At the top of such a bundle-column appeared the tufted heads or flowers of the reeds. This was the origin of the stone column with floral capital and of the three orders, Ionic, Doric, and Corinthian. This was a form which Egypt "invented," and which subsequent cultures in Palestine, Asia Minor, the Aegean, and Greece took over.[63]

The artistic expression of ancient Egypt was a native development, with its distinctive cubism, its two-dimensional representation, its idealized portrait, and its bland ignoring of precise location in space and time in order to capture eternity. Despite its flattened and static and detached qualities, it succeeded in giving the intrinsic character of Egyptian culture for twenty-five hundred years. To a very marked degree Canaanite-Phoenician art and archaic Greek art borrowed the Egyptian form of expression. We may trace from Egypt to Greece the orders of columns, certain floral and geometric designs,[64] the sphinx, or the statue which stands frozen with legs apart and with a fixed smile in clear imitation of Egyptian style. There is no doubt that there was an initial borrowing of techniques, forms, and expressions. Yet the fully developed Greek art was very different from Egyptian. Why?

We have seen that the best products of Egyptian art and architecture

63. Cf. F. von Luschan, in *Der Alte Orient*, XIII, 4 (Leipzig, 1912). Our Figs. 31*a* and 31*b*.

64. Cf. H. J. Kantor in *American Journal of Archaeology*, LI (1947), 17 ff. See our Fig. 31*c*.

came early in her history, before 1400 B.C. The older periods were normally creative, enthusiastic, and persuasive; the later periods were normally cautious, repetitive, and introverted. The most straightforward buildings, combining durability, purity of line, and artistic feeling preceded 1400 B.C.; thereafter, the showy, insecure, and over-elaborated structures were too mongrel to serve as good models. So also the most persuasive statuary, relief sculpture, and painting came in the earlier and more sensitive periods. The older art came out of the most delicate craftsmanship; it was sophisticated enough to express shades of feeling within superficially static figures; and it was still fluid and experimental enough to express active life through the medium of a hieratic and serene art. The forms were set in the Fourth and early Fifth Dynasties. Thereafter, the further the Egyptians went from the original experimental period, the more the art became repetitive and noncreative. The brief periods of innovation, like the Twelfth Dynasty or the Amarna period, were followed by times of penance, in which the artist held himself to unimaginative imitation of the old.

Thus, by the time that the Phoenicians or Aegeans or Greeks were ready to seek artistic guidance, Egypt had only form and no spirit to offer. The younger cultures took over the rather graceful but empty shell and had to find the creative impulse within themselves. If they took the orders of columns from Egypt, they used them for their own settings in buildings which expressed their own genius. Greece has hills which are lighter and more soaring than those in Egypt; Greece has a rainy season; there are forests there; the sun is not so unremitting. Greek buildings, using the same Doric, Ionic, and Corinthian capitals, lifted as do the wooded hills, instead of settling down as do the desert cliffs. Eternity was not an essential to the Greeks, as it had been to the Egyptians. Greek art therefore added the limitations of space and time to the forms which it had borrowed from Egypt. A third dimension and perspective localized the artistic composition in space, and realism localized it in time, performing the Promethean miracle of snatching art from the realm of gods and immortals and handing it over to ordinary men. Despite borrowing of form and surface technique, Greek art was essentially separated from Egyptian.

Egyptian science gave a good working basis for the culture. Its limitation was that it was practical and never ventured to be anything more. In the mythmaking world one did not pry into the affairs of the gods. Egypt worked out the 365-day calendar long centuries before it was in use elsewhere in the world. Her mathematicians and architects could lay out huge structures with an amazingly small margin of error. With a cumbersome system of notation, without any zero or complex fractions, they could make precise calculations of such volumes as that of a cylinder or that of a truncated pyramid. In the practical fields of anatomy and surgery, her physicians commanded wide respect in the ancient world. They recognized the focal importance of the heart within the human body, as a feeder of life-sustaining fluid to the entire system. It is probably significant that they came within easy distance of discovering the circulation of blood through the body and back to the heart: they had good eyes and practical sense, but their pragmatic nature in medicine and their fear of the gods prevented them from prying into matters which were not direct and useful.

The Greeks were generous enough to say that they took their science from the Babylonians and the Egyptians, and this is true in the same sense as applies to art and architecture. A young, eager, and tradition-free people was thirsting for knowledge and accepted older techniques. They took over the unwieldy arithmetical system of their predecessors, the astronomical lore of the Babylonians, and the anatomical observations of the Egyptians. However, the minds of the Greeks were not limited by a view of a world in which nature was subject to the antic whims of the gods. The ancient oriental world had been created by the gods as it was to be, so that man never tried to go forward to something new; he only tried to hold fast to that which the gods had given. In a world abounding with the presence and activity of gods and spirits, one did not study the processes of nature. The gods had given and the gods might at any time intervene with a miracle. Consequently, science was limited to measurement, building, and repair, with no interest in the future, no interest in chains of cause and effect, no interest in abstracted principles. When the Greeks freed the phenomenal world from the ever-present activity of gods and spirits, they were able to look for impersonal and regular laws as governing nature. They thereby added a third dimension to science, just as they had done for art: what man observed was no longer detached and abstracted in space and time; it was now related in a sequence of events to that which had gone before, and thus might be projected into the future along the same lines. Actually the Greeks accepted forms and techniques from the ancient oriental world but revolted against attitudes and purposes.

The same observations may be made about the treatment of man's position in space and time, that is, about the writing of history. The

Egyptians and Mesopotamians had annals and chronicles, detached records of what happened in a certain reign or a certain year, but they never tried to go back to the historical origin of a phenomenon and explain the series of events leading up to that phenomenon. In their view of the world, things happened because the gods had so willed it, and the will of the gods needed no philosophical or logical analysis. The Hebrews, although they had the same interest in the chronicles of their kings, did produce a running history from the beginnings, provided with a kind of continuing philosophy. Yet this retained the mythmaking mind, because their philosophy exposed the continuing presence and activity of God. The Greeks first wrote history as consecutive process with an exposition of the impersonal causes underlying that process. It was the genius of the Greeks—and to a lesser degree of the Hebrews —that they raised man into independent competition with the gods by permitting man to figure things out for himself. This was a disjunction with the past.

In the field of religion and ethics, it has been argued that the fountain sources of our moral heritage lie in ancient Egypt, because the Egyptians discovered the worth of the common man and insisted upon his sacred right to justice. We have seen that this had been an important issue in the first Intermediate Period. The conflict between the rights of the group and the rights of the individual—a conflict which is still under debate—had been a question at issue from the Old Kingdom to the Empire. In the reaction against the absolute centralization of the early Old Kingdom, there had come an emphasis upon the rights of the individual citizen. For a time rule ceased to be sheer right and became social responsibility, with pharaoh the good shepherd, who tended his flocks patiently and conscientiously.

However, we have seen that the era of social justice did not survive the restoration of political stability and prosperity, and that the pharaoh was restored to his high prerogatives in the later Middle Kingdom. Furthermore, the sense of national insecurity produced by the Hyksos invasion and continued by the Empire effectively ended any advocacy of the rights of the individual and forced every citizen into a disciplined and submissive acceptance of the transcendent rights of the state. The reward for such surrender on the part of an individual would come in the next world, not in this. Thus, if Egypt did discover a social conscience, she had herself forgotten that discovery long before she could transmit it to other peoples. The valuation which the Hebrews and the

Greeks put upon the individual man was a valuation which they had to discover for themselves.

We have already seen that the problem of monotheism in Egypt is a clouded one, that the allegedly monotheistic faith had no roots and no continuity within the land, and that it was a nature worship with little ethical content. If that argument be correct, Akh-en-Aton's concept of god could not have been transmitted to the Hebrews. There is a different aspect of the matter, and that is the observation that an international age produced the idea of god's universal sway, so that Egypt and her Asiatic neighbors may have shared concepts which were on the way toward monotheism. That is an argument of broader scope and has no direct bearing upon the claim of cultural transmission of the idea of a single, universal, and kindly god, in immediate and fatherly relations to all men. Akh-en-Aton did not have such a god for himself, he did not extend his god for the worship of all men, and his faith was obliterated as heresy after his death. The God whom the Hebrews discovered for themselves was fundamentally different from the Aton.

There is no evidence that the Egyptians were cultural missionaries, who sought to win over peoples to their way of life, as did the later Greeks, Arabs, or western Europeans. The means for such converting were present. The Egyptians had colonies at such places as the Fourth Cataract, Byblos in Phoenicia, and Beth-Shan in Palestine, as early as 1400 B.C. Thousands of foreign captives were brought into the Nile Valley. By 600 B.C. there were colonies of Greeks and Hebrews in Egypt. Peoples living side-by-side learn from each other. There is a tradition that Egyptian physicians were in great demand in other countries, traveling to Asia Minor and Persia to practice their superior medical lore.[65] There is no doubt that such contacts were a means of taking Egyptian forms to foreign countries and of bringing foreign forms to Egypt. In the case of the foreign captives held in Egypt, they were egyptianized by their bondage, with no conscious attempt at conversion. But we are not concerned with immigrants who were absorbed into Egyptian culture. Nor are we concerned with the transmission of forms and techniques. We are concerned with the cultural transmission of a way of life, with the essentials of spirit and intellect. There is no evidence that Egypt, when she was in active contact with other cul-

65. J. H. Breasted, *The Edwin Smith Surgical Papyrus* (*OIP*, Vol. III [Chicago, 1930]), I, 17 f.

tures, had any interest in winning them to her way of life.[66] By that time, her earlier tolerant catholicism had given way to imperial arrogance, and her earlier creative enthusiasm had given way to a jealous retentivity. After 1000 B.C., when the younger cultures may have been eager for teaching, Egyptian culture was stagnant, encysted, and tending to become mysterious about her glorious past. She had only memories left, and she clung to them with a fierce jealousy. There could be no worse teacher for a young and eager culture.

There is still one more question to deal with, and that is whether anything vitally essential can be transmitted from one culture to another. The inner essence of a society is so individual to the time and place that it will not fit anywhere else. The full expression of what makes an Egyptian or a Hebrew—or a Frenchman or an American—comes out of a unique experience in one place, one time, and one set of conditions. For example, that problem of the relative rights of the state and of the individual must be debated upon the basis of a people's own history. It is only when a culture has worked out a certain degree of its own salvation that it may borrow forms of expression from others. When a later people has attained a definite attitude toward its gods, it may borrow hymns and ceremonials from an older people. When a later people has worked out a clear relation between its government and its citizens, it may borrow structure and laws from older peoples. This provides a means for acceleration of cultural process and for accumulation of past achievements—in a word, for "progress"—from one culture to another. Further, a culture which has already attained a certain degree of maturity through its own experience may be curious about similar experiences elsewhere. Such an inquisitiveness characterized the Greeks of the time of Herodotus, when their own individuality had been established and they were comparing themselves with other peoples. These exceptions do not vitiate the general probability that the essential beliefs, ideas, and attitudes of a culture are factors of self-discovery, rather than of inheritance.

How, then, do we treat the real appreciation of Egypt by the Greeks and, to a lesser degree, by the Hebrews? The Greeks acknowledged rather simply that they had learned a great deal from Egypt and Meso-

66. There may be an exception to this generalization in Thut-mose III's policy of carrying off the sons of Asiatic princes to Egypt as hostages, with the result that their residence there egyptianized them (p. 183 above). The generalization may still be true, if the purpose of their retention in Egypt was to keep them as hostages for the good behavior of their fathers rather than to educate them to the Egyptian way of life. There is otherwise little indication of missionary zeal on the part of Egypt.

potamia, and that this had been formative in their own lives. The Hebrews were both resentful of and allured by the sophistication of the Egypt from which they had escaped. While they wrote about the "fleshpots," they also wrote about "all the wise men" of Pharaoh and how Moses had learned "all the wisdom of the Egyptians." And yet we have claimed that both cultures really revolted against the older tradition, the Hebrews socially and religiously, the Greeks morally and intellectually. Why then did they give such credit?

By the time that the Hebrews and the Greeks were writing, Egypt had become a vast and impressive legend, a colossus slumbering in a feeble old age, but still wearing a mysterious air of majesty. It was impossible to visit Egypt without respectful awe before the mighty pyramids and vast temples. The later Egyptians did nothing to dispel this sense of wonder. Their older pragmatism and easygoing tolerance had fitted their days of power. In their days of weakness they adopted an air of mysterious profundity as their defensive attitude. In that way the younger peoples were greatly impressed with visions of a vast and vague glory and wanted to become as great as Egypt had been.

Without contributing a single significant spiritual or intellectual factor, Egypt may well have stimulated the younger peoples to new ambitions and efforts. The past may not be able to teach the present how it should live in this way or believe in that way, but it may provoke a sense of dignity and ancient accomplishment, which will have a real formative effect upon the present. One may learn no one significant thing from one's grandfather, but his mere impressive presence may be formative of one's behavior and character. The influence of Egypt did not shape the Hebrews and the Greeks. They were shaped by their own experiences and their own inner dynamism. When they had thus achieved distinctive character, they were ready to receive impressions of the earlier cultures of Egypt and Mesopotamia and to modify their attitudes and behaviors on the basis of those impressions. Even though there was a real disjunction between the ancient oriental and the classical cultures, Greece and Rome were quite correct in respecting achievements of a vast and dignified antiquity. Even though there is a still wider disjunction between ancient Egypt and ourselves, we also may pay tribute to and learn from her ample and august history.

The collapse and sterility of the Egyptian way of life in her later days were tragic, but it is still legitimate to point out that the system lasted effectively for nearly two thousand years. It lasted that long because Egypt had the physical advantages of isolation, which permitted internal development and a long retention of the developed system. In geographic and spiritual security, the Egyptian could work out a way of life which had enough tolerance to permit the process of historical change. The essence of that tolerance was a series of balances or compromises, with the counterposition of forces which might have been mutually destructive. By maintaining the dogma that the movement of time was without consequence and that the *ma'at* of the creation was constantly to be reasserted through infinite ages, they achieved a balance between the inflexible maintenance of status and an erratic drifting with the flow of time. By maintaining the dogma that the king was a god, they held in working co-operation two sections of the land which were culturally and economically unsympathetic. By denying the reality of death and making the next life a triumphant continuation of this life, they set life and death in happy partnership. By capturing a blessed eternity for all good citizens, so that they might be the peers of kings and gods after death, they gave a working answer to the struggle between the rights of the king and the rights of his people. The flexibility of the Egyptian system and the means through which they found peace and security by effecting a happy balance between opposing forces show the genius of a great people.

We should not claim that they were the greatest of people, since their very tolerance robbed them of the impulse to search through problems toward solutions of full and final application. The flexibility which gave them such long happiness was a structural weakness in contrast to the unyielding intensity of the Hebrews or the deeply rooted clarity of the Greeks. Moreover, the Egyptians were unable to hold fast to their highest gifts, ultimately lost their happy and pragmatic tolerance, and became drearily inflexible in the maintenance of mere form. Yet we should judge them at their best, which lasted for a very long period of human history, and that best shows a high achievement physically, intellectually, and spiritually. The words of Isaiah in the latter, tragic days of Egypt: "Surely the princes of Tanis are fools, the counsel of the wise counsellors of Pharaoh is become brutish," come out of a correct tradition of an older wisdom and dignity: "I am the son of the wise, the son of ancient kings."

Chronology

THERE has been no attempt in this book to enter into the vexed problems of Egyptian chronology. In general, it may be said that dates proposed for the period around 3000 B.C. may have a margin of error of 100 years, those around 2500 B.C. of 75 years, those following 2000 B.C. of 10 years, those around 1500–1000 B.C. of 10–15 years, while fairly precise dates are possible around 500 B.C. This book has contented itself with round numbers for dynasties and ages. When, however, the relations of pharaohs are in question, a more precise date has been offered, with the frank confession that it is tentative and relative. Names not in this book have been omitted.

Faiyumic and Merimdean cultures	perhaps 5500 ± 500 B.C.
Tasian and Badarian cultures	perhaps 4500 ± 500
Mesopotamian stimulation	perhaps 3250 ± 150
First and Second Dynasties	3100–2700
Old Kingdom	2700–2200
Third Dynasty	2700–2650
Djoser	2700
Fourth Dynasty	2650–2500
Snefru	2650
Khufu	2600
Khaf-Re	2560
Men-kau-Re	2525
Fifth Dynasty	2500–2350
Ne-user-Re	2425
(Pyramid Texts	2350–2175)
Sixth Dynasty	2350–2200
Pepi I	2325
Pepi II	2275–2185
First Intermediate Period	2200–2050
Seventh and Eighth Dynasties	2180–2155
Ninth and Tenth Dynasties	2155–2050
Meri-ka-Re	2100
(Coffin Texts	2150–1700)
Eleventh Dynasty	2135–2000
Neb-hepet-Re Mentu-hotep	2060–2010
Middle Kingdom	2050–1800
Twelfth Dynasty	1990–1780
Amen-em-het I	1991–1961
Sen-Usert I	1971–1926
Amen-em-het II	1929–1894
Sen-Usert II	1897–1878
Sen-Usert III	1878–1840
Amen-em-het III	1840–1792

A Note on Translations

UNLESS otherwise stated, the translations of Egyptian texts in this book are the author's. The words may therefore differ from those given by the translation cited in the footnote reference. Such references will give the full setting of the passage quoted and the relevant literature, but an attempt has been made to cite convenient treatments in English, so that the citation does not always list the most detailed study of a text.

Many of the texts discussed in this volume have recently been translated in *Ancient Near Eastern Texts Relating to the Old Testament*, edited by James B. Pritchard (Princeton University Press, 1950).

Those texts which were written in the classical Egyptian language have been rendered with due respect for that style. For example, the second person singular has been translated "thou." The later chapters of the book carry some texts written in Late-Egyptian, which tended toward the colloquial. There the second person singular has been translated "you."

Parentheses ( ) inclose material not present in the original text but added by the translator as explanatory. Square brackets [ ] inclose material lost from the original text by damage and restored by the translator, with more or less certainty. A parenthetical question mark (?) usually expresses a doubt about the word or words which it immediately follows.

The spelling of personal names is the author's own contrivance.

Abbreviations

AJSL	*The American Journal of Semitic Languages and Literatures* (Chicago, 1895–1941).
Arch. Surv.	Egypt Exploration Fund. *Archaeological Survey of Egypt* (London, 1893——).
ASAE	*Annales du Service des Antiquités de l'Égypte* (Cairo, 1900——).
Berlin Abh.	*Abhandlungen der preussischen Akademie der Wissenschaften. Phil.-hist. Klasse* (Berlin).
Bibl. Aeg.	Fondation égyptologique Reine Élisabeth. *Bibliotheca Aegyptiaca* (Brussels, 1932——).
BIFAO	*Bulletin de l'Institut Français d'Archéologie Orientale du Caire* (Cairo, 1901——).
BMMA	*Bulletin of the Metropolitan Museum of Art* (New York, 1905——).
Breasted, *ARE*	James H. Breasted, *Ancient Records of Egypt* (5 vols.; Chicago, 1906–7).
Cairo Cat.	*Catalogue général des antiquités égyptiennes du Musée du Caire* (Cairo, 1901——).
EES	Egypt Exploration Society. *Memoirs* (London, 1885——).
Erman, *LAE*	Adolf Erman, *The Literature of the Ancient Egyptians*, translated from German edition (*Die Literatur der Aegypter* [1923]) by A. M. Blackman (London, 1927).
Gött. GN	*Gesellschaft der Wissenschaften zu Göttingen. Phil.-hist. Klasse. Nachrichten* (Göttingen).
JEA	Egypt Exploration Society. *Journal of Egyptian Archaeology* (London, 1914——).
JNES	*Journal of Near Eastern Studies* (Chicago, 1942——) (continuing *AJSL*).
Leip. AS	*Leipziger ägyptologische Studien* (Glückstadt, 1935——).
MIFAO	*Mémoires publiés par les membres de l'Institut Français d'Archéologie Orientale du Caire* (Cairo, 1902——).
Mün. AF	*Aegyptologische Forschungen, herausgegeben von Alexander Scharff . . . München* (Glückstadt, 1936——).
OIP	*Oriental Institute Publications* (Chicago, 1924——).
SAOC	The Oriental Institute. *Studies in Ancient Oriental Civilization* (Chicago, 1931——).
TTS	Egypt Exploration Society. *Theban Tomb Series* (London, 1915——).
Tytus	*Publications of the Metropolitan Museum of Art, Egyptian Expedition. Robb de Peyster Tytus Memorial Series* (New York, 1917——).
Untersuch.	*Untersuchungen zur Geschichte und Altertumskunde Aegyptens* (Leipzig, 1896——).
Urk.	*Urkunden des ägyptischen Altertums* (Leipzig, 1903——).
ZÄS	*Zeitschrift für ägyptische Sprache und Altertumskunde* (Leipzig, 1863——).

List of Illustrations

Index

Proper names are followed by an indication within parentheses: (G) designating a god or goddess, (K) a king of Egypt, (N) all other personal names, and (P) the name of a place or of a people.

The Arabic article *el-* has been ignored in the alphabetizing; e.g., "el-Arish" has been indexed as if only "Arish."

PHOENIX BOOKS *Titles in print*

THE UNIVERSITY OF CHICAGO PRESS